SMP interact

for GCSE mathematics

Teacher's guide for

Foundation

CAMBRIDGE
UNIVERSITY PRESS

PUBLISHED BY THE PRESS SYNDICATE OF THE UNIVERSITY OF CAMBRIDGE
The Pitt Building, Trumpington Street, Cambridge, United Kingdom

CAMBRIDGE UNIVERSITY PRESS
The Edinburgh Building, Cambridge CB2 2RU, UK
40 West 20th Street, New York, NY 10011-4211, USA
477 Williamstown Road, Port Melbourne, VIC 3207, Australia
Ruiz de Alarcón 13, 28014 Madrid, Spain
Dock House, The Waterfront, Cape Town 8001, South Africa

http://www.cambridge.org/

© The School Mathematics Project 2003
First published 2003

Printed in the United Kingdom at the University Press, Cambridge

Typeface Minion   *System* QuarkXPress®

A catalogue record for this book is available from the British Library

ISBN 0 521 89031 4 paperback

Typesetting and technical illustrations by The School Mathematics Project
Cover image © Getty Images/Nick Koudis
Cover design by Angela Ashton

No solutions to the questions were provided or approved by AQA, and the solutions
provided may not constitute the only ones. Edexcel accepts no responsibility
whatsoever for the accuracy or method of working in the answers given.

Contents

The following people contributed to the writing of the SMP Interact key stage 4 materials.

Benjamin Alldred	David Cassell	Spencer Instone	Susan Shilton
Juliette Baldwin	Ian Edney	Pamela Leon	Caroline Starkey
Simon Baxter	Stephen Feller	John Ling	Liz Stewart
Gill Beeney	Rosemary Flower	Carole Martin	Biff Vernon
Roger Beeney	John Gardiner	Lorna Mulhern	Jo Waddingham
Roger Bentote	Colin Goldsmith	Mary Pardoe	Nigel Webb
Sue Briggs	Bob Hartman	Paul Scruton	Heather West

Others, too numerous to mention individually, gave valuable advice, particularly by commenting on and trialling draft materials.

Editorial team	**Project administrator**	**Design**	**Project support**
David Cassell	Ann White	Pam Alford	Carol Cole
Spencer Instone		Melanie Bull	Pam Keetch
John Ling		Nicky Lake	Jane Seaton
Paul Scruton		Tiffany Passmore	Cathy Syred
Susan Shilton		Martin Smith	
Caroline Starkey			
Heather West			

Introduction

In this course a central place is given to discussion and other interactive work.

The students' book

Each unit of work starts with a statement of the main **learning objectives** and finishes with some questions for **self-assessment** ('Test yourself'). Revision questions are provided in periodic **reviews**.

To help build confidence, **past examination questions** appear throughout, each marked with the examination board from which it comes.

To help with preparation for **non-calculator** examination papers this symbol appears where a calculator is not intended to be used.

Starred questions are more demanding.

A **solid marginal strip** means that the objectives of an activity or suggestions on how to carry it out are set out in the teacher's guide.

A **broken marginal strip** appears next to a question or activity for which students may need teacher support.

The practice book

This optional book contains additional **practice questions** on most units of work in the students' book. It can be used for extra practice in class, for homework or as an assessment resource.

The teacher's guide

The notes for each numbered unit of work start with an **overview**, showing the title of each lettered section and, where necessary, clarifying what it covers.

Solid marginal strips match those in the students' book.

Any **equipment** or **resource sheets** (optional or essential) needed for the work is listed, together with the practice book page references.

Where appropriate for a section, **guidance notes** are provided.

In the left-hand margin, there are occasional **comments from teachers** who participated in the extensive trialling.

Opportunities to use **software** arise throughout the material. Specific guidance is marked by these symbols (spreadsheet, graph plotter and dynamic geometry package).

Answers for the students' book and the practice book appear at the end of the notes for each unit. The answers to each set of mixed questions in the practice book come after the answers to the corresponding review.

Planning a scheme of work

The precedence diagram on the following pages shows where to find any work that is assumed to have been completed before a given unit. For example, unit 61 'Substitution' assumes coverage of work in

42 Solving equations

46 Finding and using formulas

60 Calculating with fractions

The diagram can help with overall planning, particularly if you need to depart from the order of units in the book – for example in preparation for a modular GCSE or because you wish to organise units into larger blocks, such as a data handling block.

The diagram can also support lesson preparation: before starting a unit you can use it to locate earlier topics that may need to be revised.

For clarity, the diagram is divided into sections for number, algebra, space and data handling. A fifth section contains three units that each apply a range of mathematical ideas to a real-life theme. Each of these depends on mathematical work in several preceding units, but corresponding links are not shown in the diagram.

Number

Algebra

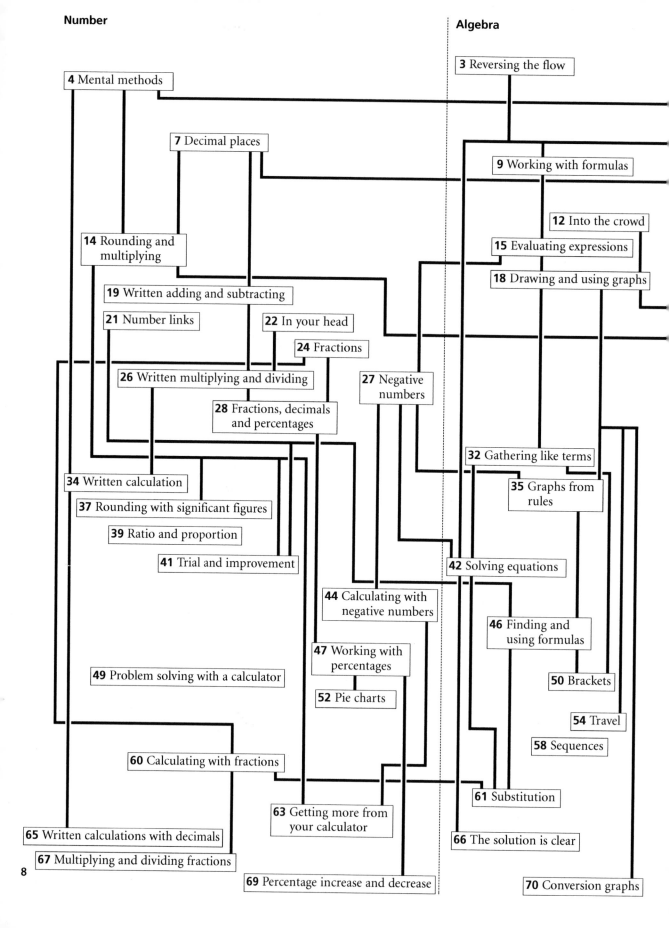

4 Mental methods

3 Reversing the flow

7 Decimal places

9 Working with formulas

12 Into the crowd

14 Rounding and multiplying

15 Evaluating expressions

18 Drawing and using graphs

19 Written adding and subtracting

21 Number links

22 In your head

24 Fractions

26 Written multiplying and dividing

27 Negative numbers

28 Fractions, decimals and percentages

32 Gathering like terms

34 Written calculation

35 Graphs from rules

37 Rounding with significant figures

39 Ratio and proportion

41 Trial and improvement

42 Solving equations

44 Calculating with negative numbers

46 Finding and using formulas

47 Working with percentages

49 Problem solving with a calculator

50 Brackets

52 Pie charts

54 Travel

58 Sequences

60 Calculating with fractions

61 Substitution

63 Getting more from your calculator

65 Written calculations with decimals

66 The solution is clear

67 Multiplying and dividing fractions

8

69 Percentage increase and decrease

70 Conversion graphs

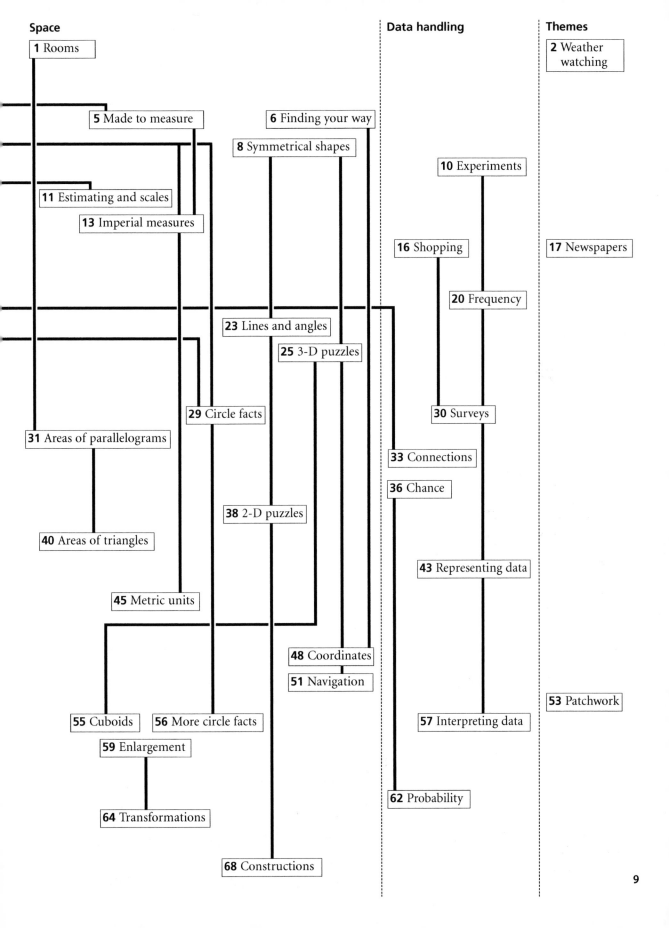

Space

1 Rooms

5 Made to measure

6 Finding your way

8 Symmetrical shapes

11 Estimating and scales

13 Imperial measures

23 Lines and angles

25 3-D puzzles

29 Circle facts

31 Areas of parallelograms

38 2-D puzzles

40 Areas of triangles

45 Metric units

48 Coordinates

51 Navigation

55 Cuboids

56 More circle facts

59 Enlargement

64 Transformations

68 Constructions

Data handling

10 Experiments

16 Shopping

20 Frequency

30 Surveys

33 Connections

36 Chance

43 Representing data

57 Interpreting data

62 Probability

Themes

2 Weather watching

17 Newspapers

53 Patchwork

9

1 Rooms

This unit revises areas of rectangles and composite shapes made from rectangles in the thematic context of decorating. Most areas are calculated using whole numbers or a whole number and a decimal with one decimal place. The work in sections A and B could mainly be carried out without a calculator.

Calculations of perimeter are interspersed in the unit.

Essential equipment

Centimetre rulers

Practice book pages 4 to 7

A *Tiles* (p 4)

This section quickly moves from examples where square counting could be used to using the formula area = length × height.

A3 It is intended that this is answered by dividing the area of the table top by the area of the tile. However, some students may find it helpful to visualise how many tiles could be placed along each edge.

B *Floor space* (p 6)

This section extends the idea of finding areas of rectangles to examples where one of the dimensions is a decimal. The diagrams on pages 6 and 7 should help students visualise the answers their calculations give them.

Questions B9 and B10 touch on cases where both dimensions are decimals.

C *Composite shapes* (p 8)

Emphasise the importance of
- drawing a sketch
- splitting the shape into rectangles
- working out and adding missing dimensions to the sketch

A *Tiles* (p 4)

A1 (a) $12\,cm^2$ (b) $18\,cm^2$ (c) $16\,cm^2$
  (d) $15\,cm^2$ (e) $20\,cm^2$ (f) $8\,cm^2$

A2 A $4\,cm^2$ B $9\,cm^2$

A3 (a) $5400\,cm^2$ (b) 1350 (c) 600

A4 (a) $49\,cm^2$ (b) $100\,cm^2$ (c) $225\,cm^2$
  (d) $300\,cm^2$ (e) $132\,cm^2$

Floor tiles

African slate	$2400\,cm^2$
Blue slate	$600\,cm^2$
Tuscan stone	$400\,cm^2$
Quarry tiles	$225\,cm^2$
Old brick	$200\,cm^2$
Ceramic tile	$900\,cm^2$
Half ceramic	$450\,cm^2$

B *Floor space* (p 6)

B1 (a) $6\,m^2$ (b) $3\,m^2$ (c) $10.5\,m^2$

B2 (a) $1.5\,m$ (b) $6\,m$ (c) $9\,m^2$

B3 (a) £52.50 (b) £67.50 (c) £45

B4 (a) The student's sketch of the kitchen split into two rectangles
  (b) The areas of the two rectangles
  (c) $10\,m^2$

B5 (a) £45 (b) £22.50 (c) £75

*B6 (a) $7.5\,m^2$ (b) Two 2 litre cans

B7 The student's check

B8 (a) $5.7\,m^2$ (b) $9.9\,m^2$ (c) $12.9\,m^2$
  (d) $4.4\,m^2$

B9 (a) Roughly 1 square metre
  (b) $1.17\,m^2$

B10 $2.99\,m^2$

C *Composite shapes* (p 8)

C1 (a) $36\,m^2$ (b) $27\,m^2$

C2 (a) $14.4\,m^2$ (b) $12.6\,m^2$ (c) $34.5\,m^2$
  (d) $40\,m^2$

C3 (a) $15.8\,m$ (b) $17.2\,m$ (c) $27.4\,m$
  (d) $34.4\,m$

C4 (a) $6.6 - 3 = 3.6\,m^2$
  (b) $6.9 - 2.4 = 4.5\,m^2$
  (c) $5.2 - 1.2 = 4\,m^2$
  (d) $6.8 - 1.2 - 1.8 = 3.8\,m^2$

C5 All except (b)

C6 (a) $11.5\,m^2$ (b) $14.1\,m^2$

D *Mixed measurements* (p 10)

D1 (a) $0.7\,m$ (b) $0.9\,m$ (c) $0.95\,m$
  (d) $1.1\,m$ (e) $1.5\,m$ (f) $2.4\,m$
  (g) $0.29\,m$ (h) $1.25\,m$ (i) $2.84\,m$
  (j) $0.05\,m$ (k) $1.05\,m$ (l) $2.08\,m$

D2 (a) $80\,cm$ (b) $60\,cm$
  (c) $25\,cm$ (d) $1\,m\ 50\,cm$
  (e) $3\,m\ 75\,cm$ (f) $2\,m\ 84\,cm$
  (g) $4\,cm$ (h) $5\,m\ 8\,cm$

D3 (a) $7.6\,\text{m}^2$ (b) $6.8\,\text{m}^2$ (c) $10\,\text{m}^2$

D4 (a) $12\,250\,\text{cm}^2$ (b) $41\,250\,\text{cm}^2$
    (c) $10\,500\,\text{cm}^2$

D5 (a) $490\,\text{cm}$ (b) $850\,\text{cm}$ (c) $430\,\text{cm}$

D6 (a) $4.9\,\text{m}$ (b) $8.5\,\text{m}$ (c) $4.3\,\text{m}$

Test yourself (p 11)

T1 (a) $12\,\text{m}^2$ (b) $13\,\text{m}$ (c) $17\,\text{m}^2$

T2 (a) $21.2\,\text{m}^2$ (b) $15.6\,\text{m}^2$
    (c) $13.8 - 1.6 = 12.2\,\text{m}^2$

T3 $37\,\text{m}^2$

T4 (a) $18\,000\,\text{cm}^2$ (b) $1.8\,\text{m}^2$

Practice book

Section A (p 4)

1 (a) $12\,\text{cm}^2$ (b) $30\,\text{cm}^2$
   (c) $40\,\text{cm}^2$ (d) $35\,\text{cm}^2$

2 (a) $80\,\text{cm}^2$ (b) $90\,\text{cm}^2$ (c) $225\,\text{cm}^2$

3 (a) $50\,\text{cm}^2$ (b) $1000\,\text{cm}^2$
   (c) $10\,000\,\text{cm}^2$

4 (a) $1100\,\text{cm}^2$ (b) $704\,\text{cm}^2$

5 512 tiles (16 up by 32 across)

Section B (p 5)

1 (a) $4\,\text{m}^2$ (b) $5\,\text{m}^2$
   (c) $14\,\text{m}^2$ (d) $10.5\,\text{m}^2$

2 About $1.5\,\text{m}^2$

3 (a) £72   (b) £252

4 (a) 6   (b) £24

Section C (p 6)

1 (a) $28\,\text{m}^2$ (b) $44\,\text{m}^2$ (c) $69\,\text{m}^2$

2 (a) $32\,\text{m}^2$ (b) $49.5\,\text{m}^2$ (c) $30.5\,\text{m}^2$
   (d) $79\,\text{m}^2$

3 (a) $24\,\text{m}$ (b) $30\,\text{m}$ (c) $44\,\text{m}$

Section D (p 7)

1 (a) $0.6\,\text{m}$ (b) $0.42\,\text{m}$ (c) $0.07\,\text{m}$
   (d) $0.98\,\text{m}$ (e) $1.12\,\text{m}$ (f) $1.73\,\text{m}$
   (g) $2.05\,\text{m}$ (h) $5.08\,\text{m}$ (i) $0.87\,\text{m}$
   (j) $1.23\,\text{m}$ (k) $4.02\,\text{m}$ (l) $12.04\,\text{m}$

2 (a) $35\,\text{cm}$ (b) $20\,\text{cm}$ (c) $80\,\text{cm}$
   (d) $190\,\text{cm}$ (e) $432\,\text{cm}$ (f) $205\,\text{cm}$
   (g) $7\,\text{cm}$ (h) $430\,\text{cm}$

3 (a) $5.4\,\text{m}^2$ (b) $10.8\,\text{m}^2$ (c) $4\,\text{m}^2$

4 (a) $51\,200\,\text{cm}^2$ (b) $10\,000\,\text{cm}^2$
   (c) $40\,000\,\text{cm}^2$

5 (a) $960\,\text{cm}$ (b) $580\,\text{cm}$ (c) $820\,\text{cm}$

6 (a) $9.6\,\text{m}$ (b) $5.8\,\text{m}$ (c) $8.2\,\text{m}$

2 Weather watching

This unit uses data sets on weather to practise a range of techniques for handling data. All the data in this unit was obtained from newspapers and websites and could easily be replaced by more recent or local data.

The unit also provides an example of a possible project using secondary data.

Essential	Optional
Graph and centimetre squared paper	Sheet G1
Practice book pages 8 to 11	

A *Winter and summer* (p 12)

'*We discussed at great length the differences between northern and southern hemisphere weather. A globe was useful!*'

The questions in this section involve finding differences between temperatures, some of which are negative. Many could be done orally.

◊ A number line or thermometer drawn on the board may be needed for some students.

◊ A globe or map of the world would be useful in this section.

◊ If you use your own data you will need to ensure that there are some temperatures below zero.

◊ The temperatures given are the highest recorded on that day.

B *Rain or shine* (p 14)

Graph paper

'In q B14, many pupils just gave their opinion rather than looking at the data!'

◊ Here, a broken line is used to connect data points where there is no meaning to intermediate points. However, this is a difficult concept for some pupils and may be better ignored.

◊ The temperatures used are the average of daily maximum temperatures for that month recorded over several years. It may be simpler to refer to these as 'average' temperatures.

C *Frequency* (p 17)

This section involves compiling frequency tables of qualitative and discrete numerical data, and then drawing frequency bar graphs from them.

Centimetre squared paper Optional: sheet G1

◊ The 'spider' graph is commonly used in travel guides and geography. Sheet G1 gives a framework for students to construct their own, or it may be useful angle revision to draw their own from scratch. Alternatively you may prefer to use a conventional bar graph.

◊ Some students may have difficulty with the use of 'modal' rather than 'mode'. 'Modal' is commonly used though, and students need to be familiar with it.

D *Comparing east and west* (p 19)

This section uses means and ranges to compare data from weather stations near the east and west coasts of the UK. A map of the UK with these places marked would be helpful, in particular to discuss whether these places are representative.

The data for the same places in January is given at the foot of page 19 to provide an opportunity for further practice in comparing east and west or winter and summer.

Ⓐ *Winter and summer* (p 12)

A1 (a) 11°C (b) 35°C (c) 3°C

A2 (a) 30°C (b) ⁻8°C (c) ⁻15°C

A3 (a) Cloudy but very hot
(b) Sunny but very cold indeed

A4 (a) Singapore
(b) Three of Buenos Aires, Johannesburg, Melbourne, Nairobi, Port Stanley, Rio de Janeiro, Santiago, Sydney and Wellington.
(c) They are in the southern hemisphere.

A5 In order Wellington (22), Dublin (6), Amsterdam (3), Berlin (⁻6), Chicago (⁻7), New York (⁻8), Moscow (⁻15)

A6 (a) Santiago was 9 degrees warmer in January than in August.
(b) Reykjavik was 11 degrees colder in January than in August.
(c) Funchal was 9 degrees colder in January than August.
(d) Copenhagen was 16 degrees colder in January than in August.
(e) Berlin was 25 degrees colder in January than in August.
(f) Moscow was 33 degrees colder in January than in August.

A7 (a) 3°C (b) 5°C (c) 18°C
(d) ⁻3°C (e) ⁻2°C (f) ⁻7°C

A8 (a) 16 degrees (b) 25 degrees
(c) 36 degrees (d) 34 degrees
(e) 35 degrees (f) 28 degrees

A9 Beijing

Ⓑ *Rain or shine* (p 14)

B1 (a) 26°C (b) 14°C (c) 17°C

B2 (a) ⁻9°C (b) 21°C (c) 16°C

B3 May, June, July and August

B4 (a) 7 degrees (b) 29 degrees
(c) 32 degrees

B5 (a) January (b) September

B6

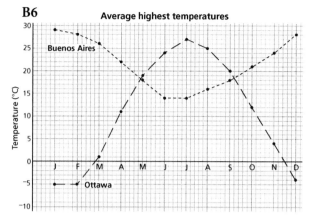

B7 2 mm or 0.2 cm

B8 (a) 5 cm (b) 5.2 cm (c) 6.3 cm

B9 (a) January and December (b) 7.3 cm

B10 August

B11 (a) 0.1 cm (b) 1.6 cm (c) 2.7 cm

B12 January, February, March, April, December

B13 19.5 cm

B14 In the winter (December until April) it rains more in London, but in the summer and autumn it rains more in Manchester. If someone went to Manchester in the summer or autumn they might think it rains more.

B15 (a) 37 cm; much more than Manchester!
(b) June (c) July and August

B16 (a) False (b) True (c) False

B17 Only A

Ⓒ *Frequency* (p 17)

C1 East

C2 1

C3 South-west

C4 (a)

Direction	Frequency
N	3
NE	3
E	0
SE	0
S	1
SW	2
W	9
NW	10

(b) North-west

(c)

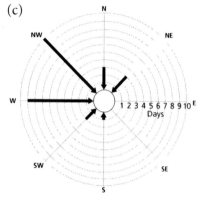

C5 (a)

Weather	Frequency
Sunny	11
Drizzle	3
Cloudy	10
Dull	3
Rain	2
Showers	1

(b) 3

(c)

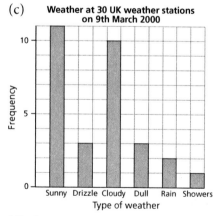

(d) Sunny

C6 (a)

Oktas	Frequency
0	1
1	4
2	1
3	1
4	1
5	3
6	5
7	10
8	5

(b) 7 oktas

(c)

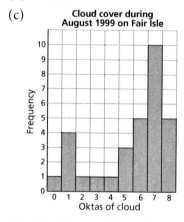

(d) (i) True   (ii) False

C7 (a)

Rainy days	Frequency
3	2
4	5
5	9
6	3
7	5
8	4
9	1
10	1

(b)

Rainy days in second half of August 1999 at 30 UK weather stations

(c) 5 rainy days

D *Comparing east and west* (p 19)

D1 (a) 19.4°C   (b) 17.5°C

(c) The east

(d) (i) 3 degrees   (ii) 5 degrees

(e) The west

D2 (a) (i) 7.96 hours   (ii) 6.88 hours

(b) East

(c) The range for the east was 6.5 hours.
The range for the west was 9.7 hours.
So the west had the greatest range.

D3 (a) East mean rainfall was 3.98 mm.
West mean rainfall was 3.06 mm.
So the east had the highest mean.

(b) The range for the east was 15.2 mm.
The range for the west was 17.8 mm.
So the west had the greatest range.

D4 (a)

East	Mean	Range
Sun (h)	2.42	3.4
Rain (mm)	1.61	2.5
Temp. (°C)	5.5	2

(b)

West	Mean	Range
Sun (h)	3.79	4.5
Rain (mm)	0.34	1.0
Temp. (°C)	8	3

(c) The student's comments

Test yourself (p 20)

T1 (a) 6 degrees   (b) 8 degrees

(c) 7 degrees

T2 31st December

T3

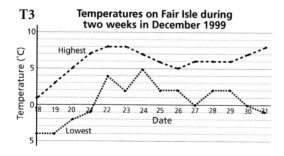

Temperatures on Fair Isle during
two weeks in December 1999

T4 (a)

Oktas	Frequency
0	0
1	0
2	1
3	1
4	1
5	2
6	0
7	5
8	4

(b)

Cloud cover on Fair Isle during
two weeks in December 1999

(c) 7 oktas

T5 (a) 5.6°C (to 1 d.p.)   (b) 7 degrees

(c) Mean 6.3°C (to 1 d.p.)
Range 3 degrees

(d) Week two

Practice book

Section A (p 8)

1 ⁻8°C

2 2°C

3 (a) 6°C   (b) 13°C

4 5th January, 15°C

5 4°C (or ⁻14°C)

Section B (p 8)

1 ⁻6°C

2 July and August

3 (a) 14°C   (b) 0°C

4 February

5

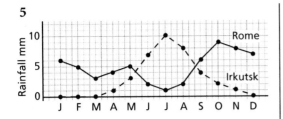

6 (a) Irkutsk   (b) 3 months

7 (a) 1.5 hours   (b) 4 hours

8 April, May, June, July, August

9

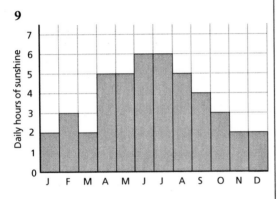

Section C (p 10)

1 (a)

Bright	|||	3
Cloudy	⸾⸾⸾⸾ ||	7
Rain	⸾⸾⸾⸾ ⸾⸾⸾⸾	10
Snow	⸾⸾⸾⸾ ⸾⸾⸾⸾ |	11

(b)

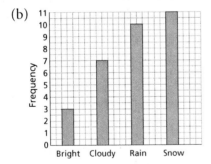

(c) Snow

2 (a)

Hours of sunshine	Tally	Frequency
1	||	2
2	|||	3
3	||||	4
4	⸾⸾⸾⸾	5
5	⸾⸾⸾⸾ ||	7
6	⸾⸾⸾⸾ |	6
7	||	2
8	||	2

(b)

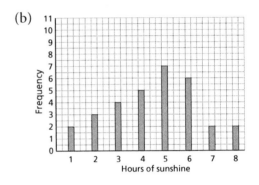

(c) 4   (d) 5 hours

Section D (p 11)

1

	Mean	**Range**
(a)	3 oktas	6 oktas
(b)	5.5 hours	5 hours
(c)	1.5 mm	2.0 mm
(d)	20.9°C	11°C
(e)	8.25 days	10 days
(f)	4.7°C or 4.6°C	4°C

2 (a) (i) Mean 3.3 mm, Range 11 mm

      (ii) Mean 1.1 mm, Range 5 mm

(b) August 17th

(c) August 17th: Mean 16°C, Range 5°C
Sept 1st: Mean 17.7°C, Range 7°C

(d) September 1st

(e) August 17th

3 Reversing the flow

This unit introduces students to solving equations using flow diagrams (here called 'arrow diagrams'). This approach will only work when the unknown appears on one side. Equations with the unknown on both sides will be dealt with by balancing in a later unit.

Optional
Sheets G2 and G3

Practice book pages 12 to 15

A *Mathematical whispers* (p 21)

Optional: sheet G2

You could start with two whole-class 'whispering' activities. The class needs to be sitting with the same number of students in each row and column. (Students left over can judge who finishes first.) It is best if students do not use a calculator for the activities.

1 Each student in a row is allotted an operation, such as 'multiply by 4' or 'subtract 5'. All the students in a row have the same operation, and should not tell it to other rows (perhaps write each operation on a slip of paper to be passed along the row). Now put a number on the board. This is the starting number.

In each column, the front student performs their operation on the starting number, and whispers the result to the student behind them. That student then performs their operation on the result and whispers the answer to the person behind them. Whispering continues along each column until the last person in the column performs their operation. The last person then writes their answer on a piece of paper and holds it up. The first column to finish (correctly) wins.

'They needed reminding about "opposite" functions and the vocabulary.'

2 Now write the operation that each row has been given on the board. So no-one else can hear, give the front student in each column a different number. Calculation and whispering begins! The last person in each column holds up the final result for that column, *and* what they think the starting number for their column was. The first correct answer wins.

These two activities lead naturally into a discussion of arrow diagrams and how to reverse them.

It is important that students realise that the arrow diagrams need only be roughly and quickly sketched. However, sheet G2 may be used if you do not wish students to spend time sketching them. Diagrams A are for question A1, B is for A2 and diagrams C are for A4.

C *Solving equations* (p 24)

Optional: sheet G3

Sheet G3 may be used if you wish students not to have to sketch their own arrow diagrams, or to help them structure their work correctly.

D *Number puzzles* (p 26)

In this section, students move from a number puzzle to an equation, and then use an arrow diagram to solve the equation.

A *Mathematical whispers* (p 21)

A1 (a) 9 $\xrightarrow{+1}$ 10 $\xrightarrow{\div 5}$ 2

(b) 4 $\xrightarrow{+2}$ 6 $\xrightarrow{\times 5}$ 30

(c) 70 $\xrightarrow{+10}$ 80 $\xrightarrow{\times 5}$ 400 $\xrightarrow{\div 2}$ 200

(d) 7 $\xrightarrow{\times 2}$ 14 $\xrightarrow{-2}$ 12 $\xrightarrow{+3}$ 15

(e) 21 $\xrightarrow{\div 7}$ 3 $\xrightarrow{+15}$ 18 $\xrightarrow{\div 6}$ 3

(f) 30 $\xrightarrow{\times 2}$ 60 $\xrightarrow{-10}$ 50 $\xrightarrow{\div 10}$ 5

(g) 80 $\xrightarrow{+20}$ 100 $\xrightarrow{\times 10}$ 1000 $\xrightarrow{+25}$ 1025

A2 (a) 4 $\xrightarrow{+6}$ 10 $\xrightarrow{\times 3}$ 30 $\xrightarrow{+10}$ 40

(b) Dave thought of 4.

A3 (a) 24 $\xrightarrow{-9}$ 15 $\xrightarrow{\div 5}$ 3 $\xrightarrow{+10}$ 13

Dave thought of 24.

(b) 40 $\xrightarrow{\div 2}$ 20 $\xrightarrow{\times 3}$ 60 $\xrightarrow{\div 12}$ 5

Dave thought of 40.

A4 (a) 9.3 $\xrightarrow{+5.6}$ 14.9 $\xrightarrow{-2.3}$ 12.6

(b) 4.7 $\xrightarrow{+7.3}$ 12 $\xrightarrow{\times 2.5}$ 30

(c) 500 $\xrightarrow{\div 10}$ 50 $\xrightarrow{\div 4}$ 12.5

(d)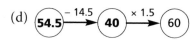

B *Using letters* (p 23)

B1 A matches R, B matches Q, C matches P.

B2 L

B3 C

B4 (a)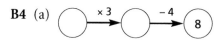

(b)

B5 Students may use their own letters.

(a) $3n + 6 = 10$ (b) $2n - 8 = 10$

(c) $\frac{n}{3} + 6 = 18$ (d) $\frac{n}{4} - 8 = 10$

C *Solving equations* (p 24)

C1 (a) $9k - 3 = 15$

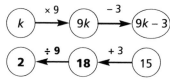

$k = 2$

(b) Check
When $k = 2$,
$$9k - 3 = 9 \times 2 - 3$$
$$= 18 - 3$$
$$= 15 \text{ which is correct.}$$

C2 $\frac{a}{4} + 12 = 20$

$a = 32$

Check
When $a = 32$,
$$\frac{a}{4} + 12 = \frac{32}{4} + 12$$
$$= 8 + 12$$
$$= 20 \text{ which is correct.}$$

C3 (Each solution should be checked.)

(a) $7n - 5 = 23$

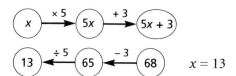

$n = 4$

(b) $5x + 3 = 68$

$x = 13$

(c) $8p - 5 = 43$

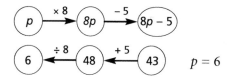

$p = 6$

(d) $4y + 12 = 60$

$y = 12$

C4 (a) $\frac{w}{4} - 16 = 4$

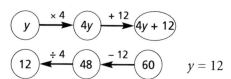

$w = 80$

(b) $\frac{m}{2} + 6 = 10$

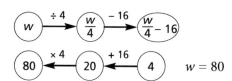

$m = 8$

(c) $\frac{x}{5} - 2 = 3$

$x \xrightarrow{\div 5} \frac{x}{5} \xrightarrow{-2} \frac{x}{5} - 2$

$25 \xleftarrow{\times 5} 5 \xleftarrow{+2} 3 \qquad x = 25$

C5 (a) $a = 2.8$ (b) $n = 6.2$

     (c) $y = 26$ (d) $k = 18$

Ⅾ **Number puzzles** (p 26)

D1 (a) $4n - 6 = 22$

(b) $n \xrightarrow{\times 4} 4n \xrightarrow{-6} 4n - 6$

(c) $7 \xleftarrow{\div 4} 28 \xleftarrow{+6} 22$

(d) $n = 7$

D2 Students may use their own letters.

(a) $5n - 8 = 97 \qquad n = 21$

(b) $\frac{n}{7} + 2 = 10 \qquad n = 56$

(c) $\frac{n}{4} - 5 = 47 \qquad n = 208$

D3 The student's number puzzle

D4 (a) The student's number puzzle for
$3n - 4 = 20$

(b) $n \xrightarrow{\times 3} 3n \xrightarrow{-4} 3n - 4$

$8 \xleftarrow{\div 3} 24 \xleftarrow{+4} 20 \qquad n = 8$

D5 (a) $x \xrightarrow{\times 4} 4x \xrightarrow{+3.5} 4x + 3.5$

$1.6 \xleftarrow{\div 4} 6.4 \xleftarrow{-3.5} 9.9 \qquad x = 1.6$

(b) $n \xrightarrow{\times 3} 3n \xrightarrow{+2.2} 3n + 2.2$

$3.5 \xleftarrow{\div 3} 10.5 \xleftarrow{-2.2} 12.7 \qquad n = 3.5$

(c) $k \xrightarrow{\times 1.5} 1.5k \xrightarrow{+4} 1.5k + 4$

$4 \xleftarrow{\div 1.5} 6 \xleftarrow{-4} 10 \qquad k = 4$

Test yourself (p 27)

T1 (a) $16 \xrightarrow{-8} 8 \xrightarrow{\times 4} 32 \xrightarrow{+5} 37$

(b) $48 \xrightarrow{\div 8} 6 \xrightarrow{+4} 10 \xrightarrow{\times 5} 50$

T2 (a) $m \xrightarrow{\times 3} 3m \xrightarrow{-6} 3m - 6$

$8 \xleftarrow{\div 3} 24 \xleftarrow{+6} 18 \qquad m = 8$

(b) $s \xrightarrow{\times 4} 4s \xrightarrow{+2} 4s + 2$

$7 \xleftarrow{\div 4} 28 \xleftarrow{-2} 30 \qquad s = 7$

(c) $w \xrightarrow{\div 2} \frac{w}{2} \xrightarrow{-4} \frac{w}{2} - 4$

$28 \xleftarrow{\times 2} 14 \xleftarrow{+4} 10 \qquad w = 28$

(d) $v \xrightarrow{\div 5} \frac{v}{5} \xrightarrow{-4} \frac{v}{5} - 4$

$50 \xleftarrow{\times 5} 10 \xleftarrow{+4} 6 \qquad v = 50$

T3 (a) $4n - 2 = 30$

$n \xrightarrow{\times 4} 4n \xrightarrow{-2} 4n - 2$

$8 \xleftarrow{\div 4} 32 \xleftarrow{+2} 30 \qquad n = 8$

(b) $\frac{n}{2} - 10 = 17$

$n \xrightarrow{\div 2} \frac{n}{2} \xrightarrow{-10} \frac{n}{2} - 10$

$54 \xleftarrow{\times 2} 27 \xleftarrow{+10} 17 \qquad n = 54$

Practice book

Section A (p 12)

1 (a) $8 \xrightarrow{+2} 10 \xrightarrow{\times 8} 80$

(b) $60 \xrightarrow{-25} 35 \xrightarrow{+12} 47$

(c) $11 \xrightarrow{-7} 4 \xrightarrow{+1} 5 \xrightarrow{\times 4} 20$

(d) $23 \xrightarrow{+12} 35 \xrightarrow{-5} 30 \xrightarrow{\times 5} 150$

(e) $32 \xrightarrow{\times 10} 320 \xrightarrow{+80} 400 \xrightarrow{+50} 450$

(f) $60 \xrightarrow{-20} 40 \xrightarrow{\div 5} 8 \xrightarrow{+3} 11$

(g) $80 \xrightarrow{\div 4} 20 \xrightarrow{\times 3} 60 \xrightarrow{-20} 40$

(h) $13 \xrightarrow{-2.5} 10.5 \xrightarrow{+0.3} 10.8 \xrightarrow{\div 2} 5.4$

2 (a) $3.4 \xrightarrow{+2.6} 6 \xrightarrow{\times 3.5} 21 \xrightarrow{\div 3} 7$

(b) $20 \xrightarrow{-8.4} 11.6 \xrightarrow{\div 2} 5.8 \xrightarrow{+4.2} 10$

(c) $60 \xrightarrow{\div 1.5} 40 \xrightarrow{\times 4.5} 180 \xrightarrow{\div 1.8} 100$

Section B (p 13)

1 (a) M (b) K (c) J (d) L

2 (a) $\bigcirc \xrightarrow{\times 3} \bigcirc \xrightarrow{+5} 14$

(b) $\bigcirc \xrightarrow{\div 3} \bigcirc \xrightarrow{-4} 6$

(c) $\bigcirc \xrightarrow{\times 4} \bigcirc \xrightarrow{-8} 36$

(d) $\bigcirc \xrightarrow{\times 10} \bigcirc \xrightarrow{+6} 46$

(e) $\bigcirc \xrightarrow{\div 4} \bigcirc \xrightarrow{+4} 7$

(f) $\bigcirc \xrightarrow{\div 5} \bigcirc \xrightarrow{+3} 5$

3 D

4 (a) $4p + 3 = 31$ (b) $\dfrac{p}{5} + 4 = 8$

(c) $\dfrac{p}{2} - 8 = 12$ (d) $6p - 30 = 30$

(e) $\dfrac{p}{5} + 30 = 36$ (f) $25p - 40 = 60$

(g) $20p + 18 = 418$

(h) $6p - 4 = 116$

Section C (p 14)

Students should check their solutions.

1 (a) $k \xrightarrow{\times 2} 2k \xrightarrow{+4} 2k + 4$

$2 \xleftarrow{\div 2} 4 \xleftarrow{-4} 8$ $k = 2$

(b) $b \xrightarrow{\times 7} 7b \xrightarrow{-2} 7b - 2$

$7 \xleftarrow{\div 7} 49 \xleftarrow{+2} 47$ $b = 7$

(c) $r \xrightarrow{\div 5} \dfrac{r}{5} \xrightarrow{-2} \dfrac{r}{5} - 2$

$20 \xleftarrow{\times 5} 4 \xleftarrow{+2} 2$ $r = 20$

(d) $z \xrightarrow{\div 3} \dfrac{z}{3} \xrightarrow{-8} \dfrac{z}{3} - 8$

$81 \xleftarrow{\times 3} 27 \xleftarrow{+8} 19$ $z = 81$

2 (a) $w \xrightarrow{\times 3} 3w \xrightarrow{+2} 3w + 2$

$7 \xleftarrow{\div 3} 21 \xleftarrow{-2} 23$ $w = 7$

(b) $d \xrightarrow{\times 2} 2d \xrightarrow{-10} 2d - 10$

$10 \xleftarrow{\div 2} 20 \xleftarrow{+10} 10$ $d = 10$

(c) $s \xrightarrow{\div 8} \dfrac{s}{8} \xrightarrow{+9} \dfrac{s}{8} + 9$

$8 \xleftarrow{\times 8} 1 \xleftarrow{-9} 10$ $s = 8$

(d)

k →(×5)→ $5k$ →(−9)→ $5k - 9$

5 ←(÷5)← 25 ←(+9)← 16 $k = 5$

(e)

b →(×5)→ $5b$ →(+2)→ $5b + 2$

5 ←(÷5)← 25 ←(−2)← 27 $b = 5$

(f)

a →(÷3)→ $\dfrac{a}{3}$ →(−2)→ $\dfrac{a}{3} - 2$

6 ←(×3)← 2 ←(+2)← 0 $a = 6$

(g)

m →(÷8)→ $\dfrac{m}{8}$ →(+4)→ $\dfrac{m}{8} + 4$

8 ←(×8)← 1 ←(−4)← 5 $m = 8$

(h)

z →(×5)→ $5z$ →(+6)→ $5z + 6$

9 ←(÷5)← 45 ←(−6)← 51 $z = 9$

(i)

e →(×7)→ $7e$ →(−7)→ $7e - 7$

2 ←(÷7)← 14 ←(+7)← 7 $e = 2$

(j)

y →(÷2)→ $\dfrac{y}{2}$ →(+10)→ $\dfrac{y}{2} + 10$

8 ←(×2)← 4 ←(−10)← 14 $y = 8$

3 (a) $b = 3.1$ (b) $c = 54$ (c) $n = 5.7$

(d) $f = 5$ (e) $g = 28$ (f) $p = 21$

Section D (p 15)

1 (a) $5n + 6 = 51,\ n = 9$

(b) $\dfrac{n}{7} + 18 = 20,\ n = 14$

(c) $2n - 9 = 11,\ n = 10$

(d) $9n - 5 = 22,\ n = 3$

(e) $\dfrac{n}{2} - 14 = 1,\ n = 30$

(f) $4n + 18 = 30,\ n = 3$

(g) $4n - 5.1 = 7.7,\ n = 3.2$

(h) $\dfrac{n}{8} + 9.5 = 14,\ n = 36$

2 (a)

I think of a number.
· I multiply by 4.
· I subtract 2.
My answer is 18.
What was my number?

$n = 5$

(b)

I think of a number.
· I divide by 3.
· I subtract 5.
My answer is 9.
What was my number?

$n = 42$

(c)

I think of a number.
· I divide by 5.
· I add 2.
My answer is 4.8.
What was my number?

$n = 14$

(d)

I think of a number.
· I multiply by 8.
· I subtract 1.
My answer is 47.
What was my number?

$n = 6$

(e)

I think of a number.
· I multiply by 8.
· I add 15.
My answer is 71.
What was my number?

$n = 7$

(f)

I think of a number.
· I divide by 10.
· I add 1.4.
My answer is 2.
What was my number?

$n = 6$

3 Any number puzzle with answer 12 and correct starting number such as $2n + 2 = 12,\ n = 5$

4 Any number puzzle with starting number 6 and answer 20 such as $2n + 8 = 20$

4 Mental methods

This unit revises multiplying by multiples of 10. It introduces rounding whole numbers to one significant figure and using rounding in estimation.

TG

p 28	**A** *Place value*	
p 29	**B** *Rounding*	Rounding to one significant figure
p 30	**C** *Multiplying by 10, 100, 1000, ...*	
p 30	**D** *Multiplying by numbers ending in zeros*	
p 31	**E** *Rough estimates*	

Practice book pages 16 and 17

B Rounding (p 29)

TG

> 'I asked them
> "If you won £27049 and could only choose one figure, which figure would it be?"
> Most soon realised it was the 2 worth £20000.'

◊ In the initial activity students can be asked to round the figures to the nearest 10, 100 etc. and discuss what is the appropriate number to use. Significant figures can be explained as using the same degree of accuracy to round numbers with different place values.

◊ Emphasise the idea of the 'most significant figure' in a written number. If, for example, it is the thousands figure, then we round to the nearest thousand, and so on. (However, when the most significant figure is 9, then rounding up inevitably involves using the next higher place value. This situation is avoided except in question B8. It will be taken up in a later unit.)

E Rough estimates (p 31)

◊ This is an elementary treatment of this topic. The work will be taken up and extended later.

With every beat of your heart

Using a life expectancy of 70, an average heart rate of 80 beats per minute, and rounding to 1 s.f., gives

$$80 \times 60 \times 20 \times 400 \times 70 = 2\,688\,000\,000 \text{ beats.}$$

Ⓐ **Place value** (p 28)

A1 (a) 3000   (b) 50

A2 (a) 400 000   (b) 90 000

A3 (a) 3618   (b) 52 763   (c) 42 371
     (d) 148 510   (e) 90 284   (f) 473 593
     (g) 95 342   (h) 274 540

A4 2000

A5 (a) 1911   (b) 3711   (c) 21 711

A6 67 275   67 342   67 531   68 200   68 752

Ⓑ **Rounding** (p 29)

B1 (a) 500   (b) 400   (c) 2600
     (c) 5800   (d) 32 400

B2 (a) 7000   (b) 8000   (c) 3000
     (d) 18 000   (e) 8000

B3 (a) 4100   (b) 4130   (c) 4000

B4 (a) 12 000   (b) 10 000
     (c) 11 700   (d) 11 680

B5 (a) 46 000   (b) 68 100
     (c) 650 000   (d) 8 000 000

B6 (a) 500   (b) 2000   (c) 30 000
     (d) 2000   (e) 90 000

B7 (a) 70   (b) 8000   (c) 800
     (d) 300 000   (e) 30 000   (f) 3000
     (g) 400   (h) 50 000
     (i) 6 000 000   (j) 600 000

*B8 1000

Ⓒ **Multiplying and dividing by 10, 100, 1000, ...** (p 30)

C1 (a) 250   (b) 43 200   (c) 6500
     (d) 560   (e) 340

C2 (a) 5000   (b) 760   (c) 34 000
     (d) 58   (e) 80 000

C3 (a) 42   (b) 5310   (c) 4.6
     (d) 5.83   (e) 0.294

C4 (a) 1800   (b) 347.2   (c) 248
     (d) 39.51   (e) 0.52

Ⓓ **Multiplying by numbers ending in zeros** (p 30)

D1 (a) 260   (b) 690   (c) 22 800
     (d) 450   (e) 8400

D2 (a) 1000   (b) 3300   (c) 7000
     (d) 1000   (e) 24 000

D3 (a) 3000   (b) 6400   (c) 48
     (d) 45   (e) 660

D4 (a) 1200   (b) 15 000   (c) 8000
     (d) 9000   (e) 2000

D5 (a) 18 000   (b) 140 000   (c) 18 000
     (d) 3600   (e) 15 000

D6 (a) 20 000   (b) 4800   (c) 35 000
     (d) 80 000   (e) 300 000

D7 £60

D8 (a) £32   (b) £100   (c) £240

D9 £80 000

Ⓔ **Rough estimates** (p 31)

E1 (a) 2000   (b) 1500   (c) 2100
     (d) 8000   (e) 12 000

E2 £1800

E3 2000

E4 (a) 5600   (b) 24 000   (c) 120 000
     (d) 48 000   (e) 280 000

E5 £15 000

E6 (a) 240 000   (b) 235 760

Test yourself (p 32)

T1 (a) 8000 (b) 30 000 (c) 900
   (d) 1000 (e) 500 000

T2 (a) 405 (b) 260 (c) 68
   (d) 31.6 (e) 0.427

T3 (a) 10 400 (b) 8800 (c) 240
   (d) 3000 (e) 34 000

T4 (a) 1800 (b) 8000 (c) 400 000
   (d) 36 000 (e) 420 000

T5 (a) 6450 (b) 400 (c) 64 530

T6 (a) 4000 (b) 15 000 (c) 14 000
   (d) 160 000 (e) 600 000

T7 £1500

Practice book

Section A (p 16)

1 (a) 2000 (b) 70 000

2 (a) 2715 (b) 32 961
  (c) 12 874 (d) 974 513

3 (a) 38 299 (b) 38 779
  (c) 41 279 (d) 58 279

4 35 141   35 432   35 675   36 002   36 143

Section B (p 16)

1 (a) 43 800 (b) 462 000 (c) 650 000

2 (a) 28 000 (b) 28 250
  (c) 28 300 (d) 30 000

3 (a) 4000 (b) 40 000 (c) 100 000
  (d) 70 000 (e) 700

4 Greenland 2 000 000 km^2
    Java 100 000 km^2
    Sri Lanka 70 000 km^2

Sections C and D (p 17)

1 (a) 137 (b) 48 (c) 37.6
   (d) 15.03 (e) 2.31 (f) 6200
   (g) 0.0572 (h) 6.2 (i) 0.583
   (j) 0.474

2 (a) 2800 (b) 660 (c) 42 600
   (d) 600 (e) 12 600 (f) 5500
   (g) 480 (h) 68 000 (i) 3200
   (j) 3060

3 (a) 2800 (b) 1800 (c) 6000
   (d) 80 000 (e) 30 000 (f) 24 000
   (g) 16 000 (h) 60 000 (i) 5600
   (j) 63 000

4 (a) £24 (b) £80
   (c) £200 (d) £1400

5 £240 000

Section E (p 17)

1 (a) 1200 (b) 1500 (c) 6000
   (d) 4800 (e) 18 000

2 £2500

3 1200 m^2

4 200 000 pints

5 Made to measure

This unit is primarily about giving students a feel for metric units. It is not anticipated that they become involved in multiplying and dividing by powers of 10 to change between units at this stage.

p 33	**A** *Metric lengths*	Writing measurements in mm, cm and metres
p 34	**B** *Thousands of them*	Using the prefix kilo- in metric units
p 35	**C** *Thousands of pieces*	Using the prefix milli- in metric units

Essential	**Optional**
Rulers marked in mm	Screws of varying sizes, old birthday cards
Metre rules or tape measures	Catalogue containing kitchen units or similar
Map of the school and local area	Ordinary mug
Scientific balance, brass drawing pins	
1 kg bags of sugar, flour or similar	
Items with known weights ranging from 250 g to 5 kg.	

Practice book pages 18 to 20

A Metric lengths (p 33)

> Rulers marked in mm, metre rules or tape measures
> Optional: screws of varying sizes, old birthday cards

◊ The aim of this section is simply to build confidence in measuring metric lengths. Some suggested activities are:

• Give students a number of screws of different sizes to measure in mm and cm. They could imagine that they have to go to a DIY shop to get more screws of the same size and need to know the lengths of each screw. Alternatively have some small labelled screw boxes (or matchboxes) that screws have to be sorted into.

• Give students some old birthday cards or similar to measure in mm and cm. They could imagine that they have to buy envelopes for these and need to know what sizes to buy.

- Ask students to measure windows in metres with a view to putting up curtains. Curtains should be 1.5 times the window's width and 20 cm longer than its depth.

A simple device, which may be useful for students who have difficulties, is to write the measurements in a boxed display with an appropriate number of boxes after the decimal point, for example:

175 cm | 0 | 1 | 7 | 5 | 1.75 m

You will need to decide whether to tackle the issue of excess zeros at this stage, for example, having 170 cm written as 1.70 m.

B *Thousands of them* (p 34)

This section looks at using the prefix kilo- in the context of kilometres and kilograms.

> Map of the school and local area
> Scientific balance, brass drawing pins
> 1 kg bags of sugar, flour or similar
> Items with known weights ranging from 250 g to 5 kg

◊ You could discuss with students if they know of any other measurements which use kilo as a prefix (such as kilowatt). Job adverts often quote salaries in terms of £K and at the turn of the century the abbreviation Y2K was widely used for the year 2000.

More or less

Remind students that a kilometre is one thousand metres and show them a metre rule. Ask them to suggest places nearby which are more or less than a kilometre from where they now are. A map with a circle drawn of scaled radius 1 km can then be used to check their guesses.

What's in a gram?

The aim of this activity is to give students a feel for what one gram is. If possible, use a balance from the science department which weighs to an accuracy of at least 0.1 g. Alternatively, if you are using kitchen scales, ten identical items could be weighed and the weight of one worked out.

Students could find the weight of a single sheet of photocopy paper (about 5 g) and work out (and check by weighing) how many sheets weigh 1 kilogram.

'I had an electronic balance. Students suggested articles that might weigh 1 g, and interest increased as we got nearer to 1 g.'

◊ Again it is not expected that students will use a formal method of changing units and a simple boxed display may be useful. Discuss some common fractions of a kilogram such as a half and a quarter and their decimal and gram equivalents.

◊ Having concentrated on a single gram, use other items with known weights so that students can familiarise themselves with weights such as 250 g, 500 g or 1 kg. Students can try estimating weights of items such as textbooks, exercise books, shoes etc by comparing them with known weights. However, it is extremely difficult to estimate weights, and this should be done more as an enjoyable investigation than a test of skill.

ℂ *Thousands of pieces* (p 35)

> Optional: catalogue containing kitchen units or similar, tape measures or metre rules, ordinary mug

TG

◊ Millimetres are commonly used in the building and engineering industries. Catalogues of kitchen units and other unit furniture usually give measurements in millimetres. To use these, converting between measurements in metres and millimetres is essential. Students could use such catalogues to work out what units they could fit along a wall of the classroom or other suitable space. This could be done by making chalk marks on floors and walls. They could also use the existing classroom furniture to create their own 'catalogue'.

◊ A handy reference is that an ordinary mug weighs about 250 grams (when empty) and holds about 250 millilitres. Students could be encouraged to find other useful references.

𝔸 *Metric lengths* (p 33)

A1 (a) 30 mm   3 cm
    (b) 10 mm   1 cm
    (c) 25 mm   2.5 cm
    (d) 53 mm   5.3 cm
    (e) 7 mm   0.7 cm
    (f) 127 mm   12.7 cm

A2

Spider	Span (mm)	Span (cm)
Bird-eating Spider	250 mm	**25 cm**
Tarantula	**240 mm**	24 cm
Raft Spider (UK)	145 mm	**14.5 cm**
House Spider (UK)	**75 mm**	7.5 cm
Wolf Spider (UK)	17 mm	**1.7 cm**
Money Spider (UK)	3 mm	**0.3 cm**

A3 Python   600 cm
    Anaconda   850 cm
    Grass Snake   125 cm
    Adder   75 cm

A4 Fruit Bat   1.70 m
    Mouse-eared Bat (UK)   0.45 m
    Pipistrelle Bat (UK)   0.25 m
    Kitti's Hog-nosed Bat   0.09 m

A5 1.4 m or 140 cm

B *Thousands of them* (p 34)

B1 (a) 5000 m   (b) 2500 m
    (c) 10 000 m   (d) 15 400 m
    (e) 200 000 m   (f) 9300 m
    (g) 600 m   (h) 250 m
    (i) 500 m   (j) 750 m

B2 (a) 5 km   (b) 20 km
    (c) 100 km   (d) 1.5 km
    (e) 5.8 km   (f) 0.5 km
    (g) 0.1 km   (h) 0.75 km

B3 14 km 200 m or 14.2 km

B4 4.5 kg   ripe bananas (mashed)
    0.5 kg   chopped nuts
    1 kg   soya margarine
    1.25 kg raisins
    0.75 kg rolled oats
    1.5 kg   wholewheat flour

B5 (a) 4000 g   (b) 2500 g   (c) 400 g
    (d) 750 g   (e) 500 g   (f) 250 g

B6 850 g or 0.85 kg

B7 (a) 2   (b) 4   (c) 10   (d) 5
    (e) 20   (f) 50   (g) 8   (h) 100

C *Thousands of pieces* (p 35)

C1 (a) 2 m   (b) 10 m   (c) 1.5 m
    (d) 1.695 m   (e) 0.5 m   (f) 0.75 m
    (g) 0.05 m   (h) 0.01 m

C2 (a) 5000 mm   (b) 50 000 mm
    (c) 2500 mm   (d) 5500 mm
    (e) 600 mm   (f) 250 mm
    (g) 4750 mm   (h) 65 mm

C3

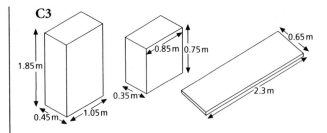

C4 (a) 2 litres   (b) 1.5 litres   (c) 5 litres

C5 (a) 0.75 litre   (b) 0.5 litre
    (c) 0.8 litre   (d) 0.1 litre

C6 (a) 1500 ml   (b) 5200 ml
    (c) 10 000 ml   (d) 500 ml

C7 (a) 3 litres   (b) 4.5 litres
    (c) 0.65 litre   (d) 0.005 litre

C8 (a) 20   (b) 150   (c) 200   (d) 100

C9 50 ml   0.5 litres   750 ml   1.2 litres
    1500 ml

C10 (a) A milligram (mg) is **a thousandth** of
       a gram. There are **a thousand**
       milligrams in a gram.

      (b) (i) 5000 mg   (ii) 50 000 mg
         (iii) 100 000 mg   (iv) 500 mg

      (c) (i) 2 g   (ii) 1.5 g
         (iii) 0.5 g   (iv) 0.05 g
      (d) 1 million

Test yourself (p 37)

T1 (a) 700 ml   (b) 1.5 litres

T2 (a) 1.25 kg   (b) 2 kg   (c) 0.75 kg

T3 650 g

Practice book

Section A (p 18)

1 (a) 20 mm, 2 cm (b) 41 mm, 4.1 cm
   (c) 66 mm, 6.6 cm

2
Bird	Length (mm)	Length (cm)
Goldcrest	90	**9**
Firecrest	**85**	8.5
Pied flycatcher	**125**	12.5
Blue tit	113	**11.3**
Long-tailed tit	**140**	14

3 (a) Firecrest (b) Long-tailed tit

4 6 mm   2.5 cm   3 cm   52 mm   5.5 cm

5
Bird	Wingspan (cm)	Wingspan (m)
Buzzard	125	1.25
Red kite	195	**1.95**
Golden eagle	**220**	2.2
Osprey	170	**1.7**
Kestrel	80	**0.8**

6 (a) Gannet (b) Green cormorant

7 (a) 300 cm (b) 450 cm (c) 645 cm
   (d) 50 cm (e) 68 cm

Section B (p 19)

1 (a) 3000 g (b) 1500 g (c) 600 g
   (d) 3200 g (e) 14 000 g

2 (a) 5 kg (b) 1.8 kg (c) 16 kg
   (d) 4.25 kg (e) 0.6 kg

3
Bird	Weight (g)	Weight (kg)
Herring gull	1200	**1.2**
Common gull	450	**0.45**
Gt black-backed gull	2000	**2**
Mute swan	**12000**	12
Canada goose	**4500**	4.5

   (a) Mute swan (b) Common gull

4 (a) 4000 m (b) 1800 m (c) 2250 m
   (d) 500 m (e) 20 000 m

5 (a) 3 km (b) 6.5 km (c) 15 km
   (d) 0.85 km (e) 1.25 km

6
	Distance (m)	Distance (km)
Anna	1200	**1.2**
Bethan	**1900**	1.9
Ron	500	**0.5**
Shamraz	650	**0.65**
James	**300**	0.3

   (a) Bethan (b) James

7 (a) 10 (b) 4 (c) 5

Section C (p 20)

1 (a) 3 m (b) 2.5 m (c) 3.26 m
   (d) 15 m (e) 0.6 m (f) 0.075 m

2 (a) 2000 mm (b) 30 000 mm
   (c) 1700 mm (d) 800 mm
   (e) 40 mm

3 No

4 250 mm   0.45 m   0.8 m   1670 mm   1.9 m

5 1 000 000

6
Capacity (litres)	Capacity (ml)
2	**2000**
1.4	**1400**
1.2	1200
0.75	750
0.05	50

7 10

8 (a) 4 (b) 3 (c) 6 (d) 12

9 250 mg   400 mg   1600 mg   2.5 g   5 g

Finding your way (p 38)

This unit is for students to practise following and giving directions using a map.

> **Optional**
> Sheet G4, an OHP transparency of sheet G4

◊ This material can be dealt with orally. The map on sheet G4 can be copied on to an OHP transparency to help with this. Students need to be reminded of four essential skills in this work:

- using simple grid references such as A2 to locate particular places – this will be developed later to two-figure grid references;
- following and giving directions to describe routes on the map;
- describing directions using the eight points of the compass – a good start to this exercise might be to draw an eight-point compass rose and ask students to add the compass directions;
- using a map scale to estimate distances – at this stage students should be able to use the edge of a piece of paper and mark off distances to read against the scale.

◊ Some students find giving left and right directions difficult and it may help if the map is orientated so that they are facing the direction they are supposed to be going.

'I asked pupils to make up some questions of their own at the end.'

◊ Students could make up their own questions and problems based on this map or one invented by themselves.

1 (a) Corporation St   (b) Boulevard St
   (c) A3
   (d) (i) C2   (ii) A1   (iii) C3

2 Left

3 (a) Left   (b) Right   (c) Left

4 (a) East (b) North-east (c) South-east

5 (a) South   (b) South-west
   (c) North-west   (d) South-west

6 The Station

7 (a) The student's directions from the Post Office to the Station
   (b) The student's directions from the Cinema to the Hospital

   (c) The student's directions from the Station to the Fire Station

8 (a) 450 m   (b) 850 m   (c) 700 m

Test yourself (p 40)

T1 (a) C2   (b) A1

T2 Right

T3 (a) East   (b) South-west

T4 The Library

T5 The student's directions from the Library to the School

T6 500 m

7   *Decimal places*

Essential

Sheets G5, G6, G7

Practice book pages 21 and 22

A   *One decimal place* (p 41)

> Sheet G5

◊   The number line in the introduction is reproduced on sheet G5.
Students could make up their own puzzles like this in order to
consolidate their understanding of the first decimal place.

C   *Two decimal places* (p 44)

> Sheets G6 and G7

◊   Use the diagrams on the page to bring out key points such as
  - 1.67 is between 1.6 and 1.7
  - 1.70 is equivalent to 1.7
  - 1.23 is less than 1.4
  - 0.09 is less than 0.7

It may help to relate the numbers on the cards to lengths in metres.
The numbers in order give the word FORMULA.

D   *At home* (p 46)

◊   You may need to point out to that the measurements of the rooms are
found by using the internal dimensions of the rectangles.

Ⓐ One decimal place (p 41)

A1 (A on sheet G5)

A2 (a) 5.2 (b) 5.8 (c) 6.3 (d) 0.3
(e) 0.7 (f) 1.2 (g) 10.5 (h) 11.5
(i) 8.8 (j) 9.9

A3 (B on sheet G5)
(a) Number line with 4.7, 4.9, 5.8, 6.3, 6.9, 7.3 marked with arrows
(b) Number line with 0.3, 0.9, 1.5, 2.3, 2.8, 3.2, 3.7 marked with arrows

A4 The 7.9 cm and 7.8 cm discs will go through the slot.

A5 3.3, 2.9, 3, 3.9

A6 (a) 0.1, 0.9, 1.2, 2, 3.4, 6.7, 7, 8.5
(b) 0.2, 0.5, 1.1, 3, 4.6, 5.6, 9.1, 11

A7 (a) 6.9 cm (b) 7.1 cm

A8 0.8, 1, 1.2

A9 1.8, 2.3, 2.8

A10 (a) 3.5 (b) 4.5 (c) 1.5 (d) 2.5

A11 Josie is right (with 3.4)

A12 (a) 7.4 (b) 8.2 (c) 8.8 (d) 0.6
(e) 1.2 (f) 1.8 (g) 2.5 (h) 3.3
(i) 5.5 (j) 6.5 (k) 7.5

A13 (C on sheet G5)
(a) Number line with 0.2, 0.6, 1.2, 1.8, 2.2, 2.4 marked with arrows
(b) Number line with 13.4, 13.8, 14.2, 14.7, 15.6, 16.4 marked with arrows

Ⓑ And it's raining ... (p 43)

B1 (a) 4.9 cm
(b) February, March and April
(c) 6.4 cm (d) 59.3 cm

*B2 (a) (i) 14.4 cm (ii) 15.5 cm
(iii) 26.1 cm
(b) 28.5 cm (c) 15.6 cm
(d) (i) 17.4 cm (ii) 8.7 cm
(iii) 23.7 cm

Ⓒ Two decimal places (p 44)

C1 (a) 5.23 (b) 5.27 (c) 5.32
(d) 0.02 (e) 0.09 (f) 0.14
(g) 1.77 (h) 1.85 (i) 1.92
(j) 3.01 (k) 3.06 (l) 3.13

C2 (On sheet G6)
(a) (i) Number line with 2.48, 2.51, 2.58, 2.65, 2.70, 2.73 marked with arrows
(ii) Number line with 1.17, 1.19, 1.20, 1.23, 1.35, 1.42 marked with arrows
(iii) Number line with 12.28, 12.34, 12.39, 12.40, 12.46, 12.51 marked with arrows
(iv) Number line with 0.03, 0.08, 0.13, 0.24, 0.29, 0.31 marked with arrows
(v) Number line with 3.99, 4.02, 4.09, 4.13, 4.16, 4.21 marked with arrows
(b) (i) The decimals in order are 4.02, 4.1, 4.12, 4.18, 4.2, 4.23 giving the word RADIUS
(ii) The decimals in order are 1.36, 1.4, 1.45, 1.50, 1.56, 2, 2.09, 2.2, 2.5, 3.0 giving the word POLYHEDRON

C3 (a) R, U (b) P, Q, R, S, U

C4 (a) R
(b) Envelope B: Q, R Envelope C: R

C5 2.67, 2.6, 3.1, 3.19, 3.07

C6 7.06, 7.1, 7.28, 7.4, 7.92, 8

C7 1.2, 1.03, 0.46, 0.45, 0.3, 0.06

C8 3.9 kg

*C9 (a) 3.3   (b) 2.57 (c) 1.4   (d) 1.25
    (e) 10   (f) 6.26 (g) 6.49 (h) 4.31

*C10

You finish on 4.1

Ⓓ **At home** (p 46)

D1 (a) 4.2 m   (b) 6.5 m
    (c) 27.3 m²   (d) £668.85

D2 2.53 m²

D3 (a) 3.0 m   (b) 3.6 m
    (c) 13.2 m   (d) Yes

D4 (a) 1.1 m   (b) 1.5 m, 1.15 m, 1.25 m

D5 Yes

D6 No

Test yourself (p 47)

T1 Arrow A

T2 3.3

T3 2.09, 2.1, 2.36, 2.7

Practice book

Section A (p 21)

1 (a) 11.3   (b) 11.7   (c) 12.2
  (d) 40.2   (e) 40.6   (f) 41.4
  (g) 59.7   (h) 0.4   (i) 1.6
  (j) 2.4   (k) 7.5   (l) 9.5

2 4, 3.9, 4.8, 5

3 0.3, 0.7, 2.7, 3, 4.8, 5.3, 6.3, 8.5

4 8.2, 4, 3.6, 2.7, 2.1, 0.9, 0.8, 0.4

5 1.2, 1.5, 1.8

6 (a) Jackie   (b) Hayley   (c) 0.8 m

7 (a) 12.2   (b) 13.6   (c) 14.8

Sections C and D (p 22)

1 (a) 6.73   (b) 6.83   (c) 6.93
  (d) 0.16   (e) 0.26   (f) 0.44
  (g) 1.73   (h) 1.84   (i) 2.03

2 0.07, 0.16, 1.75, 1.8, 1.83, 1.85
    B   U   R   G   E   R

3 3.3, 3.8, 4.25, 4.03

4 5.6, 5.89, 5.98, 6, 6.09, 6.35, 6.9

5 1.85 m, 1.83 m, 1.75 m, 1.68 m, 1.63 m, 1.57 m

6 1.8 kg

7 C and D are too wide.

8 (a) 2.55   (b) 3.47
  (c) 1.85   (d) 5.91

Symmetrical shapes

This unit deals with the symmetry of polygons.

Essential	**Optional**
Sheets G8, G9, G10, G11	Tracing paper, scissors
Practice book pages 23 to 25	

𝔸 *Describing shapes* (p 48)

The main purpose of this section is to remind students of the special types of triangles and quadrilaterals.

> Sheet G8

TG

'A good activity - it got them thinking about the properties of shapes.'

◊ The initial activity could be organised in small groups or pairs so that students can discuss the problems and produce a collective set of solutions. Possible solutions are:

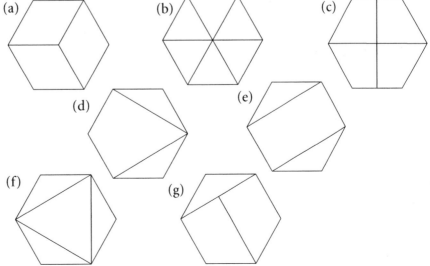

(a) (b) (c) (d) (e) (f) (g)

B *Symmetrical triangles* (p 49)

This section brings reflection and rotation symmetry together as students look at triangles and patterns in triangles.

Sheets G9, G10

◊ Describing a shape with no rotation symmetry as having order 1 is introduced here. Some may find this a difficult idea.

C *Polygon symmetry* (p 50)

In this section students look at different categories of quadrilaterals and regular polygons and describe their symmetry.

◊ Students often find the symmetry of a parallelogram difficult and assume it has reflection symmetry. Demonstrating with tracing paper or cut-out shapes that it has no reflection symmetry should encourage more careful checking of other shapes.

What am I?

This game can be played by the class or in small groups or pairs. Creating their own problems is as important as finding the solutions. The solutions to the two on the students' page are:

isosceles triangle   kite

D *Getting coordinated* (p 51)

Sheet G11
Optional: tracing paper, scissors

Use is made of coordinates in all four quadrants in this section.

𝔸 Describing shapes (p 48)

A1 (a) Equilateral triangle

(b) Rhombus

(c) Kite

(d) Pentagon

(e) Trapezium

(f) Parallelogram

𝔹 Symmetrical triangles (p 49)

B1 (a)

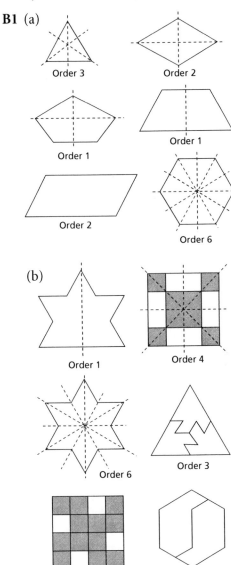

B2 (a) 3 lines of symmetry and rotation symmetry order 3

(b) 1 line of symmetry and rotation symmetry order 1

(c) 3 lines of symmetry and rotation symmetry order 3

(d) 1 line of symmetry and rotation symmetry order 1

(e) No lines of symmetry and rotation symmetry order 3

(f) 3 lines of symmetry and rotation symmetry order 3

B3 (a) The student's shading to give reflection but not rotation symmetry

(b) The student's shading to give rotation but not reflection symmetry

(c) The student's shading to give reflection and rotation symmetry

B4 (a) (i) Isosceles (ii) 1 (iii) 1

(b) (i) Right-angled (ii) 0 (iii) 1

(c) (i) Equilateral (ii) 3 (iii) 3

(d) (i) Scalene (ii) 0 (iii) 1

ℂ Polygon symmetry (p 50)

C1 (a) 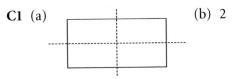 (b) 2

(c) A square has 4 lines of symmetry and rotation symmetry order 4.

C2 (a) 1 line of symmetry, no rotation symmetry

(b) The student's drawing of a non-symmetrical trapezium

C3 Rhombuses have 2 lines of symmetry and rotation symmetry order 2.

C4 Kites have 1 line of symmetry and no rotation symmetry.

C5 The student's drawing of a quadrilateral with no symmetry

C6 (a)

	Sides	Lines	Order
Equilateral triangle	3	3	3
Square	4	4	4
Regular pentagon	5	5	5
Regular hexagon	6	6	6
Regular nonagon	9	9	9

(b) 20 lines of symmetry and rotation symmetry order 20.

Ⓓ *Getting coordinated* (p 51)

D1 (a) (0, 3); square

(b) (7, 3); rhombus

(c) (4, 10), (7, 10); trapezium

(d) (12, 10); kite

D2

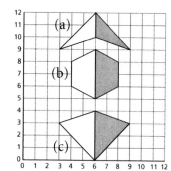

(a) Arrowhead (b) Hexagon

(c) Kite

D3 (a) (⁻2, ⁻1) (b) Parallelogram

D4 (a)

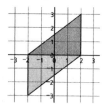

Parallelogram

(b)

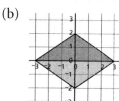

Rhombus

(c)

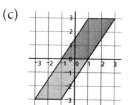

Parallelogram

D5 (a)

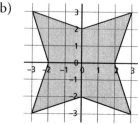

(b)

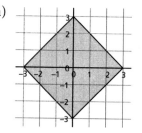

D6 (a)–(c)

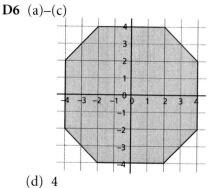

(d) 4

Test yourself (p 52)

T1 (a) B (b) D (c) A

T2 (a) A parallelogram

B kite

C trapezium

D rhombus

(b) One (c) None

(d) A and D (e) D

Practice book

Section A (p 23)

1 (a) Parallelogram
   (b) Right-angled isosceles triangle
   (c) Square   (d) Trapezium
   (e) Right-angled isosceles triangle
   (f) Right-angled isosceles triangle
   (g) Trapezium   (h) Trapezium
   (i) Hexagon   (j) Parallelogram
   (k) Equilateral triangle
   (l) Rhombus

2 (a) Right-angled isosceles
   (b) Trapezium
   (c) Kite
   (d) The student's parallelogram
   (e) The student's scalene triangle

Sections B and C (p 24)

1

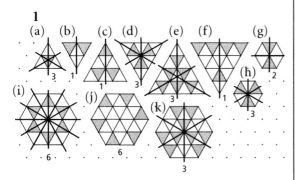

(a) (b) (c) (d) (e) (f) (g) (h) (i) (j) (k)

2 (a) Isosceles   (b) Scalene
   (c) Equilateral

3 (a) I have six equal sides.
        I am a regular **hexagon**.
        I have **6** lines of reflection symmetry.
        I have order of rotation symmetry **6**.
   (b) I have four sides.
        My opposite sides are parallel.
        I have no lines of symmetry.
        I am a **parallelogram**.
        I have order of rotation symmetry **2**.

Section D (p 25)

1 (a) (3, 11) and (5, 11) Trapezium
   (b) (3, 6) Kite
   (c) (10, 6) Rhombus
   (d) (10, 0) Square

2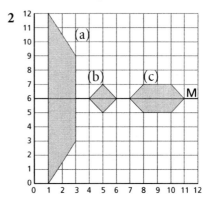

   (a) (1, 0) (3, 3) Trapezium
   (b) (5, 7) Square
   (c) (8, 5) (10, 5) Hexagon

3 (a) (⁻3, 0)   (b) Square

4 (a) (⁻2, ⁻2)

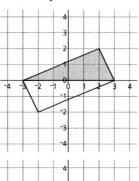

   (b) (⁻1, ⁻2)
        (1, ⁻2)

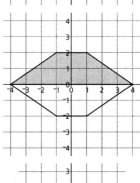

   (c) (⁻2, ⁻1)
        (⁻1, ⁻2)
        (1, ⁻2)
        (2, ⁻1)

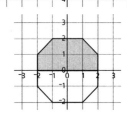

9 Working with formulas

Students draw graphs for rules found from patterns and solve equations arising from patterns.

Essential

Squared paper

Practice book pages 26 to 30

B *Know your tables* (p 54)

'We actually went to the dining room and did this with real tables and chairs.'

This section revises finding the number of one type of object in terms of the number of another type. Students find the number of chairs in a table arrangement in terms of the number of tables used.

The word 'formula' to mean a rule expressed in letters is introduced.

C *Pendants* (p 57)

'Using an OHP and making up the pendants helped them to see the "unit" that was being added on.'

This section revises finding rules in terms of a pattern number in a sequence of numbers.

C1 You may want to use this question as an introduction to finding the rules. Discussion might bring out that the 'multiplier' in the rule is 2, because the numbers in the table go up in 2s (since to go from one size to the next, we need to add another two bars). So the rule must start

number of gold bars = size number × 2 …

Then we can look at the first size to fix what we add or subtract to make the rule work.

C2 Some students may wish to draw up a table, as in question C1.

D Graphs (p 60)

Students draw graphs from pattern tables. They are told how to number and label their axes.

Squared paper

E Equations (p 62)

From patterns, students are led to using equations. They then solve these using the reverse flow diagram method introduced in unit 4 'Reversing the flow.'

A Expression review (p 53)

A1 (a) 10 (b) 30 (c) 2 (d) 12

A2 (a) 20 (b) 9 (c) 1 (d) 9

A3 (a) 9 (b) 10 (c) 10 (d) 6

A4 (a) 20 (b) 28 (c) 10 (d) 8

A5 (a) 7 (b) 16 (c) 13

A6 $2(a + 1)$ is bigger. It is 12, and $2a + 1$ is only 11.

B Know your tables (p 54)

B1 (a) 10 (b) 22 (c) 202

(d)

Number of tables	1	2	3	4	5	6	10	100
Number of chairs	4	6	8	**10**	**12**	**14**	**22**	**202**

(e) number of chairs = number of tables × 2 + 2

(f) $c = 2t + 2$

B2 (a) 24 (b) 44

(c)

Number of tables	1	2	3	4	5	6	10	100
Number of chairs	**6**	**8**	**10**	**12**	**14**	**16**	**24**	**204**

(d) number of chairs = number of tables × 2 + 4

(e) $c = 2t + 4$

B3 (a) 42 (b) 402

(c) number of chairs = number of tables × 4 + 2

(d) $c = 4t + 2$

B4 (a) 604

(b) number of chairs = number of tables × 6 + 4

(c) $c = 6t + 4$

B5 (a) number of chairs = number of tables + 2

(b) $c = t + 2$

C Pendants (p 57)

C1 (a) 3

(b) (i) 5 (ii) 7 (c) 2

(d) (i) 21 (ii) 41

(e)

SuperDrop size (n)	1	2	3	4	5	6	10	20
Number of bars (g)	**3**	**5**	**7**	**9**	**11**	**13**	**21**	**41**

(f) B: number of gold bars = (size number × 2) + 1

(g) $g = 2n + 1$

C2 (a) 15 (b) 33 (c) 303

(d) The student's explanation, for example number of bars = size × 3 + 3

(e) $3n + 3$

C3 $4n + 2$

C4 The *Triangular*: $6n + 2$
The *Simple*: $3n + 1$
The *Tri-square*: $5n + 3$

C5 (a) 5 (bars) (b) 8 (bars)

(c) The student's sketch of a size 1 and a size 2 *Expressive* pendant

Ⓓ **Graphs** (p 60)

D1 (a) The student's check

(b) 10 (bars) with the student's sketch

(c)

Size of Tribar (n)	1	2	3	4	5
Number of gold bars (g)	7	10	13	16	19

D2 (a), (b), (d)

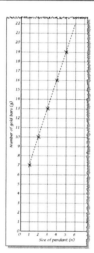

(c) The points lie in a straight line.

(e) $g = 22$ (when $n = 6$)

D3 (a) The student's check when $n = 8$

(b) 10 (bars) (c) 12 (bars)

(d)

Size of pendant (n)	1	2	3	4	5
Number of gold bars (g)	4	6	8	10	12

(e), (f), (g)

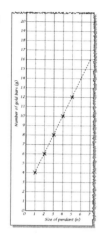

(h) $g = 14$ (when $n = 6$)

(i) $g = 16$ (when $n = 7$)

D4 (a)

Size of necklace (n)	2	3	4	5	6
Number of pearls (p)	8	11	14	17	20

(b) $3n + 2$

(c), (d)

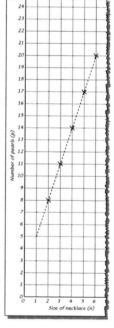

(e) There are 5 pearls in a size 1 (with the student's sketch to check).

E1 $4n + 2 = 70$

$n = 17$

Check

When $n = 17$, the necklace needs
$4 \times 17 + 2$ pearls
$= 68 + 2$
$= 70$ pearls, which is correct.

E2 $4n + 2 = 94$

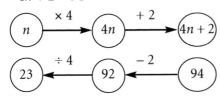

$n = 23$

Check

When $n = 23$, the necklace needs
$4 \times 23 + 2$ pearls
$= 92 + 2$
$= 94$ pearls, which is correct.

E3 $3n + 4 = 55$

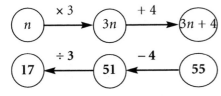

$n = 17$

Check

When $n = 17$, the necklace needs
$3 \times 17 + 4$ gold bars
$= 51 + 4$
$= 55$ bars, which is correct.

E4 $2n + 2 = 50$

$n = 24$

Check

When $n = 24$, the necklace needs
$2 \times 24 + 2$ bars
$= 48 + 2$
$= 50$ bars, which is correct.

E5 (a) $5n + 2$

 (b) $5n + 2 = 122$

$n = 24$

Check

When $n = 24$, the necklace needs
$5 \times 24 + 2$ pearls
$= 120 + 2$
$= 122$ pearls, which is correct.

*E6 Size 66

(The equation is $6n + 4 = 400$, so $n = 66$.)

Test yourself (p 65)

T1 (a) 11 (b) 14 (c) 302

(d)

Number of tables	1	2	3	4	100
Number of chairs	**5**	**8**	**11**	**14**	**302**

(e) $c = 3t + 2$

T2 (a), (b), (c)

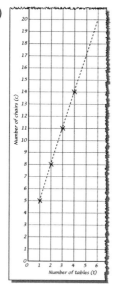

Number of chairs (c) / *Number of tables (t)*

(d) $c = 20$ (when t is 6)

T3 (a) $4n + 6$

(b) $4n + 6 = 90$

(c)

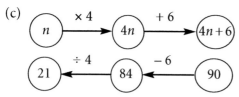

$n = 21$ so it is a size 21 necklace.

(d) The student's check

Practice book

Section B (p 26)

1 (a) 10   (b) 12   (c) 24   (d) 204

(e)

Number of rectangles	1	2	3	4	5	6	10	100
Number of squares	6	8	10	12	14	16	24	204

(f) *number of squares =*
  number of rectangles × 2 + 4

(g) $s = 2r + 4$

2 (a) 44   (b) 404

(c) *number of grey blocks =*
  number of white slabs × 4 + 4

(d) $g = 4w + 4$

3 (a) 402

(b) *number of triangles =*
  number of hexagons × 4 + 2

(c) $t = 4h + 2$

Section C (p 28)

1 (a) 10   (b) 22   (c) 102

(d) The student's explanation

(e) $2n + 2$

2 $5n + 2$

Section D (p 29)

1 (a) Student's check of size 4 *Step*

(b)

Size of *Step* design (*n*)	1	2	3	4	5
Number of blocks (*b*)	4	7	10	13	16

(c), (d)

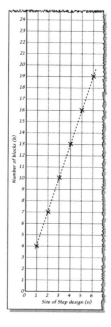

Number of blocks (b) / *Size of Step design (n)*

(e) $b = 19$ (when $n = 6$)

2 (a) 8

(b)
Size of *Cross* design (n)	2	3	4	5
Number of blocks (b)	**8**	**11**	14	**17**

(c) $3n + 2$

(d),(e)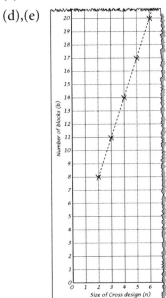

(f) $b = 20$ (when $n = 6$)

Section E (p 30)

1 (a) The student's check

(b) $4n + 1 = 61$

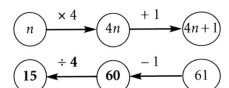

$n = \mathbf{23}$

Check

When $n = 15$, the fence needs

$4 \times 15 + 1$ posts

$= 60 + 1$

$= 61$ posts which is correct

2 $4n + 3 = 95$

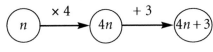

$n = 23$

Check

When $n = 23$, the fence needs

$4 \times 23 + 3$ posts

$= 92 + 3$

$= 95$ posts which is correct

3 (a) $3n + 1$ (b) size 27

Review 1 (p 67)

1 (a) $6\,m^2$ (b) $1.6\,m^2$ (c) $4.3\,m^2$

2 (a) (i) Barcelona (ii) 5 degrees

(b) Thursday

(c)

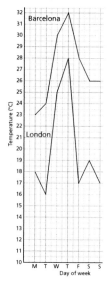

(d) Friday

(e) (i) 27°C (ii) 20°C

(f) The range in Barcelona is 9 degrees and in London 12 degrees.

3 A and Q, B and T, C and P, D and S, E and R

4 (a) 2 kg (b) 0.25 kg
(c) 3.5 kg (d) 0.05 kg

5 (a) 550 grams or 0.55 kg
(b) 1.8 km or 1800 m (c) 7.7 litres

6 (a)

$$12 \xrightarrow{\;-8\;} 4 \xrightarrow{\;\times 5\;} 20$$

(b)

$$5 \xrightarrow{\;+5\;} 10 \xrightarrow{\;\times 10\;} 100 \xrightarrow{\;\div 2\;} 50$$

7 Each answer should be checked.

(a) $4x + 1 = 29$

$$x \xrightarrow{\;\times 4\;} 4x \xrightarrow{\;+1\;} 4x+1$$

$$7 \xleftarrow{\;\div 4\;} 28 \xleftarrow{\;-1\;} 29 \qquad x = 7$$

(b) $3p - 6 = 21$

$$p \xrightarrow{\;\times 3\;} 3p \xrightarrow{\;-6\;} 3p-6$$

$$9 \xleftarrow{\;\div 3\;} 27 \xleftarrow{\;+6\;} 21 \qquad p = 9$$

(c) $\dfrac{w}{3} + 5 = 8$

$$w \xrightarrow{\;\div 3\;} \tfrac{w}{3} \xrightarrow{\;+5\;} \tfrac{w}{3}+5$$

$$9 \xleftarrow{\;\times 3\;} 3 \xleftarrow{\;-5\;} 8 \qquad w = 9$$

8 (a) 17

(b)

Size of bracelet (n)	1	2	3	4	5	10
Number of bars (b)	5	9	13	17	21	41

(c) $b = 4n + 1$ (d) 12

9 (a) 3.2 (b) 3.8 (c) 4.3 (d) 0.4
(e) 0.7 (f) 1.4 (g) 6.5 (h) 8.2
(i) 8.8 (j) 1.5 (k) 2.5

Mixed questions 1 (Practice book p 31)

1 (a) $20\,m^2$ (b) $6\,m^2$
(c) $3.75\,m^2$ (d) $10.25\,m^2$

2 15 m

3 (a) ⁻3°C (b) Wednesday
(c) Mean 7.3°C; range 6°C

4 (a)

$$7 \xrightarrow{\;\times 3\;} 21 \xrightarrow{\;-6\;} 15$$

(b)

$$5 \xrightarrow{\;+3\;} 8 \xrightarrow{\;\times 6\;} 48 \xrightarrow{\;\div 2\;} 24$$

5 (a)

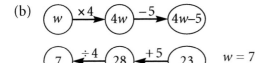

$x = 8$

(b)

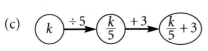

$w = 7$

(c)

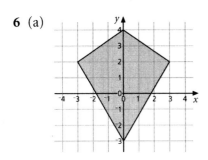

$k = 15$

6 (a)

(b) $(^-3, 2)$ (c) A kite

(d) 1

7 (a) 21

(b)

Size of bracelet (n)	1	2	3	4	5	10
Number of bars (b)	6	11	**16**	**21**	**26**	**51**

(c) $b = 5n + 1$ (d) $n = 8$

8 (a) North-east

(b) Start Street

(c) The student's directions from Paddington tube to Radnor Place

9 (a) 0.4   (b) 0.9   (c) 1.2

(d) 1.7   (e) 2.5   (f) 2.9

10 (a) 5.03, 5.05, 5.25, 5.5, 5.52

(b) 0.05, 0.08, 0.25, 0.5, 0.85, 1

(c) 250 g, $\frac{1}{2}$ kg, 0.75 kg, 1.5 kg

(d) 900 cm, 0.05 km, 500 m, 5 km

10 Experiments

This is the first of three units that consider aspects of the data handling cycle:

- specify the problem and plan what data is to be collected
- collect the data
- process and represent the data as usable information
- interpret and discuss the data and draw conclusions

These units will act as a guide to students in carrying out statistical investigations.

This first unit looks at questions that can be resolved by carrying out simple experiments. It is designed to dispel the idea that carrying out a statistical investigation always involves a questionnaire.

The outcome of this unit should be students carrying out their own experiment and writing a report on it.

TG	p 69 **A** *Specifying the problem and planning*	Designing an experiment to test memory
TG	p 70 **B** *Processing and representing*	Using various statistical techniques to interpret data
TG	p 71 **C** *Interpreting and discussing*	
TG	p 72 **D** *Ideas for your own experiment*	

> **Optional**
> OHP transparency of sheet G12
> Card and scissors, stopwatches
> Newspapers, books or magazines
> Measuring tapes, angle measurers
>
> **Practice book** pages 33 to 35

A Specifying the problem and planning (p 69)

This section asks students to think how they might carry out an experiment to compare people's memory of words, pictures and numbers.

Optional: OHP transparency of sheet G12

◊ It is intended that you carry out the memory experiment with students. First discuss how they might answer the question. They should consider what steps should be taken to ensure there is no bias. They then need to discuss what type of words, pictures and numbers to use. Possible items are:

- **Words:** car, pencil, cake, hoover, love, elephant, fire, data, cloud, history (words should not have connections with one another)
- **Pictures:** those on sheet G12
- **Numbers:** 92, 47, 81, 24, 15, 48, 30, 12, 55, 76

Practice has shown that displaying the lists for 30 seconds and then giving students 1 minute to write down their answers for each category works best. Putting the lists on an OHP transparency or A2 piece of paper makes this easier. Students will also need to consider other questions such as:

- how the answers are marked
- how the results are collated
- whether misspellings should be ignored.

◊ In research studies of memory retention, lists of 'verbal units' such as words or sets of letters are frequently used. Sets of letters are usually either:

- consonant syllables (e.g. RQK) or
- nonsense syllables which are consonant-vowel-consonant (e.g. ROK)

Students could compare remembering these sets with remembering ordinary words.

◊ There are various techniques to help remember lists, for example:

- making up a story which includes all the words or pictures in a list
- using a mnemonic such as Richard Of York Gave Battle In Vain to remember the colours of the rainbow.

Asking someone to count backward, say in fours from 50, in between seeing a list and recalling it has been shown to be a very effective destroyer of short-term memory.

Students could test these ideas using the memory experiment in the unit.

B *Processing and representing* (p 70)

This section is intended to remind students of earlier work. They can then use the techniques on this page in their own project work. You may wish students to analyse the results of their memory experiment using some of the methods on this page.

The results on page 70 of the students' book (and on page 33 of the practice book) are from a real class. Your students may like to compare them with their own data.

◊ Students find dealing with frequencies of numerical data difficult and may need help.

'Students need to plan carefully – some were too eager and failed to record whether responses were from boys or girls etc.'

'They enjoyed this part but still had to have the words (median etc.) reinforced each lesson.'

C *Interpreting and discussing* (p 71)

TG

This section gives some guidance on writing a report on a statistical investigation. Students could base their own memory experiment report on the exemplar shown here.

D *Ideas for your own experiment* (p 72)

TG

The suggestions for experiments are examples of experiments which can be carried out successfully in the classroom. Students' own suggestions need to be vetted to ensure they are practicable and will yield usable results.

Helicopter seeds

This experiment gives an opportunity for students to consider a situation where there are many variables. It will probably be easier at this stage if different groups consider a single variable such as slit length, keeping all other variables constant.

Card and scissors, stopwatches

◊ The 'helicopters' need to be dropped from a height and, although standing on a table works, dropping from a higher position gives a better range of results. Safety considerations are of course paramount.

◊ This activity gives a good opportunity to discuss various aspects of experimental design:

- ensuring consistency, for example that the same drop height is used throughout
- repeating each part of the experiment several times and taking an average of readings to obtain greater accuracy
- ensuring that external factors such as the wind do not affect the results

Word lengths

Newspapers, books or magazines

In order to carry out an unbiased experiment students will need to establish:

- how a sample is chosen from each of the newspapers etc.
- what size of sample to use
- whether to include proper names etc.

Different newspapers may surprisingly show little difference in word length but this should be seen as a worthwhile thing to discover.

Practising

> Measuring tapes, angle measurers

Guidance will be needed on how best to set up this experiment. For example, to test the effect of practice on angle estimation, two sheets can be prepared, each showing ten different angles. Students can be given the first and asked to write down their estimate of each angle. They can then be told the actual angles and asked to compare them with their own answers.

The second sheet may then be given, and students' results on this sheet compared with those on the first to see if there is any improvement.

Some students might need considerably more practice before any significant improvement is seen!

Team work

An alternative whole-class activity is to look at whether people work better in groups. Participants need to be in two groups, one of which does the task isolated, blindfolded or simply facing away. This group works in silence. The other group carries out the task facing one another and giving encouragement. Possible tasks are:

- Hold a book at arm's length. How long can it be held?
- Sitting on the edge of a desk one leg is held up in line with the top of the desk, hands on the desk. How long can the leg be kept up?
- Sort out a pack of cards into four suits and lay them out in order.

Practice book

Section B and C (p 33)

1 (a) 5   (b) 0   (c) 8

   (d)

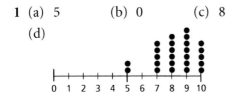

   (e) 9

2 (a)

Pictures	Tally	Frequency
3	/	1
4		0
5		0
6	/	1
7	////	4
8	///	3
9	＋＋＋ /	6
10	＋＋＋ ＋＋＋	10
	Total	**25**

(b)

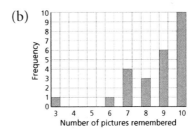

(c) 3   (d) 10

3 (a) 3 6 7 7 7 7 8 8 8 9 9 9 9 9 9
      10 10 10 10 10 10 10 10 10 10

(b) 9   (c) 7

4 (a)

Numbers	Tally	Frequency
4	//	2
5	//	2
6	////	4
7	++++	5
8	++++	5
9	////	4
10	///	3
	Total	**25**

(b)

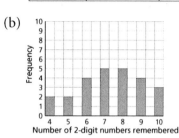

(c) Median is 7; range is 6.

5

Type	Median	Range
Words	8	5
Pictures	9	7
Numbers	7	6

(a) True   (b) False   (c) True

6 (a)

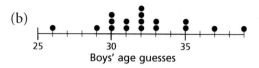

Girls' age guesses

(b)

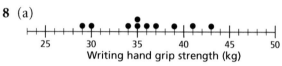

Boys' age guesses

(c) Median is 30; range is 8.

(d) Median is 32; range is 13.

(e) Boys   (f) Boys'

7 (a) 8   (b) 8.6   (c) Girls

8 (a)

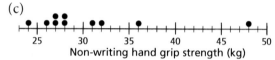

Writing hand grip strength (kg)

(b) 35.5 kg

(c)

Non-writing hand grip strength (kg)

(d) 28 kg

(e) Their writing hands

9 (a) 5.75   (b) 7.7

(c) Yes. They estimated more angles
     correctly on average after practice.

11 Estimating and scales

This unit is about ways of estimating distances by comparing with objects of known length and reading scales from a variety of measuring instruments.

TG	p 73 **A** *How long?*	Estimating lengths by comparison
TG	p 76 **B** *Reading scales*	

Essential	Optional
Metre rule, sheet G13	Sheet G13 as an OHP transparency
Practice book pages 36 and 37	

A *How long?* (p 73)

Metre rule

Without a ruler

In the key stage 3 materials students used body measurements to estimate distances, such as the nail on an index finger, which is roughly 1 cm wide. It may be useful to review these. This exercise is about estimating by visualising metres and centimetres.

Big and small

Many students may find it difficult to estimate the other heights without a prop. If a piece of paper is placed alongside Lucy and marks are made at ground level and the top of her head, the intervening distance can be divided roughly into 3 to give a 50 cm and 100 cm mark. These can then be used to estimate the other heights, which are, in order, roughly 110 cm, 260 cm, 220 cm and 200 cm.

◊ Some examination questions ask for heights to be compared against 'an average person'. A recent survey gave the average height of males as around 172 cm and females 165 cm so a figure of just under 2 metres is a useful rough approximation. Students could each measure a few of the class to find an average for their age.

B *Reading scales* (p 76)

This topic can be started by asking students to weigh or measure things using instruments with scales. Some can be hard to read so the work needs to be carefully prepared and supported.

> Sheet G13
> Optional: Sheet G13 on an OHP transparency

TG

◊ If sheet G13 is copied on to an OHP transparency a compass point or similar object can be used to indicate various readings on the scales for oral work. The use of scales needs careful introduction. For each new scale students need to answer the questions:

• How many divisions are there between the labelled marks on the scale?

• What is the numerical difference between the labelled marks?

• What does one small division stand for?

It may sometimes help for students to draw or see an enlarged part of the scale and to label every small mark on that part of the scale.

A *How long?* (p 73)

A1 (a) 10 cm (b) 6 cm (c) 4 cm
(d) 15 cm (e) 3 cm

A2 (a) 6 cm
(b) Length 4 cm, height 3 cm
(c) Length 8 cm, height 1 cm

A3 (a) 8 m (b) 16 m (c) 1.5 m
(d) 2 m

A4 (a) 200 cm = 2 m (b) 75 cm
(c) 50 cm

A5 (a) The policeman is about 2 metres tall. This makes the Bargate around 12 m high.
(b) The student's explanation of (a)

B *Reading scales* (p 76)

B1 (a) 78°F (b) 54°F (c) 36°F

B2 (a) 25 degrees
(b) (i) 250°C (ii) 125°C (iii) 275°C

B3 (a) (i) 5 km/h (ii) 125 km/h
(b) (i) 2 m.p.h. (ii) 54 m.p.h.
(c) (i) 20 knots (ii) 440 knots

B4 (a) 1.6 g (b) 5.4 cm (c) 18.6°C
(d) 0.14 mm (e) 2.34 ml (d) 4.58 mg

B5 (a)  (b)

(c)

(d)

(e)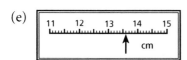

(f)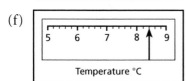

(g)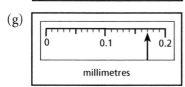

(h)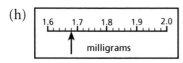

B6 (a) 5.74 grams (b) 55 km/h

(c) 26 kg

B7 (a) About 35 m.p.h.

(b) About 45 m.p.h.

(c) About 68 m.p.h.

Test yourself (p 78)

T1 1.5 m or 150 cm

T2 (a) 6 m

(b) (i) 34 m.p.h.

(ii) 47 or 48°C

Practice book

Section A (p 36)

Students' estimates may differ slightly.

1 (a) 12 cm (b) 4 cm (c) 8 cm

(d) 7 cm (e) 9 cm

2 22–23 m

3 (a) elephant: 3 m (b) hyena: 1 m

(c) giraffe: 5 m

Section B (p 37)

1 (a) 45 g (b) 10 g (c) 180 g

2 (a) 0.5 kg

(b) (i) 14 kg (ii) 28.5 kg (iii) 40.5 kg

3 (a) 0.1 kg

(b) (i) 0.5 kg (ii) 2.2 kg

Into the crowd

This unit deals with looking at the overall shape of the graph rather than specific points on it.

Essential	**Optional**
Sheet G14	Graphs cut from magazines and newspapers
Squared paper	
Practice book pages 38 and 39	

𝔸 *Noise* (p 79)

Squared paper
Optional: graphs cut from magazines and newspapers

TG

'We read the newspaper articles together and discussed the answers as a group.'

◊ You may need to mention what a decibel is (just a measure of loudness). Note that an increase of 10 dB means that the energy of the sound is increased ten-fold, though listeners would consider the sound about twice as loud. Sounds above about 120 dB can be uncomfortable.

◊ Students could be encouraged to find graphs for themselves. Technical reports in car and hi-fi magazines might be suggested.

◊ Students could be encouraged to sketch what a noise graph at other sports events might look like: a speedway meeting, a motor race, tennis, a five-day test match, chess, horse race, fishing …

A1, 2 These questions are probably best used as the basis for discussion. The times given in the answers below are, of course, only suggestions. Different interpretations of the graph may be just as valid.

𝔹 *Workout* (p 81)

Sheet G14

ℂ *Temperature* (p 82)

> Squared paper

C1 The data was produced by a thermometer measuring the air temperature in the middle of a domestic fridge. The graph shows that this temperature varied through about 15 degrees but the temperature in a piece of food would have been much more stable. In fact when the temperature probe was placed inside a carton of orange juice it recorded a steady temperature of about 3°C.

𝔸 *Noise* (p 79)

A1 (a) About 3:10 p.m.
    (b) About 3:55 p.m.
    (c) About 4:55 p.m.

A2 (a) Probably 3
    (b) Probably City 2, Ribchester 1

A3 (a) About 9:10 p.m.
    (b) About 15 minutes
    (c) About 10:05 p.m.
    (d) Between about 10:35 or 10:40 p.m. and 10:45 p.m.
    (e) About 10:45 p.m. to 10:55 p.m.
    (f) About 10:55 p.m.
    (g) It exceeded 140 dB when the band played 'Deep Fruit', between about 10:45 p.m. and 10:55 p.m.

A4 The student's sketch of playground noise

𝔹 *Workout* (p 81)

B1 (a) About 40 seconds
    (b) About 180 seconds
    (c) About 140 seconds
    (d) About 110 seconds

B2 (a) 170 beats per minute
    (b) She isn't reaching 80% of her maximum pulse rate which is 136 beats per minute.

B3 1   After about 50 seconds
   2   About 150 seconds

3 (a) About 80 seconds
    (b) 141 beats per minute
    (c) She worked harder on the treadmill.

4 About 65 beats per minute

ℂ *Temperature* (p 82)

C1 (a) It decreases rapidly.
    (b) About 5°C   (c) It rises slowly.
    (d) About ⁻12°C (e) About 8 minutes

C2 (a) Roughly 7 a.m.
    (b) Between about 11 a.m. and 12 noon
    (c) Between about 12 noon and 2 p.m.
    (d) (i) About 12 noon
        (ii) Between about 2:30 p.m. and 3 p.m.
    (e) About 25°C to 26°C   (f) 11°C

C3 The student's graph and description

Test yourself (p 84)

T1 (a) 9 a.m.   (b) 8 p.m.
    (c) About 5 p.m. (d) Fairly full
    (e) 2 p.m.

T2 The student's sketch graph like this:

Practice book

Sections A, B and C (p 38)

1 (a) About 7:29 p.m.

   (b) About 5 minutes

   (c) About 7:38–7:39 p.m.

   (d) About 7:41 p.m.

   (e) About 7:44 p.m.

2 (a) About 640 – 650

   (b) Very quiet in the early hours of the morning, then gets very busy when people go to work between 7 and 9 a.m.
   Traffic falls during the day but builds up again when people go home between 5 and 7 p.m.
   Traffic falls again during the evening.

   (c) Around 12 noon

   (d) (i)

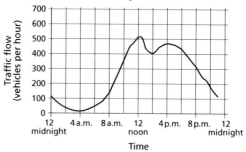

Traffic on Sundays

   (ii) There is a bigger drop around 1 p.m. and it increases again until about 4 p.m. The flow drops steadily during the evening.

13 | *Imperial measures*

This unit aims to give students a feel for some imperial units and their metric equivalents.

Essential	**Optional**
30 cm rulers	Empty 125 g, 250 g packets.
Metre rules or tape measures	Kitchen or bathroom scales
1 kg bags of sugar, flour or similar	
Items with weights ranging from	
250 g to 5 kg	
Practice book page 40	

A *How far?* (p 85)

This section provides quick mental and pencil and paper methods for converting between feet or yards and metres, and kilometres and miles.

> 30 cm rulers and metre rules

◊ In your introduction, discuss with students what imperial units they have heard of. Do they have any idea of how each unit compares with its metric equivalent?

Some that may arise (and their rough metric equivalents for your own information!) are:

inch	2.5 cm	pint	0.57 litre
foot	30 cm	gallon	4.5 litres
yard	1 m	ounce	28 g
mile	1.6 km	pound	0.45 kg
fathom	1.8 m	stone	6.4 kg
acre	0.4 hectare	ton	1 tonne

Of these, only the pound, foot, mile, pint and gallon need to be familiar to students.

B *Weighing up* (p 87)

This section is about converting between metric and imperial weights.

> 1 kg bags of sugar, flour or similar
> Items with weights ranging from 250 g to 5 kg
> Optional: empty packets which would contain 125 g, 250 g; kitchen or
> bathroom scales

◊ Students, possibly working in small groups, could be asked to hold a 1 kg bag in one hand and then hold another object in the other hand and estimate its weight in kilograms and then in pounds. The objects could be weighed using kitchen or bathroom scales to see how close the estimates were.

It may be useful also to look at packets such as 125 g and 250 g and discuss their imperial equivalents such as a 'quarter of a pound'.

◊ You may wish to introduce the more exact method at the foot of the page earlier and use it during this discussion.

A more exact method

This is a method that has been used in post-natal clinics.
The babies' weights are
Maddi 9.02 lb   Andrew 5.94 lb   Roxanne 3.96 lb   Tulip 14.3 lb

A *How far?* (p 85)

A1 (a) 9 m (b) 6 m
   (c) 70 m (d) 100 m

A2 (a) 30 ft (b) 75 ft
   (c) 300 ft (d) 4.5 ft

A3 (a) 16 km

(b)
Miles	5	10	20	50	100	200
km	8	16	32	80	160	320

   (c) (i) 40 km   (ii) 120 km
      (iii) 192 km   (iv) 264 km
      (v) 344 km

A4 (a) 24 km (b) 56 km
   (c) 88 km (d) 200 km

A5 (a)
Salisbury	90	Brighton	60
Cardiff	150	York	210
Newcastle	290		

   (b)
Salisbury	144	Brighton	96
Cardiff	240	York	336
Newcastle	464		

A6 (a) Miles ◄— Multiply by 5 ◄— Divide by 8 ◄— km

   (b) (i) 15 miles   (ii) 30 miles
      (iii) 55 miles   (iv) 85 miles

A7 (a) 25 mph (b) 50 mph (c) 75 mph

A8 James; James is 25 miles = 40 km from work; Jaqueline is 32 km = 20 miles.

A9 1725 miles

*A10 (a) 1.6 km (b) 1600 m
   (c) Less by about 100 m

Weighing up (p 87)

B1 (a) 5 kg   (b) 28 kg   (c) 90 kg
    (d) 2500 kg   (e) 1.5 kg   (f) 0.25 kg
    (g) 0.75 kg

B2 (a) 12 lb   (b) 24 lb   (c) 50 lb
    (d) 5 lb   (e) 15 lb   (f) 1 lb
    (g) 1.2 lb   (h) 1.5 lb

B3 (a) 95 kg   (b) 56 kg

B4 Preserving sugar   8 lb
    Dried apricots   3 lb
    Almonds   0.8 lb

B5 (a) 520 kg
    (b) 330 kg

Test yourself (p 88)

T1 (a) 40 km   (b) 160 km
    (c) About 48 km   (d) About 320 km

T2 (a) 25 kg   (b) 56 kg   (c) 3.5 kg

T3 8.54 metres

T4 640 km

T5 (a) Truro   24
       St Austell   56
    (b) Elgin   192
       Aberdeen   240
    (c) Lampeter   120
       Llandudno   168

T6 (a) Harry runs 15 miles = 24 km.
      Henri walks 20 km = 12.5 miles.
      So Harry's race is further.
    (b) 10 kg = 22 lb; Harriet is incorrect –
      they do not weigh the same.

Practice book

Sections A and B (p 40)

1 10 m by 25 m

2 (a) 6 feet   (b) 150 feet
    (c) 600 feet   (d) 3000 feet

3 (a) 9 km   (b) 20 miles
    (c) 100 miles   (d) 12 miles

4 (a) 48 km/h   (b) 80 km/h
    (c) 112 km/h

5 Birmingham (a) 80 miles   (b) 128 km
    Derby   (a) 60 miles   (b) 96 km
    Leeds   (a) 40 miles   (b) 64 km
    Brighton   (a) 250 miles (b) 400 km

6 (a) 0.5 kg   (b) 2 kg
    (c) 10 kg   (d) 50 kg

7 (a) 4 lb   (b) 20 lb
    (c) 0.5 lb   (d) 3 lb

8 (a) 5 kg   (b) 7 kg
    (c) 80 lb   (d) 300 g

9 Potatoes   15 kg
    Sprouts   5 kg
    Sugar   4 kg
    Salt $1\frac{1}{2}$ kg

14 Rounding and multiplying

> **Practice book** pages 41 to 43

𝔸 *Rounding to the nearest whole number* (p 89)

◊ Use the number line to revise rounding decimals with one or two decimal places to the nearest whole number. Once students have got the idea with one decimal place, ask them to locate the distance 39.37, say, and find which is the nearest phone. Students need to see that the digit in the first place of decimals is significant in determining the nearest whole number.

Point out that the diagrams is schematic and not to scale!

𝔻 *Multiplying and dividing by powers of ten* (p 92)

◊ One option is to use tracing paper and a grid to help students appreciate the movement of the digits. Draw a grid with a decimal point like this:

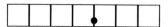

Put tracing paper over the grid and write the number to be multiplied. Then move the tracing paper to the right or left as appropriate.

For example, the diagrams below show 2.564 × 100.

◊ Students may also find it helpful to break down each calculation to repeated multiplication and division by 10, moving the figures one place to the left or right each time.

A Rounding to the nearest whole number (p 89)

A1 (a) 4   (b) 4   (c) 19
    (d) 14   (e) 27

A2 (a) 5 m   (b) 17 m   (c) 20 m
    (d) 6 m   (e) 48 m

A3 (a) 134 km   (b) 13 km   (c) 981 km
    (d) 27 km   (e) 90 km

A4 (a) 5   (b) 2   (c) 8
    (d) 5   (e) 17

A5 (a) 6 kg   (b) 1 kg   (c) 15 kg
    (d) 11 kg   (e) 18 kg

A6 (a) 18 litres   (b) 54 litres   (c) 37 litres
    (d) 1 litre   (e) 15 litres

A7 (a) 7   (b) 31   (c) 53
    (d) 20   (e) 1

B Rounding to one decimal place (p 90)

B1 6.34, 6.3   6.24, 6,2
    5.359, 5.4   6.391, 6.4
    5.312, 5.3

B2 (a) 1.2 (b) 5.7 (c) 0.2 (d) 12.4
    (e) 14.3 (f) 4.6 (g) 9.3 (h) 12.4
    (i) 0.4 (j) 1.3

B3 (a) 6.8 (b) 1.5 (c) 7.1 (d) 2.1

B4 (a) 2.9, 2.2, 2.1, 2.0
      R   E   B   A   = BEAR
    (b) 2.6, 2.3, 2.2, 2.0, 3.1
      L   H   E   A   W   = WHALE
    (c) 2.5, 2.9, 2.4, 3.0, 2.2
      G   R   I   T   E   = TIGER
    (d) 2.8, 2.2, 2.6, 2.3, 2.0, 3.0, 2.2, 2.7
      P   E   L   H   A   T   E   N
      = ELEPHANT

C Rounding to more than one decimal place (p 91)

C1 4.6125, 4.61   4.586, 4.59
    4.6189, 4.62   4.0613, 4.06
    4.598, 4.60

C2 (a) 5.63   (b) 16.13   (c) 6.40
    (d) 23.09   (e) 1.33

C3 (a) £1.68   (b) £14.93
    (c) £5.24   (d) £26.50

C4 0.6209, 0.621   0.618 24, 0.618
    0.6215, 0.622   0.620 39, 0.620
    0.618 51, 0.619

C5 (a) 1.494   (b) 1.928   (c) 3.581
    (d) 13.246   (e) 1.590   (f) 1.240
    (g) 15.479   (h) 0.880

D Multiplying and dividing by powers of ten (p 92)

D1 (a) 28.9   (b) 491   (c) 5943.6
    (d) 904   (e) 950   (f) 549
    (g) 1320   (h) 2310

D2 (a) 4.61   (b) 42.906   (c) 5.932
    (d) 0.532   (e) 0.093   (f) 0.05
    (g) 0.013   (h) 0.00012

D3 (a) 30.9   (b) 0.42   (c) 2341
    (d) 210   (e) 0.54   (f) 0.0234
    (g) 1200   (h) 0.0034

D4 (a) 6.73   (b) 100   (c) 1000

E Metric units (p 92)

E1 (a) B: 1.6 × 1000   (b) D: 1.6 ÷ 100

E2 (a) 87.2 km   (b) 450 cm
    (c) 7.2 cm   (d) 3200 m

E3 (a) 630 cm   (b) 6.3 m

E4 (a) 860 mm   (b) 86 cm

E5 (a) 4500 metres or 4.5 km   (b) No

E6 76 cm

E7 5 cm

E8 (a) 2.45 kg   (b) 1200 ml
       (c) 0.89 litres   (d) 300 grams

E9 Cat

E10 1.2 kg

E11 0.75 litre

E12 1.5 kg

E13 E, A, C, B, D

E14 60 days

E15 67 g, 0.07 kg, 300 g, 0.5 kg, 892 g,
        0.985 kg, 1.04 kg

Test yourself (p 94)

T1 (a) 75 kg   (b) 2.4

T2 1000

T3 1500 ml

T4 £2.49

T5 2.25 kg

Practice book

Section A (p 41)

1 (a) 29   (b) 7   (c) 5
       (d) 19   (e) 10

2 (a) 4 cm   (b) 9 cm   (c) 8 cm
       (d) 20 cm   (e) 21 cm

3 (a) 124 km   (b) 99 km   (c) 342 km
       (d) 984 km   (e) 128 km

4 (a) 24   (b) 30   (c) 34
       (d) 49   (e) 50

5 (a) 7 kg   (b) 3 kg   (c) 13 kg
       (d) 9 kg   (e) 11 kg

6 (a) 8   (b) 43   (c) 15
       (d) 30   (e) 1

Section B (p 41)

1 (a) 15.6   (b) 7.9   (c) 1.0
       (d) 10.7   (e) 1.4

2 (a) 4.1, 4.0, 4.2, 4.3 = CAKE
       (b) 4.5, 4.1, 4.1, 4.6, 4.2, 4.1 = CHEESE
       (c) 4.4, 4.8, 4.7, 4.1, 4.0 = BREAD

3 (a) 35.7   (b) 0.5   (c) 7.4
       (d) 2.1

Section C (p 42)

1 (a) 4.95   (b) 9.07   (c) 24.09
       (d) 1.34   (e) 47.94   (f) 14.63
       (g) 28.15   (h) 4.30

2 (a) £5.95   (b) £20.95   (c) £6.08
       (d) £32.50

3 (a) 1.235   (b) 3.568   (c) 0.885
       (d) 17.900

4 0.8334 = 0.833
       0.8345 = 0.835
       0.8235 = 0.824

Section D (p 42)

1 (a) 25.7   (b) 73.8   (c) 58 678
       (d) 984.2   (e) 23 800   (f) 178.65

2 (a) 0.48   (b) 3.6932   (c) 0.068 47
       (d) 0.097   (e) 0.014   (f) 0.09

3 (a) 7630   (b) 786.1   (c) 0.009 87
       (d) 765   (e) 0.107 69 (f) 769 300

4 (a) 7.53   (b) 100   (c) 0.045 63
       (d) 1000

5 (a) 4.3 → **43** → **0.43** → **0.043**
       (b) 8.73 → **0.873** → **87.3** → **0.0873**

Section E (p 43)

1 (a) 73.6 km   (b) 9631.2 km
   (c) 0.48 km   (d) 4.32 km
   (e) 0.063 km

2 (a) 6.3 cm   (b) 12 cm
   (c) 0.8 cm   (d) 8360 cm
   (e) 8.9 cm

3 (a) 0.68 m   (b) 7930 m
   (c) 8.456 m   (d) 95 m
   (e) 64 m

4 (a) 6.392 kg   (b) 3.92 kg
   (c) 0.75 kg   (d) 0.8 kg
   (e) 0.05 kg

5 (a) 8000 ml   (b) 4926 ml
   (c) 18 300 ml   (d) 9050 ml
   (e) 90 ml

6 0.05 kg, 77 g, 0.5 kg, 0.553 kg, 560 g, 0.763 kg, 1.055 kg

7 4.6 km

8 1.2 kg

9 (a) 7.5 cm   (b) 75 cm

10 (a) 1750 g   (b) 1150 g
   (c) 1.25 kg   (d) 750 g
   (or equivalents)

Evaluating expressions

Essential
Sheets G15, G16, dice, counters or tiles (12 per student)
Practice book pages 44 to 46

A Rules for calculations (p 95)

◊ Students can try each calculation themselves before any class discussion.

None of the questions in this section leads to negative results but it may be worth considering the difference between, say, 12 – (3 + 1) and (3 + 1) – 12. Many students interpret subtraction as an instruction to take the smaller number from the larger.

B Simple substitution (p 96)

◊ You could begin this section by asking students to fill in a table like the one in B4 and discussing the results.

Link up four (a game for two players)

> *'Good game! I put the expressions and grid on the OHP. The whole class played the game in two teams, crossing out numbers they got from the expressions on the OHP.'*

Sheets G15 and G16 (one of each per pair)
Dice (one per pair)
Each player needs about 12 counters or tiles, a different colour from their opponents'

D Rules without words (p 100)

◊ Students could express each of the rules in section C in shorthand, stating clearly what each letter stands for.

Ⓐ *Rules for calculation* (p 95)

A1 (a) 18   (b) 21   (c) 12   (d) 17
    (e) 19   (f) 6   (g) 10   (h) 12
    (i) 2   (j) 2   (k) 1   (l) 4

A2 (a) 8.5   (b) 37.5   (c) 1.4
    (d) 4.5   (e) 12   (f) 4.1
    (g) 7   (h) 39.2   (i) 7.44

A3 (a) 10   (b) 3   (c) 10   (d) 2
    (e) 15   (f) 2

Ⓑ *Simple substitution* (p 96)

B1 (a) 6   (b) 12   (c) 1   (d) 2

B2 (a) 5   (b) 30   (c) 20   (d) 3

B3 (a) 19   (b) 35   (c) 10   (d) 33
    (e) 4   (f) 4   (g) 2   (h) 2

B4 (a)

n	3	6	9	12
$3n + 4$	**13**	**22**	31	**40**
$5n - 2$	**13**	**28**	**43**	**58**
$2(n - 1)$	**4**	**10**	**16**	**22**
$4(1 + n)$	16	**28**	**40**	**52**
$\dfrac{n + 6}{2}$	**4.5**	**6**	**7.5**	**9**
$\dfrac{n}{2} - 1$	**0.5**	**2**	**3.5**	**5**

   (b) (i) $4(1 + n)$
      (ii) $3n + 4$ and $5n - 2$
      (iii) $5n - 2$ and $4(1 + n)$
      (iv) $5n - 2$
      (v) $\dfrac{n}{2} - 1$

*B5 (a) (i)

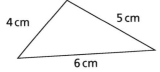

      (ii) 15 cm
   (b) 23 cm

*B6 (a) (i)

      (ii) 10 cm^2
   (b) 290 cm^2

Ⓒ *Rules* (p 98)

C1 (a) 150 cm   (b) 162 cm

C2 (a) 200 mm   (b) 480 mm
    (c) 760 mm   (d) 1180 mm

C3 (a) 8 miles   (b) 3 miles

C4 (a) 240 mm   (b) 340 mm
    (c) 440 mm   (d) 640 mm

C5 (a) 6 maps   (b) 9 maps
    (c) 16 maps

C6 (a) £120   (b) £210   (c) £270

C7 91

C8 (a) £48.60   (b) £140

C9 (a) £22.40   (b) £67.40

Ⓓ *Rules without words* (p 100)

D1 (a) 10   (b) 14

D2 (a) 10 cm   (b) 35 cm
    (c) 40 mm

D3 (a) 480 grams   (b) 680 grams
    (c) 1080 grams

D4 (a) £35   (b) £80

Test yourself (p 101)

T1 (a) 9.45 (b) 6.5 (c) 0.41

T2 (a) 6   (b) 45   (c) 14   (d) 2

T3 (a) 7   (b) 10   (c) 11   (d) 8.5

T4 (a) 20   (b) 35   (c) 53

Practice book

Section A (p 44)

1 (a) 14 (b) 22 (c) 25 (d) 11
(e) 4 (f) 6 (g) 7 (h) 12
(i) 7 (j) 3 (k) 5 (l) 1

2 (a) 6 (b) 9 (c) 3

3 (a) 19.5 (b) 5.5 (c) 3.6 (d) 7.5
(e) 5 (f) 19.8 (g) 6 (h) 4.8

Section B (p 44)

1 (a) 14 (b) 4 (c) 32 (d) 3
(e) 3 (f) 54 (g) 2 (h) 20

2 (a) 3 (b) 24 (c) 54 (d) 4

3 (a) A: 52 B: 66 C: 18 D: 32 E: 15 F: 9
(b) D (c) F (d) A and B

4 (a) The sides are 5 m and 11 m long.
(b) The student's sketch
(c) 32 m

Section C (p 45)

1 (a) £75 (b) £155

2 (a) 450p or £4.50 (b) 525p or £5.25

3 126 minutes or 2 hours 6 minutes

4 6 instructors

5 (a) 12 kilometres (b) 36 kilometres

Section D (p 46)

1 (a) £21 (b) £42

2 (a) 1080 cm or 10.8 m
(b) 1492 cm or 14.92 m

3 (a) 200 cm or 2 m
(b) 268 cm or 2.68 m

4 (a) 106 cm or 1.06 m
(b) 161 cm or 1.61 m

Shopping

This unit involves drawing and interpreting percentage pie charts and composite bar graphs.

Essential	**Optional**
Pie chart scale	Pie charts from newspapers and magazines
2 mm graph paper	

Practice book pages 47 and 48 (requires a pie chart scale)

𝔸 *In the bar* (p 102)

> 2 mm graph paper

It may be useful to have some product labels that give percentage nutritional information. They could also be used in section C.

𝔹 *In the round* (p 103)

> Pie chart scales
> Optional: pie charts from newspapers and magazines

◊ This topic can be made more relevant by using pie charts from newspapers and magazines which cover topical issues. Students could discuss what each pie chart tells them. The diameter of a pie chart should be greater than 7 cm if it is to be read with a pie chart scale.

◊ Information on the nutritional value of food is obtainable in DEFRA publications from HMSO, and may be useful in this section or for project work.

ℂ *Drawing pie charts* (p 105)

> Pie chart scales

D Comparing (p 106)

This section shows how composite bar charts can be used to compare related sets of data. Discussion of the advantages of displaying the data in this way rather than as two pie charts is very useful.

A In the bar (p 102)

A1 (a) 37% (b) 63%

(c) 28% (d) 35%

A2

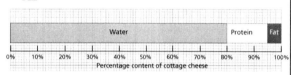

B In the round (p 103)

B1 (a) 76% (b) 13% (c) 11%

(d) A: true B: true C: false

(e) About 45 g (c) About 6 g or 7 g

B2 (a) Clothes (b) 30%

(c) 27% (d) About £10

B3 (a) 47% (b) 11%

(c) A: true B: false C: true

B4 (a) Leisure; 27%

(b) Housing and fuel

(c) 14%

C Drawing pie charts (p 105)

C1

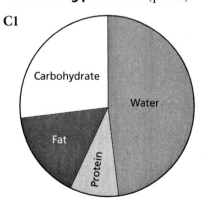

C2

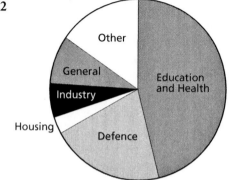

C3

D Comparing (p 106)

D1 14%. The UK has free health care.

D2 Housing and fuel, transport, clothing, and health

D3

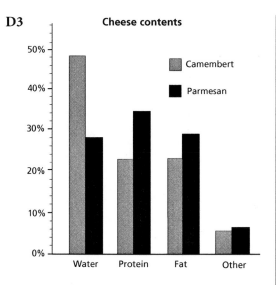

Cheese contents

Camembert has a much higher water content.

Parmesan has higher protein and fat content.

Test yourself (p 107)

T1 (a)

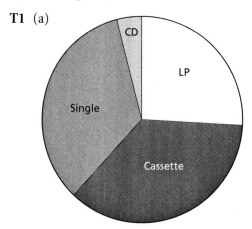

(b) Comments such as:
  • CDs were an insignificant proportion of the sales in 1986 but were over half the sales in 1996.
  • Cassettes were about the same proportion of sales in both years.
  • Sales of LPs declined a lot over the years.

T2 (a) Saturday

(b) Features such as:
  • The women generally shop more than men.
  • The women do more of their shopping on weekdays compared with men.
  • The men's weekday shopping starts very low on Monday and builds up gradually through the week, but the women's weekday shopping changes little from day to day.

Practice book

Section B (p 47)

1 (a) 41%   (b) 11%   (c) 21%

2 (a) Photocopying
  (b) 18%   (c) 10%   (d) £2000

Section C (p 47)

1

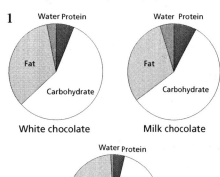

White chocolate   Milk chocolate

Plain chocolate

2

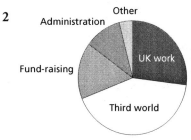

Section D (p 48)

1 (a) Mobile phone

  (b) About 19%

  (c) About 33%

  (d) Washing machines and telephones

2 (a)

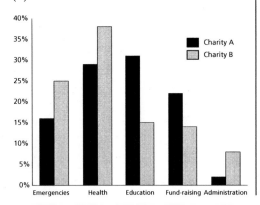

  (b) Charity A has lower administration costs.
Charity B spends more on health and emergencies than charity A.
Charity A spends more on education and fund-raising.
Any other sensible comment.

17 *Newspapers*

This unit revises and practises many numerical, spatial and data handling skills.

TG

Essential

Copies of newspapers (local and national), some tabloid, some broadsheet
It is important to have several newspapers that are not local free papers.

Ⓐ *Number search* (p 108)

Newspapers

◊ Obviously you can ask for other types of numbers. Students can suggest their own types.

Ⓑ *How long ago did the paper start?* (p 108)

'... *mainly had free papers which did not have this info*'

Daily or weekly papers with issue numbers

◊ The number of weeks in a year may not be known by to some students.

Ⓒ *Page sizes* (p 109)

Newspapers of different sizes (broadsheet, tabloid)

◊ It might be appropriate to discuss the issue of accuracy here. If the lengths of sides are rounded severely, the error may be increased when calculating the area and multiplying by the number of pages.

Ⅾ **Costs** (p 109)

Newspapers with different prices

Ⅽ **Graphs and charts** (p 109)

Newspapers

◊ Not all papers have charts in them, so it is a good idea to build up a collection of those that have! Include charts that appear misleading.

Ⅲ **Rounding numbers** (p 110)

◊ You may be lucky enough to find appropriate examples of rounding in headlines in your own collection of papers.

Otherwise, you can use the printed examples for your introduction. Ask students how each number has been rounded (nearest ten, hundred, …).

Ⅲ **Rounding numbers** (p 110)

F1 The student's headline with the number

    (a) 33 000   (b) £7200

    (c) £8 000 000   (d) £730

F2

Express	973 000
Independent	245 000
Mail	2 278 000
Mirror	1 926 000
News of the World	4 015 000
Observer	421 000
People	1 518 000
Telegraph	805 000
Times	1 347 000

F3

Express	1 062 000
Financial Times	459 000
Guardian	393 000
Independent	225 000
Mail	2 380 000
Mirror	2 271 000
Star	530 000
Sun	3 593 000
Telegraph	1 031 000
Times	719 000

Ⅻ **Mixed questions** (p 112)

G1 (a) 744 cm^2 (b) 818 cm^2 (c) 261 cm^2

G2 (a) 16   (b) 9   (c) 13

     (d) 29   (e) 60

G3

	Buy daily paper	Do not buy daily paper
Buy Sunday paper	‡‡‡‡ ////	‡‡‡‡ ‡‡‡‡ ////
Do not buy Sunday paper	‡‡‡‡ //	‡‡‡‡ ‡‡‡‡ ‡‡‡‡

G4 (a) £4.25   (b) £5.30   (c) 14

G5 (a) 50   (b) 26 cm

Review 2 (p 114)

1 (a) 90–100 km   (b) 25–30 m
   (c) 12–14 kg   (d) 1–1.25 kg

2 (a) 23 (b) 21 (c) $7\frac{1}{2}$ (d) 2 (e) 1

3 (a) 3 hours   (b) 6 hours   (c) 9 hours

4 (a) About 9:55 and 10:25
   (b) People prepared for and went to bed
   (c) About $1\frac{1}{2}$ hours

5 (a) 47.2   (b) 1073   (c) 237.5
   (d) 235   (e) 2.73   (f) 4.256
   (g) 7.352   (h) 0.027

6 7 cm

7 (a) P: 3.54   Q: 3.61   R: 3.49
   (b)
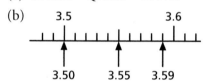

8 (a) **25** students took part in this memory experiment.
   (b) The modal number of pictures remembered was **10**.
   (c) Only **3** students remembered less than 7 pictures.
   (d) The median number of pictures remembered was **9**.
   (e) The range of the number of pictures remembered was **5**.

9 (a) 3.21   (b) 15.33   (c) 7.07
   (d) 0.03   (e) 2.70

10 (a) 26%   (b) 20%   (c) 25%
    (d) About 40–42 hours

11
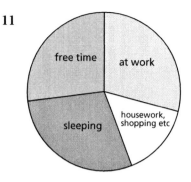

12 (a) 48°C   (b) 175°C   (c) 42°C

13 (a) About 3 m
    (b) About 1.2 to 1.3 metres

Mixed questions 2 (Practice book p 49)

1 (a)
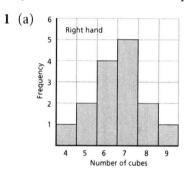

   (b)

   (c) Right hand   7
        Left hand   6

   (d)

Hand	Median	Range
Right	7	5
Left	6	3

   (e) The right hand

2 (a) 24% (b) 14%

(c) 4000 to 4500 (54%)

3 (a) (i) 6 h (ii) 7 h (iii) $4\frac{1}{2}$ h

(b)

Distance (d) km	40	80	120	160	200
Time (T) hours	4	6	8	10	12

(c) 140 km

4 (a) 15 kg (b) 12.24 (c) 0.877

5 (a) 64 kg (b) 155 g (c) 180 g

6 (a) 8 a.m. and 8 p.m.

(b) Buying sandwiches, breakfast, before they go to work

(c) About 10 a.m.

(d) About 260

(e) Around 11 a.m.

(f) Between 5 p.m. and 7 p.m.

(g) Between 8 and 8.30 a.m.

(h) About 150

18 Drawing and using graphs

> 'For some of the later questions we used a graph plotting package and they read off the answers.'

Students complete a table of values from a situation in words, or a formula in words or symbols, and then graph the values. They then read values off the graph, in both directions.

TG

p 117	**A** *Tables and graphs*	Drawing graphs from a situation in words
p 121	**B** *Graphs and rules*	Drawing a graph from a situation given as a rule

Essential	**Optional**
2 mm graph paper	Sheet G17
Practice book pages 51 to 54	

𝔸 *Tables and graphs* (p 117)

> 2 mm graph paper
> Optional: sheet G17 (ready-prepared graph paper for question A1)

TG

A1 It is intended that you use question A1 as an introduction to this topic. You may need to explain what 'extending a line' means.

Students at this level often find reading from a graph difficult, and you may need to give support. They may find using a ruler helpful; if necessary, they could draw lines on their graph.

𝔸 *Tables and graphs* (p 117)

A1 (a) 9 cm

(b)
Time (h)	0	1	2	3	4	5
Depth (cm)	5	7	**9**	**11**	**13**	**15**

(c), (d)

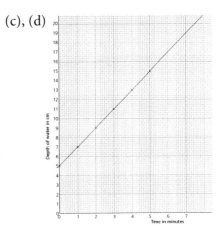

(e) 19 cm   (f) 12 cm

(g) $2\frac{1}{2}$ minutes   (h) 21 minutes past 3

18 Drawing and using graphs • **79**

A2 (a) 18 cm

(b)

Time in hours	0	1	2	3	4
Height of candle in cm	26	22	**18**	**14**	**10**

(c), (d)

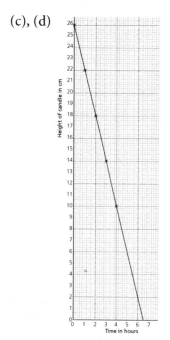

(e) 2 cm   (f) 8 cm

(g) $3\frac{1}{2}$ hours   (h) $6\frac{1}{2}$ hours

(i) 8 o'clock

A3 (a)

Time (min)	0	5	10	15	20	25
Temp. (°C)	20	28	**36**	**44**	**52**	**60**

(b), (c)

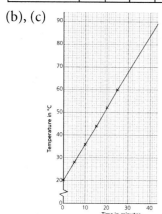

(d) 84°C   (e) 6 or 7 minutes

(f) At about 4:46

A4 (a) 11°C

(b) It will have dropped by 20 degrees, and its temperature will be about ⁻5°C.

(c)

Time (h)	0	1	2	3	4	5
Temp. (°C)	15	**11**	**7**	**3**	⁻**1**	⁻**5**

(d)

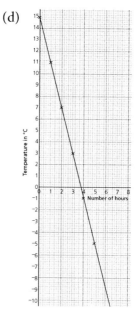

(e) 5°C   (f) ⁻9°C

(g) $4\frac{1}{2}$ hours

(h) 3:30 p.m.

B *Graphs and rules* (p 121)

B1 (a) Number of kilometres
$$= 10 \times 8 \div 5$$
$$= 80 \div 5 = 16$$

(b) (i) 32 km   (ii) 48 km   (iii) 80 km

(c)
miles	0	10	20	30	40	50
km	0	16	32	48	64	80

(d)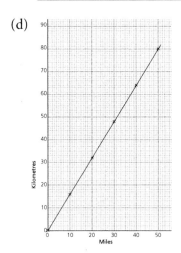

(e) (i) About 67 km   (ii) About 88 km

(f) (i) 12 or 13 miles

   (ii) About 47 miles

(g) (Answers are approximate.)

Dunkerque	17 or 18
Boulogne	21
St Omer	28
Centre ville	5
Paris	53
Versailles	49
Aéroport d'Orly	41
Fontainebleu	22 or 23
Gare TGV	9

B2 (a)
m	1	2	3	4	5	6
c	5	9	13	17	21	25

(b)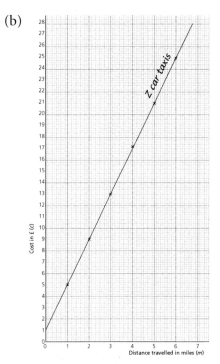

(c) (Answers are approximate.)

   (i) £8.20   (ii) £23.00

   (iii) £3.80   (iv) 3.5 miles

   (v) 5.6 miles   (vi) 3.2 miles

*B3 (a)

m	1	2	3	4	5	6
c	**7.50**	10.50	**13.50**	**16.50**	**19.50**	**22.50**

(b)
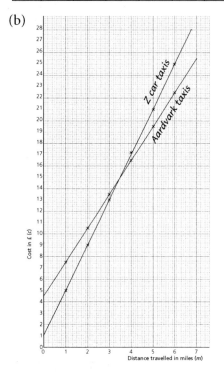

(c) (i) £7.00   (ii) £9.00

(d) Z cars are cheaper.

(e) Aardvark is cheaper.

(f) 3.5 miles

(g) Phone **Aardvark** for journeys over **3.5** miles as they are cheaper.

Test yourself (p 124)

T1 (a)

Time (min)	1	2	3	4	5	6
Charge (£)	**8**	11	**14**	17	**20**	**23**

(b)
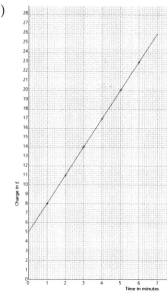

(c) £15.50   (d) $5\frac{1}{2}$ minutes

(e) (i) $\frac{1}{2}$ minute or 30 seconds

     (ii) $4\frac{1}{2}$ minutes   (iii) £24.50

Practice book

Section A (p 51)

1 (a) 8 ml

(b)

Time in minutes	0	1	2	3	4	5
Liquid collected in ml	2	5	**8**	**11**	**14**	**17**

(c), (d)

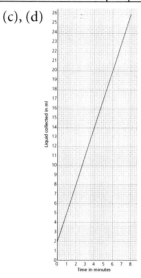

(e) 23 ml   (f) 6 minutes

(g) About $7\frac{1}{2}$ minutes

2 (a) 1080 litres   (b) 600 litres

(c)

Time in minutes	0	2	4	6	8	10
Volume of water in litres	1200	**1080**	**960**	**840**	**720**	**600**

(d), (e)

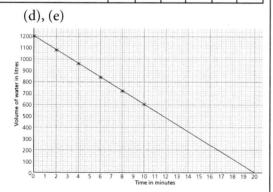

(f) 300 litres

(g) About $11\frac{1}{2}$ to 12 minutes

(h) 20 minutes   (i) 11:05 a.m.

Section B (p 53)

1 (a) $4 \div 2 + 18 = 2 + 18 = 20$

(b) (i) 19 days   (ii) 23 days

(c)

No. of years employed	0	2	4	6	8	10
No. of days holiday	18	**19**	20	**21**	**22**	**23**

(d), (e)

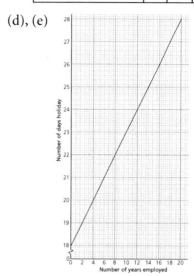

(f) 24 days holiday   (g) 16 years

(h) (i)
> **George Jones**
> **18** years
> 27 days holiday

(ii)
> **Kay Harvey**
> 11 years
> **$23\frac{1}{2}$** days holiday

(iii)
> **Abdul Hussain**
> **3** years
> $19\frac{1}{2}$ days holiday

(iv)
> **Jack North**
> 5 years
> **$20\frac{1}{2}$** days holiday

2 (a)

Hours taken (h)	1	2	3	4	5
Charge in £ (c)	**45**	55	**65**	**75**	**85**

(b)

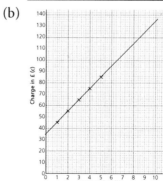

(c) (i) Charge £80   (ii) Charge £105

(iii) 6 hours work   (iv) $6\frac{1}{2}$ hours work

(v) $\frac{1}{2}$ hours work   (vi) Charge £70

Written adding and subtracting

This unit concentrates on written methods of calculation. It includes addition and subtraction of whole numbers and decimals (up to two decimal places).

It is important to include oral and mental work throughout.

> **Essential**
>
> Sheets G18, G19
>
> **Practice book** pages 55 and 56

A *Adding and subtracting whole numbers* (p 125)

TG

> Sheet G18

◊ Start with some oral work on addition and subtraction. Include problems such as 100 – 43 and emphasise that students do not have to use a written method when they can calculate mentally. For example, some students will be able to cope with 100 – 43 in their heads better than with a written algorithm.

◊ The initial activity can be approached in many different ways, both as a puzzle and as a game. Students need to draw their own blank grids to begin with.

As a puzzle, give four digits from 1 to 9 (0 can be included if you wish) and ask students to arrange them in the squares to make

  • the largest possible total

  • the smallest possible total

  • a particular total, say 102

As a game, digits can be called out one by one with the students placing them in the squares on their own grids as they are called. They can be asked to aim for the largest or smallest possible total.

The digits can be generated by using a 1 to 9 dice or cards, and the game can be played in groups.

Another option is to play it in groups in a 'nasty' way. When a digit is called out, a player can place it in *any* player's grid. This allows each player to try to lessen each other's chances of winning.

The grids for the game or puzzle can be any size.

The game or puzzle can also be played with subtractions but there is a possibility of negative numbers which you may not want to deal with at this stage. To revise subtraction, you could set students some puzzles along these lines: 'With the digits 3, 8, 6 and 4, make a subtraction with result 19'.

B *Adding and subtracting decimals* (p 126)

Sheet G19

A *Adding and subtracting whole numbers* (p 125)

A1 (a)

22	2	15
6	13	20
11	24	4

(b)

50	68	56
64	58	52
60	48	66

(c)

70	106	82
98	86	74
90	66	102

A2 (a) 82   (b) 692   (c) 5471
    (d) 125   (e) 416   (f) 176

A3 (a) A: 33 kg   B: 29 kg   C: 25 kg
      D: 33 kg   E: 29 kg
  (b) Guess C: 383 kg

A4 (a)
$$
\begin{array}{r}
7\,6 \\
-\,4\,8 \\
\hline
2\,8
\end{array}
$$

(b)
$$
\begin{array}{r}
5\,9\,6 \\
+\,3\,1\,2 \\
\hline
9\,0\,8
\end{array}
$$

(c)
$$
\begin{array}{r}
3\,5\,0 \\
-\,2\,6\,8 \\
\hline
8\,2
\end{array}
$$

(d)
$$
\begin{array}{r}
1\,3\,8 \\
+\,2\,7\,8 \\
\hline
4\,1\,6
\end{array}
$$

A5 Puzzle 1

A: 95   B: 136
C: 164   D: 530
E: 751   F: 715
G: 507   H: 601

507	746	126	601
781	711	95	715
532	530	511	751
164	75	136	134

Total 1390

Puzzle 2

A: 23   B: 142
C: 369   D: 603
E: 156   F: 388
G: 181   H: 284

369	256	284	176
231	592	156	33
603	23	388	194
244	172	142	181

Total 970

Puzzle 3

A: 428 B: 702
C: 28 D: 185
E: 773 F: 1313
G: 614 H: 2482

2482	185	773	1313
468	175	428	2612
682	702	1243	614
1023	28	834	25

Total 4753

B Adding and subtracting decimals
(p 126)

B1 8.2

B2 (a) 7.5   (b) 7.3   (c) 6 or 6.0
(d) 5.4   (e) 3 or 3.0   (f) 6.3
(g) 5.4   (h) 7.5

B3 (a) 6.48 kg   (b) 0.68 kg

B4 (a) 1.2 and 1.3   (b) 1.3 and 1.56
(c) 1.56 and 1.44 (d) 2.93 and 1.2
(e) 1.44 and 0.3   (f) 1.2 and 0.3

B5 (a) 13.1   (b) 13.37   (c) 25.74
(d) 4.86   (e) 6.23   (f) 7.71

B6 (a)
```
  2 . 8 1
+ 4 . 3
  7 . 1 1
```
(b)
```
  1 . 6
+ 1 . 5 2
  3 . 1 2
```

(c)
```
  5 . 9 3
- 4 . 1
  1 . 8 3
```
(d)
```
  3 . 6 1
- 1 . 1 3
  2 . 4 8
```

B7 (a) 2.37   (b) 2.18   (c) 4.01
(d) 11.75   (e) 36.84   (f) 2.24

B8 (a) A: 0.28 m B: 0.45 m C: 0.05 m
D: 0.15 m E: 0.11 m
(b) Guess C: 4.9 m

B9 £3.74

B10
```
  4 . 0 0
- 2 . 4 3
  1 . 5 7
```

B11 (a) 2.88   (b) 1.11   (c) 0.29

B12 Puzzle 1

A: 13 B: 5.17
C: 5.8 D: 4.51
E: 6.3 F: 16.82
G: 13.61 H: 7.6

13.61	7.2	5.32	5.17
5.8	11	2.36	13
6	4.51	6.3	16.82
4.63	5.9	16.79	7.6

Total 42.59

Puzzle 2

A: 3.3 B: 5.12
C: 5.19 D: 1.27
E: 6.6 F: 3.68
G: 3.85 H: 3.48

4.25	5.12	4.3	4.91
3.68	3.3	3.58	5.6
1.38	5.19	1.27	6.6
3.1	3.48	2.61	3.85

Total 17.09

Puzzle 3

A: 10 B: 1.28
C: 5.78 D: 22.16
E: 7.21 F: 16.15
G: 1.8 H: 4.47

1.28	12	1.5	10
6.31	5.78	1.8	3.62
22.16	16.15	7.21	4.42
5.43	9.3	16.2	4.47

Total 18.74

C Using adding and subtracting (p 127)

C1 (a) 184   (b) 69

C2 21.82 metres

C3 84°

C4 (a) 9.7 cm   (b) 16°

C5 17 cm

Test yourself (p 128)

T1

21	17	31
33	23	13
15	29	25

T2 39.5 cm

T3 (a) 0.7　　(b) 11.8　　(c) 6.7

　　(d) 16.47　(e) 1.76　　(f) 3.44

T4
$$\begin{array}{r} \mathbf{3}\,4\,9 \\ -\ \mathbf{1}\,\mathbf{8}\,2 \\ \hline 1\,6\,\mathbf{7} \end{array}$$

Practice book

Sections A and B (p 55)

1　(a)　73 + 62 = 135 or 72 + 63 = 135

　　(b)　76 − 23 = 53

2　(a)

11	**13**	21
25	15	**5**
9	**17**	19

　(b)

48	**20**	**40**
28	**36**	44
32	**52**	**24**

　(c)

3.6	**0.8**	**2.8**
1.6	2.4	**3.2**
2	**4**	**1.2**

3　(a)　84　　(b)　541　　(c)　803

　　(d)　35　　(e)　54　　(f)　156

4　(a)　870　　(b)　3.9 kg

5　(a)　5.6　(b)　2.5　(c)　11.1　(d)　2.6

　　(e)　10　(f)　4.6　(g)　2.75　(h)　0.8

6　(a)　5.75 litres　　(b)　1.55 kg

　　(c)　2.46 m

7　Jo: 7.91 kg,　David: 7.33 kg
　Jo's is heavier by 0.58 kg.

Section C (p 56)

1　(a)　384 m　　(b)　10.28 cm　(c)　10 m

2　199 m

3　(a)　65°　　　　(b)　39°

4　(a)　37°　　　　(b)　44°

5　1.55 cm

20 Frequency

Essential	**Optional**
Centimetre squared paper	Stopwatches
Sheet G20	
Practice book pages 57 to 59	

 A Stem-and-leaf (p 129)

Stem-and-leaf tables are useful as a way of recording raw data while providing a ready-made bar chart.

> Optional: Stopwatches

'*They enjoyed doing stem-and-leaf diagrams as it was new to them.*'

◊ In the initial activity students should be asked to hold their breath for as long as possible. Either a clock at the front or a partner with a stopwatch can be used to time this in seconds. Each student should keep a record of his or her own time. If a stem is placed on the board students can come and add their results to the table individually. This ensures that each student understands the format of the table. You should of course check that no student has a medical condition that precludes them from taking part.

◊ If the lengths of the rows need to be compared it may help to draw up the stem-and-leaf table on squared paper. Ordering a table can be tedious and involve transcription errors but is essential in finding the median and range.

The genuine Mayfield School data is included for illustration but may be compared with your own class data.

A2 This question uses decimal 'leaves' and students may need guidance.

B *Median and range* (p 131)

'They made a lot of mistakes finding the median when counting.'

To find the median, students need first to work out where it is. Some may find it difficult to work out that the median of 28 pieces of data lies between the 14th and 15th items. Where students have drawn their own table, crossing off values alternately from each end until one or two are left in the middle is a possible approach.

C *Comparisons* (p 132)

'I needed to intervene and check pupils' understanding frequently in this section.'

Measuring pulses is a quick way of obtaining data. As with section A, students will have a clearer idea of how the table functions if a stem is drawn on the board and they individually add their results. With this initial activity a double-sided stem-and-leaf table, as used in C2, is extremely useful for displaying and comparing the two sets of data.

D *Grouping* (p 134)

Sheet G20

◊ Students should be familiar with this topic so the initial page is intended for revision. You may wish to collect some original data for a grouped frequency table. You could ask the students to count the music CDs they own as homework. This is a good opportunity to discuss the choice of appropriate class intervals.

All the examples used in this section are discrete. On the graphs the convention of drawing columns with gaps between them and labelling the bar with the group descriptor is used. This emphasises that a continuous scale is not being used. Some exam boards may use a different approach.

D2 Because the raw data is set out in full on sheet G20, it is natural for students to count all the numbers in the 0–9 range, then in the 1–19 range, and so on, entering results in the frequency column without using the tally chart. You could instead give them a copy of the table but not the data, and read the data items out one by one for the class to tally. This gives a much better feel for the efficiency of tallying data items as they are encountered individually – as is often the case in a real project.

A Stem-and-leaf (p 129)

A1 (b)

1	3 6 8
2	1 4 7 8
3	0 4 4 7 8 9
4	0 2 4 6 7 7 9
5	0 1 2
6	0 2

Stem: 10 kg

(c) 13 kg

(d) The 40 kg row

A2 (b)

3	3
4	6
5	0 4 9
6	3 5
7	1 3 3 4 4
8	0 5
9	0 2 5 8
10	3
11	0 1

Stem: hours

(c) 11.1 hours

(d) The 7 hours row

B Median and range (p 131)

B1 (a) 5

(b) Median 163 cm

(c) Range 42 cm

B2 Median 39 kg, range 49 kg

B3 Median 7.4 h, range 7.8 h

B4 (a) 5 people

(b) Median 28.5 kg, range 32 kg

C Comparisons (p 132)

C1 (a) (i) The babies at the Post-Natal Clinic generally had **higher** pulses than the other groups.

(ii) The people in the Pensioners' Club had a **wider** range of pulses than the other groups.

(iii) The members of the Athletic Club had a **larger** number of people with pulses less than 60 than the other groups.

(b)
Group	Median (b.p.m.)	Range (b.p.m.)
A	75	40
B	65	36
C	91.5	41
D	74	61

C2 (a) Median 76 b.p.m., range 27 b.p.m.

(b) Median 68 b.p.m., range 54 b.p.m.

(c) Only A

(d) The median of those that don't smoke would stay the same but the range would drop to 38.

D Grouping (p 134)

D1 (a)
Letters	Frequency
0	2
1	3
2	5
3	7
4	4
5	2
6	0
7	1

(b)

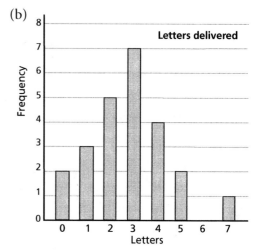

(c) 3

(d) 7

D2 (a)

Number sold	Frequency
0–9	2
10–19	8
20–29	17
30–39	15
40–49	4
50–59	2

(b)

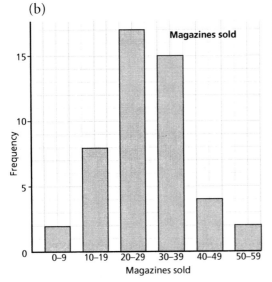

(c) 48   (d) 20–29   (e) 6

D3 (a)

Ages	Frequency
0–19	10
20–39	4
40–59	6
60–79	14
80–99	4

(b)

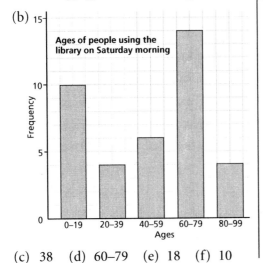

(c) 38   (d) 60–79   (e) 18   (f) 10

D4 (a) 33   (b) 60–79

(c) The student's statements such as:
More people under 20 used the library on a Saturday.
More people used the library altogether on a Saturday.

*D5 A and C

Test yourself (p 137)

T1 (a)

```
0 | 0 0 3 3 8 8
1 | 2 2 2 3 3 4 4 5 5 5 6 6 8
2 | 1 2 3 4 6 9
3 | 2 3 4 6 7 8
4 | 1 3 4
```
Stem: 10 visits

(b) Median 16 visits, range 44 visits

T2 (a) Median 14 visits, range 35 visits

(b) The student's statements, e.g.
The modal group for the women is 10–19 visits but for the men it is 0–9.
The median number of visits is higher for the women.

T3 (a)

Number of cars	Frequency
40–49	2
50–59	3
60–69	4
70–79	7
80–89	8
90–99	6

(b) 30   (c) 25

T4 (a)

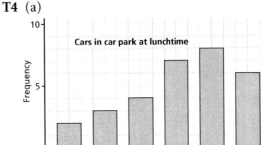

(b) 80–89

Practice book

Sections A and B (p 57)

1 (a) 0
    1   **7 3 6 9 5 6 9**
    2   **4 5 2 3 5 7 9 8 1**
    3   **6 6 4 2 7 1 9 0**
    4   **1 9 7 7**
    5

(b) 0
    1   **3 5 6 6 7 9 9**
    2   **1 2 3 4 5 5 7 8 9**
    3   **0 1 2 4 6 6 7 9**
    4   **1 7 7 9**
    5

(c) $49 - 13 = 36$

(d) 27.5

2 Median $= 25$, range $= 52 - 11 = 41$

Section C (p 58)

1 (a) Median $= 45$
    Range $= 68 - 23 = 45$

(b) Median $= 48$
    Range $= 63 - 21 = 42$

(c) A: false B: false C: false

2 (a) Black Beauty:
    Median $= 18$, range $= 28$
    Long Purple:
    Median $= 14$, range $= 21$

(b) Black Beauty, as it has a higher median.

Section D (p 59)

1 (a) 23 people   (b) 15 people
  (c) 20–39   (d) 95 people

2 (a)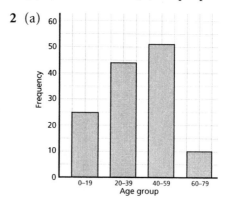

(b) (i) 130 people
    (ii) 35 more people
    (iii) The student's answers

(c) 105 people

(d) The student's answers

21 Number links

Oral and mental work should take place throughout this unit.

> **Essential**
> Dice (for 'Grid factor' game)
> Counters/tiles (for 'Prime line' game)
> **Practice book** pages 60 to 62

A *Multiples* (p 138)

Lock up (p 138)

TG

"Lock up" was enjoyable and successful. It motivated discussion on square numbers and factors. Using this as an introductory activity worked well as I referred back to it at various points in the work that followed.'

◊ This investigation is a good starter for the whole unit – it involves multiples, factors, primes and squares.

◊ You could start with ten students at the front as the 'cells' (it helps if the cell numbers are visible at all times (say, Blu-tacked above the students or pinned on their front and back). Ten more students act as the jailers. 'Cells' can face the front or back to show 'locked' and 'unlocked'. Jailers can tap cells they need to lock or unlock.

Only the prisoners in cells 1, 4 and 9 escape.

◊ Students can think of their own ways to keep track of locked and unlocked cells. One possibility is a grid like this with a tick for locked and a cross for unlocked.

Cell	1	2	3	4	5	6	7	8	9	10
Jailer 1	✗	✗	✗	✗	✗	✗	✗	✗	✗	✗
Jailer 2	✗	✓	✗	✓	✗	✓	✗	✓	✗	✓
Jailer 3	✗	✓	✓	✓	✗	✗	✗	✓	✓	✓
Jailer 4	✗	✓	✓	✗	✗	✗	✗	✗	✓	✓
Jailer 5	✗	✓	✓	✗	✓	✗	✗	✗	✓	✗
Jailer 6	✗	✓	✓	✗	✓	✓	✗	✗	✓	✗
Jailer 7	✗	✓	✓	✗	✓	✓	✓	✗	✓	✗
Jailer 8	✗	✓	✓	✗	✓	✓	✓	✓	✓	✗
Jailer 9	✗	✓	✓	✗	✓	✓	✓	✓	✗	✗
Jailer 10	✗	✓	✓	✗	✓	✓	✓	✓	✗	✓

Students may notice

- Cell 1 is unlocked and then left alone. (Can they explain why?)
- Some cells are unlocked and then locked just once. (What is the special name for these numbers? Why are they unlocked and locked just once?)
- After a while, the cells with smaller numbers get left alone. (Can they explain why?)
- The unlocked cells are square numbers. It will be difficult for many to explain why at this stage. Some students may see (especially after section B) that each square number has a factor that pairs with itself and hence an odd number of factors. So the cell door is unlocked or locked an odd number of times and hence is finally left unlocked.

Ⓑ **Factors** (p 139)

Grid factor (p 140)

> Dice

◊ Initially, it is probably easier to use the rule that once a number is entered in the grid it cannot be changed. Later this rule could be changed so that the numbers are entered into the grid once they have all been called.

◊ Students can explore what happens if they change the numbers at the edge of the grid, use a different dice, make the grid bigger and so on.

◊ Another game is 'Factor and multiple bingo'. For example, use a 3 by 3 grid and ask students to choose nine numbers between 1 and 20 to place in the grid. Then read out statements such as

- cross out one multiple of 10
- cross out one factor of 6
- cross out two factors of 10 and so on …

Play a few times, students choosing a different set of numbers each time. Suggest they think carefully about which numbers are best to choose.

C *Multiples and factors* (p 140)

◊ You could discuss various divisibility tests with students at this stage.
Most will see that you can test for divisibility by 2, 5 or 10 by just looking
at the last digit. They could investigate digit sums for various multiples
and discover that the digit sums for multiples of 3 and 9 are also
multiples of 3 and 9 respectively.

Students are usually quite impressed with the following 'trick'.

- Choose any number and multiply it by 9 (if you allow large numbers
  they may need a calculator).
- Add up the digits of the result and repeat this on each new result until
  you have a number less than 10.
- Subtract 5 from your result.
- Imagine the letters of the alphabet are coded so that A = 1, B = 2,
  C = 3 and so on. Find the letter that goes with your number.
- Now think of a European country that begins with your letter. (You
  might have to have a list of countries available!)
- Now take the second letter of your country and think of an animal
  whose name begins with that letter.
- Now picture this animal in your mind and think about its colour.

Finally ask 'Who is thinking of a grey elephant from Denmark?' Most will
be doing just that (although some may be thinking of emus, eels, elks,
…). Students can investigate how this 'trick' works.

D *Prime numbers* (p 140)

Prime line (p 141)

Counters/tiles

◊ Encourage students to look for strategies to win and to consider whether
they think the game is fair. With no errors, if you start with a 3 or a 5
you'll lose but if you start with a 2, you'll win.

◊ If a student believes a number to be prime (when it isn't), you could take
that number of counters and arrange them in a rectangle to illustrate that
it has factors other than 1 and itself.

◊ Students can vary the rules and see how the strategy for winning changes:
for example, start with 15 counters each and/or put down between 1 and
6 each time.

E *Squares and square roots* (p 141)

◊ A variety of oral questions will help emphasise the correct use of the language of squares and square roots. For example

- What is the first square number greater than 10?
- What is 3 squared?
- Is 30 a square number?
- What is the square of 4?
- What is the square root of 25?
- What are the first five square numbers?

◊ A possible extension is for students to copy, complete and continue the following pattern:

$$1$$
$$1 + 3 = 4$$
$$1 + 3 + 5 = 9$$
$$1 + 3 + 5 + 7 =$$

The fact that the square numbers occur can be illustrated by splitting up a square into 'L' shapes.

For example, this diagram shows that $25 = 1 + 3 + 5 + 7 + 9$.

Students can use these results to try to find quick ways to sum the first n odd numbers. For example, you could ask them to find the sum of the first twenty odd numbers.

How many squares?

For the 3 by 3 grid there are 1^2 3 by 3 squares, 2^2 2 by 2 squares and 3^2 unit squares. Similarly there are $1^2 + 2^2 + 3^2 + 4^2$ squares on 4 by 4 grid, and so on for larger grids. On a 10 by 10 grid there are 385 squares.

G *Number puzzles* (p 143)

◊ The puzzles all have unique solutions.

One trial school used this successfully as a whole-class activity. Students were given a question individually but, if they did not know the answer, they could 'phone a friend' or 'ask the audience'.

Ⓐ *Multiples* (p 138)

A1 36, 6, 12, 60, 600

A2 The student's six multiples of 4

A3 (a) 15, 20, 30, 45, 90
(b) 6, 20, 30, 42, 90
(c) 6, 9, 15, 21, 27, 30, 42, 45, 90
(d) 9, 27, 45, 90   (e) 20, 30, 90

Ⓑ *Factors* (p 139)

B1 6

B2 8

B3 2, 3, 4, 9, 12, 36

B4 (a) 1, 2, 3, 6   (b) 1, 3, 5, 15
(c) 1, 3, 9
(d) 1, 2, 3, 4, 6, 8, 12, 16, 24, 48
(e) 1, 17

B5 1, 2, 6

B6 (a) 1, 2, 4   (b) 1, 5   (c) 1

B7

	is a factor of 8	is a factor of 18
is a factor of 12	4	2
is a factor of 15	1	3

B8

	is a factor of 15	is a factor of 12
is a factor of 6	3	6
is a factor of 20	5	4

Ⓒ *Multiples and factors* (p 140)

C1 (a) True   (b) False   (c) True
(d) False   (e) True   (f) True

C2 (a) The student's three factors of 10
(1, 2, 5, 10)
(b) The student's three different
multiples of 10

C3 (a) Factor   (b) Multiple
(c) Multiple   (d) Factor

Ⓓ *Prime numbers* (p 140)

D1 2, 3, 5, 7, 11, 13, 17, 19

D2 32, 140, 235, 438

D3 23, 41, 47

D4 31, 37

Ⓔ *Squares and square roots* (p 141)

E1 4, 121, 49, 1

E2 (a) 36 (b) 100 (c) 49 (d) 144 (e) 1

E3 (a) 6 (b) 10 (c) 3 (d) 9 (e) 8

E4 (a) 169   (b) No

E5 11

Ⓕ *Cube numbers* (p 142)

F1 64, 125

F2 (a) 125   (b) 1000
(c) 216   (d) 729

F3 125, 216, 1000, 1331

F4 (a) 343   (b) Two (512 and 729)

Ⓖ *Number puzzles* (p 143)

G1 14

G2 36

G3 25

G4 5

G5 90

G6 49

G7 17

G8 1

G9 7

G10 64

G11 216

G12 400

Test yourself (p 143)

T1 (a) 3, 5, 9, 27, 31 (b) 3, 9, 27
(c) 2, 3, 5, 31 (d) 2, 5
(e) 9, 64, 100 (f) 27, 64

T2 (a) 4 (b) 9 (c) 125 (d) 8

T3 (a) One of 1, 2, 3, 4, 6, 12
(b) 42 or 49 (c) 1000

Practice book

Section A (p 60)

1 42, 14, 700, 35

2 12, 9, 15, 300, 24

3 Any six from
6, 12, 18, 24, 30, 36, 42, 48, 54, 60

4 Any six from
9, 18, 27, 36, 45, 54, 63, 72, 81, 90, 99

5 32, 40, 48

6 (a) 14, 21, 35, 63
(b) 8, 10, 14, 20, 24, 40
(c) 33, 55 (d) 10, 20, 35, 40, 55
(e) 8, 20, 24, 40 (f) 20, 40

Section B (p 60)

1 5

2 4, 8

3 (a) 1, 8, 2, 4 (b) 1, 12, 2, 6, 3, 4
(c) 1, 30, 2, 15, 3, 10, 5, 6
(d) 1, 16, 2, 8, 4 (e) 1, 13

4 1, 2, 4

5 (a) 1, 2, 3, 6 (b) 1, 5 (c) 1, 2, 4

6

	is a factor of 24	is a factor of 20
is a factor of 40	8	5
is a factor of 12	3	4

Section C (p 61)

1 (a) True (b) True (c) False
(d) True (e) True (f) True
(g) False (h) True

2 (a) Factor (b) Factor (c) Multiple
(d) Factor (e) Multiple (f) Factor

Section D (p 61)

1 23, 29

2 21, 86, 432, 562

3 7, 29, 5, 23

4 41, 43, 47

5 They are all even.

Section E (p 62)

1 4, 9, 25, 81, 100

2 (a) 25 (b) 16 (c) 64 (d) 121

3 (a) 7 (b) 10 (c) 12 (d) 4

4 121, 144, 169

5 12

6 13

Section F (p 62)

1 1, 8, 27, **64**, **125**

2 (a) 343 (b) 1331 (c) 512

3 64, 125, 8

4 (a) 216 $(= 6^3)$ (b) One $(7^3 = 343)$

5 (a) 2 (b) 3 (c) 6 (d) 4

Section G (p 62)

1 81

2 29

3 8

4 11

5 30

6 6

In your head (p 144)

(p 144)

'Although pupils thought they knew this, it was an area of weakness.'

Some ways of multiplying and dividing by 4 and 5 are introduced here.

1 (a) 52 (b) 92 (c) 14 (d) 100
  (e) 128 (f) 72 (g) 23 (h) 136
  (i) 27 (j) 105

2 (a) 120 (b) 140 (c) 170 (d) 360
  (e) 330 (f) 90 (g) 175 (h) 315
  (i) 130 (j) 115

3 (a) 68 (b) 96 (c) 26 (d) 84
  (e) 324 (f) 132 (g) 104 (h) 27
  (i) 43 (j) 208

4 (a) 520 (b) 240 (c) 34 (d) 41
  (e) 130

23 Lines and angles

This unit revises key stage 3 work on the sum of angles at a point, on a line and in a triangle, and introduces opposite, corresponding and alternate angles.

Essential	Optional
Tracing paper, rulers Angle measurers Sheet G21 **Practice book** pages 63 to 67	Computers or graphic calculators with a dynamic geometry package OHP transparencies of parallel lines

A *Angles in patterns* (p 145)

> 'We used the introduction to revise some key words such as equilateral, isosceles, trapezium etc.'

This section reminds students of earlier work on naming shapes and the sum of angles at a point, on a line and in a triangle. These ideas are used later in the unit and some students may need further revision. In particular they may need reminding of the angle properties of special types of triangle.

Angle measurers

B *Opposite angles* (p 147)

This section investigates angles associated with parallel lines.

Tracing paper, rulers Optional: OHP transparencies of parallel lines, computers or graphic calculators with a dynamic geometry package

◊ The initial investigation is essential to the work in this unit. By rotating two sets of parallel lines over one another, students should see that there are only ever two distinct angles and that all the angles are related. This investigation can either be undertaken by students in pairs or demonstrated on an OHP. In both situations you will need either:

• two sheets of tracing paper/transparency marked with parallel lines:

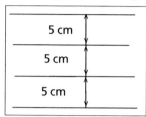 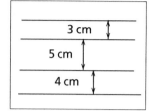

• computer(s) or graphic calculator(s) with a dynamic geometry package. Set up two sets of linked parallel lines as above. Set the package up to give the angles between lines at a range of points.

Initially place the two sets of lines at right angles so that it can be seen that all angles are right angles. By rotating one of the sets of lines it can be shown that all angles present are one or the other of a pair of supplementary angles.

E **Reasons** (p 151)

This section may be found hard by some lower-attaining students.

Sheet G21, tracing paper

◊ The notation ABC to describe an angle is used here for the first time. Other questions can be asked on the introductory diagram, such as:

• Find the value of angle EBF. Give your reason.

• Find angle CBF. Give your reason.

• Find angle DEB. Give your reason.

Tessellations

Using the properties of angles in this unit students should be able to find equal angles in tessellations. This also gives the opportunity to explore the properties of shapes that tessellate.

Ⓐ **Angles in patterns** (p 145)

A1 (a) Equilateral triangle

(b) Isosceles triangle

(c) Right-angled triangle

(d) Rhombus

(e) Parallelogram

(f) Kite

(g) Trapezium

A2 a 120° b 30° c 30° d 120°

e 60° f 60° g 30°

A3 a 70° b 140° c 55° d 150°

e 80° f 95°

A4 a 80° b 40° c 45° d 135°

e 65° f 70° g 110° h 40°

Ⓑ **Opposite angles** (p 147)

B1

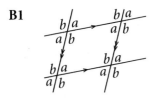

B2 a 50° b 130° c 50° d 100°

e 80° f 100° g 30° h 150°

i 30° j 105° k 75° l 105°

m 47° n 47° o 133°

B3 a 110° b 110° c 96° d 84°

e 96° f 130° g 50° h 50°

B4 a 65° b 65° c 35° d 110°

e 110°

B5 (a) (i) 100° (ii) 80°

(b) Angle r must be less than 60°.

(c) Angle q must greater than 120°.

*B6 (a) y is acute, x and z are obtuse.

(b) y would be obtuse, x and z would be acute.

(c) They would all be right angles.

Ⓒ **Corresponding angles** (p 149)

C1 Any four from: a and c, e and g, f and h, i and k, j and l, m and o, n and p

C2 a 125° b 35° c 115° d 65°

e 110° f 70° g 80° h 100°

i 100° j 110° k 110°

C3 x 104° y 104°

Ⓓ **Alternate angles** (p 150)

D1 (a) Angles c and e are alternate angles.

(b) Angles b and f are alternate angles.

D2 r and w, s and v, t and y, u and x

D3 a 35° b 88° c 128° d 128°

D4 (a) Angle b must be less than 35°.

(b) Angle a must be greater than 145°.

Ⓔ **Reasons** (p 151)

E1 (a) IJ (b) 90°

(c) Right-angled (d) 35°

(e) A trapezium

(f) LHI is 55° as ILH is 90°, HIL is 35° and the angles in a triangle add up to 180°.

E2 (a) HK and LO (b) MIJ

E3 (a) Angle KJN is **60°** since angle KJN is an alternate angle to **MNJ**.

(b) Angle JNO is **120°** since angles JNO and **MNJ** are on a straight line and must add up to **180°**.

(c) Angle IML is **110°** since angle IML is an **alternate** angle to **JIM** .

E4 A trapezium because it has two parallel sides, IJ and MN

E5 (a) (i) SU and VY   (ii) WT and XT
      (iii) VWZ

     (b) (i) STW is 70° since STW is a corresponding angle to VWZ.
        (ii) TWX is 70° since TWX is opposite to VWZ.
        (iii) TXW is 70° since TWX and TXW are equal angles in an isosceles triangle.
        (iv) WTX is 40° since WTX, TWX and TXW are the angles of a triangle which must add to 180°.

E6 (a) (i) 145°
        (ii) a and 35° are on a line and must add up to 180°.

     (b) (i) 83°
        (ii) b, 35° and 62° are the angles of a triangle so add up to 180°.

     (c) (i) 35°
        (ii) c is opposite to 35°.

Test yourself (p 153)

T1 a 56° b 108° c 95° d 112°
     e 33° f 72° g 108°

T2 a 147° b 65° c 115° d 84°
     e 63° f 124° g 56° h 108°
     i 108°

T3 (a) Isosceles triangle
     (b) (i) 70°   (ii) 110°

T4 (a) (i) 109°
        (ii) PSQ, QSR and x (RST) are on a straight line so must add up to 180°.

     (b) (i) 24°
        (ii) PQS is an alternate angle to QSR.

Practice book

Section A (p 63)

1 A: right-angled triangle
   B: right-angled triangle
   C: right-angled triangle
   D: equilateral triangle
   E: right-angled triangle
   F: isosceles triangle

2 $a = 110°, b = 60°, c = 30°,$
   $d = 120°, e = 90°, f = 30°$

3 $a = 50°, b = 125°, c = 20°,$
   $d = 135°, e = 70°, f = 55°$

4 $a = 60°, b = 110°, c = 70°, d = 45°,$
   $e = 45°, f = 135°, g = 75°, h = 30°$

Section B (p 64)

1 $a = 90°, b = 90°, c = 90°, d = 155°,$
   $e = 25°, f = 155°, g = 70°, h = 110°,$
   $i = 70°, j = 126°, k = 54°, l = 126°$

2 $a = 70°, b = 110°, c = 70°, d = 108°,$
   $e = 72°, f = 108°, g = 84°, h = 96°, i = 84°$

3 $a = 40°, b = 90°, c = 50°, d = 40°, e = 60°,$
   $f = 60°, g = 60°, h = 60°$

Section C (p 65)

1 $a = 75°, b = 80°, c = 40°, d = 140°,$
   $e = 115°, f = 115°, g = 115°, h = 65°,$
   $i = 88°, j = 88°, k = 92°, l = 92°$

2 (a) $y = 114°, z = 66°$ (b) 60°

Section D (p 66)

1 $a = 78°, b = 102°, c = 72°, d = 108°,$
   $e = 72°, f = 72°$

2 (a) Angles a and e are alternate angles.
   (b) Angles b and d are alternate angles.

3 $a = 50°, b = 50°, c = 42°, d = 44°$

Section E (p 67)

1 (a) c

  (b) $c = 40°$ (alternate to a)
     $d = 40°$ (alternate to b)
     $e = 100°$ (sum of angles in a triangle
             is 180°)

2 (a) a and d, a and f, b and g

  (b) $b = 105°$, $c = 75°$, $d = 105°$, $e = 75°$,
     $f = 105°$, $g = 105°$

3 (a) 48° (alternate to ABD)

  (b) 132° (angles on a straight line)

  (c) 45° (angles on a straight line)

  (d) 93° (angles BDE + EDG)

  (e) 45° (alternate to EDG)

4 (a) Trapezium

  (b) (i) 85° since CBE is an alternate
        angle to 85°

     (ii) 130° since the 4 angles of a
         quadrilateral add up to 360°

     (iii) 95° since ABE and CBE are on a
         straight line

     (iv) 50° since BEA and BED are on a
         straight line

     (v) 35° since the angles of a triangle
        must add up to 180°

24 Fractions

Much of this work will have been met before, but experience shows that it usually needs reinforcement.

p 154 **A** *Recognising fractions*

p 155 **B** *Equivalent fractions*

p 156 **C** *Simplifying fractions*

p 157 **D** *Writing one number as a fraction of another*

p 158 **E** *Finding a fraction of a number*

Optional
Sheets G22 and G23 (for section E)

Practice book pages 68 and 69

Ⓐ *Recognising fractions* (p 154)

A1 (a) Yes   (b) Yes   (c) Yes
    (d) No, $\frac{1}{8}$ (e) Yes   (f) No, $\frac{1}{2}$
    (g) Yes   (h) Yes

A2 (a) $\frac{1}{3}$ (b) $\frac{1}{4}$ (c) $\frac{5}{6}$ (d) $\frac{3}{5}$
    (e) $\frac{2}{5}$ (f) $\frac{1}{2}$ (g) $\frac{1}{4}$ (h) $\frac{3}{4}$

Ⓑ *Equivalent fractions* (p 155)

B1 $\frac{1}{3}$ and $\frac{2}{6}$

B2 $\frac{6}{8}$ and $\frac{3}{4}$

B3 $\frac{4}{10}$ and $\frac{2}{5}$

B4 (a) 5   (b) $\frac{15}{20}$

B5 (a) $\frac{2}{3} = \frac{10}{15}$ (b) $\frac{5}{6} = \frac{20}{24}$ (c) $\frac{3}{4} = \frac{9}{12}$
    (d) $\frac{2}{5} = \frac{12}{30}$ (e) $\frac{3}{7} = \frac{9}{21}$

B6 (a) $\frac{3}{8} = \frac{12}{32}$ (b) $\frac{5}{7} = \frac{25}{35}$ (c) $\frac{4}{9} = \frac{8}{18}$
    (d) $\frac{5}{8} = \frac{15}{24}$ (e) $\frac{3}{10} = \frac{18}{60}$

Ⓒ *Simplifying fractions* (p 156)

C1 (a) $\frac{4}{5}$ (b) $\frac{1}{2}$ (c) $\frac{3}{4}$
    (d) $\frac{3}{4}$ (e) $\frac{3}{8}$

C2 (a) $\frac{3}{10}$ (b) $\frac{1}{2}$ (c) $\frac{1}{5}$
    (d) $\frac{4}{5}$ (e) $\frac{3}{4}$

C3 $\frac{3}{4}$

C4 (a) $\frac{1}{4}$ (b) $\frac{5}{12}$ (c) $\frac{1}{5}$
    (d) $\frac{1}{4}$ (e) $\frac{1}{2}$ (f) $\frac{1}{6}$
    (g) $\frac{1}{4}$ (h) $\frac{1}{5}$ (i) $\frac{4}{9}$

C5 (a) $\frac{6}{8}, \frac{15}{20}, \frac{30}{40}, \frac{18}{24}$
    (b) $\frac{10}{15}, \frac{16}{24}, \frac{40}{60}, \frac{12}{18}$ (c) $\frac{3}{8}$

Ⓓ *Writing one number as a fraction of another* (p 157)

D1 $\frac{1}{4}$

D2 $\frac{2}{3}$

D3 $\frac{1}{3}$

D4 $\frac{2}{5}$

D5 (a) 15   (b) $\frac{1}{3}$ (b) $\frac{2}{3}$

D6 (a) $\frac{1}{4}$ (b) $\frac{3}{4}$

D7 $\frac{1}{4}$

D8 (a) $\frac{3}{8}$ (b) $\frac{2}{7}$ (c) $\frac{2}{5}$
    (d) $\frac{2}{5}$ (e) $\frac{1}{7}$

E *Finding a fraction of a number* (p 158)

E1 (a) 27   (b) 120   (c) 18   (d) $8\frac{1}{2}$
    (e) 240   (f) $25\frac{1}{2}$ (g) 120   (h) $16\frac{1}{2}$
    (i) 45   (j) 90

E2 (a) TRICKS   (b) PRECIOUS
    (c) DISAPPEAR   (d) THIRSTY
    (e) COMPANION

E3 16

E4 (a) $\frac{1}{3}$ of **24** = 8   (b) $\frac{1}{4}$ of 12 = 3
    (c) $\frac{3}{5}$ of 20 = 12   (d) $\frac{1}{8}$ of 40 = 5
    (e) $\frac{5}{8}$ of 24 = 15   (f) $\frac{2}{3}$ of 18 = 12
    (g) $\frac{3}{5}$ of 30 = 18   (h) $\frac{3}{10}$ of 80 = 24

****E5** (a) $\frac{2}{3}$ of 6 = 4   (b) $\frac{3}{4}$ of 12 = 9
    (c) $\frac{3}{8}$ of 24 = 9

Fraction maze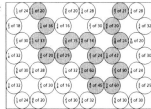

Test yourself (p 159)

T1 (a) $\frac{3}{5}$
    (b)   (any 9 rectangles shaded)

T2 (a) (i) (any 4 squares shaded)
    (ii) $\frac{2}{3}$

(b) (i)   (any 12 squares shaded)

    (ii) 12

T3 200 ml

Practice book

Sections A, B and C (p 68)

1 (a) $\frac{1}{4}$ (b) $\frac{2}{6}$ or $\frac{1}{3}$

2 $\frac{8}{12}$ and $\frac{2}{3}$

3 (a) $\frac{1}{2} = \frac{4}{8}$ (b) $\frac{1}{3} = \frac{4}{12}$
   (c) $\frac{2}{5} = \frac{6}{15}$ (d) $\frac{3}{4} = \frac{12}{16}$

4 (a) $\frac{3}{5}$ (b) $\frac{1}{3}$ (c) $\frac{2}{3}$
   (d) $\frac{3}{5}$ (e) $\frac{3}{7}$

5 (a) $\frac{3}{4}$ (b) $\frac{3}{8}$ (c) $\frac{1}{5}$ (d) $\frac{8}{25}$

6 (a) $\frac{3}{9}, \frac{6}{18}, \frac{2}{6}, \frac{8}{24}$ (b) $\frac{5}{20}, \frac{6}{24}, \frac{4}{16}$

Section D (p 68)

1 $\frac{1}{3}$

2 $\frac{1}{5}$

3 $\frac{2}{3}$

4 $\frac{1}{5}$

5 (a) $\frac{1}{3}$ (b) $\frac{1}{2}$ (c) $\frac{1}{6}$ (d) $\frac{1}{4}$

6 $\frac{5}{8}$

7 (a) $\frac{5}{12}$ (b) $\frac{1}{3}$ (c) $\frac{1}{4}$

8 (a) $\frac{2}{5}$ (b) $\frac{1}{3}$ (c) $\frac{4}{15}$

Section E (p 69)

1 (a) 6   (b) 12   (c) 7
   (d) 21   (e) 24

2 (a) 25   (b) 27   (c) 60
   (d) 200   (e) 250

3 (a) CAVE   (b) POLITICS

4 45

5 16

25 3-D puzzles

Students use different ways of representing three-dimensional objects in two-dimensions. They also learn about reflection symmetry in 3-D objects.

Essential

Sheets G24, G25, G26, G27, G28, G29
Multilink cubes, mirrors
Triangular dotty paper (sheet 2)
Centimetre squared paper

Practice book pages 70 to 72

Optional

Scissors, compasses
Soma Cube pieces

A **The Soma Cube** (p 160)

> Triangular dotty paper
> Optional: multilink cubes, Soma Cube pieces

◊ Students' interest will be enhanced by inviting them to put together the Soma Cube, which can be bought from mathematical suppliers or made from multilink cubes. The set in the photograph was made very simply from a 25 mm square-section length of wood.

B **Views** (p 161)

> Centimetre squared paper

◊ In conventional technical drawing the three views are arranged in a particular way. Here any correct view is accepted, regardless of orientation.

ℂ **Nets** (p 164)

> Centimetre squared paper, triangular dotty paper
> Sheet G24
> Optional: scissors, compasses

◊ There are 12 distinct nets for a cube.

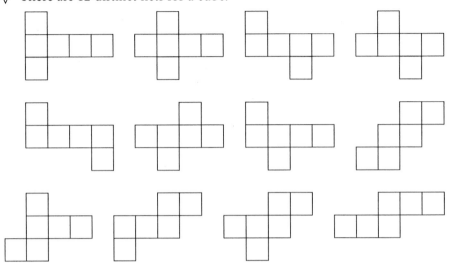

Looking for these as a group exercise is valuable as it will involve discussion of reflection symmetry and the requirement that every 'outside' edge on the net must pair up with another outside edge.

𝔻 **Prisms** (p 166)

> Centimetre squared paper
> Sheet G25

◊ Students should be encouraged to arrive at their own definition of a prism. Familiarity with the term 'cross-section' is assumed in the questions.

𝔼 **Reflection symmetry** (p 167)

> Multilink cubes – two different coloured sets of five per pair of students
> Mirrors, triangular dotty paper
> Sheet G26

Test yourself (p 169)

> Sheets G27, G28, G29

B **Views** (p 161)

B1 B and C

B2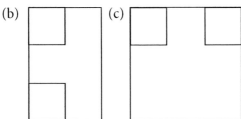

B3 B

B4 The student's plan, front and side views of another Soma Cube piece

B5 (a) R

(b) 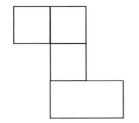 (c)

B6 (a) 9

(b) (Orientation may vary.)

B7 Mug A, G

Spoon B, D

Toilet roll C, E

Book F, H

or

B8 (a) A P, B R, C S, D Q

(b) View from T

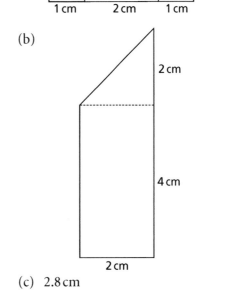

B9 (a)

1 cm   2 cm   1 cm

2 cm

(b)

2 cm

4 cm

2 cm

(c) 2.8 cm

C **Nets** (p 164)

C1 The student's four nets of a cube (See main text for complete set.)

C2 B and D

C3 The student's accurate net of 6 cm by 8 cm by 4 cm cuboid

C4 (a) 8

(b) 4

(c)

Ⓓ **Prisms** (p 166)

D1 (a) B, C and E

(b)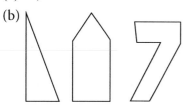

D2 The student's accurate net of an equilateral triangular prism

D3 (a)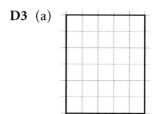

(b)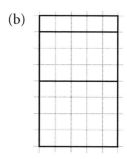

Ⓔ **Reflection symmetry** (p 167)

E1 D

E2 A and G, B and H, C and E, D and F

E3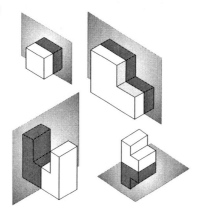

E4 (a) 2 planes of symmetry

(b) No symmetry

(c) 3 planes of symmetry

(d) 1 plane of symmetry

E5 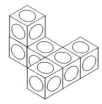   or similar

E6 A 4 planes   B 4 planes
     C 1 plane   D 6 planes

Test yourself (p 169)

T1 The student's accurate net of 3 cm by 2 cm by 1 cm cuboid

T2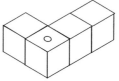

T3 The student's plane of symmetry shown on each shape

T4 (Half size)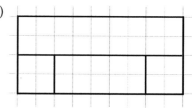

Practice book

Sections A and B (p 70)

1 (a) Diagram drawn on triangular dotty paper

  (b)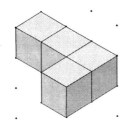

plan view

  (c)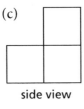

side view

2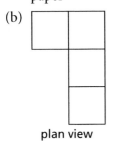

3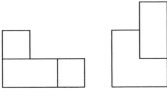

plan view   front view

4

5 (a) 18 cubes

  (b)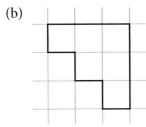

Sections C and D (p 71)

1 A and D are nets of a cube.

2 (a) 2   (b) 3

3 (a)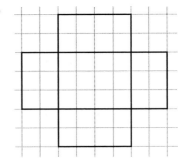

  (b) The area of the net is $40 \, \text{cm}^2$.

4 A is opposite E   B is opposite D
  C is opposite F

5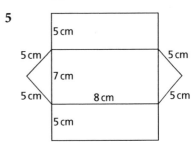

Section E (p 72)

1 A: yes   B: yes   C: no

2 (a) 1 plane of symmetry
  (b) 4 planes of symmetry
  (c) 1 plane of symmetry

3 (a) 3 planes   (b) 2 planes
  (c) 1 plane

26 Written multiplying and dividing

This unit concentrates on written methods of calculation. It includes multiplication and division of whole numbers and decimals by a single digit.

It is important to include oral and mental work throughout.

p 170 **A** *Multiplying whole numbers*

p 171 **B** *Multiplying decimals*

p 172 **C** *Dividing whole numbers*

p 173 **D** *Dividing decimals*

p 175 **E** *Mixed questions*

Essential

Sheets G30, G31

Practice book pages 73 to 76

Ⓐ *Multiplying whole numbers* (p 170)

> Sheet G30

Ⓑ *Multiplying decimals* (p 171)

> Sheet G31

Ⓐ Multiplying whole numbers (p 170)

A1 (a) 160 (b) 144 (c) 428 (d) 3762

A2 Puzzle 1

A: 84 B: 81 C: 115 D: 45

E: 112 F: 155 G: 172

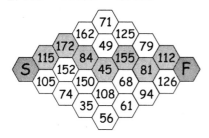

Puzzle 2

A: 585 B: 270 C: 185 D: 348

E: 432 F: 828 G: 492 H: 540

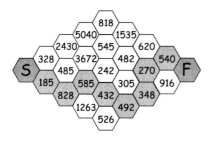

Puzzle 3

A: 686 B: 306 C: 1216 D: 695

E: 654 F: 2410 G: 3008 H: 2560

I: 3339

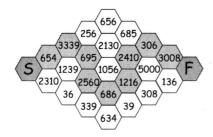

A3 (a) 102   AUK
     (b) 570   EMU
     (c) 964   OWL
     (d) 398   ROC
     (e) 4132   LARK
     (f) 8396   CROW
     (g) 71816   MACAW
     (h) 83125   CRAKE

A4 (a)
```
    1 5
  ×   7
  1 0 5
```
(b)
```
    2 8
  ×   4
  1 1 2
```

(c)
```
    4 7 9
  ×     3
  1 4 3 7
```
(d)
```
    3 2 6
  ×     9
  2 9 3 4
```

A5 168

A6 1704

A7 £996

Ⓑ Multiplying decimals (p 171)

B1 (a) 3 (b) 1.8 (c) 7.5 (d) 4.8

B2 (a) **0.2** × 4 = 0.8 (b) 1.4 × **3** = 4.2
     (c) 0.3 × **5** = 1.5 (d) **5** × 0.8 = 4
     (e) **0.6** × 4 = 2.4 (f) 5 × **0.2** = 1

B3 (a) **1.5** × 3 = 4.5 (b) **0.1** × **8** = 0.8
     (c) **1.2** × **8** = 9.6 (d) **1.5** × **8** = 12
     (e) **1.2** × 5 = 6 (f) **0.4** × 5 = 2

B4 £9.12

B5 (a) 6.98 (b) 127.8 (c) 12.9
     (d) 70.53 (e) 16.72 (f) 13
     (g) 31.15 (h) 87.36

B6 Puzzle 1

A: 6.8 B: 29.2 C: 15.3 D: 4.2

E: 11.6 F: 22.5 G: 16.1

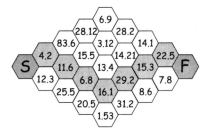

Puzzle 2

A: 6 B: 18 C: 62.1 D: 6.4

E: 62.15 F: 2.1 G: 0.39 H: 2.56

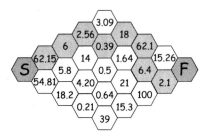

Puzzle 3

A: 5 B: 28.2 C: 17.2 D: 26

E: 24.9 F: 54.27 G: 4.02 H: 16.45

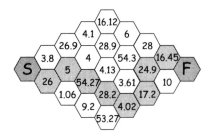

B7 29.16 metres

B8 (a) 12.8 km (b) 4.2 miles
  (c) 13.2 pounds (d) 4.05 kg
  (e) 12.7 cm

C Dividing whole numbers (p 172)

C1 (a) 23 (b) 51 (c) 29 (d) 34
  (e) 204 (f) 48 (g) 29 (h) 53

C2 28

C3 27

C4 16

C5 (a) 1580   (b) 369
  (c) 324   (d) 504

C6 A and D (562)   B and E (104)
  C and I (136)   F and H (263)
  The odd one out is G (25).

C7 (a) 25 (b) 2

C8 (a) 4 (b) 1 (c) 5 (d) 6
  (e) 1 (f) 7 (g) 8 (h) 0
  (i) 5
  giving the letters PLOVLERIO
  and the city of LIVERPOOL

C9 21

C10 12

C11 34

D Dividing decimals (p 173)

D1 (a) 6.4 (b) 2.9 (c) 1.6 (d) 3.67
  (e) 3.14 (f) 4.29 (g) 0.41 (h) 0.38

D2 1.32 kg

D3 A and E (1.63)   C and G (0.53)
  D and H (1.04)   F and I (2.03)
  The odd one out is B (1.5)

D4 (a) 3.65 (b) 1.35 (c) 2.15 (d) 0.26

D5 (a) 1.29, 2.6, 2.6, 1.56
YLLI → LILY

(b) 6.13, 5.02, 0.39, 12.3
SROE → ROSE

(c) 8.95, 6.13, 1.56, 1.29, 24.2
ASIYD → DAISY

(d) 0.85, 2.6, 4.81, 1.56, 3.08
PLUIT → TULIP

(e) 2.6, 0.39, 2.55, 12.3, 1.56, 3.08
LOVEIT → VIOLET

D6 (a) 6.5 (b) 3.5 (c) 3.8 (d) 3.5

D7 1.5 litres

D8 £3.25

D9
$$4\overline{)5\,.\,{}^10{}^20}\quad 1.25$$

D10 (a) 2.25 (b) 2.5 (c) 0.75

E **Mixed questions** (p 175)

E1 £1.69

E2 $216\,cm^2$

E3 (a) 375 kg (b) 75 kg

E4 (a) False (b) True (c) True
(d) False (e) True

E5 $22.5\,cm^3$

E6 18

E7 $48\,cm^3$

E8 11.6 metres

E9 10.63 kg

Test yourself (p 176)

T1 (a) 184 (b) 136 (c) 31

T2 (a) £20.55 (b) £86.25

T3
$$\begin{array}{r} 5\;6\;1 \\ \times\;\;3 \\ \hline 1\;6\;8\;3 \end{array}$$

T4 75 miles

T5 1.45 metres

T6 (a) 1.5 (b) 12.8 (c) 3.8

Practice book

Sections A and B (p 73)

1 (a) 190 (b) 568 (c) 1720 (d) 4203

2 (a) CORK (b) TASK (c) STOP
(d) SHOW (e) CHART (f) CROWS

3 135 packets

4 (a) 5280 feet (b) 112 pounds
(c) 192 pints

5 (a) 1.2 (b) 6 (c) 6.3 (d) 10

6 (a) 2 (b) 0.3 (c) 9
(d) 1.6 (e) 6 (f) 0.5

7 £8.40

8 20.7 cm

9 (a) 7.25 (b) 6.42
(c) 17.12 (d) 37.74

10 (a) 15.4 pounds (b) 8.75 pints

Section C (p 74)

1 (a) 17 (b) 19 (c) 63
(d) 418 (e) 154

2 35

3 26

4 (a) 1453 (b) 316
(c) 145 (d) 423

5 550

6 A and G (34)   B and F (125)
C and E (732)   Odd one out D (325)

7 (a) 16 packs   (b) 4 bars

8 A and F (rem. 3)   B and D (rem. 4)
C and G (rem. 5)
Odd one out E (rem. 6)

9 (a) 93   (b) 2

10 (a) 85 tables   (b) 5 seats

11 226

Section D (p 75)

1 (a) 4.3 (b) 1.8 (c) 0.9 (d) 0.7
(e) 0.25 (f) 1.18 (g) 2.47 (h) 1.7

2 0.69 m

3 (a) 3.15 (b) 1.25 (c) 1.28 (d) 2.15

4 A and D (2.9)   B and E (0.48)
C and G (0.85) Odd one out F (1.75)

5 0.65 kg

6 1.5 m

7 3.75 kg

8 (a) 4.5   (b) 1.75   (c) 1.24
(d) 1.75   (e) 2.5   (f) 4.5
(g) 4.5   (h) 3.2   (i) 2.5

9 (a) CHERRY   (b) APPLE
(c) PEACH   (d) GRAPE

Section E (p 76)

1 2.55 litres

2 (a) 228 cm^2 (b) 18.2 m^2

3 6%

4 17.6 cm

5 0.9 m

6 5.75 cm

7 (a) 22.8 m   (b) 4.56 m

Review 3 (p 177)

1 (a) £8 (b) $5 \div 2 + 3 = 5.5$

(c)

w	5	10	15	20	25	30
c	5.50	8.00	10.50	13.00	15.50	18.00

(d)

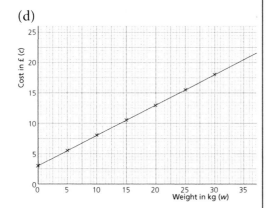

(f) £7.00 to £7.50

(g) About £20.50

(h) About 17 kg

2 (a) Yes, one

(b)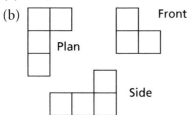

3 (a) 100 4 36 6 24 8 2

(b) 13 3 5 2

(c) 36 24

(d) 4 6 3 2

(e) 100 4 36 49

(f) 8 27

4 (a) $\frac{1}{3}$ (b) 15 (c) $\frac{1}{6}$

5 (a)

```
6 | 9 8 5
7 | 5 9 5 0 6 3 7
8 | 9 8 8 2 1 7
9 | 8 3 6 9
```
Stem = 10 kg

(b)

```
6 | 5 8 9
7 | 0 3 5 5 6 7 9
8 | 1 2 7 8 8 9
9 | 3 6 8 9
```
Stem = 10 kg

(c) 80 kg (d) 34 kg

6 (a)

```
5 | 9 8
6 | 5 3 9 9 1
7 | 7 1 5 1 8 9 0
8 | 2 4 0 3
9 | 5 5
```
Stem = 10 kg

```
5 | 8 9
6 | 1 3 5 9 9
7 | 0 1 1 5 7 8 9
8 | 0 2 3 4
9 | 5 5
```
Stem = 10 kg

(b) Medians: before 80 kg, after 73 kg, down 7 kg

Ranges: before 34 kg, after 37 kg, up 3 kg

7 Means: before 81.4 kg, after 74.2 kg

8 (a) 424 (b) 206 (c) 408

(d) 206 (e) 3.15 (f) 1.76

(g) 29.8 (h) 1.49

9 $a = 115°$ $b = 25°$ $c = 155°$

$d = 55°$ $e = 125°$

10 They are alternate.

Mixed questions 3 (Practice book p 77)

1 (a) 7   (b) 32   (c) 0–19

2 (a)

0	
1	
2	
3	
4	6 2 5 8
5	6 9 9 9 3
6	5 6 8 3 6 0 5 1 2 8 9

Stem = 10 years

(b)

0	
1	
2	
3	
4	2 5 6 8
5	3 6 9 9 9
6	0 1 2 3 5 5 6 6 8 8 9

Stem = 10 years

(c) $60\frac{1}{2}$ (d) 27 years

(e) A much older age group uses the pool on Monday morning.

3

	factor of 24	multiple of 8	prime number	square number	cube number
8	✔	✔			✔
16		✔		✔	
27					✔
32		✔			
36				✔	
64		✔		✔	✔

4 (a) 88   (b) 170   (c) 52
    (d) 115   (e) 68   (f) 18
    (g) 415   (h) 52   (i) 45
    (j) 66

5 (a) 553   (b) 324   (c) 432
    (d) 402   (e) 7.16   (f) 3.46
    (g) 15   (h) 1.23

6 $a = 55°$ $b = 125°$ $c = 75°$
   $d = 30°$ $e = 115°$ $f = 115°$

7 PBC = 65° with valid reasons

8 (a) $\frac{1}{4}$ (b) $\frac{1}{3}$ (c) $\frac{1}{2}$
   (d) $\frac{1}{5}$ (e) $\frac{3}{10}$

9 (a) $\frac{3}{5}$ (b) 9   (c) $\frac{3}{5}$

10 (a) Yes   (b) Yes, 2
    (c) Plan

Front   Side

27 *Negative numbers*

This unit covers all operations except multiplying two negative numbers, and division. These are dealt with later.

p 179 **A** *Up and down*		Revising use of temperature scale
p 180 **B** *Adding negative numbers*		
p 181 **C** *Subtracting a negative number*		
p 182 **D** *Multiplying a negative by a positive number*		
p 183 **E** *Evaluating expressions*		

> **Optional**
> Sheets G32 and G33
> Dice (coloured, or see section B below)
> Counters of two different colours
>
> **Practice book** pages 79 to 81

B *Adding negative numbers* (p 179)

> Optional for the Three in a row games: sheet G32, dice of two different colours, or put stickers on dice to show ⁻1, ⁻2, …, counters of two different colours

◊ As a class activity, you can write a grid of, say, eight numbers on the board (similar to the grid in 'Target practice' below). Ask students to find two numbers which add up to …

Target practice

You can choose different numbers for the grid.

Three in a row games

◊ It is obviously better to use prepared dice for the negative numbers rather than rely on colour.

Games of this kind not only provide palatable practice, but also give opportunities for strategy. This is especially so in games 2 and 3, where players have to decide which dice to roll.

ℂ **Subtracting a negative number** (p 181)

> Number cards ⁻5 to 5
> Optional: Sheet G33

◊ Depending on whether students have done this before, you could bring this to life by scoring, say, pop groups, songs or TV shows. For example, you could ask students each to write the name of a group or show on a piece of paper and give it to you. As you read out each in turn, a panel of judges give positive or negative scores (or abstain!). You can then discuss the effect of 'subtracting' a negative score.

𝔼 **Evaluating expressions** (p 183)

◊ This is sometimes the point at which students who have appeared to cope with each operation separately lose their way.

Insist that students first write down the expression, then the expression with the number substituted and then the result.

𝔸 **Up and down** (p 179)

A1 (a) ⁻2°C (b) ⁻6°C (c) ⁻3.5°C
(d) ⁻9°C (e) ⁻12°C (f) ⁻20°C

A2 (a) ⁻7°C, ⁻4°C, 0°C, 3°C, 10°C
(b) ⁻5°C, ⁻4.5°C, ⁻1°C, 6°C, 7.5°C

A3 9 degrees

A4 ⁻5°C

A5 (a) fall, 6 degrees (b) rise, 5 degrees
(c) rise, 7 degrees (d) fall, 5 degrees
(e) fall, 10 degrees (f) rise, 20 degrees

A6 (a) 11°C (b) 2°C (c) ⁻4°C
(d) ⁻9°C (e) ⁻2°C (f) ⁻10°C

A7 (a) ⁻5 (b) ⁻13 (c) ⁻11
(d) ⁻5 (e) ⁻8 (f) ⁻16
(g) ⁻17 (h) ⁻11 (i) ⁻16

𝔹 **Adding negative numbers** (p 180)

B1 (a) 1 (b) 3 (c) ⁻1 (d) ⁻6
(e) ⁻7 (f) ⁻6 (g) ⁻15 (h) ⁻25
(i) 3 (j) 2

B2 (a) JAGUAR (b) SUBARU
(c) CITROEN

B3 (a) ⁻1 + 2 (b) ⁻5 + ⁻1
(c) ⁻5 + 4 (d) ⁻1 + 4

B4 (a) 5 (b) ⁻9 (c) ⁻1 (d) ⁻9
(e) ⁻8 (f) 2 (g) ⁻7 (h) ⁻6

ℂ **Subtracting a negative number** (p 181)

C1 (a) 9 (b) ⁻3 (c) ⁻3 (d) 11
(e) ⁻8 (f) ⁻1 (g) 13 (h) ⁻1
(i) 11 (j) 4

C2 ⁻4 + 6 and 1 − ⁻1
⁻3 − 2 and ⁻10 + 5
3 − ⁻2 and ⁻2 + 7
5 − 8 and ⁻6 − ⁻3

C3 (a) $^-10$ (b) 4 (c) $^-10$ (d) 10
(e) $^-4$ (f) 10 (g) $^-4$ (h) $^-10$
(i) $^-4$ (j) $^-4$

C4 (a) 3 (b) 8 (c) $^-5$ (d) 6

C5 (a) $^-10$ (b) $^-24$ (c) $^-25$ (d) 8

Ⓓ *Multiplying a negative by a positive number* (p 182)

D1 (a) $^-8$ (b) $^-15$ (c) $^-35$
(d) $^-24$ (e) $^-9$

D2 (a) $^-12$ (b) $^-40$ (c) $^-6$
(d) $^-27$ (e) $^-56$

D3 (a) $^-70$ (b) $^-60$ (c) $^-28$
(d) $^-80$ (e) $^-60$

D4 (a) 2 (b) $^-2$ (c) 5 (d) $^-3$
(e) $^-1$ (f) 5 (g) $^-4$ (h) 5

D5 (a) COW (b) SHEEP
(c) RABBIT (d) GOAT
(e) HAMSTER

*D6 (a) PRETORIA (b) AUCKLAND
(c) HIROSHIMA

Ⓔ *Evaluating expressions* (p 183)

E1 (a) $^-3$ (b) $^-1$ (c) 2
(d) 3 (e) $^-6$

E2 (a) 2 (b) $^-5$ (c) 6
(d) $^-2$ (e) $^-7$

E3 (a) $^-4$ (b) $^-7$ (c) $^-5$

E4 (a) $^-12$ (b) $^-15$ (c) $^-20$

E5 (a) $^-6$ (b) $^-20$ (c) $^-24$

E6 (a) $^-5$ (b) $^-3$ (c) 0
(d) 1 (e) $^-8$

E7 (a) $^-7$ (b) $^-9$ (c) $^-11$
(d) 1 (e) $^-6$

E8 (a) $^-10$ (b) 1 (c) $^-3$
(d) $^-8$ (e) 8

E9 $n + 2 = {}^-2$ $2n = {}^-8$ $5 - n = 9$
$4 + 2n = {}^-4$ $2n - 1 = {}^-9$

E10 (a) 4 (b) $^-30$ (c) 8
(d) $^-7$ (e) $^-22$

E11 $4 - t \ (= 14)$

E12 $r - 10 \ (= {}^-18)$

E13 (a) 3 (b) $^-1$ (c) 7
(d) $^-5$ (e) $^-19$

E14 (a) 23 (b) $^-9$ (c) $^-25$
(d) 3 (e) $^-1$

E15 (a) $^-16$ (b) $^-10$ (c) $^-4$
(d) $^-1$ (e) $^-22$

E16 (a) $^-25$ (b) $^-11$ (c) 0
(d) $^-16$ (e) $^-22$ (f) $^-10$

E17 (a) ALBANIA (b) BELGIUM

E18 (a) COW (b) PIG (c) GOAT
(d) HORSE (e) MOUSE (f) OTTER

Test yourself (p 185)

T1 (a) $^-8°C$ (b) $9°C$ (c) 16 degrees

T2 $^-4°C$

T3 (a) (i) $^-6$ (ii) 3
(b) 18

T4 (a) $68°F$ (b) $24°F$

T5 (a) $^-11$ (b) $^-11$ (c) $^-2$
(d) $^-2$ (e) $^-13$ (f) 9

Practice book

Section A (p 79)

1 (a) $^-7°C, ^-2°C, 0°C, 3°C, 5°C$

  (b) $^-7.5°C, ^-4°C, ^-1°C, 2.5°C, 5°C$

2 $4°C$

3 (a) 6 (b) $^-3$ (c) $^-8$ (d) 2

  (e) $^-7$ (f) $^-6$ (g) $^-3$ (h) $^-3$

  (i) $^-5$ (j) $^-2$

4 (a) 5 (b) $^-8$ (c) $^-7$ (d) $^-13$

  (e) $^-10$ (f) $^-9$ (g) 13 (h) $^-15$

  (i) $^-7$ (j) $^-16$

Section B (p 79)

1 (a) 2 (b) 5 (c) $^-6$ (d) 7

  (e) 8 (f) $^-8$ (g) $^-10$ (h) 9

  (i) $^-12$ (j) $^-6$

2 (a) $^-6 + ^-4$ (b) $^-6 + 5$ (c) $^-4 + 5$

  (d) $^-6 + 2$ (e) $^-4 + 2$

3 (a) $^-10 + 3$ (b) $^-6 + 3$ (c) $^-10 + 5$

  (d) $^-6 + 5$ (e) $^-10 + ^-6$

4 (a) 5 (b) $^-12$ (c) $^-2$ (d) $^-7$

Section C (p 80)

1 (a) 8 (b) 6 (c) 13 (d) 6 (e) 14

2 (a) $^-3$ (b) 3 (c) 5 (d) 7 (e) 2

3 (a) 6 (b) $^-12$ (c) $^-12$ (d) 6

  (e) $^-9$ (f) 5 (g) $^-5$ (h) 9

  (i) $^-4$ (j) $^-12$ (k) 4 (l) 12

4 $^-5 + ^-3$ and $^-10 - ^-2$

  $3 - 7$ and $^-1 + ^-3$

  $^-4 - ^-2$ and $2 - 4$

Section D (p 80)

1 (a) $^-15$ (b) $^-28$ (c) $^-16$

  (d) $^-12$ (e) $^-25$ (f) $^-30$

  (g) $^-100$ (h) $^-48$ (i) $^-120$

  (j) $^-45$

2 (a) PERU (b) SPAIN

  (c) ITALY (d) RUSSIA

Section E (p 81)

1 (a) $^-21$ (b) $^-16$ (c) $^-60$

  (d) $^-7$ (e) $^-13$ (f) $^-19$

2 (a) $^-14$ (b) 1 (c) $^-13$

  (d) $^-16$ (e) $^-3$ (f) $^-43$

3 $p + 5 = 2$

  $3p = ^-9$

  $2p + 2 = ^-4$

  $6 - p = 9$

  $3 + 2p = ^-3$

4 FRANCE

5 ENGLAND

28 Fractions, decimals and percentages

The main aim of this unit is to familiarise students with the decimal and percentage equivalents of a range of common fractions.

Essential

Sheet G34
Dice (preferably with labelled faces, see below)
Counters (two different colours)

Practice book pages 82 to 84

𝔸 *Fractions and percentages* (p 186)

'I drew a number on the board and asked pupils to come up and mark where $\frac{1}{2}$, 75%, 0.2 etc. were.'

The FP game

◊ It is better to use sticky labels to label the faces of the dice 10%, 20%, 25%, 50%, 100% and 'Roll again'.

ℂ *Fractions, decimals and percentages* (p 188)

Sheet G34, dice

TG

◊ Explain to students that sheet G34 shows number lines from 0 to 1 (in decimals) and from 0% to 100%. The bars in between show fractions: the students' first task is to label the fraction bars correctly.

Ask them to have a good look at, say, the tenths bar and use it to give the decimal equivalent for, say, $\frac{3}{10}$. After a while make them cover up the sheet or turn it over and give them, orally, questions to answer without it.

Repeat for other sets of fractions and gradually move to the point where they can answer mixed oral questions without having to refer to the sheet.

As with all work of this kind, constant reinforcement through oral questions at regular intervals is necessary!

The FDP game

As before, it is better to label the dice.

Ⓓ **Thirds** (p 190)

◊ Some students may not be ready for this section. Omitting it will not cause problems in the rest of the unit.

◊ It is probably easier to deal with percentages first, as dividing 100 by 3 and getting '33 and a bit' is more tangible than dividing 1 by 3 and getting a recurring decimal.

Ⓐ **Fractions and percentages** (p 186)

A1 70%

A2 (a) 75% (b) 40% (c) 90%
(d) 80% (e) 60%

A3 (a) (i) $\frac{1}{4}$ (ii) 25%
(b) (i) $\frac{3}{5}$ (ii) 60%
(c) (i) $\frac{3}{10}$ (ii) 30%

A4 $\frac{1}{10}$, 20%, $\frac{1}{4}$, $\frac{3}{10}$, 50%

A5 (a) $\frac{1}{5}$, 30%, 40%, $\frac{1}{2}$, $\frac{3}{4}$
(b) 10%, $\frac{1}{4}$, $\frac{3}{10}$, $\frac{2}{5}$, 50%
(c) $\frac{1}{5}$, 25%, 30%, $\frac{2}{5}$, $\frac{1}{2}$
(d) $\frac{1}{2}$, 60%, 70%, $\frac{3}{4}$, $\frac{4}{5}$

Ⓑ **Decimals and percentages 1** (p 188)

B1 (a) 20% (b) 50% (c) 25%
(d) 80% (e) 75%

B2 (a) 0.1 (b) 0.7 (c) 0.9
(d) 0.3 (e) 0.45

B3 40% and 0.4, 0.1 and 10%, 0.6 and 60%, 0.8 and 80%
25% matches 0.25

B4 10%, 25%, 0.4, 50%, 0.7

Ⓒ **Fractions, decimals and percentages** (p 188)

C1 $\frac{4}{5}$, 80%, 0.8 $\frac{3}{4}$, 75%, 0.75 $\frac{2}{5}$, 40%, $\frac{4}{10}$

C2 0.75 is larger. 0.75 is 75%, $\frac{7}{10}$ is 70%, and 75% is larger.

C3 0.1 is smaller. 0.1 is 10%, $\frac{1}{5}$ is 20% and 10% is smaller.

C4 (a) MARS (b) SATURN
(c) VENUS (d) URANUS

C5 20%, $\frac{1}{4}$, 0.3, $\frac{2}{5}$, 50%

C6 0.6, 70%, $\frac{3}{4}$, $\frac{4}{5}$, $\frac{9}{10}$

C7 $\frac{1}{5}$, $\frac{1}{4}$, $\frac{3}{10}$, 0.4, $\frac{1}{2}$, 60%

C8 (a) $\begin{array}{r} 0.4 \\ 5\overline{)2.0} \end{array}$ (b) $\begin{array}{r} 0.25 \\ 4\overline{)1.00} \end{array}$

Ⓓ **Thirds** (p 190)

D1 (a) 30%, $\frac{1}{3}$, 40%, 0.45, $\frac{1}{2}$
(b) 0.65, $\frac{2}{3}$, 70%, $\frac{3}{4}$, 0.8
(c) 20%, $\frac{1}{4}$, $\frac{1}{3}$, 0.35, 50%
(d) 25%, 0.3, $\frac{1}{3}$, $\frac{2}{5}$, 0.5

E *Percentages in your head* (p 191)

E1 (a) 25 (b) 1 (c) 4 (d) 6

E2 (a) 6 (b) 20 (c) 8 (d) 2.5

E3 (a) 12 (b) 18 (c) 6 (d) 100

E4 (a) $\frac{1}{5}$ (b) 5

E5 10% of 40 = 20% of 20
20% of 50 = 25% of 40
50% of 6 = 10% of 30
25% of 60 = 50% of 30

E6 (a) 18 (b) 14 (c) 6 (d) 24 (e) 24

E7 250 g

E8 40 prizes

E9 (a) 60 (b) 30 (c) 24 (d) 6

F *Decimals and percentages 2* (p 192)

F1

Percentage	Fraction	Decimal
21%	$\frac{21}{100}$	**0.21**
57%	$\frac{57}{100}$	**0.57**
41%	$\frac{41}{100}$	0.41
9%	$\frac{9}{100}$	**0.09**
3%	$\frac{3}{100}$	**0.03**
8%	$\frac{8}{100}$	0.08

F2 (a) 0.65 (b) 0.73 (c) 0.08
(d) 0.8(0) (e) 0.94

F3 (a) 85% (b) 17% (c) 33%
(d) 2% (e) 10%

F4 (a) 0.15 (b) 0.4
(c) 0.09, 15%, 0.2, $\frac{2}{5}$

F5 (a) 0.18, $\frac{1}{4}$, 28%, 0.3
(b) 8%, 0.55, 0.6, $\frac{7}{10}$
(c) 0.09, $\frac{3}{4}$, 78%, 0.8
(d) 0.19, 0.4, 48%, $\frac{1}{2}$

Test yourself (p 193)

T1 (a) $\frac{2}{3}$ (b) (or equivalent)
(c) $\frac{2}{8}$, 0.25

T2 (a) $\frac{3}{10}$ (b) 30%
(c) (or equivalent)

T3 (a) 0.2 (b) $\frac{1}{4}$
(c) 0.17 (d) 17%, $\frac{1}{5}$, 0.25

Practice book

Section A (p 82)

1 (a) $\frac{2}{5}$ (b) 40%

2 30%, 40%, $\frac{1}{2}$, $\frac{3}{5}$, 70%, $\frac{8}{10}$

3 (a) $\frac{3}{10}$ (b) $\frac{1}{4}$ (c) $\frac{3}{5}$ (d) $\frac{4}{5}$

4 '20% extra' and '$\frac{1}{5}$ more'
'60% increase' and '$\frac{3}{5}$ more'
'50% extra' and 'Extra $\frac{1}{2}$'
'25% more' and '$\frac{1}{4}$ extra'

Section B (p 82)

1 (a) 30% (b) 60% (c) 90%

2 (a) 0.2 (b) 0.75 (c) 0.8

3 25%, 0.3, 0.4, 50%, 60%, 0.75

4 0.2 and 20%; 0.7 and 70%;
0.5 and 50%; 0.25 and 25%

Sections C and D (p 83)

1 $\frac{3}{10}$ and the student's explanation

2 $\frac{1}{4}$ and the student's explanation

3 (a) 10%, 20%, $\frac{1}{4}$, 0.3, $\frac{2}{5}$
(b) $\frac{6}{10}$, 70%, $\frac{3}{4}$, 0.8, 90%

4 (a) LION (b) TIGER
(c) RHINO (d) PYTHON

5 Equivalents of $\frac{1}{4}$, 0.3, 80%, 80%, $\frac{3}{4}$

6

Fraction	Decimal	Percentage
$\frac{3}{4}$	**0.75**	**75%**
$\frac{3}{5}$	0.6	**60%**
$\frac{7}{10}$	**0.7**	**70%**
$\frac{2}{5}$	**0.4**	40%
$\frac{9}{10}$	0.9	**90%**

7 (a) $\frac{1}{2}$, 70%, $\frac{3}{4}$, $\frac{4}{5}$, 0.9

   (b) 40%, $\frac{1}{2}$, $\frac{3}{5}$, $\frac{3}{4}$, 0.8

8 (a) 0.75   (b) 0.6

   (c) 0.125   (d) 0.875

9 25%, $\frac{1}{3}$, 0.4, 50%, 0.6, $\frac{2}{3}$

Section E (p 84)

1 (a) £4   (b) £8   (c) £28

   (d) £6   (e) £20   (f) £24

2 (a) £1.50   (b) £16.50

3 16 g

4 50 g

5 (a) £20 (b) £15 (c) £12 (d) £13

Section F (p 84)

1

Fraction	Decimal	Percentage
$\frac{81}{100}$	**0.81**	**81%**
$\frac{1}{100}$	0.01	**1%**
$\frac{87}{100}$	**0.87**	87%
$\frac{6}{100}$	**0.06**	6%

2 (a) $\frac{1}{5}$, $\frac{1}{4}$, 0.27, 30%, 0.4

   (b) $\frac{3}{5}$, 0.67, $\frac{3}{4}$, 0.8, $\frac{9}{10}$

   (c) 0.06, 0.1, $\frac{1}{5}$, 25%, $\frac{1}{2}$

   (d) 60%, $\frac{3}{4}$, $\frac{4}{5}$, 0.85, 0.9

29 Circle facts

> **Essential**
>
> Cylindrical objects (tins etc.)
> Thin strips of paper 40 cm or more long
>
> **Practice book** pages 85 to 87

𝔸 *Round about* (p 194)

TG

This activity is designed to familiarise students with the descriptive terms of a circle. A useful initial activity is to ask them to define a circle.

The diameter of the clockface of Big Ben is 6.8 m.

𝔹 *Finding the circumference* (p 195)

In this section students use the approximate relationship $C = 3d$ to find the circumference.

> Cylindrical objects (tins etc.)
> Thin strips of paper at least 40 cm long

TG

'Well worth doing.'

◊ Give students a range of cylindrical objects which they can use to check the relationship between diameter and circumference. This method avoids any measuring and should enable them to see the 'three times' rule directly.

◊ After the initial exercise it may be useful to measure the diameter and circumference (with a tape measure) to confirm the results.

◊ Some schools have used the strips to make a graph of circumference against diameter.

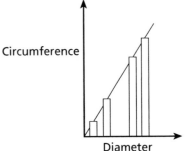

☾ **Finding the diameter and radius** (p 197)

◊ You will need to give an introduction to the idea of dividing as the reverse process. Again, a value of 3 is intended to be used as students gain confidence. You may need to discuss the degree of accuracy for the answers to C8 and C9, given that students are only using a rough method.

𝔻 **Becoming more accurate** (p 199)

π is introduced, together with the idea of obtaining greater accuracy.

> 'We cut pieces of string, formed circles and measured the diameter.'

◊ Students may find it difficult to see that they are getting a multiplier that can be applied to any circle, especially since measurement errors and other factors will preclude getting the same exact value every time.

◊ If students do not have a π key on their calculator they can use 3.142. Different degrees of rounding are asked for in this section including 'to one decimal place' and 'to a sensible degree of accuracy'. This is a good place to discuss limitations of the accuracy of measurements.

D3 Identifying the correct arrow on the scale provides a way in to seeing what happens when we round to the nearest 0.1. It may be worth doing D3 with the whole class and, if necessary, supplementing it with further teacher-led work using a decimal scale.

𝔹 **Finding the circumference** (p 195)

B1 (a) 21 cm (b) 30 cm (c) 18 cm

B2 (a) 45 cm (b) 24 cm (c) 69 cm

B3 (a) 12 cm (b) 15 cm (c) 7.5 cm

B4 (a) Diameter 3 cm, circumference 9 cm
(b) Diameter 1 cm, circumference 3 cm
(c) Diameter 4.5 cm, circumference 13.5 cm

B5 6 cm

B6 66 cm

B7 The student's sketch of a 10 cm by 27 cm rectangle

B8 12 cm

*B9** About 225 metres

ℂ **Finding the diameter and radius** (p 197)

C1 20 cm

C2 4 cm

C3 7 cm

C4 30 cm

C5 16 cm

C6 250 m

C7 12 cm

C8 18 m (or an answer close to this)

C9 1.5 cm

C10 4 m (or an answer close to this)

C11 8 cm

C12 (a) 8 cm (b) 4 cm

C13 7 cm

C14 40 cm

C15 1.1 m

C16 190 paces

C17 (a) About 2 m (or a bit less)
    (b) About 20 m (or a bit less)
    (c) About 6 m (or close to this)

Ⓓ *Becoming more accurate* (p 199)

D1 (a) 6.283 185...   (b) 6.3 cm

D2 (a) 10.053 096...   (b) 10.1 cm

D3 (a) W   (b) 11.6 cm

D4 (a) 8.2 cm   (b) 10.7 cm
    (b) 5.7 cm   (d) 13.8 cm

D5 (a) Diameter 2.8 cm,
       circumference 8.8 cm
    (b) Diameter 1.8 cm,
       circumference 5.7 cm
    (c) Diameter 3.2 cm,
       circumference 10.1 cm
    (d) Diameter 3.8 cm,
       circumference 11.9 cm

D6 (a) 3.6 cm   (b) 11.3 cm

D7 (a) Diameter 4.7 cm,
       circumference 14.8 cm
    (b) Diameter 2.7 cm,
       circumference 8.5 cm
    (c) Diameter 3.9 cm,
       circumference 12.3 cm
    (d) Diameter 3.2 cm,
       circumference 10.1 cm

D8 (a) 25.1 cm (b) 13.2 cm (c) 35.2 cm

D9 (a) 28.0 cm   (b) 88.0 cm

D10 (a) 180 cm   (b) 565 cm

D11 8.5 m

D12 25.1 m

D13 (a) 37.7 m (b) 7 m   (c) 44.0 m

*D14 Inside 628.318... m, outside 678.584... m,
     difference 50 m

*D15 (a) 3.14 cm (b) 3.14 cm (c) 314 cm

Test yourself (p 203)

T1 8.8 cm

T2 5.0 km

T3 (a) 60 cm   (b) 188.5 cm

T4 11.3 cm

T5 25.1 cm

T6 80 m

T7 (a) 157 cm   (b) 50 (nearly 51)

Practice book

Section B (p 85)

1 (a) 15 cm   (b) 36 cm   (c) 48 cm

2 (a) 90 cm   (b) 60 cm   (c) 45 cm

3 300 cm is needed altogether (120 cm for
   the top and 180 cm for the bottom.)

4 90 kerbstones

5 (a) 75 cm   (b) 225 cm

6 (a) 80 m   (b) 240 m

Section C (p 86)

1
Type of tree	Diameter	Radius
Oak	40 cm	20 cm
Siver Birch	20 cm	10 cm
Horse Chestnut	50 cm	25 cm
Yew	70 cm	35 cm
Beech	25 cm	$12\frac{1}{2}$ cm

Section D (p 87)

1 (a) 10.1 cm   (b) 6.0 cm
   (c) 11.9 or 12.0 cm (d) 4.4 cm
   (e) 6.6 cm

2 A diameter 2 cm, circumference 6.3 cm
   B diameter 2.8 cm, circumference 8.8 cm
   C diameter 6 cm, circumference 18.8 cm

3 The circumference is 81.67 cm,
   so Harry's piece is not long enough.

4 26.7 cm
               6 cm

30 Surveys

This unit is intended as a guide to carrying out statistical surveys. It covers designing a questionnaire, choosing a sample, analysing results and writing a report. Much of it is designed to stimulate discussion about these processes.

Examples and data are provided, but the topic will become much more interesting if students use material from their own class or individual projects.

Essential	Optional
Pie chart scales	Copies of real-life questionnaires

A *Starting a project* (p 204)

This section deals with two processes:

- writing a statement or question for a data handling project;
- deciding which statements or questions are suitable to be tested by carrying out a survey.

Some of the statements and questions posed in the initial activity will need an experimental approach or will require secondary data. Unit 10 'Experiments' dealt with carrying out experiments and unit 43 contains further work on secondary data.

Students may already know about surveys, particularly from other subject areas, but they often think that a survey can be used to test any statement or question. The initial discussion should encourage them to think where a survey is the most appropriate technique.

Examination boards' coursework guides should be checked for their particular requirements.

B *Questionnaires* (p 205)

This section deals with the design of questionnaires, in particular writing suitable questions.

> Optional: copies of real-life questionnaires

You could use some examples of real-life questionnaires of varying quality which students could comment on, for example the detailed 'customer service' questionnaires sent as junk mail and designed to provide market research profiles on individuals for future targeted promotions.

C *Choosing a sample* (p 207)

This section looks at ways of choosing a sample and how questionnaires are distributed and collected. Many students think that they only need to give the questionnaire to a few friends.

The initial discussion should encourage students to think about:

- how to select a sample that is 'representative' – students should ask themselves whether their method gets a fair cross-section of people;
- how many people should be included in the survey – numbers should be sufficient to ensure a representative sample but realistic in terms of what is feasible and manageable for analysis;
- whether the method of collecting the data is efficient, and ensures that most of the questionnaires are returned properly completed.

Boards' coursework guides give information on what size samples are considered appropriate. A sample of 30 is often considered the minimum.

The right choice?

The survey described was carried out by a local council in the east of England. This phenomenon is known as 'non-response bias'. In fact, shortly after the survey was carried out, toxic waste was discovered at the site and twenty years later there is no public access.

Students may be interested in how professional surveys are conducted. These facts may be useful:

- In the 1990s Gallup, the best-known market research and opinion poll company, changed their survey method. Previously they had canvassed opinion in the street in certain areas and asked canvassers to ensure a representative sample. Under the new system canvassing is carried out over the phone to carefully selected households all over the UK.
- Newspapers often publish details about the most watched TV programmes quoting the number of people who watched a particular programme. This information is usually provided by the National Viewers Survey which uses a representative sample from around the

UK who have a monitor connected to their TV which records the programmes that are being watched and even how many people are in the room watching them. These figures are then multiplied up to estimate the total number of viewers nationally.

• Record charts were at one time compiled from sales figures from a small number of outlets. When it was discovered that record companies were sending people to particular shops to buy large numbers of the companies' own records to boost their chart positions, the pollsters had to increase the number of outlets covered. Charts are now based on sales from 75% of all outlets.

Ⓓ *Looking at results* (p 208)

This section gives students an opportunity to revise some techniques and apply them to data collected in surveys.

Pie chart scales

◊ You may wish to take this opportunity to revise other topics such as the dot plot, stem-and-leaf diagram and median.

 ◊ This a good opportunity to use a spreadsheet to display data and calculate statistics.

Ⓔ *Writing a report* (p 209)

This section contains useful hints for students writing reports on surveys they have conducted and some suggestions for surveys they could carry out themselves.

Ⓑ *Questionnaires* (p 205)

B1 The student's question

B2 The student's question

B3 The student's question

B4 (a) Difficult to answer precisely or embarrassing

    (b) Embarrassing

    (c) Leading

B5 C is the most useful as it gives a limited range of choices but has an 'open' box at the end.

B6 The student's questionnaire

Ⓒ *Choosing a sample* (p 207)

C1 Key points that should be made are:

    (a) Too small a sample; very limited representation of all pet owners

    (b) Will probably give a representative sample, but it is unlikely that many questionnaires will be returned

    (c) Generally a good idea

C2 (a) At least 30 would be appropriate

(b) The student's suggestion; should ensure that students are chosen from all ages in the school

D *Looking at results* (p 208)

D1 (a) 10   (b) $\frac{10}{25} = \frac{2}{5}$

(c) 40%   (d) 60%

D2 (a) 28%   (b) 72%

D3 (a) Should school uniform be compulsory?

	Yes	No	Total
Male	6	4	10
Female	12	3	15
Total	18	7	25

(b) Males $\frac{6}{10} = \frac{3}{5}$

Females $\frac{12}{15} = \frac{4}{5}$

D4 (a)

Colour	Tally	Frequency
Black	ⵚⵚ ‖	7
Blue	ⵚⵚ ‖	6
Grey	‖‖‖‖	4
Red	ⵚⵚ	5
Other	‖‖‖	3
	Total	25

(b) Black   (c) 6

(d)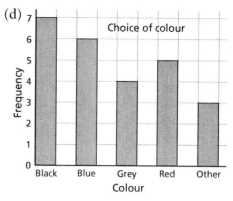

D5 (a) Mean 2.7   range 3

(b) Mean 1.3   range 2

(c) Boys

D6 (a)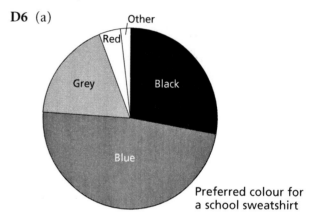

Preferred colour for a school sweatshirt

(b) Around 384

31 Areas of parallelograms

This unit introduces students to finding the area of a parallelogram.

Essential

Sheets G35 and G36
Scissors, rulers, set squares

Practice book pages 88 to 89

A Areas of rectangles (p 211)

◊ In this section and throughout this unit decimals are largely avoided unless they give whole-number answers.

B Areas of parallelograms (p 212)

This section leads students to a visual recognition that a parallelogram has the same area as a rectangle with the same base and perpendicular height.

> Sheets G35 and G36, scissors, rulers, set squares

Squaring off

'I put the sheets on an OHP and the kids came up and did these for everyone to see.'

In this activity students should realise that by cutting a parallelogram along a perpendicular height the two pieces can be made into a rectangle. This is easy to see when the parallelogram is drawn on squared paper. Parallelograms C and D can be cut in two ways but E 'overhangs' in one orientation. The areas are:

A 24 cm²   B 15 cm²   C 30 cm²   D 36 cm²   E 24 cm²

By comparing their results students should see that there are a number of ways the parallelograms can be cut but all give the same result.

◊ Weaker students may find it useful to draw and cut the parallelograms in B2 and B3 to check their results.

C *Finding the perpendicular* (p 214)

This section uses the standard formula to find the area of a parallelogram.

> Set squares

◊ Questions C1 and C2 should establish that the area of a parallelogram can be found using any side as the base provided the height is measured perpendicular to it.

D *Overhangs* (p 216)

This section deals with the case where the top edge overhangs the bottom edge and the perpendicular height cannot be measured directly. When measuring, this problem can always be avoided by using the longest side as the base.

◊ The second diagram reinforces the principle that any two parallelograms with the same base and perpendicular height will always have the same area, even in the overhanging case. This can be usefully illustrated by a pile of books or by using a dynamic geometry package.

E *Parallelogram problems* (p 217)

E4 Some teachers have preferred to use this question as a class activity or in small groups. Students could make up their own questions.

A *Areas of rectangles* (p 211)

A1 (a) $15\,\text{cm}^2$ (b) $10\,\text{cm}^2$ (c) $28\,\text{cm}^2$

A2 (a) $40\,\text{cm}^2$ (b) $35\,\text{cm}^2$
    (c) $150\,\text{cm}^2$ (d) $20\,\text{cm}^2$

A3 (a) $80\,\text{m}^2$ (b) $18\,\text{m}^2$
    (c) $22\,\text{m}^2$ (c) $52\,\text{m}^2$

B *Areas of parallelograms* (p 212)

B1 Possible solutions are:

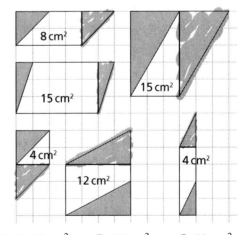

B2 A $12\,\text{cm}^2$ B $16\,\text{cm}^2$ C $28\,\text{cm}^2$
    D $8\,\text{cm}^2$ E $12\,\text{cm}^2$ F $20\,\text{cm}^2$
    G $6\,\text{cm}^2$

B3 (a) All have area 12 cm².

(b) Comment such as 'they all make a 3 by 4 rectangle when cut and re-joined'.

B4 (a) The student's drawing of a parallelogram with area 20 cm²

(b) The student's drawing of a different parallelogram with area 20 cm²

(c) The student's drawing of a parallelogram with area 10 cm²

ℂ *Finding the perpendicular* (p 214)

C1 (a) 4 cm

(b) Area = base × perp. height
$= 4\frac{1}{2}$ cm × 4 cm = 18 cm²

C2 (a) 6 cm

(b) 3 cm

(c) Area = base × perp. height
= 6 cm × 3 cm = 18 cm²

C3 The answers are the same. It does not matter which side you choose as the base.

C4 (a) 35 cm² (b) 30 cm² (c) 72 cm²

(d) 40 cm² (e) 21 cm² (f) 66 cm²

C5 (a) 40 cm² (b) 28 cm² (c) 63 cm²

(d) 42 cm² (e) 8 cm²

𝔻 *Overhangs* (p 216)

D1 (a) 48 cm² (b) 18 cm² (c) 80 cm²

(d) 40 cm² (e) 21 cm² (f) 22 cm²

𝔼 *Parallelogram problems* (p 217)

E1 (a) A (3, 5) B (7, 5) C (5, 2) D (1, 2)

(b) 12 cm²

E2 (a)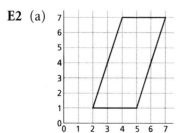

(b)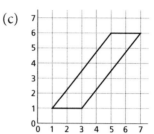

(c)

E3 (a) 18 cm² (b) 20 cm² (c) 10 cm²

E4 (a) (i) F (ii) D (iii) I

(b) A and E both have area 12 cm².

(c) A/E and G, B and H, C and I

Test yourself (p 218)

T1 75 m²

T2 (a) A parallelogram

(b) 2.8 cm (c) 13.6 cm (d) 8 cm²

Practice book

Sections B and C (p 88)

1 (a) 10 cm² (b) 6 cm² (c) 16 cm²

(d) 8 cm² (e) 12 cm² (f) 10 cm²

2 (a) 3 parallelograms with area 12 cm²

(b) 3 parallelograms with area 15 cm²

3 (a) 12 cm² (b) 15 cm²

4 (a) 63 cm² (b) 12 cm² (c) 48 cm²

(d) 120 cm² (e) 252 cm² (f) 504 cm²

Section D (p 89)

1 (a) 60 cm² (b) 40 cm² (c) 24 cm²

(d) 84 cm² (e) 200 cm² (f) 72 cm²

32 Gathering like terms

> **Practice book** pages 90 to 92

A Revisiting expressions (p 219)

◊ The introduction may be used to remind students of gathering like terms where only numbers and a single letter are involved. If it does not come out in discussion, you may wish to remind them that, for example, $5a + 2$ and $2 + 5a$ are both valid simplifications.

◊ Some students may find it helpful to write like terms together when simplifying. For example

$$2x + 10 + 3x - 3$$
$$= 2x + 3x + 10 - 3$$
$$= 5x + 7$$

C Letters away! (p 222)

◊ It can be helpful to check that both the original and the simplified expressions give the same result if the same number is substituted into them. In this case, where the expressions represent lengths, care must be taken to choose a number so that they do not turn out to be negative. In the introduction, choosing $m = 1$, $a = 1$, $x = 2$ and $y = 1$ will avoid this pitfall.

D Forming expressions and formulas (p 223)

◊ Examination questions sometimes ask for an expression and sometimes for a formula. The wording in this section is deliberately varied, and you may wish to draw students' attention to the two possible ways of asking for an answer.

◊ To help students form an expression or formula you might suggest that they first think of the problem with the letters replaced by numbers. What would they do to the numbers to get the answer? Then they should try doing the same thing but using the letters instead of their numbers.

◊ Students may find the language used in this type of problem confusing. It may help them if they realise that statements like 'There are n sheep in a field' is short for 'There are some sheep in a field. Let n stand for the number of sheep.'

A *Revisiting expressions* (p 219)

A1 (a) A and G, B and C, E and F

(b) A 31, B 18, C 18, D 19, E 13, F 13, G 31

A2 (a) $3p$ (b) $2e + 1$ (c) $3h + 5$
(d) $3f + 3$ (e) $3g + 8$ (f) $3y - 5$

A3 (a) $9a$ (b) $5b + 11$ (c) $6c + 42$
(d) $5d + 2$ (e) $16e + 23$ (f) $19f - 15$

A4 (a) $2x + 3x = \mathbf{5x}$
(b) $2y + \mathbf{6y} = 8y$
(c) $k + 3 + \mathbf{k} + \mathbf{2} = 2k + 5$
(d) $\mathbf{3h} + 2 + 2h - 1 = 5h + 1$
(e) $5d - 2 + 3d - 4 = \mathbf{8d} - 6$
(f) $\mathbf{2b} + 2 + b + \mathbf{5} = 3b + 7$

A5 (a) $2s + 4$ (b) $3d$ (c) $4k + 10$

A6 (a) $4m + 2$ (b) 3 (c) $2m$
(d) $5m + 4$

A7 (a) $6x + 3$ (b) $18x + 3$ (c) $5x + 5$
(d) $6x + 4$ (e) $7x + 3$ (f) $9x + 3$

B *More than one letter* (p 221)

B1 (a) $4a + 6b$ (b) $4x + 4y$
(c) $4p + 6q + 3$ (d) $4e + 5f + 4$
(e) $11j + 11k - 6$ (f) $5h + 8m + 2$

B2 (a) $7a + 5b$ (b) $4x + 10y$
(c) $3p + 7q + 3$ (d) $2e + 7f$
(e) $7j + 15k - 6$ (f) $5h + 8m - 7$

B3 (a) $7p + 8q$ (b) $6a + 4b + 13$
(c) $4a + 4b + 4c$

*B4 (a) $3z + 4y + z + 5y = 4z + 9y$
(b) $2u + v + \mathbf{u} + 3v = 4v + 3u$
(c) $5j + \mathbf{2k} + j + 4k = \mathbf{6j} + 6k$
(d) $12 + 2h + \mathbf{4g} + h + g - \mathbf{6} = 6 + \mathbf{3h} + 5g$

*B5

C *Letters away!* (p 222)

C1 (a) $2 - 3s$ (b) $15 - 6p$ (c) $30 - 9d$
(d) $6 - 3e$ (e) $2f$ (f) $2t$

C2 (a) $7k - 3h$ (b) $5s - r$
(c) $9 - 5b - 4a$ (d) $7e - c - d$
(e) $m + 10n - 2p$ (f) $11z - 2y - x$

C3 (a)

(b)

(c)

*C4 (a) $2a - \mathbf{3b} + b + 2a = 4a - 2b$
(b) $2w + x - \mathbf{5w} + 3x = 4x - 3w$
(c) $3k - \mathbf{4j} - j - k = 2k - 5j$
(d) $10 - 2k + \mathbf{3j} - k - 8j - \mathbf{4} = 6 - \mathbf{3k} - 5j$

*C5 $2 - 5d$

D Forming expressions and formulas
(p 223)

D1 (a) 24   (b) $100 - n$ (c) $m - p$

D2 (a) 8×35 (b) $35d$ (c) $40m$

    (d) $35d + 40m$

D3 $20 - 2n$

D4 (a) £37   (b) $T = 10 + 5d$

    (c) The student's check that $T = 50$

D5 (a) $w + 5$ (b) $P = 10 + 4w$

D6 (a) £130   (b) $10 + 20h$

D7 (a) 6 metres   (b) $10 - x$ metres

    (c) $y - z$ metres

D8 $C = 20 - 4n$

D9 $T = g + 2h + 5i$

D10 $C = 65n$

D11 (a) £10.03   (b) $18x$ pence

    (c) $3n + 2m$ pence

Test yourself (p 225)

T1 (a) $4t$ (b) $2r + 1$ (c) $5 + 2u$

    (d) $10f$ (e) $3a + 8$ (f) $1 + 7g$

T2 (i) $4a$ (ii) $7b - 4c$

T3 (a) $12a - 6$ (b) $2s + 14$

    (c) $2k - l + 5$

T4 A and R, B and T, C and P, D and S,
    E and Q

T5 (a) $2m + 6n$ (b) $6u + 6v + 3$

    (c) $3a - 2b - 3c$ (d) $10 - 2f + 2g$

    (e) $2t - 4s$ (f) $12 - 16l$

T6 $25r + 45s$ pence

T7 $100 - 2l$ centimetres

T8 (a) £95   (b) $T = a + 6b$

Practice book

Section A (p 90)

1 (a) $4s$ (b) $8x$ (c) $3w + 3$ (d) $16d$

2 (a) $3x$ (b) $3e + 3$ (c) $4j - 6$

    (d) $3m - 1$ (e) $8w + 10$ (f) $110w + 7$

3 (a) $x + 6$ (b) $x + 8$ (c) $x - 2$

4 (a) $p + 9$ (b) $2p + 5$ (c) 3

5 (a) $3x + 15$

    (b) (i) $9x + 15$ (ii) $6x + 9$ (iii) $6x + 21$

Sections B and C (p 91)

1 (a) $3b + 2c + 4$ (b) $2w + 4l + 6$

    (c) $3a + 2d + 3$ (d) $2p + 3q - 6$

2 (a) $2w + 2l + 6$ (b) $4w + 2l + 6$

3 (a) $3n + 4m$ (b) $7r + 3s$

    (c) $8p + 3q$ (d) $3a + 3b + 3$

    (e) $3f + 5g + 9$ (f) $9j + 5k + 1$

4 (a) $g + 15$ (b) $12 - t$

5 (a)   (b)

    (c)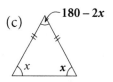

6 (a) $4a + 4b$ (b) $4r + 2s$ (c) $2c + 2d$

    (d) $10 - 5m - n$ (e) $2p + q + 2$

Section D (p 92)

1 (a) $w + 4$ (b) $P = 4w + 8$

2 (a) $x + 4$ (b) $x - 2$

3 (a) $12c$ (b) $p + 12$ (c) $3p + 36$

4 (a) $10 - x$ metres   (b) $w - 2x$ metres

5 $c = 20 - 3x$

33 Connections

This unit deals with bivariate data including drawing scatter diagrams, describing correlation and drawing lines of best fit.

TG	p 226 **A** *Scatter diagrams*	Drawing scatter diagrams
	p 230 **B** *Correlation*	Identifying the types of correlation
TG	p 233 **C** *Lines of best fit*	

Essential

Graph paper
Sheets G37, G38, G39, G40, G41, G42

Practice book pages 93 to 95

𝔸 *Scatter diagrams* (p 226)

This section deals with drawing scatter diagrams and the relationships they may show.

> Sheets G37, G38

TG

◊ The students should try both word puzzle tests and record the number of correct answers. It may be useful to have half the class doing the word square test and the others the anagram test and then swap over. This would counteract any tendency for students to do better in the first or second test they take. The timings for the tests were found in trialling to give a good range of results for students likely to be using this material but you may wish to adjust them for some groups.

Once the data is collated it can be presented to the students. Ask them if they think there is any connection between the two tests and how they might examine this. This should lead on to the drawing of a scatter diagram for their own data. Obtaining no correlation, if it happens, should be seen as a worthwhile result. Ask students what type of pattern they might expect if there was a connection.

◊ Crosses are used in the student's book as they clearly indicate where a point is. However, dots can also be used; a dot with one or more rings may be used to show repeated values.

A5 Using jagged lines to show that a scale does not start at zero is introduced in this question.

B **Correlation** (p 230)

> Graph paper, sheet G39

◊ The questions should lead to some discussion of 'strong' and 'weak' correlation.

Are you fit then?

This range of simple physical tests could be used to examine different types of correlation. This would be an ideal opportunity too to introduce the use of a spreadsheet to draw scatter diagrams – a much easier process than plotting by hand. Students should be encouraged to manipulate the scales to give roughly square graphs with sensible ranges on the axes.

C **Lines of best fit** (p 233)

> Graph paper, sheets G40, G41, G42

◊ Emphasise that it is only sensible to draw a line of best fit when there is a good correlation present. There is no definite rule at this level about what is 'good' correlation but this should indicate that the data clearly follows a straight line.

Predicting values from a line of best fit within the range of existing data (interpolation) is generally more reliable than doing so outside the range of data (extrapolation) and students need to be aware of this. Question C2(f) highlights this.

Find the connection

Students can use the data on the sheets to investigate any possible correlation between the various characteristics of the cars listed. Using a spreadsheet or other software for plotting scatter diagrams is ideal for this.

If all the data is entered beforehand into separate columns on the spreadsheet, then students can choose which pair of columns to check.

Further and more up-to-date information can easily be found using the internet.

Ⓐ *Scatter diagrams* (p 226)

A1 (a) Bob, yes (b) Hal, no (c) Guy

(d)
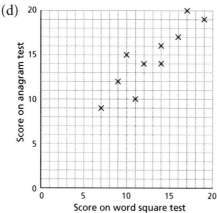

(e) Yes

A2 (a)
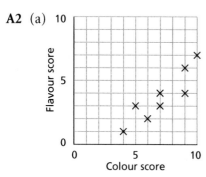

(b) B

A3 (a)

(b) Those who did well on the number puzzle did poorly on the picture puzzle and vice versa.

A4 (b)

Moth	Length	Wingspan
A	2.6	6.3
B	1.5	4.2
C	1.8	4.3
D	2.0	5.6
E	1.6	4.5
F	1.9	5.0
G	1.8	4.2
H	1.1	2.9
I	1.7	3.9
J	2.3	4.1
K	1.3	3.0
L	1.4	3.9
M	1.5	3.1
N	0.9	2.9
O	1.4	2.7
P	1.4	3.8
Q	2.1	3.4
R	1.7	4.8

(c)
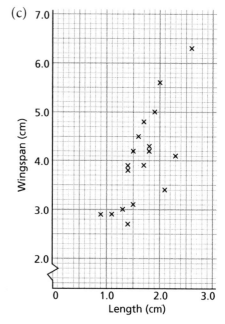

(d) Yes, it is generally true.

A5 The taller girls are likely to have taller mothers and vice versa.

Ⓑ *Correlation* (p 230)

B1 (a) • Positive correlation

   • The cars with larger engines generally had faster top speeds.

(b) • Negative correlation

   • Students with longer legs generally had shorter (i.e. faster) 100 m times.

(c) • Zero correlation

• There is no connection between the students' heights and maths test results.

B2 (a)

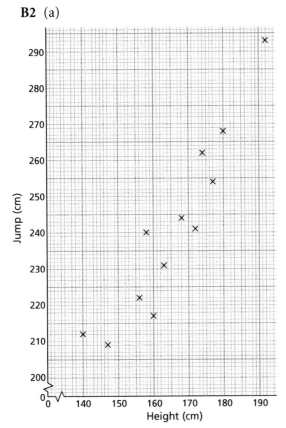

Jump (cm) vs Height (cm)

(b) Positive correlation

(c) Taller students can usually do a higher standing jump.

B3 (a)

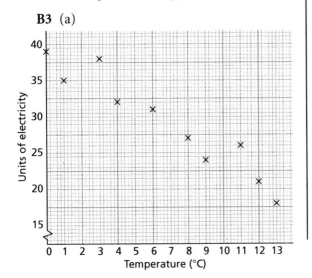

Units of electricity vs Temperature (°C)

(b) Negative correlation

(c) When the temperature is lower at 7 p.m. more electricity is generally used that day and vice versa.

B4 (a)

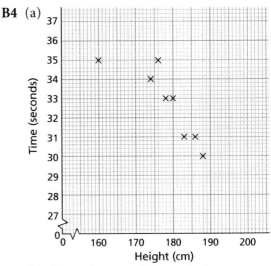

Time (seconds) vs Height (cm)

(b) There is a negative correlation, so taller people generally had a shorter (i.e. faster) 200 m time.

ℂ *Lines of best fit* (p 233)

C1 (a) The student's line of best fit

(b) (i) 170 cm   (ii) 190 cm

    (iii) 200 cm   (iv) 145 cm

(c) (i) 54 cm   (ii) 40 cm

    (iii) 60 cm   (iv) 27 cm

(d) 215 cm

This is well outside the range of the data so cannot be reliable.

C2 (a) and (c)

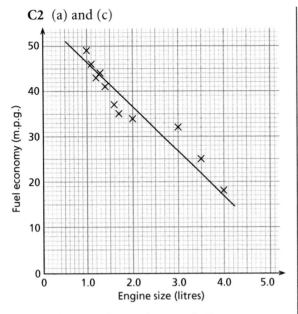

(b) Good negative correlation

(d) 32 m.p.g.   (e) 0.7 litres

(f) 0 m.p.g. according to the graph
This is very unreliable!

C3 (a), (b)

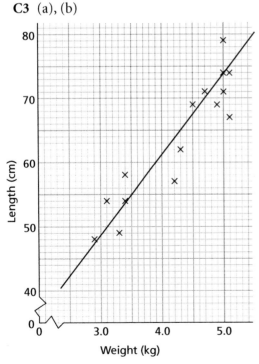

(c) (i) 61 cm   (ii) 48 cm
    (iii) 57 cm   (iv) 80 cm

(d) 5.1 kg

(e) 7 kg; the student's comment (unreliable)

C4 (a)

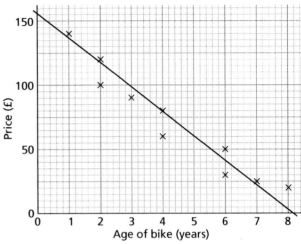

(b) Older bikes cost less.

(c) About £60

(d) About £150; probably not very realistic

Test yourself (p 236)

T1 (a) and (c)

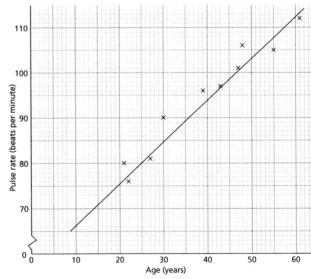

(b) Good positive correlation

(d) 90 beats per minute

(e) 132 b.p.m.; very unreliable

T2 (a)

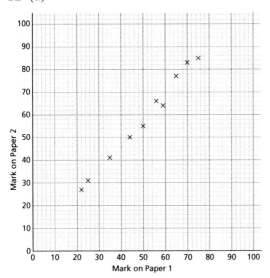

(b) There is a good positive correlation.

(c) About 48

Practice book

Section A (p 93)

1 (a) C   (b) F

(c)

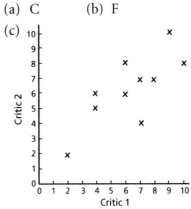

(d) Yes

They both give the films similar scores.

2 (a) 7 cm   (b) Yes

(c)

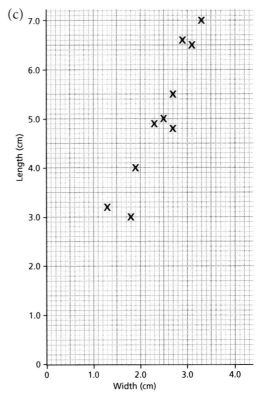

(d) The wider the leaf, the longer the leaf. (The leaves are about twice as long as they are wide.)

Section B (p 46)

1 (a)

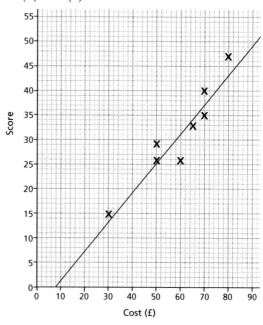

(b) Positive correlation

(c) Those who did well in year 6 were likely to do well in year 7.

(d) Dan

2 (a)

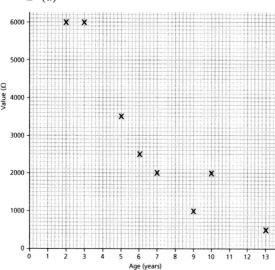

(b) Negative correlation

(c) As cars get older, their value decreases.

Section C (p 95)

1 (a) and (c)

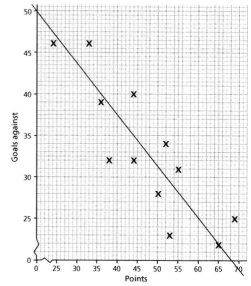

(b) Positive correlation

(d) About 20   (e) About £95

2 (a) and (b)

(c) The more points you have, the fewer goals you are likely to have let in.

(d) 32–33 goals   (e) About 43 points

34 Written calculation

Essential

Sheets G43, G44

Practice book pages 96 to 99

Ⓐ *Multiplying* (p 237)

Sheet G43

Table method

◊ Students may need to revise multiplying multiples of 10 first.

◊ Some students find it easier to add sets of numbers 'across' the table and then add these results, for example:

	50	2			
30	1500	60	→	1500 + 60 =	1560
7	350	14	→	350 + 14 =	364
					1924

Long multiplication

◊ Remind students that we can work out 37×52 by working out the sum of 37×2 and 37×50 and that the numbers 74 and 1850 are the results of these multiplications.

Lattice method

◊ This is popular and, despite its complex 'look', many students are able to apply it correctly. You may need to remind students to:

  • place the numbers to be multiplied at the top and right-hand side of the grid;

  • draw the diagonal lines from the top right to the bottom left of the squares;

  • add up the diagonal 'columns'.

B **Dividing** (p 238)

Sheet G44

TG ◊ The traditional long division algorithm is notoriously difficult. Students often find it helps, say, to write out the 23 times table if dividing by 23.

A **Multiplying** (p 237)

A1 (a) 255   (b) 1952
     (c) 1272   (d) 1846

A2 (a) 6278   (b) 8004
     (c) 5135   (d) 4554

A3 (a) 7052   (b) 12 272
     (c) 36 792   (d) 43 985

A4 (a) 304 cm^2 (b) 1032 m^2

A5 (a) (i) 30 × 40
         (ii) 1200p or £12.00
     (b) £11.89

A6 (a) 10 × 60 = 600 (b) 684

A7 6588

A8 Puzzle 1

A: 390   B: 377
C: 735   D: 672
E: 425   F: 1326
G: 814

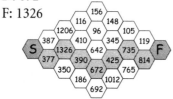

Puzzle 2

A: 2592   B: 3645
C: 1829   D: 2208
E: 4263   F: 2262
G: 6794

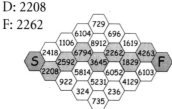

Puzzle 3

A: 3266   B: 2394
C: 2010   D: 2205
E: 3234   F: 7900
G: 13 088   H: 18 816

B **Dividing** (p 238)

B1 (a) 19 (b) 23 (c) 29 (d) 33

B2 (a) 16 (b) 23 (c) 18 (d) 22

B3 (a) 31 (b) 41 (c) 56 (d) 29

B4 Puzzle 1

A: 16   B: 17
C: 18   D: 19
E: 23   F: 25
G: 33

Puzzle 2

A: 23   B: 21
C: 24   D: 15
E: 17   F: 32
G: 29

Puzzle 3

A: 34   B: 26
C: 45   D: 38
E: 28   F: 21
G: 23   H: 52

B5 26

B6 28

B7 26

B8 (a) 17   (b) 6

B9 (a) 21   (b) 28

B10 12

B11 23

       ℂ *Mixed questions* (p 239)

C1 384

C2 24

C3 (a) £6.30   (b) 25

C4 (a) 12   (b) £1140

C5 (a) 150 × 40 = 6000p = £60
    (b) £59.28   (c) 25

C6 39

Test yourself (p 240)

T1 1288

T2 28

T3 £3.48

T4 £11 985

T5 12

T6 25 words per minute

T7 (a) (i) 800 × 30 × 10 = £240 000
       (ii) More, as 800 is more than 792
          and 30 is more than 29
    (b) 22 968

Practice book

Section A (p 96)

1 (a) 252 (b) 943 (c) 1470 (d) 999

2 (a) 4088 (b) 6068 (c) 4216 (d) 7553

3 (a) 3675   (b) 12 528
    (c) 66 332   (d) 14 553

4 (a) 280   (b) 4480

5 (a) 20 × 40 = 800 (b) 738

6 (a) £7872   (b) £9.90
    (c) (i) £46.74 (ii) £108.68

Section B (p 97)

1 (a) 35 (b) 32 (c) 34 (d) 16

2 (a) 31 (b) 19 (c) 17 (d) 27

3 (a) 69 (b) 54 (c) 95 (d) 26

4 (a) 80 (b) 45

5 35

6 56

7 (a) 27 (b) 36

8 27p

9 (a) 19p for the large bag and
      21p for the small bag
    (b) Yes, 2p each

10 (a) 36 cm   (b) 39 cm

11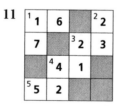

12 7

13 (a) 29   (b) 35 ml

14 (a) 2000 g   (b) 57 m²

Section C (p 99)

1 47

2 (a) 36 litres (b) £33.12

3 £23

4 (a) 18 (b) 24 (c) 432 (d) £155.52

5 (a) 50 × 40 = 2000   (b) 1872

Review 4 (p 241)

1 (a) 0.4   (b) $\frac{3}{4}$ (c) 0.4

2 0.75, $\frac{6}{8}$ and 75%

3 The student's rectangles with $\frac{3}{5}$, 40% and 0.3 shaded

4 (a) 2°C   (b) ⁻8°C
   (c) ⁻1°C   (d) ⁻16°C

5 (a) ⁻10   (b) ⁻11   (c) ⁻9
   (d) ⁻5   (e) ⁻25

6 ⁻4

7 (a)

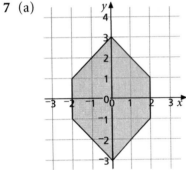

   (b) (⁻2, 1) and (⁻2, ⁻1)   (c) Order 2

8 (a) 10.5 m   (b) 117 m   (c) 47 m

9 (a) 1.03, 1.1, 1.15, 1.25, 1.4
   (b) 0.05, 0.09, 0.11, 0.20, 0.7, 1
   (c) 99 g, $\frac{1}{4}$ kg, 500 g, 0.7 kg
   (d) 450 cm, 5 m, 0.01 km, $\frac{1}{2}$ km, 35 km

10 (a) 5f   (b) 3x + 8   (c) a + 4b

11 (a) 2n   (b) n + 5

12 (a) 24 cm²   (b) 48 cm²   (c) 90 cm²

13 (a)

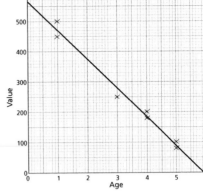

   (b) (Strong) negative correlation
   (c) The student's line of best fit
   (d) About £375

14 (a) 124   (b) 230   (c) 68   (d) 205
   (e) 82   (f) 17   (g) 340   (h) 36
   (i) 30   (j) 24

15 (a) 1026   (b) 34

16 (a) Too much accuracy is asked for. People will not remember.
   (b) This is a leading question.

17 (a) 10p + 4   (b) 6a + 5b + 5
   (c) 10x + 2y

18 (a)

No. of weeks	Tally	Frequency
5–9	//	2
10–14	//	2
15–19	///	3
20–24	₶₶ /	6
25–29	₶₶	5
30–34	//	2

(b)

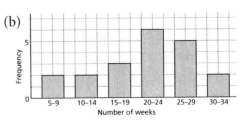

(c) 20–24 weeks

Mixed questions 4 (Practice book p 100)

1 (a) 20%, 0.25, $\frac{1}{2}$, 65%, $\frac{3}{4}$
   (b) 10%, 0.15, 20%, $\frac{1}{4}$, $\frac{1}{3}$

2 (a) 6   (b) 12   (c) 16
   (d) 15   (e) 50

3 (a) £40   (b) £16
   (c) £12   (d) £12

4 (a) ⁻6°C, ⁻3°C, 1°C, 2°C, 5°C
   (b) ⁻3.2°C, ⁻1.5°C, 0°C, 2.5°C, 3.8°C

5 (a) ⁻1 and 2   (b) ⁻4 and 6
   (c) ⁻4 and 2   (d) ⁻2 and 2

6 (a) ⁻9   (b) ⁻6   (c) ⁻2

7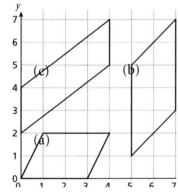

   (a) Area = 6 cm²   (b) Area = 8 cm²
   (c) Area = 8 cm²

8 90 cm

9 (a) 19 m   (b) 10 times

10 (a) 2.5 cm   (b) 7.9 cm

11 (a) This is a leading question.
    (b) Too little information is asked for.
    (c) Student's suggestion, such as 'How much pocket money did you get last week? Tick one.' with five or more choices for participants to choose from

12 Area = 40 cm²

13 (a) $7a$ (b) $6k + 4$ (c) $8h - 4$

14 (a) 68 cm   (b) 1.5 kg
    (c) Positive   (d) Strong

15 (a) Estimate 20 × 30 = 600; 589 m²
    (b) Estimate 800 ÷ 20 = 40; 39 rows

35 Graphs from rules

Essential	**Optional**
2 mm graph paper Sheets G46, G47, G49, G50, G51	Sheets G45, G48
Practice book pages 102 to 104	

We have provided resource sheets with axes for almost all questions.
Some of these sheets are optional.

𝔸 *Finding patterns* (p 244)

In your introduction, ask the students which of the rules at the start of this section fits the table, and why each of the others cannot be correct.

Then ask students to think of a different but similar rule of their own, and to work out their own table of values connecting the x- and y-coordinates (using $x = 0, 1, 2, 3, 4$ and 5). Individuals can then come up to the board and write their own y values in a table. The rest of the class can try to spot a rule that works for the student's table. There may be a variety of ways of expressing the rule, which is to be encouraged.

Students may give the connection in words, but should be encouraged to try to give it using the letters x and y.

B *Drawing the line* (p 245)

> 2 mm graph paper
> Sheets G46, G47
> Optional: sheet G45

Students will need to multiply a positive number by a negative in this section, so some revision may be necessary.

In the introduction, emphasise that the tables are tables of coordinates, and that formulas such as $y = 2x + 1$ connect x- and y-coordinates.

B1 Grid A on sheet G45 is optional.

B2 Grid B on sheet G45 is optional.

B3, 4 Sheet G46 is required.

B5, 6, 8 Sheet G47 is required.

B7, 8 Students need to draw up a table of their own for these questions. They also need to draw their own axes. You will find more questions of this type in the practice materials.

C *A different type of equation* (p 247)

◊ Students often find it difficult to think of $y = 3$ as meaning the set of points where the y-coordinate is always 3. It may be necessary to deal with a few equations of this type in discussion.

D *On different lines* (p 248)

> 2 mm graph paper
> Optional: sheet G48

◊ In the introduction, concentrate on spotting pairs of values that fit the equation, trying especially the cases where $x = 0$ and $y = 0$. The pairs are usually fairly easy to spot in the types of example the students are likely to come across. Students could simply find only the points where $x = 0$ and $y = 0$, but completing the full table is less likely to lead to errors.

When they do need to solve a simple equation (for example, to find the value of y when $4 + 2y = 12$), encourage them to treat it as a puzzle and to try to spot the solution straight away; there is no need for them to solve the equation formally.

Introduction, D1–3, 5 Optional sheet G48 contains axes for these.

Test yourself (p 250)

Sheets G49, G50, G51

T2 Sheet G49 is required.

T3, 4 Sheet G50 is required.

T6, 7 Sheet G51 is required.

A Finding patterns (p 244)

A1 $y = 3x$

A2 $y = x + 2$ and $x = y - 2$

A3 $y = 2x + 1$

A4 A is $y = 2x + 3$ B is $y = 2x + 4$

C is $y = 4x$ D is $y = 4x + 1$

B Drawing the line (p 245)

B1 (a) 4   (b) 6

(c)

x	0	1	2	3	4	5
y	3	4	5	6	7	8

(d)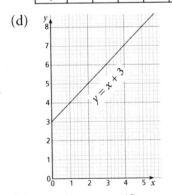

(e) $y = 5.5$ (f) $x = 4.5$

B2 (a) $y = 6$ (b) $y = -2$

(c)

x	-2	-1	0	1	2	3
y	-4	-2	0	2	4	6

(d)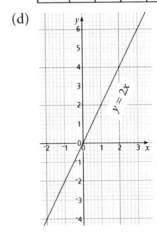

(e) $(0.5, \mathbf{1})$ $(2.5, \mathbf{5})$ $(^-1.5, ^-3)$

B3 (a)

x	0	1	2	3	4	5
y	0	4	8	12	16	20

(b)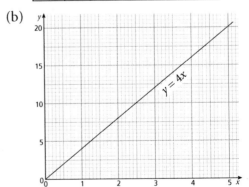

(c) $x = 2.5$

B4 (a)

x	⁻1	0	1	2	3
y	⁻2	1	4	7	10

(b)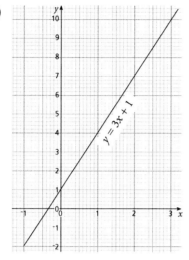

(c) $x = 1.3$

B5 (a)

x	⁻3	⁻2	⁻1	0	1	2
y	⁻3	⁻1	1	3	5	7

(b)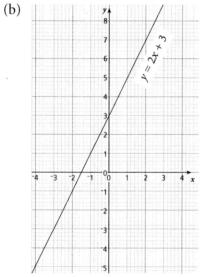

(c) (i) $y = 6$ (ii) $x = {}^-1.8$

B6 (a)

x	⁻1	0	1	2
$y = 3x - 1$	⁻4	⁻1	2	5

(b)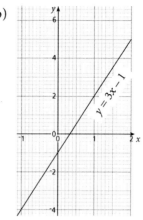

(c) $x = 1.3$

B7 (Different scales may have been used.)

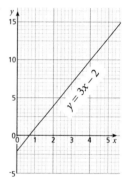

B8 (Different axes may have been used.)

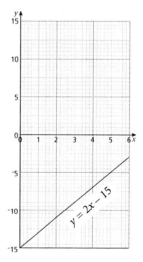

𝐶 **A different type of equation** (p 247)

C1 (a)

x	2	2	**2**	**2**	2
y	-1	0	1	2	3

(b) The x-coordinates are all 2.

(c) $x = 2$

C2 (a), (b)

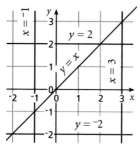

(c) $(-2, -2)$

C3

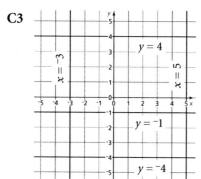

𝔻 **On different lines** (p 248)

D1 (b) The student's checks

(c) $x = 6$ (d) $x = 5$

(e)

x	0	1	2	3	4	5	6	7
y	7	6	5	4	3	2	1	0

(f)

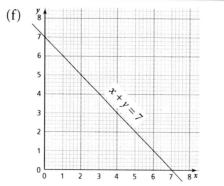

(g) $(2.5, \mathbf{4.5})$ $(\mathbf{1.5}, 5.5)$

D2 (b) $y = 10$ (c) $y = 8$

(d)

x	0	1	2	3	4	5
y	**10**	**8**	**6**	**4**	**2**	**0**

(e)

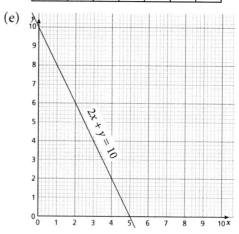

(f) $y = 3$ (g) $x = 1.5$

D3 (a) $y = 4$ (b) $y = 2$

(c)

x	0	3	6	9	12
y	**4**	**3**	**2**	**1**	**0**

(d)

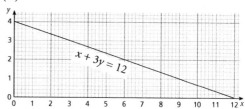

(e) $y = 2.7$ (f) $x = 4.5$

D4

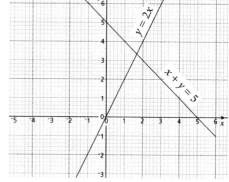

*D5 (b), (c) The student's checks

(d) $y = 4$

(e)

x	0	3	6	9	12
y	8	6	**4**	**2**	**0**

(f)

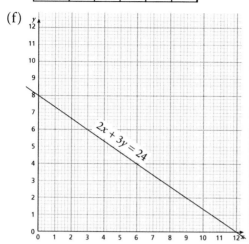

Test yourself (p 250)

T1 $y = x + 4$

T2

x	$^-2$	$^-1$	0	1	2	3	4
y	$^-10$	$^-5$	**0**	5	**10**	**15**	**20**

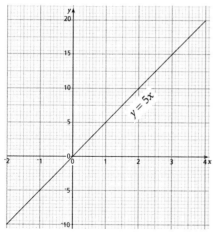

When $y = 18$, $x = 3.6$

T3 (a) The student's point on $y = x + 1$

(b)

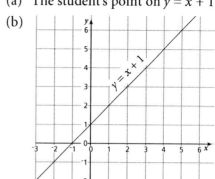

T4 (a)

x	$^-1$	0	1	2
y	$^-3$	$^-1$	**1**	**3**

(b)

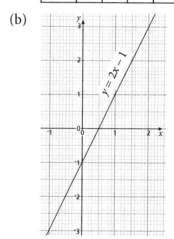

(c) $x = 1.7$ or 1.8

T5 A is $x = ^-2$ B is $y = 1$
       C is $x = 1$ D is $y = ^-3$

T6 (a)

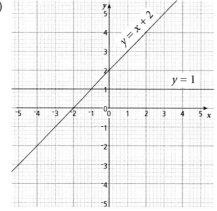

(b) P is $(^-1, 1)$

T7 (a) $y = 6$

(b)

x	0	1	2	3	4
y	12	9	**6**	**3**	**0**

(c)

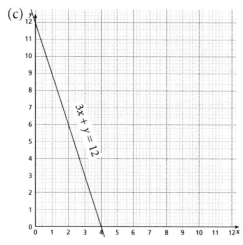

(d) $x = 2.7$

Practice book

Section A (p 102)

1 $y = 4x$

2 $y = x + 5$

3 A: $y = 2x + 4$ B: $y = 7x$

   C: $y = 3x + 5$ D: $y = 4x + 3$

Section B (p 102)

1 (a)

x	0	1	2	3	4	5
y	**6**	**7**	**8**	**9**	**10**	**11**

(b)

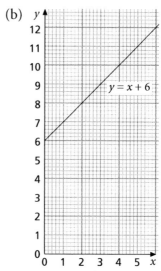

(c) $y = 9.5$ (d) $x = 1.5$

2 (a)

x	-2	-1	0	1	2	3
y	**-6**	**-3**	**0**	**3**	**6**	**9**

(b) See graph

(c) $(0.5, \mathbf{1.5})$, $(2.5, \mathbf{7.5})$, $(^-1.5, ^-4.5)$

3 (a)

x	-2	-1	0	1	2	3
y	-8	-6	-4	-2	0	2

(b) See graph

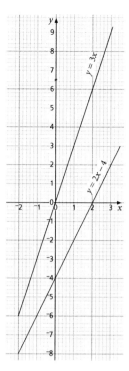

5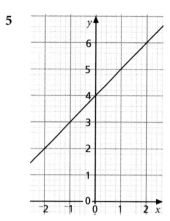

6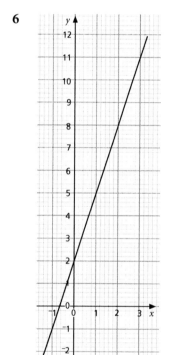

4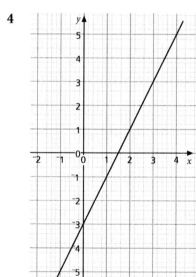

Section C (p 103)

1 (a), (b)

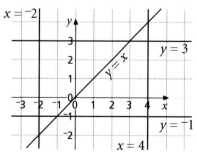

(c) (⁻2, ⁻2) (⁻1, ⁻1) (3, 3)

2 (a)

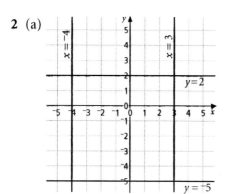

(b) A square

(c) (⁻4, 2) (3, 2) (3, ⁻5) (⁻4, ⁻5)

Section D (p 104)

1 (a) $y = 12$ (b) $x = 12$

(c)

x	0	2	4	6	8	10	12
y	12	10	8	6	4	2	0

(d)

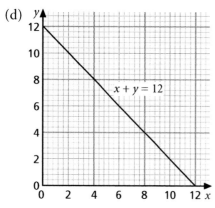

(e) (4.5, **7.5**) (**2.5**, 9.5)

2 (a)

x	10	6	2
y	0	1	2

(b)

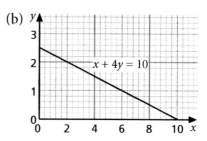

(c) $y = 2\frac{1}{2}$ (d) $x = 4$

3 (a)

x	0	1	2	3	4	5
y	15	12	9	6	3	0

(b)

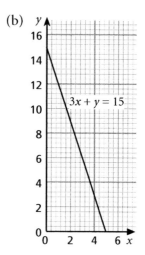

36 Chance

This unit uses simple trials with equally likely outcomes to revise earlier work on expressing probability as a fraction. Different ways of listing are then used to find probabilities in multi-event trials.

Essential	Optional
Sheets G52, G53	Sheet G53 on an OHP transparency
Dice, counters or tiles	
Practice book pages 105 to 108	

A *Probability* (p 251)

◊ This section assumes that students are familiar with expressing probability as a fraction, but this may need revising. You may also wish to revise equivalent fractions and simplifying.

A7, 8 Some students may think that B is a better bag to choose from as it contains more beads. Doing an experiment may help convince them.

B *Listing* (p 253)

◊ The essential point of this section is that students learn to be systematic about their listing so that all possibilities are included. A tree diagram approach could be used. Using abbreviations is encouraged to make the task of listing less onerous.

◊ Some students may find it easier to list the possible choices as blocks, rather than in one long list. For example, in B2 the possibilities are

PB	BP	MP	AP
PM	BM	MB	AB
PA	BA	MA	AM

C Listing outcomes (p 254)

TG

The big bad wolf game

Students should be allowed to play this game until they feel reasonably sure about whether the game is fair or not. You could collate the results of the whole class or groups of players to reinforce this. The analysis in C1 to C3 shows that this is in fact a fair game.

C8 A common misconception is for students to think that there are three outcomes – both heads, both tails, and both different; therefore the probability of getting two heads is $\frac{1}{3}$. If so, it is worth doing an experiment, then listing the outcomes to explain the unexpected result.

D Using grids (p 256)

This section shows how a grid can be used where the total score is some combination of two numbers from separate random processes.

TG

Skyscraper

This can be played in small groups or with the whole class, using the sheet on an OHP transparency. Some students may know that the most likely sum of two dice is 7 but few will be aware that the most likely difference is 1. Before starting the game, it may be worth asking the students what the possible differences are. Playing the game should cause the students to think about listing the outcomes and this should lead to the more efficient way of showing them in a grid, as in question D1.

A Probability (p 251)

A1 (a) $\frac{1}{5}$ (b) $\frac{4}{5}$ (c) $\frac{2}{5}$ (d) $\frac{3}{5}$
(e) $\frac{2}{5}$ (f) 0

A2 (a) $\frac{1}{6}$ (b) $\frac{2}{6} = \frac{1}{3}$ (c) $\frac{3}{6} = \frac{1}{2}$
(d) $\frac{5}{6}$ (e) $\frac{3}{6} = \frac{1}{2}$

A3 (a) 8 (b) $\frac{3}{8}$ (c) $\frac{5}{8}$

A4 (a) (i) $\frac{4}{7}$ (ii) $\frac{3}{7}$
(b) (i) $\frac{5}{9}$ (ii) $\frac{4}{9}$
(c) (i) $\frac{6}{10} = \frac{3}{5}$ (ii) $\frac{4}{10} = \frac{2}{5}$
(d) (i) $\frac{8}{12} = \frac{2}{3}$ (ii) $\frac{4}{12} = \frac{1}{3}$

A5 (a) $\frac{1}{5}$ (b) $\frac{3}{5}$ (c) $\frac{2}{5}$

A6 (a) $\frac{5}{10} = \frac{1}{2}$ (b) $\frac{3}{10}$
(c) $\frac{2}{10} = \frac{1}{5}$ (d) $\frac{7}{10}$

A7 It doesn't matter.
probability of red = $\frac{3}{5}$ from A or B

*A8 A: probability of red = $\frac{4}{6} = \frac{8}{12}$
B: probability of red = $\frac{7}{12}$
So A has a higher chance of red being chosen at random.

Ⓑ *Listing* (p 253)

B1 (a) A C
A D
A E
B C
B D
B E

(b) 6   (c) ✔ against BD and BE only

B2 (a)

Top	Bottom
P	B
P	M
P	A
B	P
B	M
B	A
M	P
M	B
M	A
A	P
A	B
A	M

(b) 12   (c) 6

*B3 (a)

ACF	BCF
ACG	BCG
ADF	BDF
ADG	BDG
AEF	BEF
AEG	BEG

(b) 12   (c) 4

Ⓒ *Listing outcomes* (p 254)

C1 (a)

1st	2nd		1st	2nd	
W	W		G	W	✔
W	S	✔	G	S	✗
W	G	✔	G	G	✗
W	R		G	R	
S	W	✔	R	W	
S	S	✗	R	S	
S	G	✗	R	G	
S	R		R	R	

(b) 16   (c) 4   (d) $\frac{4}{16} = \frac{1}{4}$

C2 (a) 4   (b) $\frac{4}{16} = \frac{1}{4}$

C3 (a) 8   (b) $\frac{8}{16} = \frac{1}{2}$
(c) They have equal chances of winning.

C4 (a)

R R	B R	G R
R B	B B	G B
R G	B G	G G

(b) 9   (c) $\frac{3}{9} = \frac{1}{3}$ (d) $\frac{6}{9} = \frac{2}{3}$

C5 (a)

1 5	2 5	3 5	4 5
1 6	2 6	3 6	4 6
1 7	2 7	3 7	4 7

(b) 12

(c) (i) $\frac{4}{12} = \frac{1}{3}$ (ii) $\frac{2}{12} = \frac{1}{6}$ (iii) $\frac{3}{12} = \frac{1}{4}$

C6 (a)

A A	B A	C A	D A	E A
A B	B B	C B	D B	E B
A C	B C	C C	D C	E C
A D	B D	C D	D D	E D
A E	B E	C E	D E	E E

(b) 25   (c) $\frac{5}{25} = \frac{1}{5}$ (d) $\frac{4}{25}$ (e) $\frac{9}{25}$

C7 (a)

A	B	Score
1	6	7
1	7	8
1	8	9
1	9	10
2	6	8
2	7	9
2	8	10
2	9	11
3	6	9
3	7	10
3	8	11
3	9	12

(b) 12   (c) $\frac{3}{12} = \frac{1}{4}$ (d) $\frac{2}{12} = \frac{1}{6}$

(e) $\frac{6}{12} = \frac{1}{2}$ (f) 0

C8 (a) HH
HT
TH
TT

(b) 4   (c) $\frac{1}{4}$ (d) $\frac{2}{4} = \frac{1}{2}$

*C9 (a) HHH   TTH
HHT   THT
HTH   HTT
THH   TTT

(b) 8   (c) $\frac{1}{8}$ (d) $\frac{3}{8}$

C10 (a) BBB
BBG
BGB
GBB
GGB
GBG
BGG
GGG

(b) $\frac{1}{8}$ (c) $\frac{3}{8}$

Ⓓ *Using grids* (p 256)

D1 (a)

	1	2	3	4	5	6
1	0	1	2	3	4	5
2	1	0	1	2	3	4
3	2	1	0	1	2	3
4	3	2	1	0	1	2
5	4	3	2	1	0	1
6	5	4	3	2	1	0

(b) 36   (c) $\frac{6}{36} = \frac{1}{6}$ (d) $\frac{10}{36} = \frac{5}{18}$

(e) probability of $2 = \frac{8}{36} = \frac{2}{9}$,
probability of $3 = \frac{6}{36} = \frac{1}{6}$,
probability of $4 = \frac{4}{36} = \frac{1}{9}$,
probability of $5 = \frac{2}{36} = \frac{1}{18}$

(f) 5 is least likely.

(g) Skyscraper 1

D2 (a)

+	1	2	3	4	5	6
1	2	3	4	5	6	7
2	3	4	5	6	7	8
3	4	5	6	7	8	9
4	5	6	7	8	9	10
5	6	7	8	9	10	11
6	7	8	9	10	11	12

(b) $\frac{3}{36} = \frac{1}{12}$ (c) $\frac{5}{36}$

(d) $\frac{3}{36} = \frac{1}{12}$ (e) 7; $\frac{6}{36} = \frac{1}{6}$

D3 (a)

+	1	2	3	4	5
1	2	3	4	5	6
2	3	4	5	6	7
3	4	5	6	7	8
4	5	6	7	8	9
5	6	7	8	9	10

(b) (i) $\frac{1}{25}$ (ii) 0   (iii) $\frac{5}{25} = \frac{1}{5}$

D4 (a)

+	1	2	3	4
5	6	7	8	9
6	7	8	9	10
7	8	9	10	11

(b) $\frac{3}{12} = \frac{1}{4}$ (c) $\frac{6}{12} = \frac{1}{2}$ (d) $\frac{6}{12} = \frac{1}{2}$

D5 (a) (i)

×	1	2	3	4
1	1	2	3	4
2	2	4	6	8
3	3	6	9	12
4	4	8	12	16
5	5	10	15	20
6	6	12	18	24

(ii) 0

(b) $\frac{8}{24} = \frac{1}{3}$

Test yourself (p 259)

T1 (a) $\frac{10}{20} = \frac{1}{2}$ (b) $\frac{7}{20}$

T2 (a)

1st	2nd		1st	2nd
O	O		B	O
O	L		B	L
O	B		B	B
O	S		B	S
L	O		S	O
L	L		S	L
L	B		S	B
L	S		S	S

(b) (i) $\frac{1}{16}$ (ii) $\frac{4}{16} = \frac{1}{4}$ (iii) $\frac{12}{16} = \frac{3}{4}$

T3 (a) $\frac{1}{4}$

(b) (i)

+	1	2	3	4
4	**5**	**6**	7	**8**
5	**6**	7	**8**	9
6	7	**8**	9	10

(ii) $\frac{3}{12} = \frac{1}{4}$

Practice book

Section A (p 105)

1 (a) $\frac{2}{6} = \frac{1}{3}$ (b) $\frac{1}{6}$ (c) $\frac{3}{6} = \frac{1}{2}$

   (d) $\frac{4}{6} = \frac{2}{3}$ (e) 0

2 (a) $\frac{1}{7}$ (b) $\frac{6}{7}$ (c) $\frac{3}{7}$

   (d) $\frac{4}{7}$ (e) $\frac{2}{7}$ (f) 0

3 (a) 13   (b) $\frac{8}{13}$ (c) $\frac{5}{13}$

4 (a) $\frac{3}{12} = \frac{1}{4}$ (b) $\frac{5}{12}$ (c) $\frac{7}{12}$

   (d) $\frac{8}{12} = \frac{2}{3}$

5 (a) $\frac{2}{7}$ (b) $\frac{2}{7}$ (c) $\frac{4}{7}$

   (d) $\frac{3}{7}$ (e) $\frac{6}{7}$

Section B (p 106)

1 (a)

Shirt	Tie
W	R
W	M
G	**R**
G	**M**
P	**R**
P	**M**

(b) 6

2 (a) (i)

Cereal	Marmalade
C	O
C	L
C	T
W	O
W	**L**
W	**T**
R	**O**
R	**L**
R	**T**
P	**O**
P	**L**
P	**T**

(ii) 12

(b) 9

3 (a)

Bread	Filling
W	H
W	C
W	P
W	E
B	H
B	C
B	P
B	E
G	H
G	C
G	P
G	E
H	H
H	C
H	P
H	E

(b) 16

(c) No

Section C (p 107)

1 (a)

W1	W2	W3	W4	W5
G1	G2	G3	G4	G5
B1	B2	B3	B4	B5

(b) 15   (c) $\frac{1}{15}$ (d) $\frac{2}{15}$ (e) $\frac{2}{15}$

2 (a)

− −	− =	− +	− ×	− ÷
= −	= =	= +	= ×	= ÷
+ −	+ =	+ +	+ ×	+ ÷
× −	× =	× +	× ×	× ÷
÷ −	÷ =	÷ +	÷ ×	÷ ÷

(b) 25   (c) $\frac{1}{5}$ (d) $\frac{2}{25}$

3 (a)

CC CS CD CP
SC SS SD SP
DC DS DD DP
PC PS PD PP

(b) 16

(c) (i) $\frac{1}{16}$ (ii) $\frac{4}{16}=\frac{1}{4}$ (iii) $\frac{12}{16}=\frac{3}{4}$

4 (a)

AAB AAC ABB ABC ACB ACC
BAB BAC BBB BBC BCB BCC
CAB CAC CBB CBC CCB CCC

(b) (i) $\frac{2}{18}=\frac{1}{9}$ (ii) $\frac{12}{18}=\frac{2}{3}$

(iii) $\frac{4}{18}=\frac{2}{9}$ (iv) $\frac{8}{18}=\frac{4}{9}$

(v) $\frac{2}{18}=\frac{1}{9}$

Section D (p 108)

1 (a)

First dice

+	1	2	3	4	5	6
1	2	3	4	5	6	7
1	2	3	4	5	6	7
3	4	5	6	7	8	9
3	4	5	6	7	8	9
5	6	7	8	9	10	11
6	7	8	9	10	11	12

(Second dice down the left)

(b) $\frac{2}{36}=\frac{1}{18}$ (c) $\frac{19}{36}$

(d) 7   (e) $\frac{6}{36}=\frac{1}{6}$

2 (a)

Spinner

−	1	2	3	4	5
1	0	1	2	3	4
2	1	0	1	2	3
3	2	1	0	1	2
4	3	2	1	0	1
5	4	3	2	1	0
6	5	4	3	2	1

(Dice down the left)

(b) $\frac{1}{30}$ (c) $\frac{4}{30}=\frac{2}{15}$

(d) 1, $\frac{9}{30}=\frac{3}{10}$ (e) $\frac{16}{30}=\frac{8}{15}$

3 (a)

First spinner

×	1	1	2	3	4
1	1	1	2	3	4
2	2	2	4	6	8
3	3	3	6	9	12
4	4	4	8	12	16
4	4	4	8	12	16

(Second spinner down the left)

(b) (i) $\frac{8}{25}$ (ii) $\frac{19}{25}$ (iii) $\frac{5}{25}=\frac{1}{5}$

37 Rounding with significant figures

> **Practice book** pages 109 to 112

B *Rounding to one significant figure: decimals* (p 261)

◊ A short revision of place value is likely to be useful. You could write on the board a number with several decimal places and ask for the value of each digit. Then ask for the digit with the highest value (the most significant figure), which will be the first non-zero figure reading from left to right.

C *Multiplying decimals* (p 262)

◊ The mistake '0.2 × 0.3 = 0.6' is so common that it is worth spending time on a careful introduction to multiplying decimals. You could start by asking for the answer to 0.2 × 0.3. If someone says '0.6', then ask for the answer to 2 × 0.3, which can of course be thought of as 0.3 + 0.3. It should appear odd that 0.2 × 0.3 and 2 × 0.3 have the same answer!

Two approaches to 0.2 × 0.3 are suggested in the students' book. One involves area, the other uses the effect of dividing by 10. The latter is generally useful although in practice the rule about counting decimal places is likely to take over.

Ⓐ Rounding to one significant figure: whole numbers (p 260)

A1 (a) 700   (b) 4000   (c) 700
     (d) 2000   (e) 80   (f) 5000
     (g) 400   (h) 2000   (i) 9000
     (j) 500

A2 (a) The student's headline including '5000'
     (b) The student's headline including '40 000'

A3 (a) 800   (b) 1500   (c) 14 000
     (d) 20 000

A4 (a) 800   (b) 10 000   (c) 4200
     (d) 15 000   (e) 3000   (f) 8000
     (g) 3200   (h) 18 000   (i) 24 000
     (j) 30 000

A5 £1500

A6 (a) £6000
     (b) Bigger, because 300 is bigger than 288 and £20 is bigger than £19

Ⓑ Rounding to one significant figure: decimals (p 261)

B1 (a) 20   (b) 2   (c) 70   (d) 200   (e) 9

B2 (a) 0.5   (b) 0.8   (c) 0.04
     (d) 0.07   (e) 0.005

B3 (a) 70   (b) 9   (c) 0.06   (d) 200   (e) 0.4

B4 (b) The area of Egypt is roughly 400 000 square miles.
     (c) An ounce is roughly 30 grams.
     (d) A metre is roughly 40 inches.
     (e) A cubic foot is roughly 0.03 cubic metres.

B5 (a) 20 000   (b) 0.06   (c) 7
     (d) 300   (e) 0.008   (f) 300 000
     (g) 30   (h) 200   (i) 90   (j) 0.1

*B6 (a) 1000   (b) 0.1   (c) 10 000

Ⓒ Multiplying decimals (p 262)

C1 (a) $0.4 \times 0.3 = 0.12$
     (b) $0.4 \times 0.5 = 0.2(0)$
     (c) $0.4 \times 0.2 = 0.08$
     (d) (i) 0.24   (ii) 0.3   (iii) 0.49
        (iv) 0.09   (v) 0.4   (vi) 0.09

C2 (a) $5 \times 3 = 15$
        $5 \times 0.3 = 1.5$
        $0.5 \times 0.3 = 0.15$
     (b) $3 \times 7 = 21$
        $3 \times 0.7 = 2.1$
        $0.3 \times 0.7 = 0.21$
     (c) $6 \times 5 = 30$
        $6 \times 0.5 = 3$
        $0.6 \times 0.5 = 0.3$

C3 (a) 0.24   (b) 0.07   (c) 0.01

C4 (a) 22
     (b) (i) 2.2   (ii) 0.22   (iii) 0.22
        (iv) 0.022   (v) 0.022

C5 (a) 36
     (b) (i) 3.6   (ii) 0.36   (iii) 0.36
        (iv) 0.036   (v) 0.036

C6 (a) 84
     (b) (i) 8.4   (ii) 0.084   (iii) 0.084
        (iv) 0.84   (v) 0.0084

C7 (a) 3.22   (b) 3.22   (c) 0.322
     (d) 0.322   (e) 0.0322

C8 (a) 972   (b) 9.72   (c) 97.2
     (d) 0.972   (e) 0.972

C9 (a) 12   (b) 270   (c) 1.2   (d) 20
     (e) 300   (f) 12   (g) 120   (h) 180
     (i) 40   (j) 0.04

*C10 (a) A: $2\,m^2$ B: $0.6\,m^2$ C: $0.8\,m^2$
       D: $0.24\,m^2$
     (b) $3.64\,m^2$

*C11 2.76

D Rough estimates with decimals (p 264)

D1 (a) 8   (b) 30   (c) 0.8   (d) 35

D2 (a) $30 \times £20 = £600$

     (b) Bigger, because 30 is bigger than 28 and £20 is bigger than £19.75

D3 Because $40 \times £2 = £80$, and this is bigger than the exact amount

D4 (a) $60 \times 0.5 = 30\,\text{kg}$

     (b) Smaller, because 60 is less than 62 and 0.5 is less than 0.51

D5 (a) 1.6   (b) 1.6   (c) 20   (d) 160

     (e) 2.7   (f) 45   (g) 18   (h) 1

D6 (a) 2   (b) 6   (c) 4   (d) 10

D7 (a) 9   (b) 15   (c) 300   (d) 8

E Rounding answers (p 265)

E1 (a) 43.27   (b) 3.9   (c) 0.747

     (d) 2.07   (e) 5.21   (f) 18.0

E2 3.02

E3 (a) 25.24   (b) 34.5   (c) 0.02

     (d) 0.112

E4 (a) $30 \times £4 = £120$ (b) £114.17

E5 (a) $20 \times 10 = 200\,\text{m}^2$ (b) $182.9\,\text{m}^2$

E6 (a) $1 \times 0.8 = 0.8\,\text{m}^2$ (b) $0.92\,\text{m}^2$

E7 91.4 cm

F Exchange rates (p 266)

F1 (a) NZ$112.00   (b) £31.25

F2 (a) HK$613.60   (b) £29.66

F3 (a) US$583.80   (b) £179.86

F4 (a) EGP277.50   (b) £102.76

F5 £21.49

F6 £16.57

F7 (a) 192.42 kroner (b) £15.37

Test yourself (p 267)

T1 $\frac{600 \times 30}{90} = \frac{18\,000}{90} = 200$

T2 $\frac{6 \times 20}{10} = 12$

T3 (a) 20   (b) 0.52   (c) 0.08

     (d) 0.036   (e) 4

T4 (a) 15   (b) 28   (c) 0.06

     (d) 40

T5 720 Swiss francs

T6 (a) 4950 Rand

     (b) (i) 945 Rand   (ii) £90

Practice book

Section A (p 109)

1 (a) 600   (b) 400   (c) 2000

   (d) 80   (e) 4000   (f) 6000

   (g) 60   (h) 90 000   (i) 300

   (j) 9000

2 (a) Student's headline including £3 000 000

   (b) Student's headline including 50 000

3 (a) 1200   (b) 1200   (c) 15 000

4 (a) $50 \times 20 = 1000$

   (b) $70 \times 30 = 2100$

   (c) $200 \times 20 = 4000$

   (d) $60 \times 300 = 18\,000$

   (e) $100 \times 400 = 40\,000$

5 $30 \times £20 = £600$

Section B (p 109)

1 (a) 60   (b) 5   (c) 0.5   (d) 90

   (e) 8   (f) 0.8   (g) 0.4   (h) 0.08

   (i) 0.07 (j) 0.005

2 (a) 5000   (b) 100   (c) 0.2

   (d) 0.3   (e) 0.08

3 (b) The world's largest pancake was about 50 feet in diameter and weighed about 3 tons.

(c) In 1999 a pumpkin was grown that weighed about 500 kg.

(d) The largest pyramid of champagne glasses contained about 30 000 glasses.

(e) The world's smallest spider has a length of about 0.4 mm.

Section C (p 110)

1 (a) $0.4 \times 0.4 = 0.16$ (b) $0.3 \times 0.6 = 0.18$

(c) $0.1 \times 0.9 = 0.09$

2 (a) $3 \times 4 = 12$
$3 \times 0.4 = \mathbf{1.2}$
$0.3 \times 0.4 = \mathbf{0.12}$

(b) $8 \times 4 = 32$
$8 \times 0.4 = \mathbf{3.2}$
$0.8 \times 0.4 = \mathbf{0.32}$

(c) $4 \times 5 = 20$
$4 \times 0.5 = \mathbf{2}$
$0.4 \times 0.5 = \mathbf{0.2}$

3 (a) 0.16   (b) 0.06   (c) 0.45

4 (a) 24

(b) (i) 2.4 (ii) 0.24 (iii) 2.4 (iv) 0.24

5 (a) 66

(b) (i) 6.6 (ii) 0.66 (iii) 0.66
(iv) 0.066

6 (a) 2.85   (b) 2.85

(c) 0.285   (d) 0.0285

7 (a) 153 (b) 15.3 (c) 15.3 (d) 1.53

8 (a) 15 (b) 80 (c) 42 (d) 400

(e) 0.36 (f) 36 (g) 30 (h) 810

Section D (p 111)

1 (a) $3 \times 0.6 = 1.8$ (b) $0.7 \times 20 = 14$

(c) $0.3 \times 30 = 9$ (d) $60 \times 0.5 = 30$

2 (a) $50 \times £20 = £1000$

(b) Smaller, both numbers are rounded down

3 (a) $7\,m \times 4\,m = 28\,m^2$ (b) Larger

4 $50 \times 0.5 = 25\,kg$

5 (a) $8 \times 0.3 = 2.4$ (b) $0.6 \times 30 = 18$

(c) $5 \times 0.03 = 0.15$ (d) $70 \times 0.2 = 14$

(e) $0.07 \times 30 = 2.1$ (f) $300 \times 0.4 = 120$

(g) $0.1 \times 20 = 2$ (h) $0.02 \times 100 = 2$

6 $\dfrac{38 \times 0.62}{2.9} \approx \dfrac{40 \times 0.6}{3} = 8$

$\dfrac{0.38 \times 620}{2.9} \approx \dfrac{0.4 \times 600}{3} = 80$

$\dfrac{0.038 \times 620}{29} \approx \dfrac{0.04 \times 600}{30} = 0.8$

7 (a) $\dfrac{40 \times 0.3}{3} = 4$ (b) $\dfrac{50 \times 0.8}{4} = 10$

(c) $\dfrac{200 \times 0.6}{30} = 4$ (d) $\dfrac{0.9 \times 50}{3} = 15$

(e) $\dfrac{0.7 \times 60}{6} = 7$ (f) $\dfrac{0.01 \times 800}{40} = 0.2$

Section E (p 112)

1 (a) 51.5   (b) 6.75   (c) 8.36

(d) 24.1   (e) 12.61   (f) 0.06

2 (a) 8.66   (b) 10.8

(c) 37.10   (d) 0.087

3 (a) $10 \times £1 = £10$ (b) £9.77

4 (a) $20\,cm \times 30\,cm = 600\,cm^2$

(b) $617.8\,cm^2$

5 9.1 litres

6 54.0 kg

Section F (p 112)

1 (a) US$ 94.72   (b) £135.14

2 (a) 4451.50 yen   (b) £36.50

3 A$ 816.50

4 £17.74

2-D puzzles

This unit revises the basic properties of triangles and quadrilaterals and invites the investigation of the angle properties of all polygons.

Essential	Optional
Sheets G54, G55	Sheet G56
Scissors, ruler, compasses and angle measurer	
Practice book pages 113 to 116	

Ⓐ *Different shapes* (p 268)

This section consists of two puzzles which can be used to revise the names and properties of different types of triangles and quadrilaterals.

Sheet G54, ruler and scissors

◊ Students should be encouraged to explain how their solutions meet the requirements so that they become familiar with the properties of the shapes used.

Squaring off

The term 'congruent' is used and students may need reminding of its meaning.

These are possible solutions to the problems.

A B C D

E F G H

Being square

These are the solutions to the puzzles on sheet G54.

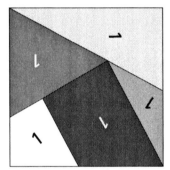 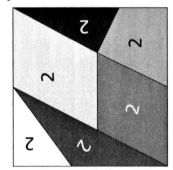

> 'This was an opportunity to recap so much earlier work.'

Ⓑ *Angles in a triangle* (p 269)

TG

◊ The introduction is intended as a demonstration on the board or OHP. Ask students to mark angles the same as *a*, *b* and *c* on the diagram. This exercise should lead students to recognise the 'proof' that the angles in a triangle must add up to 180°. The same exercise could also lead to the fact that the exterior angle is the sum of the two opposite angles.

Ⓒ *Angles in a quadrilateral* (p 270)

> Sheet G55

TG

◊ The introductory activity should lead to the fact that any quadrilateral can always be split into two triangles and hence the sum of the angles in a quadrilateral is always 360°.

D **At the centre** (p 271)

> Ruler and compasses

◊ Students may want to extend the pentagram design in 'A tangled web' by replicating it inside the inner pentagon.

E **Exterior angles** (p 272)

> Scissors

◊ The introductory activity is best carried out by the whole class, with each student using a different polygon, so they can see the general truth of the result.

◊ This topic can easily be investigated on a computer or graphic calculator.

• Using dynamic geometry software, draw a polygon on the screen. Add lines to the polygon to give all the exterior angles in one direction. 'Measure' the exterior angles and list these with their sum. Show that as points on the shape are moved around the angle sum remains 360°.

• In LOGO students could be given polygons drawn with the exterior angles given for all but one side. Students have to work out what the final exterior angle is.

F **Interior angles** (p 273)

> Optional: sheet G56

◊ Sheet G56 has examples of polygons to start the investigation into the number of triangles that can be produced by drawing lines from each corner to all other corners.

G **Problems and puzzles** (p 275)

> Ruler, compasses and a set square

◊ 'Making squares' offers an opportunity to practise drawing shapes from given sketches.

◊ In 'Design your own puzzle' centimetre squared or triangular dotty paper could be used.

B *Angles in a triangle* (p 269)

B1 $a = 70°$ $b = 30°$ $c = 100°$ $d = 50°$
$e = 80°$ $f = 70°$ $g = 50°$

B2 $a = 80°$ (angles in a triangle add up to 180°)

$b = 35°$ (alternate angles)

$c = 65°$ (angles in a triangle add up to 180° or symmetry)

$d = 100°$ (opposite angles)

$e = 80°$ (angles in a triangle add up to 180° or symmetry)

C *Angles in a quadrilateral* (p 270)

C1 $a = 69°$ $b = 95°$ $c = 55°$ $d = 96°$ $e = 84°$

C2 (a) 122°   (b) 22°

C3 (a) 360°

(b) (i) 67°   (ii) 65°

D *At the centre* (p 271)

D1 (a) 5   (b) 360°   (c) 72°

D2

Polygon	Hexa-	Penta-	Octa-	Deca-	Dodeca-
Sides	6	5	8	10	12
Angle	60°	72°	45°	36°	30°

D3 The student's drawings of regular polygons

E *Exterior angles* (p 272)

E1 $a = 53°$ $b = 79°$ $c = 37°$

E2 (a) 6   (b) 60°

E3 (a) 72°   (b) 45°

F *Interior angles* (p 273)

F1 (a) The student's pentagon divided
(b) 3   (c) $3 \times 180° = 540°$

F2 (a)

Polygon	Hexa-	Penta-	Octa-	Deca-	Dodeca-
Triangles	4	3	6	8	10
Angles sum	720°	540°	1080°	1440°	1800°

(b) number of triangles
= number of sides − 2

(c) $t = n - 2$

F3 (a) 5   (b) $5 \times 180° = 900°$

F4 (a) 18   (b) $18 \times 180° = 3240°$

F5 (a) 720°   (b) 120°

F6

Polygon	Hexa-	Penta-	Octa-	Deca-	Dodeca-
Angle sum	720°	540°	1080°	1440°	1800°
Interior	120°	108°	135°	144°	150°

F7 (a) The interior angle is 120° and $3 \times 120° = 360°$.

(b) (i) No (ii) Yes (iii) Yes
(iv) No (v) Yes

F8 (a) 18°

(b)

Regular polygon	Interior angle	Exterior angle	Total
Hexagon	120°	60°	180°
Pentagon	108°	72°	180°
Octagon	135°	45°	180°

(c) For any regular polygon the sum of the interior and exterior angle is always 180°.

G *Problems and puzzles* (p 275)

G1 (a) Isosceles   (b) 70°
(c) Trapezium
(d) 110° (supplementary to ABE)
(e) One

G2 (a) 120°   (b) 60°
(c) An equilateral triangle, since both CAB and ACB must be 60°

G3 (a) 72° (b) Isosceles (c) 54°
(d) No; its internal angle 108° does not go into 360° an exact number of times

Test yourself (p 277)

T1 $a = 70°$ $b = 115°$ $c = 105°$ $d = 50°$

T2 (a) $7 \times 180° = 1260°$ (b) $40°$
(c) $140°$

T3 (a) (i) C or D (ii) B (iii) A or F
(b) Trapezium (c) C and D (d) $135°$

T4 (a) $135°$ (b) $45°$ (c) $90°$

Practice book

Sections B and C (p 113)

1 $a = 45°$ $b = 70°$ $c = 31°$
$d = 52°$ $e = 75°$

2 $a = 70°$ $b = 45°$ $c = 124°$
$d = 56°$ $e = 50°$ $f = 45°$
$g = 35°$ $h = 35°$ $i = 145°$
$j = 35°$ $k = 85°$ $l = 145°$

3 $a = 58°$ $b = 122°$ $c = 58°$
$d = 150°$ $e = 155°$ $f = 119°$
$g = 95°$ $h = 85°$ $i = 125°$
$j = 55°$ $k = 55°$

Sections D and E (p 114)

1 (a) $90°$ (b) $120°$ (c) $45°$

2 (a) Angle at centre =
$360° \div$ number of sides
(b) $36°$

3 $a = 121°$ $b = 39°$

4 (a) $90°$ (b) $60°$ (c) $36°$

5 $a = 72°$ $b = 72°$ $c = 54°$

Section F (p 115)

1 number of sides → -2 → $\times 180$ → sum of interior angles

2 (a) $540°$ (b) $900°$

3 $a = 100°$ $b = 64°$

4 $140°$

5 (a) $120°$ (b) $135°$ (c) $144°$

6 (a) $p = 108°$ $q = 144°$
(b) A regular decagon

7 (a) $120°$ (b) $150°$
(c) $120° + 150° + 90° = 360°$

Section G (p 116)

1 $a = 105°$ $b = 75°$ $c = 75°$
$d = 105°$ $e = 150°$ $f = 30°$

2 (a) Trapezium (b) Kite
(c) Isosceles (d) $135°$
(e) $45°$ (f) $45°$

3 (a) Isosceles (b) $72°$
(c) $108°$ (d) $36°$
(e) $72°$

Ratio and proportion

This unit asks students to multiply up and divide down proportions such as in recipes, and to use the unitary method, in particular to compare prices using unit costs. It also asks students to use ratios given in the form $a:b$. This includes expressing problems as ratios, dividing amounts in a given ratio and recognising equivalent ratios. This may be too much in one go for some students and you may wish to split the unit after section D.

> **Optional**
> Sheet G57 on card, scissors
>
> **Practice book** pages 117 to 121

A *Recipes* (p 278)

'I made a grid on acetate and covered much of this as a class exercise.'

◊ The recipes at the start of this section can be used for oral work on multiplying up and dividing down the proportions. None of the written questions uses the recipe for Lemon Ice Cream. The questions should be structured to cover

• multiplying up where there are discrete quantities, for example 'How many egg yolks would you need to make 12 servings of ice cream?'

• multiplying up with measured quantities, for example 'How much caster sugar would you need to make ice cream for 24 people?'

- dividing down, for example
  'How much double cream would you need to make ice cream for 3 people?'
- asking how many people you could make the recipe for, given a limited quantity of one ingredient, for example
  'If you had plenty of all the other ingredients but only 100 ml of lemon juice, how many people could you make ice cream for?'

Encourage students to explain how they arrived at their results.
Other recipes could be used for the students to produce their own sets of problems and answers.

A7 This question leads towards the unitary method in section C.

B *Comparisons* (p 280)

This section asks students to use informal methods to compare costs of different quantities of the same item, where one quantity is a simple multiple of the other. Questions at this stage give answers to whole pence.

C *The unitary method* (p 281)

◊ You may wish to use the recipe material in section A to ask students how they might produce say a recipe for fish pie for 10 people.

D *Unit costs* (p 282)

◊ The latter part of this section deals with cases where using a 'unit' cost would produce unwieldy decimals and uses units such as 100 g instead. The alternative to this is to look at the amount bought per unit of money but this may lead to confusion.

E *Mixing* (p 284)

Optional: sheet G57 on card, scissors

◊ There are four different ratios of squash to water on the trays.

1:2 Tom, Rauridh
1:1 Eva, Mischa, Angie
2:1 Rani, Lisa
2:3 Annabel, Terry

Sheet G57 could be printed on card and cut into separate cards. Groups could then sort the cards into trays which show the same ratio of squash to water. Alternatively this could be done with a set of cards on a transparency on an OHP.

F **Simplest form** (p 287)

◊ Asking students to say which of the ratios in the picture are the same (as with those at the start of section E) should lead to discussion of what is the simplest way each of the ratios can be written. It is useful to show how all the other ratios can then be multiplied up from these.

The ratios are:
- A, E   1 : 3
- C, D   3 : 1
- B, F   2 : 3

G **Sharing in a ratio** (p 288)

◊ Martin's and David's suggestions need reducing to simplest form first. This could be demonstrated with 40 counters representing pounds and sharing on the basis of the 2 : 3 suggestion '2 for David, 3 for Martin' until all the counters are used up. Students could then be asked to suggest quicker ways of doing this.

A **Recipes** (p 278)

A1 4

A2 (a) 9   (b) 40   (c) 30
     (d) 1   (e) 5   (f) $1\frac{1}{2}$

A3 (a) 120 g   (b) 600 g   (c) 960 g
     (d) 12 kg   (e) 0.9 kg   (f) 200 g

A4 (a) 6 kg gooseberries
        9 kg sugar
        3 litres of water
     (b) 250 g haddock
        200 ml milk
        30 g butter
        100 ml single cream
        1 egg
        400 g potatoes

A5 (a) 12   (b) 20   (c) 8

A6 (a) 12   (b) 24   (c) 20

A7 (a) 15 g
     (b) (i) 90 g   (ii) 150 g   (iii) 210 g

A8 (a) 100 g
     (b) (i) 300 g   (ii) 500 g
        (iii) 1000 g or 1 kg

B **Comparisons** (p 280)

B1 (a) Buying separately costs £3.84, so multipack doesn't save money
     (b) Buying separately costs £3.70, so multipack saves money
     (c) Buying separately costs £11.40, so multipack saves money
     (d) Buying separately costs £10.32, so multipack doesn't save money

B2 (a) 5   (b) £7.50   (c) Yes

B3 (a) 3 smaller make up larger which would cost £2.55 so the larger unit is dearer

(b) 5 smaller make up larger which would cost £6 so the larger unit is not cheaper

(c) 4 smaller make up larger which would cost £5.20 so the larger unit is cheaper

(d) $2\frac{1}{2}$ smaller make up larger which would cost £2 so the larger unit is cheaper

B4 2 smaller make up larger which would cost £2.50 so the large size is cheaper.

C *The unitary method* (p 281)

C1 (a) 5 kg   (b) 50 kg

C2 (a) 30 g   (b) 600 g

C3 15 miles

C4 35 m of wood
7 wooden trays
84 nails

C5 28 veggie sausages
1050 g of rice
7 litres

C6 (a) (i) 750 g   (ii) 270 g   (iii) 360 g

(b) 6

D *Unit costs* (p 282)

D1 (a) £8   (b) £7   (c) Hedges & Co

D2 (a) 52p (b) 49p (c) Value Pack

D3 (a) 3 litres costs 45p per litre,
2 litres costs 47p per litre,
so 3 litres is cheaper.

(b) 5 kg costs 30p per kg,
2 kg costs 31p per kg,
so 5 kg is cheaper.

(c) 3 kg costs 72p per kg,
5 kg costs 65p per kg,
so 5 kg is cheaper.

(d) 12 metres costs 55p per metre,
14 metres costs 60p per metre,
so 12 metres is cheaper.

D4 (a) 64p   (b) 60p

(c) The large bottle

(d) The student's sensible reason

D5 (a)

Size	Cost per litre
Large	£1.44
Standard	£1.49
Economy	£1.42
Travel	£1.56

(b) Economy, Large, Standard, Travel

D6 (a) 0.81   (b) 81p

D7 (a) 91p (b) 71p (c) 44p (d) £2.63

D8 (a)

Size	Cost per litre
1 litre	93p
0.5 litres	96p
1.5 litres	91p
3 litres	92p

(b) The 1.5 litres size

D9

Size	Cost per 100 g
200 g	45p
300 g	38p
500 g	41p
800 g	44p

So the 300 g size is the best value.

D10 Large size costs 25p for 100 ml,
family size costs 26p for 100 ml,
so the large size is better value.

D11 (a) Small 82p for 50 g
Large 85p for 50 g

(b) The small size is best value.

D12 400 g size costs 15p per 50 g,
250 g size costs 14p per 50 g,
so the 250 g jar gives better value.

E *Mixing* (p 284)

E1 (a) No, 1 : 5 (b) Yes   (c) Yes

(d) No, 1 : 3 (e) Yes   (f) Yes

E2 (a) False   (b) False

     (c) True   (d) True

E3 (a) (i) 12 cups   (ii) 30 cups

        (iii) $4\frac{1}{2}$ cups

     (b) (i) 2 cups   (ii) 5 cups

        (iii) 200 ml

E4 (a) 250 g   (b) 300 g

     (c) (i) 150 g   (ii) 450 g

E5 (a)

Job	Cement	Ballast	Ratio
General	1 part	5 parts	1 : 5
Foundations	1 part	**6 parts**	1 : 6
Paving	1 part	4 parts	**1 : 4**

     (b) (i) General   (ii) Paving

     (c) (i) 18 buckets   (ii) 50 wheelbarrows

     (d) (i) 2 shovels   (ii) 4 bags

     (e) (i) 48 pots   (ii) 60 pots

E6 (a) 6   (b) 27   (c) 2 : 3   (d) 4 : 3

*E7 (a) 300 g   (b) 800 g   (c) 150 g

     (d) 80 g   (e) 750 g   (f) 1.33 kg

𝔽 *Simplest form* (p 287)

F1 (a) 1 : 3   (b) 7 : 5   (c) 1 : 2

     (d) 2 : 5   (e) 12 : 5   (f) 1 : 3

     (g) 2 : 5   (h) 5 : 24

F2 3 : 5

F3 (a) 4 : 5   (b) 1 : 15

     (c) 3 : 4   (d) 8 : 1

𝔾 *Sharing in a ratio* (p 288)

G1 (a) £20 and £16

     (b) 24 marbles and 40 marbles

     (c) £100 and £20

     (d) 6 deliveries and 9 deliveries

G2 Geraint 15, Idris 9

G3 21 milk chocolates

G4 (a) 100 g   (b) 250 g

G5 36

G6 Maize flour 150 g, water 600 g

G7 Copper 16 kg, zinc 4 kg

G8 Yukon £8 million, Skelly £6 million

G9 50 kg salt, 400 kg sugar

G10 (a) Saltpetre 250 g, charcoal 100 g

     (b) Sulphur 20 g, charcoal 40 g

     (c) Saltpetre 150 g, sulphur 30 g, charcoal 60 g

G11 Cheese straws – makes 500 g

     Flour   200 g

     Margarine   150 g

     Cheese   150 g

G12 48 kg of iron

     16 kg nickel

     16 kg chromium

Test yourself (p 290)

T1 (a) 50 g

     (b) 300 g of chocolate

        30 g unsalted butter

        6 eggs

     (c) 3 people

T2 5 litres

T3 (a) Sack costs 90p per kg,

        handy-pack costs 98p per kg

        so the sack is better value.

     (b) 200 ml tin costs £2.33 for 100 ml,

        500 ml tin costs £2.39 for 100 ml,

        so the 200 ml tin is better value.

T4 £28

T5 (a) 250 g caster sugar

        150 g butter

        50 g cocoa powder

     (b) 60 g

Practice book

Section A (p 117)

1 160 g

2 (a) 240 ml (b) 25 g (c) 30 ml
  (d) 800 g (e) 600 g

3 (a) 50 g peeled prawns, 20 g butter,
      2.5 ml lemon juice, 5 ml chopped
      parsley
  (b) (i) 300 g peeled prawns, 120 g
          butter, 15 ml lemon juice,
          30 ml chopped parsley
      (ii) 500 g peeled prawns,
          200 g butter, 25 ml lemon juice,
          50 ml chopped parsley

4 (a) 20 g
  (b) (i) 80 g (ii) 240 g (iii) 500 g

5 300 g plain flour, 12 ml baking powder,
   600 g mixed dried fruit,
   30 ml sunflower oil

Sections B and C (p 118)

1 (a) A: £1.75, B: £1.60, B
  (b) A: £0.75, B: £0.76, A
  (c) A: £0.50, B: £0.45, B

2 £0.39 × 5 = £1.95 so 50 g bar better value

3 £1.49 × 3 = £4.47 so packet better value

4 (a) 4 (b) £7.44 (c) Yes, 9p

5 (a) 40 (b) 200

6 60

7 360 kilometres

Section D (p 119)

1 (a) £4 (b) £3.80 (c) Quikpix

2 (a) 4 pack: £0.75, 8 pack: £0.65,
      12 pack: £0.60, 20 pack: £0.55
  (b) 20 pack
  (c) 4 pack

3 (a) 5 kg for £1.35 (27p, 28p)
  (b) 2 kg for £5.80 (£3, £2.90)
  (c) 8 litres for £4 (50p, 55p)
  (d) 8 metres for £9.60 (£1.25, £1.20)

4 (a) £2.66 (b) 67p (c) £1.33 (d) 12p

5 (a) 500 ml for £2.45 (52p, 49p)
  (b) 200 ml for £2.52 (£1.26, £1.30)
  (c) 400 ml for £25.20 (£6.30, £6.40)
  (d) 800 ml for £6.96 (88p, 87p)

6 (a) £4.76, £4.77 (b) Large: 125 ml

Section E (p 120)

1 (a) 3:1 (b) 4:1 (c) 5:2 (d) 7:3
  (e) 6:2 or 3:1 (f) 9:3 or 3:1 (g) 10:3
  It is is 3:1 in (a), (e) and (f)

2 (a) (i) 15 (ii) 25 (iii) 100
  (b) (i) 2 (ii) 4 (iii) 10

3 (a) (i) 400 (ii) 650
  (b) (i) 30 (ii) 58

4 (a) 150 ml (b) 1 litre (c) 4 glassfuls

5 (a) (i) 10 (ii) 20 (iii) $2\frac{1}{2}$
  (b) (i) 6 (ii) 10 (iii) 40

Section G (p 121)

1 10

2 (a) £8, £12 (b) £12, £48
  (c) £2.50, £2 (d) £150, £250

3 100

4 27

5 8

6 (a) 300 g, 500 g (b) 750 g, 1250 g

7 £80

8 (a) 1 kg, 2 kg, 1.5 kg (b) 300 g, 600 g, 450 g

9 (a) 1200 g, 800 g (b) 2 kg, 6 kg
  (c) 500 g, 1500 g (d) 250 g, 750 g, 500 g

40 Areas of triangles

In this unit students see that a triangle is half a parallelogram and therefore the area of a triangle is half that of a parallelogram with the same base and perpendicular height.

> **Essential**
>
> Sheets G58, G59, G60
> Scissors
>
> **Practice book** pages 122 to 125

𝔸 *Review* (p 291)

◊ Some students may need reminding that the perpendicular height of a parallelogram is used, particularly in 1(d) where the parallelogram overhangs.

𝔹 *Half and half* (p 292)

◊ The purpose of this section is to emphasise that when a shape is half of a rectangle or a parallelogram its area is exactly half. This includes triangles. The areas of the shaded shapes are 12 cm^2 and 10 cm^2.

◊ In 'Design your own' students will need to realise that the shape must have rotational symmetry order 2.

C *Into triangles* (p 293)

Sheets G58, G59
Scissors

TG

> 'This is not my usual way of teaching areas of triangles but it worked well and I will use it again because it reinforces the areas of parallelograms.'

◊ The purpose of the initial activity is to establish that all triangles can be made by cutting a parallelogram (or rectangle) along one diagonal. Hence the area of a triangle is half the area of a parallelogram with the same base and perpendicular height. This definition should avoid problems about how the height of a triangle is measured when the apex overhangs the base.

D *Composite shapes* (p 296)

Sheet G60, scissors

TG

◊ The purpose of the initial activity is to allow students to see that a variety of other shapes can be constructed from rectangles and triangles and that the areas of these shapes can be found by adding together the areas of the separate pieces. The subsequent questions ask students to draw sketches of how they calculated the area of a composite shape.

E *Converting* (p 297)

TG

◊ Many students will be surprised and uneasy at the orders of magnitude that are involved in comparing areas in cm^2 and m^2. Having a sheet of paper 1 metre square with centimetre squares marked on may be helpful.

A *Review* (p 291)

A1 (a) 15 cm^2　　　(b) 8 cm^2
　　　(c) 6 cm^2　　　(d) 10 cm^2

A2 (a) 48 cm^2　(b) 70 cm^2　(c) 96 cm^2
　　　(d) 70 cm^2　(e) 18 m^2　(f) 180 m^2

B *Half and half* (p 292)

B1 (a) 10 cm^2　(b) 7.5 cm^2　(c) 6 cm^2
　　　(d) 8 cm^2　(e) 4 cm^2　(f) 9 cm^2

C *Into triangles* (p 293)

C1 (a) 9 cm^2　　　(b) 10 cm^2
　　　(c) 6 cm^2　　　(d) 14 cm^2

C2 (a) The student's parallelograms
　　　(b) A 8 cm^2　B 15 cm^2　C 12 cm^2
　　　(c) A 4 cm^2　B 7.5 cm^2　C 6 cm^2

C3 (a) 24 cm^2　(b) 35 cm^2　(c) 108 cm^2
　　　(d) 31.5 cm^2　(e) 13.5 cm^2　(f) 150 cm^2

C4 A $7.5\,\text{cm}^2$ B $20\,\text{cm}^2$

C $14\,\text{cm}^2$ D $6.25\,\text{cm}^2$

C5 A and H, B and G, C and D, E and F

C6 (a) $1000\,\text{cm}^2$ (b) $1800\,\text{cm}^2$

(c) $1200\,\text{cm}^2$

C7 (a) $7.525\,\text{cm}^2$ (b) $28.83\,\text{cm}^2$

(c) $23.37\,\text{cm}^2$

Ⓓ **Composite shapes** (p 296)

D1 (a) $10.5\,\text{cm}^2$ (b) $10\,\text{cm}^2$ (c) $16\,\text{cm}^2$

D2 (a) $35\,\text{cm}^2$ (b) $35\,\text{cm}^2$

(c) $35\,\text{cm}^2$ (d) $156\,\text{cm}^2$

Ⓔ **Converting** (p 297)

E1 A and G: $10\,000\,\text{cm}^2 = 1\,\text{m}^2$

B and L: $500\,000\,\text{cm}^2 = 50\,\text{m}^2$

C and I: $100\,000\,\text{cm}^2 = 10\,\text{m}^2$

D and K: $1000\,\text{cm}^2 = 0.1\,\text{m}^2$

E and J: $0.5\,\text{m}^2 = 5000\,\text{cm}^2$

F and H: $5\,\text{m}^2 = 50\,000\,\text{cm}^2$

E2 (a) $40\,000\,\text{cm}^2$ (b) $200\,000\,\text{cm}^2$

(c) $250\,000\,\text{cm}^2$ (d) $2\,000\,000\,\text{cm}^2$

(e) $25\,000\,\text{cm}^2$ (f) $48\,000\,\text{cm}^2$

(g) $6000\,\text{cm}^2$ (h) $9000\,\text{cm}^2$

(i) $2500\,\text{cm}^2$ (j) $500\,\text{cm}^2$

E3 (a) $7\,\text{m}^2$ (b) $2\,\text{m}^2$ (c) $15\,\text{m}^2$

(d) $30\,\text{m}^2$ (e) $4.5\,\text{m}^2$ (f) $8.5\,\text{m}^2$

(g) $0.3\,\text{m}^2$ (h) $0.8\,\text{m}^2$ (i) $0.75\,\text{m}^2$

(j) $0.04\,\text{m}^2$

E4 (a) $30\,000\,\text{cm}^2 = 3\,\text{m}^2$

(b) $20\,000\,\text{cm}^2 = 2\,\text{m}^2$

(c) $60\,000\,\text{cm}^2 = 6\,\text{m}^2$

(d) $200\,000\,\text{cm}^2 = 20\,\text{m}^2$

Test yourself (p 298)

T1 (a) $21\,\text{cm}^2$ (b) $24\,\text{cm}^2$ (c) $10.5\,\text{cm}^2$

T2 $102.96\,\text{cm}^2$

T3 (a) $230\,\text{cm}^2$ (b) $80\,\text{cm}^2$ (c) $44\,\text{cm}^2$

T4 (a) $15\,\text{cm}^2$ (b) $30\,\text{cm}^2$

T5 (a) $120\,000\,\text{cm}^2$ (b) $12\,\text{m}^2$

Practice book

Section C (p 122)

1 (a) $7.5\,\text{cm}^2$ (b) $5\,\text{cm}^2$ (c) $7.5\,\text{cm}^2$

(d) $6\,\text{cm}^2$ (e) $9\,\text{cm}^2$

2 (a) $6\,\text{cm}^2$ (b) $6\,\text{cm}^2$ (c) $6\,\text{cm}^2$

3 (a) $8\,\text{cm}^2$

(b) 2 triangles with an area of $8\,\text{cm}^2$

4 (a) $21\,\text{cm}^2$ (b) $44\,\text{cm}^2$ (c) $108\,\text{cm}^2$

(d) $384\,\text{cm}^2$ (e) $28.5\,\text{cm}^2$ (f) $18.4\,\text{cm}^2$

(g) $92.4\,\text{cm}^2$

5 (a) A: $18\,\text{cm}^2$ B: $9\,\text{cm}^2$ C: $9\,\text{cm}^2$

D: $4.5\,\text{cm}^2$ E: $9\,\text{cm}^2$ F: $18\,\text{cm}^2$

(b) $72\,\text{cm}^2$

(c) Total area of A to F = $67.5\,\text{cm}^2$

Missing triangle has area $4.5\,\text{cm}^2$.

Sections D and E (p 124)

1 (a) $52\,\text{cm}^2$ (b) $144\,\text{cm}^2$

2 (a) $45\,\text{cm}^2$ (b) $36\,\text{cm}^2$

3 (a) $18\,\text{cm}^2$ (b) $18\,\text{cm}^2$

4 (a) $560\,\text{cm}^2$

(b) G: $104\,\text{cm}^2$ H: $110\,\text{cm}^2$ I: $97\,\text{cm}^2$

(c) $249\,\text{cm}^2$

5 (a) $80\,000\,\text{cm}^2$ (b) $500\,000\,\text{cm}^2$

(c) $1\,000\,000\,\text{cm}^2$ (d) $45\,000\,\text{cm}^2$

(e) $36\,000\,\text{cm}^2$ (f) $5000\,\text{cm}^2$

(g) $7500\,\text{cm}^2$ (h) $100\,\text{cm}^2$

6 (a) $6\,\text{m}^2$ (b) $15\,\text{m}^2$ (c) $200\,\text{m}^2$

(d) $2.5\,\text{m}^2$ (e) $0.6\,\text{m}^2$ (f) $0.05\,\text{m}^2$

7 (a) $60\,000\,\text{cm}^2$ (b) $6\,\text{m}^2$

41 *Trial and improvement*

Practice book pages 126 to 128

Ⓐ *Searching with your calculator* (p 299)

These problems are intended to introduce the idea that some problems can be solved just by trying out possible solutions (although some, such as 'Missing numbers', can be solved by a more direct method).

◊ Students can try these problems for themselves and their methods can be discussed. Some can be solved easily by an exhaustive search and others will involve some element of trial and improvement. There is no need to discuss in detail the idea of 'getting closer' to a solution at this stage.

Solutions are:

Missing digits

$29 \times 38 = 1102$, $53 \times 136 = 7208$, $744 \div 24 = 31$, $8.5 \times 3.2 = 27.2$, $115.2 \div 24 = 4.8$

Rectangles

The whole-number pairs are (1 cm, 112 cm), (2 cm, 56 cm), (4 cm, 28 cm), (7 cm, 16 cm), (8 cm, 14 cm).

Magic triangle

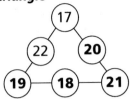

Missing numbers

18 × 59 = 1062, 893 ÷ **19** = 47, 71 × **93** = 6603, **943** ÷ 23 = 41

B **Strips** (p 300)

The idea of solving a problem by trial and *improvement* (rather than trial and *error*) is introduced in the context of 'addition strips'.

◊ Discuss the completed strip and how it has been made. Students can try to complete the other strips. To complete the last strip, students will probably need to try a variety of numbers in the second square. Start to discuss the idea of a number being 'too small' or 'too large' and hence some trials being pointless.

◊ Students can make up similar addition strip problems for each other to solve.

B3 Decimals are necessary here.

C **Squares and cubes** (p 300)

◊ Some of the problems involving squares can be solved using the square root key; this method is, of course, far more efficient than trial and improvement. You can decide whether to talk about the appropriateness of trial and improvement as a method here or leave this discussion till later.

◊ Students who have scientific calculators can use the square and power keys to speed up their work.

E **Being systematic** (p 302)

The problems in this section have whole number or exact decimal solutions.

◊ Students could start by playing a game in threes as follows:
  • One player thinks of two numbers that the other two players have to find and multiplies them together.

- The player then tells the other two players the product of and the difference between the two numbers.
- The other two players try to find the numbers and the winner is the one who finds them first.

◊ A spreadsheet can be used to help solve these problems. Alternatively, students can set their work out in tables such as the ones on page 303.

F *Not exactly* (p 303)

These problems have non-exact decimal solutions.

'We worked the example in the introduction on an OHP and discussed when to stop.'

◊ The main problem here is deciding if the width is 8.7 or 8.8 correct to one decimal place. One way to decide this is to consider 8.75 (the half way point); the result it gives is too big so the width must be closer to 8.7. Students should be aware of the fact that they must try lengths with two decimal places to be sure of their answer to one decimal place. They could work out the area when the width is 8.71, 8.72, 8.73, … if they prefer.

A *Searching with your calculator* (p 299)

A1 (a) $19 \times 23 = \mathbf{437}$

(b) $975 \div 39 = \mathbf{25}$

(c) $1.7 \times 4.\mathbf{6} = \mathbf{7}.82$

A2 13 and 19

A3 All possible pairs are:

1 cm, 210 cm	2 cm, 105 cm
3 cm, 70 cm	5 cm, 42 cm
6 cm, 35 cm	7 cm, 30 cm
10 cm, 21 cm	14 cm, 15 cm

A4 6

A5 27 years

B *Strips* (p 300)

B1 (a)

2	7	9	16	25

(b)

1	5	6	11	17	28

B2 (a)

3	4	7	11

(b)

6	5	11	16

(c)

9	2	11	13	24

(d)

4	7	11	18	29

(e)

5	8	13	21	34

(f)

6	0	6	6	12

B3 (a)

6	1.5	7.5	9

(b)

3	2.5	5.5	8	13.5	21.5	35

C *Squares and cubes* (p 300)

C1 C: 3^2

C2 A, Q ($2^3 = 8$)   B, S ($3^3 = 27$)

C, R ($4^2 = 16$)   D, T ($8^2 = 64$)

E, P ($3^2 = 9$)

C3 (a) 144 (b) 216 (c) 196 (d) 1000

C4 100, 256 and 441

C5 225

C6 324, 361

C7 7 cm

C8 9 cm

C9 (a) 125 (b) 512 (c) 1331

C10 (a) 12 (b) 20

C11 (a) 3.375 (b) 0.729
(c) 9.261 (d) 1157.625

C12 (a) 1.2 (b) 0.8

***C13**

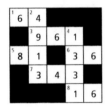

Ⅾ *Consecutive number puzzles* (p 302)

D1 92, 93

D2 (a) 18, 19 (b) 41, 42
(c) 25, 26 (d) 87, 88

D3 12, 13, 14

D4 43, 44, 45

D5 56, 58

D6 99, 101

D7 20, 22, 24

Ⅽ *Being systematic* (p 302)

E1 49, 52

E2 15, 15.4

E3 2.5, 5.5

E4 6.2, 6.3

E5 7.7, 2.3

Ⅎ *Not exactly* (p 303)

F1 5.8 cm

F2 12.7 cm

F3 7.4 cm

F4 1.59 cm

***F5** 3.7

Ꮐ *Deciding on your own method* (p 304)

G1 13

G2 1, 663 3, 221 13, 51 17, 39

G3 11 cm

G4 37

G5 11 cm

G6 12.2 cm

G7 4.6 cm

Test yourself (p 305)

T1 (a) 64, 400 (b) 64, 1728, 9261

T2 23, 24

T3 37, 39

T4 49, 54

T5 10.5

T6 4.2 cm

Practice book

Sections A and B (p 126)

1 16 m and 15 m

2 (a) 18 × 27 = 486 (b) 966 ÷ 23 = 42
(c) 58 × 48 = 2784

3

×	**43**	**39**
37	1591	1443
41	1763	1599

4 24 and 36

5 12 cm and 10 cm

Section C (p 126)

1 (a) 169 (b) 512 (c) 225 (d) 23

2 256 and 289

3 484

4 (a) 576 cm^2 (b) 27 cm

5 343

6 (a) 13 (b) 19

7 (a) 8 cm (b) 64 cm^2

Section D (p 126)

1 63, 64

2 (a) 19, 20, 21 (b) 28, 29, 30
   (c) 109, 110, 111 (d) 1419, 1420, 1421

3 (a) 16, 17 (b) 25, 26
   (c) 45, 46 (d) 77, 78

4 (a) 14, 15 (b) 5, 6, 7

5 44, 46

6 73, 75

Section E (p 127)

1 The student's table, leading to 38, 44

2 47, 94

3 16, 16.5

4 5.2, 11.8

5 62.7, 37.3

Section F (p 127)

1 The student's table, leading to 6.4 cm

2 5.8 cm

3 The student's table, leading to 4.6 cm

Section G (p 128)

1 (a) 38 (b) 47

2 32 cm and 37 cm

3 27 cm

4 81 years old

5 14 cm and 8 cm

6 18 cm

42 Solving equations

Practice book pages 129 to 132

B *Balancing and equations* (p 308)

TG

The emphasis here is on matching each equation with an appropriate balance puzzle and then finding the value of *x* by solving the balance puzzle.

The puzzle at the top of the page is the puzzle in A2 (c) and you may wish to refer students back to this.

D *Strips* (p 310)

This section deals with solving equations in a more formal way, thinking of them as balance puzzles and writing down intermediate steps in algebraic form.

The first few problems can be solved easily without formally forming and solving an equation but, towards the end of the section, the problems become more difficult and forming and solving an equation is clearly helpful.

You may wish students to form and solve equations from the start or let them decide for themselves when it becomes useful to do this. In any case, encourage them to use equation solving rather than trial and improvement.

E *Undoing subtractions* (p 311)

◊ The image of a balance does not apply easily to equations such as $4x - 3 = x + 12$. The balance idea has however emphasised 'doing the same thing to both sides' and this process is used here.

Some students may find it easier to use flow chart ideas developed in the earlier unit 'Reversing the flow' to solve equations such as $3x - 7 = 5$.

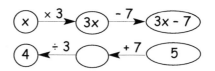

However, this will not help when the unknown appears on both sides of the equation and so the unit uses balancing methods throughout.

◊ If we wish to isolate the $4x$ on the left-hand side of $4x - 3 = x + 12$, then we must add 3 to both sides. Students' experiences in 'Reversing the flow' should help them see that, in order to 'get back' from $4x - 3$ to x, we have first to 'undo' the '– 3'.

A common error is for students to think they should subtract 3 from both sides leaving just $4x = x + 9$.

◊ If it does not arise naturally in discussion, point out that there is no one correct thing to do first. You could add 3 to both sides first or subtract x from both sides.

F *Problem solving* (p 312)

◊ You may wish to revise simplifying expressions such as $x + 2x + 3 + x - 5$ before you begin this section.

◊ Students could try to solve the problem in small groups and discuss their methods with the rest of the class. Some may use trial and improvement.

By the end of the discussion, they should see that the perimeter of the triangle is equivalent to $4x + 8$. Hence, the problem can be solved by solving the equation $4x + 8 = 40$.

You may wish to begin with easier examples such as

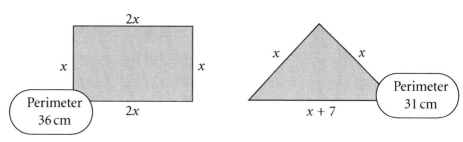

Ⓐ *Balancing puzzles* (p 306)

A1 (a) 2   (b) 5   (c) 10   (d) 8
     (e) 10   (f) 6   (g) 9   (h) 3

A2 (a) 5   (b) 12   (c) 5   (d) 5
     (e) 2   (f) 8   (g) 7   (h) 17
     (i) 4   (j) 4

Ⓑ *Balancing and equations* (p 308)

B1 (a) C, $x = 2$ (b) B, $x = 3$ (c) F, $x = 8$
     (d) E, $x = 6$ (e) A, $x = 4$ (f) D, $x = 4$

Ⓒ *Solving equations* (p 309)

C1 (a) $x = 3$ (b) $x = 7$ (c) $x = 4$
     (d) $x = 5$ (e) $x = 3$ (f) $x = 5$

C2 (a) $x = 7$ (b) $x = 4$ (c) $x = 9$
     (d) $x = 3$ (e) $x = 10$ (f) $x = 3$

C3 (a) $x = 8$ (b) $x = 5$ (c) $x = 3$
     (d) $x = 2$ (e) $x = 2$ (f) $x = 4$
     (g) $x = 4$ (h) $x = 1$ (i) $x = 2$

C4 (a) $7x + 6 = 2x + 41$ (b) $x = 7$

Ⓓ *Strips* (p 310)

D1 $x = 6$

D2 $x = 5$

D3 $x = 6$

D4 $x = 7$

D5 $x = 14$

D6 $x = 8$

D7 $x = 4$

D8 $x = 7$

D9 $x = 3$

D10 $x = 2$

D11 $x = 2$

D12 $x = 5$

D13 $x = 4$

D14 $x = 3$

Ⓔ *Undoing subtractions* (p 311)

E1 (a) $x = 9$ (b) $x = 15$ (c) $x = 6$
     (d) $x = 4$ (e) $x = 3$ (f) $x = 4$
     (g) $x = 9$ (h) $x = 7$ (i) $x = 1$

E2 (a) $x = 4$ (b) $x = 8$ (c) $x = 3$
     (d) $x = 2$ (e) $x = 3$ (f) $x = 5$
     (g) $x = 10$ (h) $x = 6$ (i) $x = 7$

E3 (a) $x = 5$ (b) $x = 3$

*E4 (a) $x = 3$ (b) $x = 6$ (c) $x = 5$
     (d) $x = 5$ (e) $x = 3$ (f) $x = 8$

Ⓕ *Problem solving* (p 312)

F1 (a) $6x + 2$ (b) $6x + 2 = 44$, $x = 7$

F2 (a) $3x + 2$ (b) $3x + 2 = 23$, $x = 7$

F3 (a) $4x + 20$ (b) $4x + 20 = 180$, $x = 40$

F4 (a) $6x = 180$ (b) $x = 30$

Ⓖ *Not always wholly positive* (p 313)

G1 (a) $x = 3.5$ (b) $n = 0.2$ (c) $x = 2.5$
     (d) $p = 1.5$ (e) $x = 2.5$ (f) $y = 1.4$

G2 (a) $x = {}^-1$ (b) $n = {}^-3$ (c) $x = {}^-2$
     (d) $y = {}^-2$ (e) $x = {}^-3$ (f) $a = {}^-7$

G3 (a) $p = {}^-3$ (b) $x = 3$ (c) $n = 4$
     (d) $n = {}^-4$ (e) $y = {}^-4$ (f) $x = {}^-3$

G4 (a) $x = \frac{3}{5}$ (b) $p = \frac{1}{2}$ (c) $y = \frac{5}{7}$
     (d) $x = \frac{3}{4}$ (e) $n = \frac{1}{3}$ (f) $z = \frac{5}{8}$

Test yourself (p 313)

T1 (a) $x = 7$ (b) $x = 4$

T2 (a) $x = 18$ (b) $y = 7$ (c) $n = 3$

T3 (a) $x = 4$ (b) $x = 6$

T4 (a) $x = 5$ (b) $y = 4$ (c) $p = 3.2$

T5 (a) $4x + 20$
     (b) (i) $4x + 20 = 180$
         (ii) $x = 40$ so the smallest angle is 44°

T6 (a) $x = {}^-2$ (b) $x = {}^-1$ (c) $x = \frac{4}{5}$

Practice book

Section A (p 129)

1 4
2 8
3 11
4 6
5 9
6 2
7 3
8 12
9 8
10 6

Sections B, C and D (p 130)

1 (a) A, $x = 4$ (b) D, $x = 5$
   (c) B, $x = 2$ (d) C, $x = 1$

2 (a) $x = 5$ (b) $x = 3$ (c) $x = 6$
   (d) $x = 4$ (e) $x = 12$ (f) $x = 2$

3 (a) $5x + 10 = 3x + 22$ (b) $x = 6$

4 (a) $x = 4$ (b) $x = 3$ (c) $x = 2$
   (d) $x = 5$ (e) $x = 1$ (f) $x = 3$

5 (a) $x = 14$ (b) $x = 6$ (c) $x = 9$
   (d) $x = 3$ (e) $x = 2$ (f) $x = 6$
   (g) $x = 5$ (h) $x = 4$

Section E (p 131)

1 (a) $x = 5$ (b) $x = 12$ (c) $x = 3$
   (d) $x = 4$ (e) $x = 1$ (f) $x = 5$
   (g) $x = 5$ (h) $x = 4$ (i) $x = 2$
   (j) $x = 2$ (k) $x = 7$ (l) $x = 4$

2 (a) $x = 6$ (b) $x = 2$

*3 (a) $x = 5$ (b) $x = 9$ (c) $x = 2$
    (d) $x = 1$ (e) $x = 4$ (f) $x = 3$

Section F (p 132)

1 (a) $6x + 12$ (b) $6x + 12 = 48, x = 6$

2 (a) $3x + 60°$ (b) $3x + 60° = 180°, x = 40°$

3 (a) $3x + 4 = 49$ (b) $x = 15$
   (c) 10 cm, 15 cm, 24 cm

4 (a) $6x + 8$ (b) $6x + 8 = 62, x = 9$

Section G (p 132)

1 (a) $y = 1.5$ (b) $p = 0.1$ (c) $n = 0.8$
   (d) $x = 1.5$ (e) $y = 2.5$ (f) $a = 0.6$

2 (a) $b = ^-2$ (b) $y = ^-4$ (c) $a = ^-2$
   (d) $p = ^-1$ (e) $s = ^-2$ (f) $n = ^-3$

3 (a) $t = ^-5$ (b) $y = ^-1$ (c) $m = 4.5$
   (d) $x = ^-2$ (e) $n = 5.5$ (f) $p = ^-4$

Review 5 (p 314)

1 (a) 2

(b)

x	0	1	2	3	4	5
y	-4	-2	0	2	4	6

(c)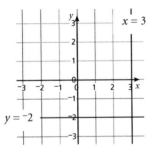

(d) 3   (e) 1.5

2

3 (a) 400   (b) 400   (c) 0.5
  (d) 0.08   (e) 1

4 (a) 80 kg   (b) 18 kg   (c) 80
     tonnes

5 $a = 45°$ $b = 80°$ $c = 108°$ $d = 144°$

6 Area A $= 6\,\text{m}^2$ Area B $= 2\,\text{m}^2$

7 56 and 57

8 4.3 cm

9 (a) $\frac{1}{3}$ (b) $\frac{8}{30} = \frac{4}{15}$

10 (a) $x = 3$ (b) $x = 7$ (c) $x = 5$
   (d) $x = 4$ (e) $x = 3$ (f) $x = 2$

11 (a) $5x - 30$ (b) $5x - 30 = 180$
   (c) $x = 42$; the angles are 42°, 84°
        and 54°.

12 (a) 20 grams
   (b) 200 grams plain flour
        500 ml milk
        2 eggs
        1 teaspoon salt
   (c) 20 pancakes
        (he is limited by the milk)

13 (a) John would get 40, Harriet 80.
   (b) John would get 48 and Harriet 72.

Mixed questions 5 (Practice book p 133)

1 (a), (b) $x = {}^-2$ $x = 1$

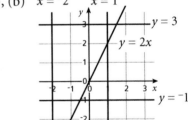

(c) $(1\frac{1}{2}, 3)$

2 (a) US$177.31   (b) £248.23

3 (a) Roughly $50 \times 5 = 250$
  (b) Roughly $50 \div 2 = 25$
  (c) Roughly $\dfrac{100 \times 0.1}{2} = 5$
  (d) Roughly $\dfrac{0.1 \times 4000}{20} = 20$

4 (a) $a = 65°$, an alternate angle
  (b) $b = 75°$, angles on a straight line add
       up to 180°

5 $p = 108°, q = 72°, r = 36°$

6 (a) $40\,\text{cm}^2$ (b) $24\,\text{cm}^2$ (c) $168\,\text{cm}^2$

7 Width $= 29.7$ cm

8 (a)

Score on dice

		1	2	3	4	5	6
Score on coin	1	2	3	4	5	6	7
	2	3	4	5	6	7	8

(b) $\frac{2}{12} = \frac{1}{6}$ (c) $\frac{5}{12}$

9 (a) $2:1$ (b) $2:3$ (c) $9:2$ (d) $2:5$

10 (a) (i) 6 litres   (ii) 2 litres

(b) 9 litres red wine, 6 litres lemonade and 3 litres orange juice

11 (a) $a = 9$ (b) $b = 6$ (c) $c = 11$

(d) $d = 4$ (e) $e = 8$ (f) $f = 2$

12 (a) $n = 3$ (b) $n = 3$ (c) $n = 5$

13 (a) $4x + 4$

(b) $4x + 4 = 64$, $x = 15$

(c) Sides are 15 m and 17 m, area is 255 m^2

Representing data

This unit is about interpreting data presented in tables and diagrams.

Essential

Sheets G61, G62

Practice book pages 135 to 138

A **Reading tables** (p 316)

◊ The data for boys' names is available from the ONS (Office for National Statistics) website so more recent information or girls' names data could be used for questions.

Current postal charges can be obtained in leaflets at any post office.

B **Two-way tables** (p 318)

TG

◊ The important idea that should come from the initial discussion is that totals are important if you want to gain a true interpretation of a two-way table. At first glance Elisa's statement appears true but overall there were twice as many town houses as country houses. The *proportions* of detached houses in the town and country are respectively 24% and 36%. The proportions of other types could be discussed using percentages in the same way. Students should be encouraged to add totals of rows and columns and check that these add up to the same overall figure.

C Diagrams (p 320)

◊ The initial data can be presented in either a pictogram or a bar chart. Students will need to be asked what one 'house' represents in the pictogram. It is useful to discuss the relative merits of each type of diagram: the pictogram is visually more engaging but cannot display the information to the same degree of accuracy.

C4 Historically a 'stick' diagram has been used when showing discrete numerical data (as in C5) but modern practice is to use bars as here.

D Composite bar charts (p 322)

◊ Bar charts can be drawn in either horizontal or vertical format and this section uses both. Stacked bar charts (where the separate sections are placed in one bar) are not used here as they show the overall totals more clearly but make individual comparisons more difficult.

E Line graphs (p 323)

Sheet G61

◊ The line on the graph on page 323 could be dotted to indicate that in-between points have no meaning.

F Index numbers (p 325)

◊ Care needs to be taken with index numbers as a change from 135 one year to 145 the next does not show a rise of 10%. The factor would be $(145 \div 135) \times 100 = 107.4$ or a rise of 7.4%. However, this may be beyond students at this level.

Test yourself (p 326)

Sheet G62

A Reading tables (p 316)

A1 Christopher

A2 Mark

A3 David

A4 No

A5 Route 3

A6 7

A7 6

A8 (a) 7   (b) 35 minutes

A9 38%

A10 90%

A11 (a) False   (b) True   (c) True

A12 (a) £1.09   (b) £1.90
      (c) 72p   (d) £4.94

A13 (a) 8p   (b) 24p   (c) 28p   (d) 65p

A14 £2.16

Ⓑ *Two-way tables* (p 318)

B1 (a)

	How they get to school			
	Walk/ cycle	Bus	Car	Total
Boys	32	48	**20**	100
Girls	12	**28**	10	50
Total	44	**76**	**30**	150

     (b) 32%   (c) 24%   (d) Boys

B2 (a) Girls – 56% of girls use a bus but only 48% of boys.
     (b) They are the same proportion (20%).

B3 (a)

	Wear glasses	Don't wear glasses	Totals
Boys	5	**8**	13
Girls	**7**	10	**17**
Totals	12	**18**	30

     (b) $\frac{5}{13}$ (c) 17   (d) $\frac{7}{17}$

B4 (a) 28   (b) 30

B5 (a)

	Number of bedrooms				
	2	3	4	5	Total
Detached	0	10	8	2	20
Semi-detached	2	8	5	0	15
Terraced	10	15	0	0	25
Total	12	33	13	2	60

     (b) 8   (c) 25   (d) 50%

B6 (a) 30   (b) 8   (c) None

B7 (a) 47   (b) 9   (c) 17

Ⓒ *Diagrams* (p 320)

C1

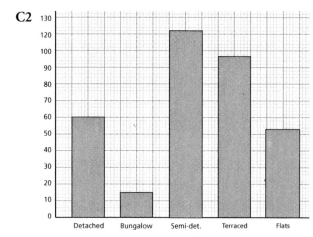

represents 20 houses

C2

C3 (a) (i) 60   (ii) 50
     (b)

C4 (a) 3   (b) 66   (c) 6   (d) 192

C5 (a) 2   (b) 31   (c) 96

C6 (a) The student's diagram
     (b) Although a bar chart or stick diagram is more accurate a pictogram might make a better presentation.

Ⓓ *Composite bar charts* (p 322)

D1 (a) Semi-detached   (b) Detached

D2 Semi-detached and terraced

D3 (a) Going down   (b) Army; yes
     (c) 1978 and 1988

D4 (a) Watching TV

(b) Boys watched more videos and went to clubs;
Girls read books more than boys.

E *Line graphs* (p 323)

E1 To show that the scale does not start at zero

E2 (a) £1.20   (b) £1.25   (c) £1.88

E3 (a) 1994 and 1995

(b) Between 1992 and 1994

E4 It generally went up between 1989 and 1999.

E5 (a)

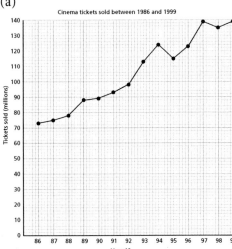

(b) The student's two statements about the graph, for example: The number of tickets steadily rose between 1986 and 1999 apart from a drop in 1995 and 1998.
Sales in 1999 were almost double those in 1986.

E6 (a) The months of the year

(b) July and August

(c) February

(d) Generally got better

(e) In 1994 there was a drop between March and April.

F *Index numbers* (p 325)

F1 (a) 32%   (b) Tree Sparrow

(c) Spotted Flycatcher

F2 (a) 58%

(b)

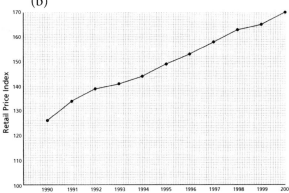

Test yourself (p 326)

T1 (a) German   (b) 492

(c) Religious studies

T2 (a) 36   (b) $\frac{12}{36} = \frac{1}{3}$

(c) Boys
The fraction for girls is $\frac{6}{27} = \frac{2}{9}$.

T3 (a) 90   (b) 25   (c) $\frac{1}{10}$

T4 (a) Friday

(b) Yes. The student's reason

(c) Yes. 51% shopped on Friday, Saturday and Sunday.

T5 (a)

(b) It is the hottest month of the six.

Practice book

Sections A and B (p 135)

1 (a) Margaret   (b) Christine

  (c) Mary, Dorothy, Margaret, Jessica, Rebecca

2 (a) 0730 train. It takes 33 minutes.

  (b) 4 trains

  (c) 0742 is the slowest train.
(It takes 40 minutes.)

3 (a)

	Play a musical instrument	Do not play a musical instrument	Totals
Boys	7	9	16
Girls	9	5	14
Totals	16	14	30

  (b) 16 boys   (c) 14 girls

  (d) $\frac{9}{14}$ (e) $\frac{16}{30} = \frac{8}{15}$

Sections C and D (p 136)

1 (a)

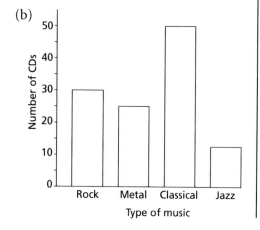

  ⊙ represents 10 CDs

(b)

2 (a) 7   (b) 14   (c) 2

  (d)

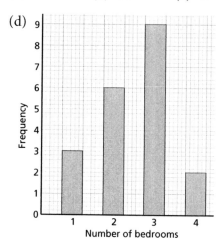

3 (a) Ice cream, sweets and chocolates

  (b) Computer games

  (c) Mobile phones are more popular with girls.

  (d) 25%

Section E (p 137)

1 (a) (i) £4   (ii) £4.30   (iii) £7.10

  (b) It went down in the years 1992–1993, 1993–1994 and 1998–1999.

  (c) It rose steeply in the years 1997–1998, 1999–2000 and 2000–2001.

2 (a) The bills are

Quarter	1	2	3	4
	£82	£87	£67	£88

  (b) The fourth quarter, Oct, Nov, Dec

  (c) The third quarter Jul, Aug, Sept
They probably are out more and go away on holiday.

  (d) The bills have increased.

Calculating with negative numbers

Essential

Sheets G63, G64, G65

Practice book pages 139 to 143

B *Multiplying* (p 329)

Sheets G63 and G64

TG

◊ One way to structure the introduction is described below.

Ask students to try to match the expressions in the first box and hence calculate the answers to each multiplication.

Continuing to think of multiplication of a positive by a negative as a repeated addition, students can copy and complete the first pattern in the second box and then try to complete the second pattern. Discuss possible answers to $^-2 \times {}^-1$ and show that the pattern of results $^-6, {}^-4, {}^-2, 0, \ldots$ leads to $^-2 \times {}^-1 = 2, {}^-2 \times {}^-2 = 4$ etc.

Students can now use patterns to fill in the table on sheet G63 to establish the rules at the top of page 330.

C *Dividing* (p 331)

TG

Establish the rules for division on page 332.

E *Substitution* (p 334)

Sheet G65

Ⓐ *Adding and subtracting* (p 328)

A1 (a) ⁻5   (b) 3   (c) ⁻4   (d) 6
     (e) 0   (f) ⁻4   (g) ⁻10   (h) ⁻4
     (i) ⁻13   (j) ⁻9

A2 (a) 3   (b) ⁻3   (c) 0   (d) ⁻10
     (e) ⁻10   (f) ⁻6   (g) ⁻9   (h) ⁻5

A3 (a) ⁻1   (b) ⁻7   (c) 8   (d) ⁻3
     (e) ⁻9   (f) ⁻1

A4 (a)

4	⁻3	2
⁻1	1	3
0	5	⁻2

(b)

1	0	5
6	2	⁻2
⁻1	4	3

(c)

⁻1	4	⁻3
⁻2	0	2
3	⁻4	1

(d)

1	⁻6	⁻1
⁻4	⁻2	0
⁻3	2	⁻5

A5 (a) 5   (b) 10   (c) 10   (d) 7
     (e) 5   (f) 3   (g) 0   (h) ⁻6
     (i) ⁻7   (j) ⁻3

A6 (a) ⁻3   (b) 5   (c) ⁻9   (d) ⁻11
     (e) 4   (f) 9   (g) ⁻8   (h) 6
     (i) 5   (j) ⁻2

A7 (a) 2 – 6 = ⁻4 or ⁻7 – ⁻3 = ⁻4
     (b) 2 + ⁻7 = ⁻5   (c) ⁻5 + 1 = ⁻4
     (d) ⁻5 – 1 = ⁻6   (e) 1 – ⁻7 = 8
     (f) ⁻3 + ⁻7 = ⁻10

*A8 (a) ⁻8 + ⁻5 = ⁻13   (b) 2 + ⁻8 = ⁻6
     (c) 2 – 7 = ⁻5   (d) ⁻8 – 2 = ⁻10
     (e) 7 – ⁻5 = 12

Ⓑ *Multiplying* (p 329)

B1 (a) ⁻12   (b) ⁻6   (c) ⁻9   (d) 0
     (e) ⁻4   (f) 6   (g) 12   (h) 4
     (i) 9   (j) 8

B2 (a) ⁻24   (b) 15   (c) ⁻10   (d) 21
     (e) ⁻21   (f) 21   (g) ⁻21   (h) ⁻36
     (i) 70   (j) ⁻8

B3 (a)

×	4	⁻3	2
5	20	⁻15	**10**
⁻2	**⁻8**	6	⁻4
⁻4	**⁻16**	12	⁻8

(b)

×	⁻10	8	⁻4
⁻5	50	⁻40	20
6	⁻60	48	⁻24
⁻1	10	⁻8	4

B4 ⁻50

B5 (a) 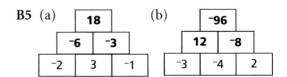 (b)

(c)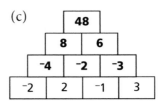

B6 (a) ⁻6   (b) 7   (c) ⁻5   (d) ⁻6

B7 (a) 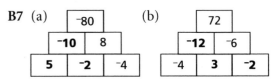 (b)

(c)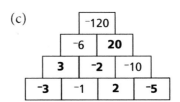

B8 (a) (⁻5)² = ⁻5 × ⁻5 = **25**
     (b) (i) 9   (ii) 16   (iii) 36

B9 (a)

×	5	-3
2	10	**-6**
-3	-15	**9**

(b)

×	**-5**	5	**6**
-3	**15**	-15	**-18**
-1	5	**-5**	-6
4	-20	20	**24**

(c)

×	**-3**	0	**-2**
1	**-3**	0	-2
-4	12	0	**8**
5	**-15**	**0**	-10

*B10 (a) -15   (b) M

(c) (i) PACK   (ii) FIND

    (iii) GLOBE

*B11

1   2

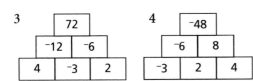

3   4

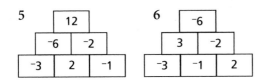

5   6

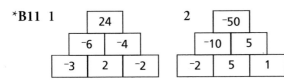

7   8

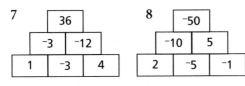

9   10

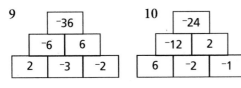

11

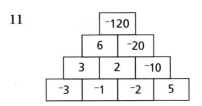

12

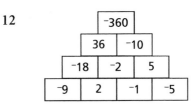

C *Dividing* (p 331)

C1 (a) -6   (b) -2   (c) 2   (d) 7

(e) -4   (f) -3   (g) 3   (h) 2

C2 (a) -2   (b) 5   (c) -12   (d) -24

(e) -5   (f) 18

C3 (a) -15 ÷ 5 = -3   (b) -10 ÷ -5 = 2

(c) -12 ÷ -3 = 4   (d) -15 ÷ 3 = -5

C4 (a) -10   (b) 2   (c) -5   (d) 32

(e) -40   (f) 7   (g) -24   (h) -2

(i) 5   (j) 63

C5 (a) -4   (b) -6   (c) -12   (d) -4

(e) 14   (f) 10   (g) 3   (h) -5

(i) -8

C6 (a) -25   (b) 20   (c) 5

C7 (a) 21 ÷ -7 = -3   (b) -7 × -2 = 14

(c) -2 × 3 = -6   (d) 10 ÷ -2 = -5

(e) -10 ÷ -2 = 5   (f) -3 × 21 = -63

C8 (a) 6 ÷ 3 = 2   (b) 6 ÷ -3 = -2

(c) 3 × -3 = -9   (d) -15 × -3 = 45

(e) -15 ÷ -3 = 5

C9 (a) -12 ÷ -6 = 2   (b) -12 × -6 = 72

(c) -12 ÷ 3 = -4

(d) 12 ÷ -6 = -2 or -6 ÷ 3 = -2

(e) -12 × 3 = -36

*C10 (a) -6   (b) 24

Ⓓ *Mixed calculations* (p 333)

D1 (a) ⁻7   (b) ⁻30   (c) ⁻4   (d) ⁻5
    (e) ⁻9   (f) 20   (g) ⁻2   (h) 100
    (i) 2   (j) 7

D2 (a) ⁻7   (b) ⁻5   (c) 24   (d) ⁻42

D3 (a) ⁻5   (b) ⁻28   (c) 9   (d) 15
    (e) ⁻3   (f) ⁻2   (g) 3   (h) ⁻4

D4 (a) 10   (b) ⁻9   (c) ⁻20   (d) ⁻1
    (e) 9   (f) ⁻8

D5 (a) Monday and Saturday
    (b) 10 degrees
    (c) ⁻3°C

D6 42, ⁻86

D7 (a) ⁻3   (b) 11   (c) 23

D8 (a) (i) Any pair from
          ⁻1, 10
          ⁻10, 1
          ⁻2, 5
          ⁻5, 2

      (ii) Any pair of numbers n and $⁻n$
    (b) ⁻196

*D9 (a) 6 + ⁻10 = ⁻4   (b) ⁻2 – 9 = ⁻11
    (c) 6 – ⁻10 = 16   (d) ⁻2 × 9 = ⁻18
    (e) ⁻10 ÷ ⁻2 = 5

Ⓔ *Substitution* (p 334)

E1 (a) 1   (b) ⁻4   (c) ⁻11
    (d) 1   (e) ⁻2

E2 (a) 4   (b) ⁻12   (c) ⁻8
    (d) ⁻3   (e) 8

E3 (a) 1   (b) ⁻11   (c) 16
    (d) ⁻1   (e) ⁻6

E4 (a) ⁻15   (b) 23   (c) 0
    (d) 7   (e) 11

E5 (a) 3   (b) 24   (c) ⁻12
    (d) 36   (e) 4

E6 Puzzle 1

  A   ⁻5   B   ⁻1   C   ⁻2
  D   ⁻10   E   13   F   ⁻16
  G   ⁻4

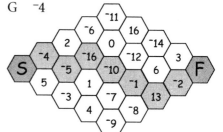

Puzzle 2

  A   ⁻9   B   ⁻1   C   5
  D   3   E   ⁻12   F   18
  G   2   H   10

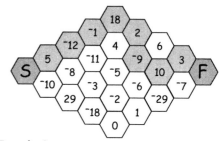

Puzzle 3

  A   ⁻15   B   1   C   ⁻2
  D   4   E   22   F   0
  G   ⁻6   H   36   I   ⁻3

E7 (a) 0, 1, ⁻2, ⁻4 → NOJH → JOHN
    (b) ⁻5, ⁻5, 4, 2 → EETP → PETE
    (c) 0, ⁻1, 3, ⁻3, 1 → NMSIO → SIMON
    (d) 1, ⁻4, ⁻5, ⁻2, 3, 2 → OHEJSP →
        JOSEPH
    (e) 2, ⁻4, 0, ⁻5, 4, 3, ⁻5 → PHNETSE →
        STEPHEN

E8 (a) 50   (b) 8   (c) 0   (d) ⁻6

Test yourself (p 335)

T1 (a) ⁻12   (b) ⁻25   (c) 18
  (d) 25   (e) 24

T2 (a) ⁻3   (b) 2   (c) ⁻2
  (d) 9   (e) ⁻4

T3 (a) 18   (b) 2   (c) ⁻24
  (d) ⁻6   (e) ⁻6

T4 (a) ⁻8   (b) ⁻6   (c) ⁻12
  (d) ⁻15   (e) ⁻3   (f) 3

T5 (a) ⁻2   (b) ⁻7   (c) 5
  (d) 3   (e) ⁻2

T6 (a) 2 + ⁻8 = ⁻6   (b) 3 × ⁻5 = ⁻15
  (c) ⁻5 − 3 = ⁻8   (d) ⁻8 ÷ 2 = ⁻4
  (e) ⁻8 + ⁻5 = ⁻13   (f) ⁻8 × ⁻5 = 40

T7 (a) 6   (b) 3   (c) ⁻16   (d) 15

T8 (a) ⁻3   (b) ⁻2   (c) 9   (d) ⁻8
  (e) 12   (f) ⁻5   (g) ⁻2   (h) 13
  (i) ⁻2   (j) 18

T9 5

Practice book

Section A (p 139)

1 (a) ⁻4   (b) 1   (c) ⁻7   (d) ⁻8
  (e) ⁻3   (f) 0   (g) ⁻18   (h) 14

2 (a) 1   (b) ⁻4   (c) ⁻5   (d) ⁻13
  (e) 2   (f) ⁻10   (g) 0   (h) ⁻12
  (i) ⁻8

3 (a) 8 + ⁻3 = 5   (b) 7 + ⁻8 = ⁻1
  (c) ⁻6 + ⁻3 = ⁻9   (d) 7 + ⁻4 = 3

4 (a)

⁻3	**1**	8
13	2	**⁻9**
⁻4	**3**	7

(b)

⁻4	3	⁻5
⁻3	**⁻2**	**⁻1**
1	**⁻7**	**0**

(c)

⁻4	1	**0**
3	**⁻1**	**⁻5**
⁻2	**⁻3**	2

5 (a) 8   (b) 11   (c) ⁻1   (d) 3
  (e) 8   (f) 10   (g) 0   (h) 18

6 (a) 5   (b) 3   (c) ⁻7   (d) ⁻7
  (e) 7   (f) ⁻12   (g) ⁻6   (h) 6

7 (a) **1 − 5** = ⁻4   (b) **⁻4 − 1** = ⁻5
  (c) **5 + ⁻4** = 1   (d) **⁻3 − ⁻4** = 1

8 ⁻4 + 6 = 2   ⁻4 − 6 = ⁻10   6 − ⁻4 = 10

9 ⁻3 + ⁻5 = ⁻8   ⁻3 − ⁻5 = 2   ⁻5 − ⁻3 = ⁻2

10 (a) POTATO   (b) CARROT
  (c) BEETROOT

Sections B and C (p 140)

1 (a) ⁻15   (b) ⁻8   (c) ⁻18   (d) 6
  (e) ⁻6   (f) 4   (g) ⁻24   (h) 60

2

×	⁻1	⁻3	4
3	⁻3	**⁻9**	12
⁻2	**2**	6	**⁻8**
⁻5	**5**	15	**⁻20**

×	⁻4	6	8
2	**⁻8**	**12**	**16**
⁻3	**12**	**⁻18**	**⁻24**
⁻10	**40**	**⁻60**	**⁻80**

×	⁻1	2	**⁻4**
2	⁻2	**4**	**⁻8**
⁻3	**3**	**⁻6**	12
⁻4	**4**	**⁻8**	**16**

3 (a) 8 × **⁻3** = ⁻24   (b) ⁻5 × **⁻7** = 35
  (c) **⁻6** × ⁻6 = 36   (d) ⁻4 × **⁻8** = 32

4 (a) 25 (b) 9 (c) 100

5 (a)

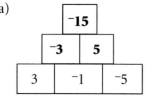

(b)

```
        ┌─────┐
        │ 80  │
      ┌──┴──┬──┴──┐
      │ ⁻8  │ ⁻10 │
   ┌──┴──┬──┴──┬──┴──┐
   │ ⁻4  │  2  │ ⁻5  │
   └─────┴─────┴─────┘
```

(c)

```
        ┌─────┐
        │ 48  │
      ┌──┴──┬──┴──┐
      │ ⁻6  │ ⁻8  │
   ┌──┴──┬──┴──┬──┴──┐
   │ ⁻3  │  2  │ ⁻4  │
   └─────┴─────┴─────┘
```

6 (a) ⁻5 (b) ⁻5 (c) 2
   (d) 8 (e) ⁻7

7 (a) ⁻45 (b) 24 (c) ⁻4
   (d) 8 (e) 40 (f) ⁻5
   (g) ⁻16 (h) ⁻4 (i) ⁻1
   (j) 1

8 (a) ⁻4 × ⁻3 = 12 (b) ⁻70 ÷ 7 = ⁻10
   (c) ⁻8 × ⁻5 = 40 (d) ⁻6 × ⁻1 = 6
   (e) 56 ÷ ⁻7 = ⁻8 (f) 90 ÷ ⁻10 = ⁻9
   (g) ⁻4 × ⁻4 = 16 (h) ⁻48 ÷ 6 = ⁻8

9 (a) ⁻6 ÷ 3 = ⁻2 (b) 3 × ⁻4 = ⁻12
   (c) ⁻24 ÷ ⁻6 = 4 (d) ⁻4 × ⁻6 = 24

10 (a) 3 × ⁻5 (b) ⁻20 ÷ ⁻5
   (c) ⁻5 × ⁻20 (d) ⁻5 × 5
   (e) ⁻5 ÷ 5 or 5 ÷ ⁻5
   (f) 3 × ⁻20

Section D (p 141)

1 (a) ⁻5 (b) ⁻21 (c) ⁻7 (d) ⁻4
   (e) 18 (f) 6 (g) 7 (h) 6
   (i) ⁻4 (j) 6

2 (a) 2 (b) ⁻2 (c) 30 (d) ⁻6

3 (a) 9 (b) ⁻14 (c) 5 (d) 16
   (e) ⁻2 (f) ⁻3 (g) 2 (h) 25

4 (a) 9 + ⁻7 = 2 (b) 4 × ⁻9 = ⁻36
   (c) ⁻21 ÷ 7 = ⁻3 (d) ⁻4 − ⁻5 = 1
   (e) 8 + ⁻3 + ⁻6 = ⁻1
   (f) ⁻45 ÷ ⁻9 = 5

5 (a) Thursday (b) 5°C (c) ⁻2°C

6 (a) ⁻7, ⁻12 (b) ⁻6, 1 (c) ⁻40, 80

7 (a) ⁻22 (b) 18 (c) ⁻42

8 (a) SKIING (b) KARATE
   (c) KARTING (d) SKATING

Section E (p 142)

1 (a) ⁻5 (b) ⁻11 (c) 11
   (d) ⁻16 (e) ⁻24

2 (a) ⁻6 (b) 3 (c) ⁻9
   (d) 9 (e) ⁻40

3 (a) $x + y = ⁻5, x − y = 1, y − x = ⁻1$
   ATE
   (b) $2x − y = ⁻1, 2x + 1 = ⁻3, xy = 6,$
   $2y + 1 = ⁻5$
   TEAM
   (c) $5 + x = 3, 2 − y = 5, x^2 = 4, 3y = ⁻9$
   ICED

4 (a) ⁻3 (b) ⁻6 (c) ⁻2
   (d) 25 (e) 6

5 (a) ⁻18 (b) ⁻2 (c) 10
   (d) ⁻9 (e) 1

6 ⁻15

7 3

8 MATHS CAN BE A PUZZLE

45 Metric units

This unit deals with metric equivalents of imperial measurements not met in 'Made to measure'. It also gives students the opportunity to practise estimating a range of measures in everyday settings.

Essential

Bags of sugar, empty litre cartons, packets of 50 teabags (weight 125 g)
Objects to guess the weight and capacity of
5 ml spoons, metre rules, bathroom and kitchen scales

Practice book pages 144 and 145

A *Estimating* (p 336)

Bags of sugar, empty litre cartons, packets of 50 teabags (weight 125 g)
Objects to guess the weight and capacity of
5 ml spoons, metre rules, bathroom and kitchen scales

◊ Before doing the examples students need to do some practical estimating to gain a feel for the different metric units. One kilogram bags of sugar (inside ziplock plastic bags or similar to prevent spillage) are an ideal way of estimating the weights of items in kilograms. Have a set of objects whose weights are in the range 2 kg to 10 kg and are to be guessed by holding a bag of sugar in one hand and the object in another. For other comparisons use the 5 ml spoon and containers with capacity between 10 ml and 80 ml, 1 litre cartons and containers with capacity between 2 and 10 litres, 50 tea bags and objects with weights between 200 g and 1 kg.

This could be set up as a guessing competition and then the objects weighed or measured properly to see who was closest.

◊ Students may need reminding of earlier work using kilo- and milli-.

Have you got the bottle?

'cl' stands for centilitre so 75 cl is 75/100 of a litre or 0.75 litre.

B *Liquid conversions* (p 338)

◊ You could discuss the implications of the article and demonstrate this with a litre carton and a pint beer glass.

C *A mixed bag* (p 339)

All the conversions in this section should be familiar to students and this provides further practice.

A *Estimating* (p 336)

A1 (a) Desk width to nearest 20 cm
   (b) About 25 cm
   (c) Probably about 20 cm
   (d) Chair seat height to nearest 20 cm

A2 (a) The rough weight of student's bag
   (b) The rough weight of a chair
   (c) The rough weight of pile of exercise books

A3 (a) The rough weight of book (about 250 g)
   (b) The rough weight of full pencil case
   (c) The rough weight of a ruler (about 50 g)

A4 (a) The rough capacity of a school bag
   (b) The rough capacity of rubbish bin

A5 (a) Roughly 150 ml
   (b) Roughly 250 ml
   (c) Less than 5 ml

A6 (a) m (b) km (c) cm (d) mm

A7 (a) kg (b) g (c) tonne

A8 (i) cm (ii) g (iii) km (iv) ml

A9 (a) 500 cm (b) 250 cm (c) 5000 cm
   (d) 5 cm (e) 20 cm (f) 0.5 cm

A10 (a) 8 m (b) 1.5 m (c) 0.8 m
   (d) 7000 m (e) 25 000 m (f) 750 m

A11 (a) 2000 g (b) 10 000 g
   (c) 500 g (d) 250 g

A12 (a) 3 kg (b) 1.5 kg
   (c) 0.6 kg (d) 0.75 kg

A13 (a) 5000 ml (b) 2500 ml (c) 500 ml
   (d) 0.25 litre (e) 2 litres (f) 1.25 litres

B *Liquid conversions* (p 338)

B1 (a) 4 litres (b) 10 litres
   (c) 3.5 litres (d) 7.5 litres

B2 (a) 12 pints (b) 30 pints
   (c) 5 pints (d) 25 pints

B3 (a) 500 ml (b) 250 ml
   (c) 125 ml (d) 375 ml

B4

	(a)	(b)
Witney's Pale	96 pints	48 litres
Adlard's O.S.	32 pints	16 litres
Khronicberg	120 pints	60 litres
Bugwiper	68 pints	34 litres

B5 (a) 45 litres (b) 22.5 litres
   (c) 11.25 litres (d) 9 litres
   (e) 27 litres (f) 20.25 litres

C *A mixed bag* (p 339)

C1 (a) 150 cm (b) 60 cm
   (c) 180 cm (d) 300 cm

C2 (a) 50 m (b) 10 m
   (c) 30 m (d) 2000 m

C3 (a) Our school swimming pool is **25 m** long.

(b) Our aeroplane flew at **4000 m**.

(c) The peak of Mount Everest is nearly **10 000 m** above sea level.

(d) An Anaconda grows to about **7 m** in length.

(e) The highest waterfall in the world is Angel Falls in Venezuela and is **1000 m** high.

C4

Age	Birth	10	30	50	80
(lb)	8	56	164	220	185
(kg)	**4**	**28**	**82**	**110**	**92.5**

C5

Detford	64	Walford	24
Malpeth	40	Ardale	80

Midworth 32
Frotton 16

C6 (a) 71 to 72 kg (b) 1.55 m

Test yourself (p 340)

T1 The student's estimates for

(a) the width of a chair back (40 cm)

(b) the weight of a chair (2 kg)

(c) the weight of a trainer (400 g)

T2 (a) kilograms (b) kilometres

(c) millilitres (possibly litres)

(d) metres

T3 (a) 2 litres (b) 5 litres (c) 20 litres

T4 (a) My gran lives at Crumford which is about **56 kilometres** away.

(b) Heavyweight boxers must weigh over **95 kilograms**.

(c) The current long jump record is nearly **10 metres**.

T5 (a) 6 pints (b) 1 kilogram

Practice book

Section A (p 144)

1 (a) Sensible (b) 5 kg (c) 330 ml

(d) 2 m (e) Sensible (f) 50 litres

2 (a) cm (b) km (c) kg (d) ml

3 (a) 700 cm (b) 6 cm (c) 270 cm

(d) 35 cm (e) 80 cm (f) 0.3 cm

4 (a) 3000 m (b) 2.5 m (c) 0.28 m

(d) 5200 m (e) 700 m (f) 0.09 m

5 (a) 5000 g (b) 700 g

(c) 15 000 g (d) 750 g

6 (a) 4 kg (b) 3.4 kg

(c) 0.2 kg (d) 0.355 kg

7 (a) 3000 ml (b) 4500 ml

(c) 800 ml (d) 3 litres

(e) 1.23 litres (f) 0.65 litres

Sections B and C (p 145)

1 (a) 2 litres (b) 9 litres

(c) 15 litres (d) $4\frac{1}{2}$ litres

2 (a) 8 pints (b) 36 pints

(c) 17 pints (d) 51 pints

3 (a) 2000 ml (b) 100 ml

(c) 375 ml (d) 50 ml

4 (a) Gold top 36 pints
Silver top 144 pints
Semi-skimmed 128 pints
Skimmed 72 pints

(b) Gold top 18 litres
Silver top 72 litres
Semi-skimmed 64 litres
Skimmed 36 litres

(c) Gold top 20.25 litres
Silver top 81 litres
Semi-skimmed 72 litres
Skimmed 40.5 litres

5 (a) 240 cm (b) 120 cm (c) 105 cm

(d) 15 m (e) 80 m (f) 3000 m

6 (a) 640 km (b) 67.5 litres

(c) 50 kg (d) 2.5 m

46 Finding and using formulas

Essential	**Optional**
Sheets G66, G67	Counters
Coloured pencils	Sheets G68, G69
2 mm graph paper	
Practice book pages 146 to 149	

Ⓐ *Review: substitution* (p 341)

> Sheet G66

◊ This section revises substituting into expressions of the type that students have previously met, such as

$$3n + 4, \quad 3(n + 4), \quad \frac{n + 3}{4}, \quad \frac{n}{4} + 3$$

and the equivalents involving subtraction.

The two games on sheet G66 give students plenty of enjoyable practice in substituting into expressions of the above type.

Ⓑ *Taking off* (p 342)

Students may need reminding that multiplication and division are done before addition or subtraction when evaluating expressions.

C **Areas** (p 343)

TG

After your introduction, the students should know that

- $a \times a$ is written as a^2
- $3a \times 2b$ is written as $6ab$

Ensure that they are confident in substituting numbers into expressions like these.

D **More letters** (p 344)

Sheet G67, coloured pencils
Optional: counters

TG

◊ This section moves on to slightly more complicated expressions. When explaining how to work out such expressions, you may find it useful to tell students to

- replace all the letters with the numbers
- where two letters appeared next to each other, or in front of a bracket, insert a multiplication sign

They may also need to be reminded about the order of performing operations when working out expressions.

You can enlarge the playing boards on sheet G67 so that students can use counters instead of coloured pencils.

E **Arrow diagrams** (p 345)

TG

In the introduction, ensure that the form of words 'a formula for r in terms of n' is understood, as it is commonly used.

G **Graphs using formulas** (p 347)

Optional: sheet G68

G2 Grid A on sheet G68 is optional.

G3 Grid B on sheet G68 is optional.

Test yourself (p 349)

Optional: sheet G69

T12 Optional sheet G69 contains a grid for this question.

A *Review: substitution* (p 341)

A1 (a) $3n$ (b) $\frac{1}{2}n$ (c) $2n$

A2 (a) 25 (b) 27 (c) 7 (d) 0
(e) 3 (f) 30 (g) 6 (h) 1

A3 (a) $2a + 1$ (b) $2a + 2$

A4 (a) $5a - 20$ (b) $4a - 10$

A5 $3(a + 2)$ when $a = 5$
$= 3 \times (\mathbf{5 + 2})$
$= 3 \times \mathbf{7}$
$= \mathbf{21}$

A6 (a) 16 (b) 24 (c) 40 (d) 15

A7 $2(x + 3)$

B *Taking off* (p 342)

B1 (a) $10 - 3a$ when $a = 2$
$= 10 - 3 \times 2$
$= 10 - \mathbf{6}$
$= \mathbf{4}$

(b) (i) 34 (ii) 2 (iii) 40 (iv) 50

B2 (a) 35

(b) (i) 13 (ii) 15 (iii) 95 (iv) 25

B3 (a) (i) 30° (ii) 5° (iii) 145°

(b) (i) ACB $= 80°$, ABC $= 80°$,
CAB $= 20°$

(ii) Isosceles

C *Areas* (p 343)

C1 (a) $15pq$ (b) 10 and 9

(c) $15pq = 15 \times 2 \times 3 = 90$, which
checks

C2 (a) $8ab$ (b) $12h$ (c) $16k^2$

C3 (a) $15ab$ (b) $20x$ (c) $12y^2$
(d) $5kl$ (e) $20e^2$ (f) $4n^2$
(g) $20m$ (h) $30jk$ (i) $6rs$
(j) $5ab$

C4 (a) $4c$ (b) $6k$ (c) $2h$

D *More letters* (p 344)

D1 (a) 6   (b) 11   (c) 2
(d) 30   (e) 40

D2 (a) 2   (b) 12   (c) 5
(d) 16   (e) 14

D3 (a) 24   (b) 30   (c) 30
(d) 6   (e) 2

D4 (a) 12   (b) 50   (c) 16
(d) 10   (e) 8

D5 (a) A H T W = WHAT
(b) U F N = FUN
(c) B G L R A A E = ALGEBRA

D6 40

D7 (a) 32   (b) 8   (c) 25
(d) 41   (e) 9

D8 (a) 8   (b) 27   (c) 1

E *Arrow diagrams* (p 345)

E1 (a) $19; r = 2n + 3$ (b) $31; r = 4n - 1$
(c) $26; r = 3n + 2$ (d) $30; r = 3(n + 2)$

E2 A and K, B and J, C and L

E3 $y = 4x + 1$

F *Using and making formulas* (p 346)

F1 (a) $R = 3L + 2S$ (b) 36 cm

F2 (a) $6a + 4b$ (b) $6ab$

F3 (a) 650   (b) £600
(c) £1200   (d) £0

F4 (a) $^-1$ (b) $2x - 7$

F5 (a) £350   (b) $C = 8n + 100$

F6 (a) 340   (b) $N = 2T + 20$

F7 (a) 30 (b) 60 (c) $N = \dfrac{p}{2} + 10$

Ⓖ **Graphs using formulas** (p 347)

G1 (a) 0.2 m or 20 cm

(b) 2 squares

(c) 4 kg   (d) 6 kg

(e) 4.7 to 4.8 kg   (f) 3 kg

G2 (a)

d	40	45	50	55	60	65
h	120	135	**150**	**165**	**180**	**195**

(b)

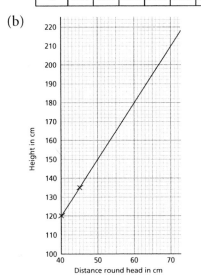

(c) 174 cm   (d) 46 to 47 cm

(e) Yes, probably, as the distance round her head is likely to be 55 cm.

G3 (a) $c = 35 + 10 \times 4 = \mathbf{75}$
The charge is £75.

(b) It will cost £155.

(c)

w	2	4	6	8	10	12
c	55	**75**	**95**	**115**	**135**	**155**

(d)

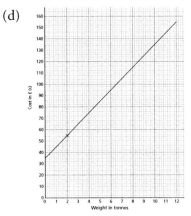

(e) £105   (f) £85

(g) 9.4 to 9.6 tonnes

Test yourself (p 349)

T1 (a) 40   (b) 20   (c) 2
(d) 5   (e) 4

T2 (a) 16   (b) 42   (c) 8
(d) 4   (e) 23

T3 (a) 24 (b) 10 (c) 24 (d) 40
(e) 11 (f) 2 (g) 0 (h) 7

T4 £105

T5 (a) $9x$ (b) $8e + 2f$ (c) $4ef$

T6 (a) 12 (b) 6 (c) 70 (d) 33
(e) 10 (f) 19 (g) 25 (h) 50
(i) 16 (j) 11

T7 (a) 1   (b) 8   (c) 2
(d) 8   (e) 4

T8 (a) 18   (b) $\frac{1}{2}$

T9 £34

T10 (a) £60 (b) £16 (c) $C = 8n + 12$

T11 (a) 8   (b) $\dfrac{x + 7}{3}$

T12 (a)

w	0	2	4	6	8	10
l	16	**20**	**24**	28	**32**	36

(b)

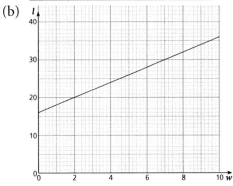

(c) 6.5 kg

Practice book

Section A (p 146)

1

2 (a) 16   (b) 33   (c) 15

    (d) 12   (e) 40   (f) 40

3 (a) 31   (b) 9   (c) 7

    (d) 10   (e) 21   (f) 22

    (g) 15   (h) 25   (i) 60

Sections B and C (p 146)

1 (a) 4   (b) 0   (c) 18

    (d) 35   (e) 27   (f) 17

2 (a) Angle BAC = 40°

    (b) Angle ACB = 40°

    (c) Angle ABC = 100°

3 A: s^2 B: $4ab$ C: $12b$ D: $15a^2$

4

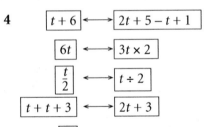

$2t$ is the odd one out.

5 (a) 12   (b) 60   (c) 24   (d) 400

Sections D and E (p 147)

1 (a) 24   (b) 45   (c) 120

    (d) 24   (e) 10

2 (a) 16   (b) 16   (c) 15   (d) 8

3 (a) 9   (b) 18   (c) 100

    (d) 92   (e) 27

4

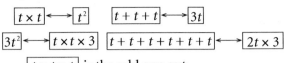

$t \times t \times t$ is the odd one out.

5 (a) (i) 23   (ii) $2n + 3$

    (b) (i) 36   (ii) $3(n + 2)$

    (c) (i) 9   (ii) $\frac{n}{2} + 4$

    (d) (i) 3   (ii) $\frac{n + 2}{4}$

Section F (p 148)

1 (a) 5 metres   (b) $10 - p$ metres

2 (a) $8n$ (b) $n + 8$ (c) $3(n + 8)$

3 (a) £90   (b) £130   (c) £60

4 (a) 39   (b) $7n + 4$

5 (a) 31 matches   (b) 12 squares

Section G (p 149)

1 (a) 6.6 lb   (b) 1.8 kg   (c) 3.2 kg

2 (a)

n	5	10	15	20	25	30
C	70	80	90	100	110	120

    (b)

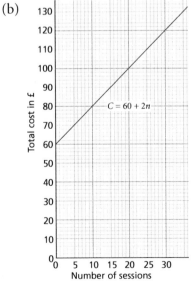

    (c) (i) £84   (ii) £116

    (iii) 19 sessions

Working with percentages

This unit covers finding a percentage of a given amount (sections B and C) and expressing one number as a percentage of another (sections D and E). The unit could be dealt with by tackling the two non-calculator sections B and D first, and then the calculator sections C and E.

Practice book pages 150 to 152

B *In your head* (p 352)

◊ The key facts in this section are that 50% is half, 25% is a quarter and 10% is one tenth. Based on these, many other percentages can be found by pencil and paper methods. So 50% is found by halving, 25% by halving again and the two added together gives 75%.

C *Percentages on a calculator* (p 354)

◊ Three alternative methods are suggested here but it is not intended that all are used. All are essentially the same method with the order of operations changed. It is assumed in the 'On a calculator' descriptions that the operations are carried out in the right order; this may need emphasising, possibly with the use of brackets.

D One number as a percentage of another (p 355)

◊ In expressing one number as a percentage of another without a calculator the key is recognising when to multiply or divide the parts of the fraction. Questions D9 and D10 suggest a method for dealing with some two-part cases but this is probably too much for most students.

E Calculating percentages (p 356)

◊ If method 3 was used in section C students may recognise the decimal equivalents of percentages (i.e. that 0.36 is the same as 36%) and may not need to multiply by 100. Care will need to be taken, however, to avoid mistakes like interpreting 0.9 as 9%.

A Fractions and percentages (p 351)

A1 (a) A and G, B and I, C and E, F and H

　　 (b) The student's sign equivalent to '20% bonus'

A2 (a) 89%　　(b) 7%　　(c) 50%

　　 (d) 25%　　(e) 75%　　(f) 10%

　　 (g) 70%　　(h) 40%

A3 (a) $\frac{37}{100}$ 　　　　(b) $\frac{9}{100}$

　　 (c) $\frac{25}{100} = \frac{1}{4}$ 　　(d) $\frac{30}{100} = \frac{3}{10}$

　　 (e) $\frac{20}{100} = \frac{1}{5}$ 　　(f) $\frac{85}{100} = \frac{17}{20}$

　　 (g) $\frac{16}{100} = \frac{4}{25}$ 　　(h) $\frac{15}{100} = \frac{3}{20}$

A4 (a) $\frac{3}{50} = \frac{6}{100} = $ **6%**

　　 (b) $\frac{12}{25} = \frac{48}{100} = $ **48%**

　　 (c) $\frac{68}{200} = \frac{34}{100} = $ **34%**

　　 (d) $\frac{150}{200} = \frac{75}{100} = $ **75%**

　　 (e) $\frac{7}{20} = \frac{35}{100} = $ **35%**

　　 (f) $\frac{27}{50} = \frac{54}{100} = $ **54%**

B In your head (p 352)

B1 (a) £20　　(b) 42p　　(c) 15 kg

　　 (d) 100 ml　　(e) 35 litres

B2 (a) £4　　(b) 10 kg　　(c) 16p

　　 (d) 125 g　　(e) 7.5 cm

B3 (a) £15　　(b) 60 kg　　(c) 150 ml

　　 (d) 18p　　(e) 13.5 m

B4 (a) £25　　(b) 9 kg

　　 (c) 45 pens　(d) 120 g

B5 (a) £125　　(b) £2000　　(c) £450

B6 (a) £7　　(b) 30 ml　　(c) 15 g

　　 (d) 5 litres　(e) 85p

B7 (a) £6　(b) £12　(c) £54　(d) £24

B8 (a) £18　　(b) 21 kg

　　 (c) 12 g　　(d) 48 g

B9 (a) 60 g　　(b) 50 g　　(c) 75 ml

B10 (a) £4　(b) £2　(c) £6　(d) £14

B11 (a) 12 g　(b) 6 g　(c) 42 g　(d) 102 g

B12 (a) £3　(b) £10　(c) 7 g　(d) 12 ml

B13 (a) 3 kg　　(b) 105 g

　　 (c) 39 eggs　(d) 72 g

B14 25 g

B15 60 g

B16 285 g

B17 (a) 75 g　　(b) 575 g

B18 (a) 25 g   (b) 6 g   (c) 60 g
     (d) 160 g   (e) 60 g   (f) 125 g
     (g) 175 g   (h) 9 g   (i) 105 g

B19 (a) 15%   (b) 60 g

C Percentages on a calculator (p 354)

C1 (a) 72   (b) 185   (c) 154   (d) 396

C2 (a) 17.6   (b) 76.8   (c) 33.6
     (d) 292.4   (e) 40.8   (f) 343.2
     (g) 96.6   (h) 754.4

C3 (a) £19.55   (b) £26.32
     (c) £27.72   (d) £44.82

C4 (a) 33.84 litres   (b) 378 g
     (c) 59.5 ml   (d) 139.5 km

C5 6.3 g

C6 64 g

C7 (a) 90 g   (b) 54 g   (c) 30.1 g
     (d) 40.8 g   (e) 50.4 g   (f) 22.5 g

D One number as a percentage of another (p 355)

D1 (a) 35%   (b) 48%
     (c) 26%   (d) 65%

D2 (a) 75%   (b) 15%
     (c) 65%   (d) 40%

D3 20%

D4 (a) 50%   (b) 30%
     (c) 20%   (d) 80%

D5 (a) 12%   (b) 64%
     (c) 16%   (d) 8%

D6 Mel; Tina scored 60%.

D7 80%

D8 15%

D9 (a) $\frac{60}{80}$ (b) $\frac{3}{4}$ (c) 75%

D10 (a) $\frac{30}{60} = \frac{1}{2} = 50\%$
     (b) $\frac{10}{40} = \frac{1}{4} = 25\%$
     (c) $\frac{33}{60} = \frac{11}{20} = 55\%$
     (d) $\frac{36}{80} = \frac{9}{20} = 45\%$

E Calculating percentages (p 356)

E1 (a) 35%   (b) 28%   (c) 75%
     (d) 65%   (e) 90%   (f) 30%
     (g) 4%   (h) 95%

E2 (a) 65%   (b) 35%

E3 Miriam   85%
    Charles   45%
    Adam   70%
    Tak Man 90%
    Celia   55%

E4 Black   54%
    Blue   18%
    Grey   20%
    Green   8%

E5 (a) (i) 150 m^2 (ii) 21 m^2
     (b) 14%

E6 (a) 56%   (b) 54%   (c) 45%
     (d) 31%   (e) 80%   (f) 43%
     (g) 38%   (h) 52%

E7 Sleeping   33%
    School   29%
    Eating   8%
    Homework   13%
    Television   17%
    Total   **100%**

F Mixed questions (p 357)

F1 (a) 16.5 ml   (b) 13.2 ml

F2 (a) 37.5 g   (b) 137.5 g

F3 (a) 75 m^2 (b) 41.25 m^2 (c) 8%

F4 62% of 4.2 m^2 = 2.6 m^2 (to 1 d.p.)

F5 (a) 80 (b) 41.25% (c) 26.25%

*F6 (a) 25; 36% (b) 24; 29% (c) 49; 51%

Test yourself (p 358)

T1 (a) 75% (b) $\frac{3}{10}$

T2 (a) 95 g (b) 44.8 g

T3 (a) 40% (b) Simon Smith
(c) 14 000

T4 (a) 26 (b) 45%

T5 (a) 75%
(b) Gladiators; the Allstars scored from only 70% of corners.

T6 38.2%

Practice book

Section B (p 150)

1 (a) £6 (b) 16p (c) 9 litres
(d) £17.50 (e) 5.5 m (f) 7.5 kg

2 (a) £75 (b) £350 (c) £600

3 (a) £8 (b) £24 (c) £56 (d) £32

4 (a) £14 (b) £12 (c) 54 g (d) 88 g

5 (a) 10p (b) £9 (c) £140

6 (a) £32 (b) 8 g (c) 54 ml

7 (a) 4.5 kg (b) 180 g (c) £44

8 (a) 35% fat (b) 175 g

9 (a) 15% (b) 68

Section C (p 151)

1 (a) 27 (b) £14.40 (c) 151.2
(d) £16.90 (e) £8.74 (f) 44.64 kg

2 (a) £87 (b) £81 (c) £145.20

3 39 g

4 (a) £6678 (b) £5922

5 (a) £97.92 (b) £57.84

6

A*	A	B	C	D	E	F	G
5	10	35	80	55	40	10	15

Section D (p 151)

1 (a) 48% (b) 55% (c) 28%
(d) 35% (e) 70% (f) 35%

2 24%

3 45%

4 (a) 20% (b) 30% (c) 50% (d) 70%

5 8%

6 (a) $\frac{45}{90} = \frac{1}{2} = 50\%$ (b) $\frac{9}{60} = \frac{3}{20} = 15\%$
(c) $\frac{21}{70} = \frac{3}{10} = 30\%$

Section E (p 152)

1 (a) 8% (b) 75% (c) 16%
(d) 40% (e) 35% (f) 42%

2 (a) 48% (b) 52%

3 English 85% French 88%
Maths 55% Science 80%

4 (a) 73% (b) 86% (c) 39%
(d) 79% (e) 91% (f) 73%

5 CDs 42%
Books 27%
Stationery 13%
Make-up 18%
Total 100%

6 Everyday 22%
Sometimes 35%
Never 43%

48 Coordinates

This unit introduces students to various uses of coordinates, including completing shapes based on geometric information, finding the midpoint of a line segment and using 3-D coordinates. 3-D coordinates will be challenging for many at this level.

Essential	Optional
Sheets G70, G71, G72	Metre rules, chalk or tape
Centimetre squared paper	OHP transparency of sheet G70
Scissors, glue	
Practice book pages 153 and 154	

Ⓐ *Shapes on grids* (p 359)

Some aspects of this topic have been developed in earlier units on shape and symmetry. Students may need reminding about the properties of the different quadrilaterals and denoting lines in the form $x = a$ and $y = a$.

◊ In the initial activity students will need to recognise lines that are parallel. This idea should be familiar from earlier work. When they suggest a point that gives the corner of a rectangle or parallelogram, they could be asked how they know this is true. In some cases they should realise there is a range of points which give the desired shape.

Ⓑ *Midpoints* (p 361)

Sheet G70 (possibly on an OHP transparency)

Stuck in the middle

To introduce this game a copy of sheet G70 could be displayed on an OHP. Students could suggest points, with the teacher or another student placing them on the grid. Keeping a table of results or establishing one once students have played the game themselves will be useful in developing this topic.

First point	Target	Second point
(4, ⁻1)	(3, 1)	(2, 3)

You could add new sets of values, or alternatives for scoring particular targets, and ask students how they know whether they are correct. You could look at methods of calculating the mid-value but this may prove difficult when negative numbers are involved.

B4 It is intended that from B4 onwards students calculate midpoints but some may need to draw a grid to get the answer or to check it.

Side splitting

This is a fairly well-known investigation and should lead to the conclusion that a parallelogram is always formed by joining the bisectors of the sides of any quadrilateral.

ℂ *3-D coordinates* (p 363)

This section introduces simple 3-D coordinates in the positive sector only.

> Sheets G71, G72 (possibly on card)
> Scissors, glue

◊ The grid and accessories provide a simple model to introduce 3-D coordinates. A rod of the kind shown in the first diagram can be made from a drinking straw and fixed with a blob of Blu-tack. The separate rectangle from G72 can be used to show how the z-coordinate simply defines the height the point is above the base plane. The cuboid on G72 is marked with labels at each corner and on three faces so that it can be correctly aligned. A large-scale demonstration model of the grid and cuboid would be a great asset.

In the room

The classroom could be established as a large-scale 3-D coordinate grid by marking off three 'axes', where floor and walls meet, at one-metre intervals. The students could then be asked to give the coordinates of points in the room. Walk around the room holding a small object at different heights and ask students to give you its coordinates.

Ⓐ *Shapes on grids* (p 359)

A1 (a) The student's point N to make MN parallel to FG, e.g. (6, 1)

(b) The student's two points K and L giving a line parallel to EF

A2 (a) The point (3, ⁻2) labelled H

(b) The *x*-axis or $y = 0$

A3 (a) The point (⁻2, ⁻1) labelled L

(b) (⁻2, 2)

(c) The *y*-axis or $x = 0$

A4 (a)

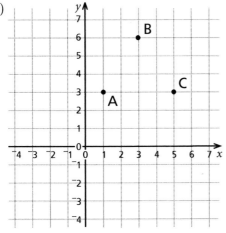

(b) (3, 0)

(c) Any point on the line $x = 3$ where $y < 3$

(d) $x = 3$

A5 (a)

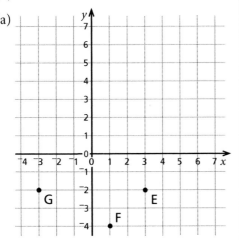

(b) (⁻1, 0)   (c) (1, 0)

(d) The line $y = ⁻2$

A6 (a)

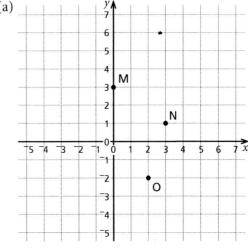

(b) (⁻3, 1) and (⁻2, ⁻2)

Ⓑ *Midpoints* (p 361)

B1 The student's three pairs of coordinates where (6, 5) is exactly in the middle

B2 The student's three pairs of coordinates where (2, ⁻3) is exactly in the middle

B3 (a) 3   (b) 8   (c) 16   (d) 2

(e) 3   (f) 16   (g) $3\frac{1}{2}$ (h) $14\frac{1}{2}$

(i) ⁻3   (j) $⁻3\frac{1}{2}$ (k) $⁻7\frac{1}{2}$ (l) ⁻1

(m) 1   (n) $\frac{1}{2}$ (o) $⁻1\frac{1}{2}$ (p) 2

B4 (a) (4, 5)   (b) (4, 4)

(c) (3, 1)   (d) $(2, 3\frac{1}{2})$

B5 (a) $(4\frac{1}{2}, 1)$ (b) (0, ⁻3)

(c) $(⁻2, \frac{1}{2})$ (d) $(2\frac{1}{2}, 4\frac{1}{2})$

B6 (a), (b), (c)

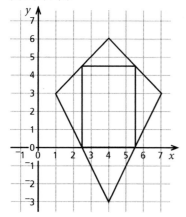

(d) The new shape is a rectangle.

B7 (a), (c)

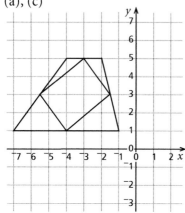

(b) The original shape is a trapezium.

(d) The new shape is a parallelogram.

ℂ **3-D coordinates** (p 363)

C1 (a) F (3, 0, 2)   (b) C (3, 4, 0)
     (c) E (0, 0, 2)   (d) H (3, 4, 2)

C2 (a) B (0, 0, 4)   (b) G (2, 3, 0)
     (c) E (2, 3, 4)   (d) A (0, 3, 4)

C3 (a) G (1, 2, 2)   (b) B (5, 5, 0)
     (c) F (5, 5, 2)   (d) H (1, 5, 2)

C4 A   (0, 1, 1)   B   (2, 2, 1)
     C   (1, 2, 2)   D   (1, 4, 1)
     E   (2, 3, 0)

Test yourself (p 364)

T1 (a)

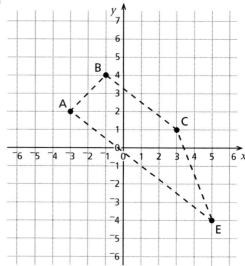

(b) (1, ⁻1) or (5, 3)   (c)   Trapezium

T2 (a)   (1, 1)   (b) $(5, \frac{1}{2})$ (c) $(2, ⁻1\frac{1}{2})$

T3 B (0, 1, 2)   C (1, 4, 1)

Practice book

Section A (p 153)

1 (a) Isosceles triangle (3, 1) (5, 5) (7, 1)
   (b) Kite (7, ⁻2) (7, ⁻4) (5, ⁻4) (2, 1)
   (c) Square (1, 5) (3, 3) (1, 1) (⁻1, 3)
   (d) Parallelogram (⁻4, ⁻1) (⁻1, ⁻1)
        (2, ⁻4) (⁻1, ⁻4)
   (e) Trapezium (⁻5, 1) (⁻5, 4) (⁻3, 4)
        (⁻1, 1)

2 (a) Isosceles triangle
   (b) The student's four points, each with
        4 as the *x*-coordinate
   (c) *x* = 4
   (d) (4, 0)

3 (a), (b), (d)

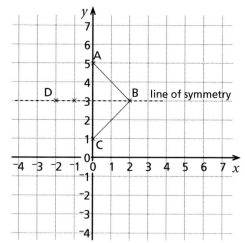

(c) E could be (⁻4, 3), (⁻3, 3) or (⁻1, 3),
for example.

(e) The equation of the line is $y = 3$.

Sections B and C (p 154)

1 (a) (i) (0, 4)   (ii) $(2, 2\frac{1}{2})$

    (iii) $(3\frac{1}{2}, 2\frac{1}{2})$ (iv) $(^-1, 2\frac{1}{2})$

(b) (2, ⁻2)

2 (a)

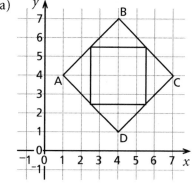

(b) ABCD has area $18\,\text{cm}^2$

(c) Square

(d) $9\,\text{cm}^2$

3 B has coordinates (2, 2, 0).
C has coordinates (3, 2, 1).
D has coordinates (0, 2, 2).

49 Problem solving with a calculator

Practice book pages 155 and 156

Ⓐ **Which calculation?** (p 365)

TG

◊ Matching the calculations to problems can be done either as a class activity or by individuals (as a check on their readiness for the later work in the unit).

◊ The questions in this section are all one-stage problems, or multi-stage problems broken down into steps.

Ⓐ **Which calculation?** (p 365)

A1 $48 \times 27 = 1296$

A2 $405 - 188 = 217$ miles

A3 $420 \div 28 = 15$

A4 $14.6 \times £13.45 = £196.37$

A5 $£600 \div 48 = £12.50$

A6 $£6.75 \div £0.27 = 25$

A7 (a) £17.60   (b) £2.20

A8 (a) £4.50   (b) £2.20   (c) 55p

A9 (a) £7.05   (b) £2.76   (c) 4

A10 (a) £84.50   (b) £7.25

Ⓑ **Showing working** (p 367)

B1 7 adults cost $7 \times £19 = £133$
15 children cost $15 \times £13 = £195$
Total cost = £328

B2 Cost of desk and chair =
$£57.95 + £24.75 = £82.70$
Cost of lamp =
$£101.25 - £82.70 = £18.55$
Or: Cost of lamp =
$£101.25 - £57.95 - £24.75 = £18.55$

B3 (a) $73 + 89 + 112 = 274$ miles
(b) $274 \times £0.34 = £93.16$

B4 Total cost = £72.40
Each person pays £9.05

B5 Cost of paint = £58.68
Total cost of wallpaper =
£93.60 − £58.68 = £34.92
Each roll of wallpaper cost
£34.92 ÷ 9 = £3.88

B6 (a) Total cost of ingredients = £39.05
Money taken = 24 × £3.75 = £90.00
Profit = £90.00 − £39.05 = £50.95

(b) Dried fruit for one cake cost
£13.20 ÷ 24 = £0.55

B7 Cost of felt-tips =
£11.42 − £3.49 − £2.75 = £5.18
Number bought = 5.18 ÷ 0.37 = 14

B8 Normal cost =
2 × £14.80 + 3 × £8.20 = £54.20
Cost with Railcard =
£20 + 2 × £9.90 + 3 × £2.00 = £45.80
Amount saved = £54.20 − £45.80 = £8.40

ℂ **Changing money** (p 368)

C1 (a) 278.40 Canadian dollars
(b) £31.68

C2 (a) £79.97 Swiss francs (b) £37.27

C3 (a) 11 392 yen (b) £4.78

C4 (a) 708 dollars (b) £288.14

𝔻 **Comparing costs** (p 369)

D1 Steve paid 64p per disk.
Sheila paid 65p per disk.
Steve got the better bargain.

D2 1 kg from the smaller bag costs £1.50.
1 kg from the larger bag costs £1.54
(to nearest penny).
So the smaller (3.5 kg) bag gives you
more for your money, because 1 kg costs
less.

D3 (a) £0.93 (b) £0.90 (c) £0.88
(d) The 1.5 litre bottle

D4 (a) 2.4 g (b) 2.5 g
(c) The big pack, because you get more
for 1p

D5 1 kg from the bag costs 24p,
1 kg from the sack costs 19p,
so 5p is saved.

D6 (a) 29p (b) 23p (c) £3.50

Test yourself (p 370)

T1 51p

T2 1956 − 1742 = 214 units used
214 × 41p = £87.74
92 × 7p = £6.44
Total bill = £94.18

T3 Cost of 12 copies, one a month =
12 × £2.99 = £35.88
Cost of 4 times 3 months =
4 × £5.49 = £21.96
Saving = £13.92

T4 (a) 495 NZ dollars (b) £23.90

T5 Yum grams per penny =
227 ÷ 27 = 8.4 (to 1 d.p.)
Core grams per penny =
432 ÷ 52 = 8.3 (to 1 d.p.)
Yum gives more grams per penny.

Practice book

Section A (p 155)

1 (a) £27.54 (b) £4.59

2 (a) £41.40 (b) £10.35

3 (a) £8.33 (b) 7

Section B (p 155)

1 (a) £6.87 (b) 31

2 £2.49

3 16.5 miles

Section C (p 156)

1. 124 dollars

2. £116.24

3. (a) 13 190 rupees   (b) £26.74

4. £81.42

Section D (p 156)

1. 1 glass in A costs 45p, in B 47.5p, so A is better.

2. 1 bag in A costs 3.5p, in B 3.2p, so B is better.

3. 1 litre in Greenfingers costs £1.30.
   1 litre in Ace of Spades costs £1.24.
   So Ace of Spades is better.

4. 50 ml in the 200 ml bottle costs 45p.
   50 ml in the 350 ml bottle costs 42p.
   So the 350 ml bottle is better value.

5. (a) Golden charges £8.75, Silver £8.40, so Silver is cheaper.

   (b) Golden charges £11.75, Silver £12.60, so Golden is cheaper.

50 Brackets

Essential

Sheets G73, G74

Practice book pages 157 to 160

B *Expressions with brackets* (p 372)

◊ Use the introduction to explain why $3(n + 2) = 3n + 6$.

An arithmetical shortcut that may help some students understand how to expand brackets is

$$3 \times 99 = 3(100 - 1) = 3 \times 100 - 3 \times 1$$
or $\quad 3 \times 102 = 3(100 + 2) = 3 \times 100 + 3 \times 2$

You could also appeal to the idea of area:

	a	3
4	$4a$	12

$4(a + 3) = 4a + 12$

C *Factorising* (p 373)

◊ Emphasise that, when factorising, we are looking for a number (or a letter in section D) that will divide into each term of the expression to be factorised. Of course the common factor may involve both a number and a letter, but at Foundation level this is unlikely.

◊ There are a number of unwritten rules when factorising, and you may wish to make some of these explicit.

- While it is true that $12a - 16 = 2(6a - 8)$, the expression has not been *fully* factorised. We generally expect the largest whole number possible outside the brackets.
- It is also true that $12a - 18 = 12(a - 1\frac{1}{2})$, but in factorising it is understood that only whole numbers are to be used.

E Simplifying (p 375)

Sheet G73

G Mixed examples (p 376)

Sheet G74

A Review (p 371)

A1 (a) 6   (b) 20   (c) 14   (d) 10
    (e) 2   (f) 3   (g) 8   (h) 2
    (i) 4   (j) 6

A2 (a) $3u$ (b) $2v + 4$ (c) $2w + 8$
    (d) $2u + 2$ (e) $3v + 2$ (f) $3w + 7$

A3 (a) $11a$ (b) $8b + 14$ (c) $4c + 8$
    (d) $6d + 7$ (e) $4e + 3$ (f) $3f + 3$

A4 (a) $6a + 8b$ (b) $7b + 3c + 10$
    (c) $7c + 8d + 4$ (d) $7d + 4e - 1$
    (e) $14e + 3f$ (f) $7f + 5g + 5h$

A5 (a) $6a + 4b$ (b) $9p + 3$
    (c) $3r + 3s + 15$

A6 (a) $11x$ (b) $9y - 4$

A7 $5x + 10y$

A8 (a) n^2 (b) $2a^2$ (c) $6s^2$
    (d) $5k^2$ (e) $20u^2$

A9 (a) $2xy$ (b) $3ab$ (c) $6st$
    (d) uv (e) $20uv$

B Expressions with brackets (p 372)

B1 $2(x + 4) = 2x + 8$; $2x + 4 = 2(x + 2)$;
$2(x + 8) = 2x + 16$
The odd one left over is $2(x + 16)$.

B2 $3a + 18 = 3(a + 6)$; $3(a - 2) = 3a - 6$;
$3a - 18 = 3(a - 6)$
The odd one left over is $3a - 2$.

B3 (a) $2x + 10$ (b) $3y + 9$ (c) $5p - 30$
    (d) $70 + 10q$ (e) $4v - 20$

B4 (a) $6x + 12$ (b) $8y - 6$ (c) $6 + 18p$
    (d) $6 - 18p$ (e) $40 - 24v$

B5 (a) $2(a + 6) = 2a + \mathbf{12}$
    (b) $\mathbf{3}(b + 2) = 3b + 6$
    (c) $4(c + \mathbf{5}) = 4c + 20$

C Factorising (p 373)

C1 (a) 4   (b) 2   (c) 12   (d) 7

C2 (a) $6a + 8 = \mathbf{2}(3a + 4)$
    (b) $10b - 15 = \mathbf{5}(2b - 3)$
    (c) $14c + 6 = \mathbf{2}(7c + 3)$

C3 (a) $2(x + 4)$ (b) $3(y + 3)$
(c) $5(p - 3)$ (d) $4(5 + q)$
(e) $12(v - 2)$

C4 (a) $3(2x + 3)$ (b) $4(2x + 3)$
(c) $5(5 - 3x)$ (d) $3(3x + 4)$
(e) $4(2x - 7)$

C5 ORANGE

C6 (a) ROSE   (b) CROCUS
(c) SNOWDROP

Ⓓ *More letters* (p 374)

D1 (a) $a(a + 4) = a^2 + \mathbf{4a}$
(b) $b(2b - 3) = 2b^2 - \mathbf{3b}$
(c) $c(1 + c) = c + \mathbf{c^2}$

D2 (a) $n^2 + 3n$ (b) $m^2 - 4m$
(c) $r + 2r^2$ (d) $4s^2 - 3s$
(e) $3x^2 + 4x$ (f) $3y - 5y^2$

D3 (a) $4v^2 + 20v$ (b) $2w^2 - 8w$
(c) $2x^2 + 2x$ (d) $6y - 3y^2$

D4 $n(2n + 3) = 2n^2 + 3n$
$n^2 + n = n(n + 1)$
$n(3n + 2) = 3n^2 + 2n$
Odd one: $n(2n + 1) = 2n^2 + n$

D5 (a) $n(\mathbf{n} + 2) = n^2 + 2n$
(b) $\mathbf{n}(n + 3) = n^2 + 3n$
(c) $n(n + \mathbf{4}) = n^2 + 4n$

D6 (a) $m(m + 9)$ (b) $n(n - 5)$
(c) $x(2x + 1)$ (d) $y(3y - 5)$
(e) $p(3 + 4p)$ (f) $q(2 - 5q)$
(g) $v(v + 4)$ (h) $w(4w - 1)$

D7 (a) $2a + 2b$ (b) $3f - 3e$
(c) $8g + 4h$ (d) $3k - 9g$
(e) $8h + 12j$ (f) $10w + 5u$

D8 (a) $3(a + b)$ (b) $3(g - 2h)$
(c) $7(k + 2l)$ (d) $5(w + 3z)$

Ⓔ *Simplifying* (p 375)

E1 (a) $3z + 19$ (b) $10b + 25$
(c) $5x + 16$ (d) $5y + 12$
(e) $8a - 18$ (f) $2c + 8$

E2 (a) $7x + 8$ (b) $15w + 8$
(c) $6z + 25$ (d) $8u - 6$
(e) $2 - 20v$ (f) $36w + 2$

E3 P and R, Q and U, S and T

E4 (a) $5a + 12$ (b) $6b + 2$
(c) $10c + 2$

E5 ELEPHANT
GIRAFFE
TIGER

Ⓕ *Subtracting* (p 375)

F1 (a) $13 - a$ (b) $6b - 5$ (c) $16 - c$
(d) $3d + 2$ (e) $11 - 3e$ (f) $8f - 8$

F2 (a) $6 - 2n$ (b) $4n + 6$ (c) $20 - 5n$
(d) $5n - 6$ (e) $11n - 6$ (f) $3n$

F3 (a) $x + 3$ (b) $h + 9$ (c) $j - 5$
(d) $2x + 9$ (e) $y + 22$ (f) $2z + 4$

F4 $3(x + 2) - 2(x + 1)$ is the odd one out.

Ⓖ *Mixed examples* (p 376)

G1 (a) $3s + 12$ (b) $2a - 6$ (c) $8 + 4t$
(d) $10u - 20$ (e) $8e + 12$

G2 (a) $3(r + 2)$ (b) $5(s - 5)$
(c) $2(3a + 4)$ (d) $2(2 - 3u)$
(e) $6(3t + 2)$

G3 (a) $s(s + 4)$ (b) $d(d + 3)$
(c) $h(h - 8)$ (d) $h(4h - 1)$
(e) $6j(j + 1)$

G4 (a) $2a$ (b) $2b^2$ (c) $4c$
(d) $6a$ (e) $2a^2$

G5 (a) $5f + 8$ (b) $3a + 6$
     (c) $15 - 5b$ (d) $10g - 12$
     (e) $10 - t$ (f) $11u - 4$
     (g) $12 - 3s$ (h) $2a + 19$

G6 (a) $4s + 3t$ (b) $5a + 6b$ (c) $5n$

G7 (a) (i) $3a$ (ii) $7p$ (iii) $5s + 4t$
     (b) $4m + 6$

G8 (a) $9a$ (b) $b = 8$

G9 (a) $2a + 6b$ (b) $a + 4$

G10 (a) $6p$ (b) $4s + 2t$ (c) $4m + 12$

G11 (a) $5x - 20$ (b) $3x - x^2$

*G12 COMPUTER
GRAPH
SYMMETRY

Test yourself (p 377)

T1 (a) $3d + 12$ (b) $5u - 10$
     (c) $4s + 8$ (d) $6 - 2y$

T2 (a) $6e + 4$ (b) $18p - 12$
     (c) $6w + 3$ (d) $3 - 6w$

T3 (a) $3(x + 2)$ (b) $7(a - 2)$
     (c) $6(1 + 2b)$ (d) $5(1 - 2t)$

T4 (a) $2a + 14$ (b) $6a + 6$
     (c) $8 - t$ (d) $4x + 3$
     (e) $9a - 6$ (f) $12a + 18$
     (g) $2v - 8$ (h) $6h + 12$

T5 (a) $d^2 + 2d$ (b) $u^2 - 4u$
     (c) $2h^2 + 3h$ (d) $3j^2 - 7j$
     (e) $3s + 6t$ (f) $4d - 12w$
     (g) $6e - 6f$ (h) $15k + 10g$

T6 (a) $x(x + 6)$ (b) $a(a - 14)$
     (c) $6(a + 2b)$ (d) $5(s - 2t)$

T7 (a) (i) $5x$ (ii) $3x$ (iii) $3y^2$
     (b) (i) $4x + 4y$ (ii) $5x - 10y$

T8 (a) $5x - 20$ (b) $6x + 3$

Practice book

Section A (p 157)

1 (a) 12 (b) 15 (c) 18
     (d) 9 (e) 6 (f) 15
     (g) 4 (h) 0 (i) 21
     (j) 28

2 (a) $4p$ (b) $2p + 3$ (c) $3q + 5$
     (d) $q + 1$ (e) $3r + 6$

3 (a) $8a$ (b) $7b + 4$ (c) $3c + 5$
     (d) $d + 4$ (e) $7e + 2$ (f) $f + 4$

4 (a) $4r + 6s$ (b) $7s + 2t + 5$
     (c) $4t + 10u$ (d) $5u + 2v + 3$
     (e) $9w$

5 (a) $8x + 4y$ (b) $5z + 2$
     (c) $c + 7d + 7$ (d) $4t + 8$
     (e) $8r + 3s + 2$

6 (a) a^2 (b) $3b^2$ (c) $10c^2$
     (d) $7d^2$ (e) $36e^2$

7 (a) $2fg$ (b) $5hj$ (c) $21kl$
     (d) mn (e) $35pq$

Sections B and C (p 158)

1 $5(c + 1) = 5c + 5$
     $5(c + 2) = 5c + 10$
     $5c + 50 = 5(c + 10)$
     $5c + 2$ is the one left over.

2 (a) $2a + 6$ (b) $4b - 20$ (c) $8c - 16$
     (d) $20 + 5d$ (e) $7e - 21$

3 (a) $10a + 15$ (b) $6b - 8$
     (c) $14 + 21c$ (d) $12d - 3$
     (e) $45e + 63$

4 (a) $4(3v - 8) = 12v - \mathbf{32}$
     (b) $\mathbf{2}(3w + 5) = 6w + 10$
     (c) $5(x - \mathbf{4}) = 5x - 20$

5 (a) $4a + 6 = \mathbf{2}(2a + 3)$

   (b) $15b - 12 = \mathbf{3}(5b - 4)$

   (c) $40 + 70c = \mathbf{10}(4 + 7c)$

6 (a) $2(p + 6)$ (b) $3(q + 2)$ (c) $6(r + 1)$

   (d) $7(s - 2)$ (e) $5(t + 4)$

7 (a) $2(2u + 5)$ (b) $3(2v - 3)$

   (c) $5(2w + 1)$ (d) $5(3x - 2)$

   (e) $2(6y + 1)$

8 (a) $4(2a + 1)$ (b) $5(2b - 5)$

   (c) $4(4c - 3)$ (d) $5(4d + 5)$

   (e) $8(3e - 4)$

9 (a) $5(2x + 3)$ $3(2x + 1)$ NAIL

   (b) $2(x + 1)$ $3(x + 2)$ $6(x + 2)$
      HAMMER

   (c) $6(2x + 1)$ $2(3x + 2)$ $4(2x + 3)$
      CHISEL

Sections D and E (p 159)

1 (a) $x(x + 5) = x^2 + \mathbf{5x}$

   (b) $y(y - 7) = \mathbf{y^2} - 7y$

   (c) $z(3z - 2) = 3z^2 - \mathbf{2z}$

2 (a) $a^2 + 9a$ (b) $b^2 - 6b$

   (c) $4c + c^2$ (d) $3d^2 + 5d$

   (e) $e - 2e^2$ (f) $10f^2 - 9f$

3 $c(2c + 1) = 2c^2 + c$

  $2c^2 + 5c = c(2c + 5)$

  $c(3c + 5) = 3c^2 + 5c$

  One left over: $c(c + 1) = c^2 + c$

4 (a) $s(s + 4)$ (b) $t(t - 9)$

   (c) $v(7 + v)$ (d) $x(x + 8)$

   (e) $y(y + 5)$ (f) $z(12 + z)$

   (g) $u(2u + 3)$ (h) $w(3 - 5w)$

5 (a) $3c + 3d$ (b) $2x - 2y$

   (c) $10r + 5t$ (d) $12g - 8h$

   (e) $8p - 14q$ (f) $30m + 24n$

6 (a) $4(u + v)$ (b) $2(a + 4b)$

   (c) $5(m - 4n)$ (d) $3(3c + 4d)$

7 (a) $2a + 10$ (b) $3 + 5b$ (c) $5c + 12$

   (d) $5d + 12$ (e) $5e + 8$ (f) $3f - 15$

8 (a) $11u + 3$ (b) $9 + 15v$

   (c) $10w + 24$ (d) $20x$

   (e) $2y + 8$ (f) $31z - 30$

9 (a) $8c + 7$ (b) $4 + 20d$ (c) $29e - 3$

Sections F and G (p 160)

1 (a) $11 - a$ (b) $11 - b$ (c) $3c + 3$

   (d) $4d - 7$ (e) $5 + 4e$ (f) $13f - 3$

2 (a) $9 - 2m$ (b) $6n + 6$ (c) $12p - 20$

   (d) $2 - 4q$ (e) $11r + 10$ (f) $3s - 4$

3 (a) $2g + 3$ (b) $4h + 18$ (c) $22 + 2j$

   (d) $3k + 41$ (e) $10l - 2$ (f) $7m - 2$

4 $(4x - 3) - 2(x - 1)$ is the odd one out.

5 (a) $4a + 28$ (b) $5b - 30$ (c) $18c + 2$

   (d) $18 - 12d$ (e) $35e + 14$

6 (a) $5(r + 4)$ (b) $4(t - 2)$

   (c) $3(3v + 1)$ (d) $2(4w + 3)$

   (e) $4(5x - 2)$

7 (a) $t(t - 5)$ (b) $k(k + 10)$

   (c) $k(5k + 8)$ (d) $c(6c + 1)$

   (e) $k(3k - 7)$

8 (a) $2a$ (b) $4b^2$ (c) $3x$

   (d) $5y^2$ (e) $3z^2$

9 (a) $7a + 4$ (b) $5b + 5$ (c) $9c - 6$

   (d) $3 + 3d$ (e) $6e - 12$ (f) $13 - f$

   (g) $2g + 4$ (h) $3h + 9$

10 (a) $3a + 2b$ (b) $5x + 2y$ (c) $6p - 3q$

51 Navigation

This unit reviews earlier work on scale drawing and compass directions and introduces four-figure grid references and bearings.

Essential	Optional
Sheets G75, G76, G77, G78, G79, G80, G81, G82 Angle measurers **Practice book** pages 161 and 162	String

A *Grid references* (p 378)

> Optional: string

◊ Some examination boards require the use of four-figure references and students will need to know the convention that the reference refers to the square to the right and above the given lines. Only questions A1 and A2 specifically require the use of these. Some students may already be familiar with six-figure references.

This section also revises the use of

• Simple scales – students can use paper to mark the distance between two points and then measure against the grid squares. A piece of string or the edge of a piece of paper can also be used to measure curved distances like those in questions A6 and A7.

• Compass directions – the eight-pointed rose is used.

B *Scales* (p 380)

> Sheets G75, G76, G77, G78

Ⓓ *Bearings* (p 383)

> Sheets G79, G80, G81
> Ruler, angle measurer

The important point to emphasise is that bearings are always measured from a 'north line' through the point the bearing is measured from. Where a grid is used on the map it is not usually difficult to establish the north line from a point. In some exam questions students may be asked to draw a north line without a grid and they may need to be reminded of how to draw lines parallel to a marked north line or other line.

Seeing from the Eye

The sides of the map on sheet G80 run north-south, though you could point out that this isn't always true of city maps. Information can be obtained from British Airways, who manage the London Eye, about what can be seen from the top. Webcams at sites such as the Tyne Bridge offer other opportunities for similar localised work. www.multimap.com provides maps of local areas with key features.

Tower Bridge is 3 km from the Eye. Students could use this to get the approximate scale of the map and hence the distances to the other features.

Test yourself (p 386)

> Sheet G82
> Angle measurer

Ⓐ *Grid references* (p 378)

A1 (a) Hynish   (b) Ruaig
   (c) Ballevullin   (d) Scarinish

A2 (a) 1445 and 1545
   (b) 1044   (c) 0840
   (d) 1548

A3 (a) North   (b) East
   (c) West   (d) South-west
   (e) North-west   (f) North-east

A4 (a) South   (b) South-west
   (c) North-east   (d) South-east

A5 (a) 7 km   (b) 5 km
   (c) 8 km   (d) 13 km

A6 11 or 12 km

A7 Roughly 60 km

A8 (a) Loch à Phuill
   (b) Balephetrish Bay
   (c) Loch Bhasapoll
   (d) Gott Bay

A9 (a) 3 km north
   (b) 12 km south-west
   (c) 6 km north-east

B Scales (p 380)

B1 9 m by 15 m

B2 (a) 7 m by 5 m   (b) 6 m by 4 m

     (c) 4.5 m by 4 m   (d) 2.5 m by 2 m

B3 (a) Rectangle around door 4 cm by 2 cm

     (b) Rectangle in living room
        4 cm by 6 cm

     (c) Rectangle in bedroom
        2 cm by 1.5 cm

     (d) Rectangle in dining room
        1 cm by 2 cm

B4 (a) 35 m   (b) 55 m   (c) 170 m

B5 (a) 210 m   (b) 105   (c) £1575

B6 A rectangle 2 cm by 1 cm running along
the edge of the car park

B7 (a) East   (b) North-west

     (c) South-west   (d) North

B8 (a) 400 km   (b) 550 km

     (c) 250 km   (d) 1000 km

B9 All of the cities but not Land's End or
John o'Groats

B10 (a) Butter Lump

     (b) Long Bay

     (c) White Bay

     (d) Skate Point/Gavin's Glen

B11 1 km

B12 (a) 2 km   (b) 6 km

     (c) 4.5 km   (d) 3 km

B13 (a) Aird Hill

     (b) Butter Lump

     (c) Doughend Hole

     (d) Sheanawally Point

C Using angles (p 382)

C1 (a) 90°   (b) 180°   (c) 270°

     (d) 30°   (e) 210°   (f) 240°

C2 (a) Angle is between 90° and 180°

     (b) Angle is between 180° and 270°

     (c) Angle is between 270° and 360°

     (d) Angle is between 0° and 90°

     (e) Angle is between 180° and 270°

C3 (a) 270°   (b) 180°

     (c) 135°   (d) 315°

C4 (a) East   (b) North-east

     (c) South-west

C5

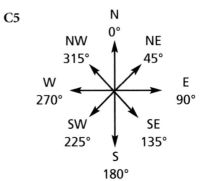

D Bearings (p 383)

Note: bearings may be given ± 2°
from those given here.

D1 (a) 037°   (b) 111°   (c) 222°

D2 (a) 152°   (b) 261°   (c) 111°

D3 (a) E   (b) D   (c) B

D4 (a) 10 km   (b) 21 km   (c) 25 km

D5 (a) 8 km on a bearing of 150°

     (b) 24 km on a bearing of 242°

     (c) 22 km on a bearing of 082°

     (d) 8 km on a bearing of 357°

     (e) 9 km on a bearing of 105°

     (f) 16 km on a bearing of 308°

D6 and **D7**

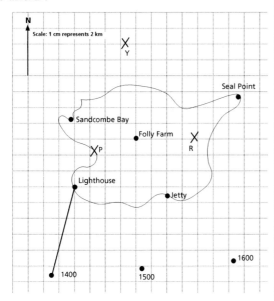

D7 (e) 133°   (f) 12 km

Test yourself (p 386)

T1 (a) 4223

   (b) (i) North-west   (ii) 36 km

T2 (a) 2.4 km

   (b)

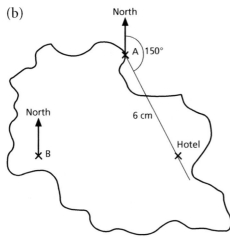

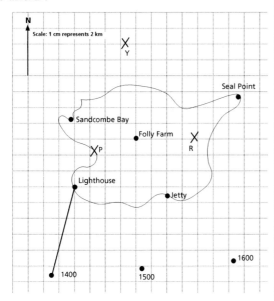

Practice book

Section B (p 161)

1 (a) (i) 4 m   (ii) 6 m

      (iii) 13 m   (iv) 5 m

   (b) 1.5 cm

   (c) (i) 18 m   (ii) 6   (iii) £33.00

2 (a) (i) 25 km   (ii) 20 km   (iii) 15 km

   (b) Lighthouse

   (c) 15 km

   (d) North west

Section D (p 162)

1 16 km

2 E

3 032°

4 190°

5 (a) 10 km   (b) 16 km   (c) 6 km

   (d) 087°   (e) 169°

6 D

7 289°

52 Pie charts

Most examination boards encourage the use of an angle measurer to draw pie charts, while others favour the use of a pie chart scale (and percentages). Hence, section D provides work on drawing pie charts where the numbers are convenient for working with 360° and in section E the numbers are convenient for working with 100%.

Many students find a pie chart scale with percentages useful when handling real data and we recommend it for this.

TG
TG
TG
TG

Essential

Sheet G83
Angle measurers or pie chart scales
Compasses

Practice book pages 163 to 167

B *Reading pie charts, simple fractions and percentages* (p 388)

Angle measurers

C Reading pie charts: the unitary method (p 390)

> Angle measurers

◊ The example on the page shows the unitary method of working out what is represented by 1° each time. It can be used in all cases although you need to emphasise that any rounding is only done at the very end of a calculation. For example, if you were trying to figure out what was represented by an angle of 75° where the whole chart represented 24 hours, working out what 1° represents leads to $24 \div 360 = 0.0666666...$ which musn't be rounded.

It is possible to work out that 1 hour is represented by $360° \div 24 = 15°$ and then do $75 \div 15$ to get 5 hours. But students often find it difficult to know what to do with the 15 and will multiply instead (or divide but do it the wrong way round)!

If they stick to the method of working out what 1° stands for first by dividing by 360°, then *multiplying* by the size of the angles is always the correct operation.

The remaining angles for the other sectors are: have a drink – 70°, watch TV – 140°, other – 30°, start homework – 40°. Students can measure and work out the numbers for the other sectors.

C3 Using the method outlined above leads to 1° representing 0.2 ducks. However, some students will quite naturally work out that 1 duck is represented by 5°. Some can consider this alternative method and *divide* the angles by 5 to work out the number of ducks. Others may well find it confusing and for reading pie charts are best encouraged to stick to the method of finding what is represented by 1° and then multiplying.

D Drawing pie charts: angles (p 392)

This section is for students preparing for an examination where angle measurers are used.

> Angle measurers, sheet G83

◊ The method on the page is again a unitary method where you work out what angle is represented by 1 of whatever units you are dealing with.

Here we have a total of £20 so we need to work out what angle represents £1. One advantage of this method is that again we end up multiplying to find the angles.

We could of course work the other way round, working out what is represented by 1°, but this leads to divisions to work out angles, which students find harder to understand and do in the correct order.

◊ Students can be confused about which way round to do the initial division; use of the 'arrow diagrams' can help. If they know the angles (when reading pie charts) then they need to find what is represented by 1 degree and the angles can be placed on the left. For example:

$$\div 360 \left\{ \begin{array}{l} 360° \\ \\ 1° \\ \\ 80° \end{array} \right. \times 80 \qquad \begin{array}{l} \text{shows} \\ \text{shows} \\ \text{shows} \end{array} \qquad \begin{array}{l} 90 \\ \\ ? \\ \\ ? \end{array} \left. \right\} \div 360 \\ \left. \right\} \times 80$$

If they know, say, the amounts of money (when drawing pie charts) for each sector then they need to find what angle represents £1 and the amounts of money can be placed on the left. For example:

$$\div 20 \left\{ \begin{array}{l} £20 \\ \\ £1 \\ \\ £8 \end{array} \right. \times 8 \qquad \begin{array}{l} \text{is shown by} \\ \text{is shown by} \\ \text{is shown by} \end{array} \qquad \begin{array}{l} 360° \\ \\ ? \\ \\ ? \end{array} \left. \right\} \div 20 \\ \left. \right\} \times 8$$

E *Drawing pie charts: percentages* (p 394)

This section is for students preparing for an examination where pie chart scales are used.

Pie chart scales

◊ The example on the page is again a unitary method where you work out what percentage is equivalent to 1 of whatever units you are dealing with.

Here we have a total of £20 so we need to work out what percentage is equivalent to £1. One advantage of this method is that again we end up multiplying to find the percentages for the sectors.

We could of course work the other way round, working out what is represented by 1%, but this leads to divisions to work out the total percentages which students find harder to understand and do in the correct order.

F *Handling real data* (p 396)

Students tackle problems where the total frequency is not a convenient multiple or factor of 360 or 100, which is very likely to happen in their own data handling projects. They can either work with angles and use the memory facility in their calculators to avoid error or use percentages (with or without use of a pie chart scale).

Beth's data leads to percentages and angles that add up to 100% and 360°, but Geeta's does not. This gives the opportunity to think about what to do if the totals are not exactly 100% or 360°.

> Pie chart scales or angle measurers

◊ In analysing data as part of a project, students may well convert their results to percentages and then want to present their results as pie charts. Using a pie chart scale in this case will simplify their work considerably. If a pie chart scale is not available, students can turn their (unrounded) percentages into angles by finding those percentages of 360°.

◊ Beth's data leads to the following percentages and angles.

Number of people	Percentage	Angle
8	17%	63°
10	22%	78°
23	50%	180°
5	11%	39°
Totals 46	100%	360°

◊ Geeta's data leads to the following percentages and angles.

Number of people	Percentage	Angle
5	8%	30°
11	18%	65°
43	70%	254°
2	3%	12°
Totals 61	99%	361°

Point out that, due to rounding errors, the sum of the percentages is not 100% or the sum of the angles is not 360°. When this happens the simplest solution is to adjust the largest sector by 1% or 1°.

A *Review* (p 387)

A1 (a) $\frac{1}{2}$ (b) 50%

A2 (a) $\frac{1}{4}$ (b) 25%

A3 $\frac{1}{6}$

A4 (a) $\frac{1}{3}$ (b) 150° (c) 25%

A5 (a) 120 (b) 90   (c) 40   (d) 20

A6 800 students

A7 (a) 45   (b) 60   (c) 120

A8 (a) 52   (b) 140   (c) 392

B *Reading pie charts, simple fractions and percentages* (p 388)

B1 (a) Mint   (b) $\frac{1}{4}$ (c) 150
       (d) $\frac{1}{3}$ (e) 200   (f) 120°
       (g) 200   (h) 50

B2 (a) 120°   (b) $\frac{1}{3}$ (c) 8 hours

   (d) (i) Sleeping   120°   8
           In paid work   90°   6
           Looking after her son 60°   4
           Household jobs   45°   3
           Watching TV   30°   2
           Other   15°   1

       (ii) 8 + 6 + 4 + 3 + 2 + 1 = 24

B3 (a) In school   (b) 25%
   (c) $\frac{1}{6}$

B4 (a) £2400
   (b) (i) 120°   (ii) £800

B5 (a) $\frac{1}{3}$
   (b) (i) 320   (ii) 80

C *Reading pie charts: the unitary method* (p 390)

C1 (a) UK   (b) 2 cars
   (c) (i) 80° (ii) 160
   (d) (i) 190 (ii) 110 (iii) 240 (iv) 20

C2 (a) Blue
   (b) (i) 105° (ii) 84 people
   (c) (i) 120   (ii) 48   (iii) 24

C3 (a) $\frac{1}{2}$ (b) 72   (c) 20
   (d) (i) 25°   (ii) 5

C4 (a) $\frac{1}{3}$ (b) 1836   (c) 357

D *Drawing pie charts: angles* (p 392)

D1 (a) 18   (b) 20°   (c) 80°
   (d) The student's labelled pie chart with sectors
       Brown   200°
       Blue   80°
       Green   60°
       Grey   20°

D2 The student's labelled pie chart with sectors
       Ford   160°
       Rover   100°
       Vauxhall   60°
       BMW   40°

D3 The student's labelled pie chart with sectors
       A   90°
       E   45°
       I   75°
       O   120°
       U   30°

D4 The student's labelled pie chart with sectors
       Muesli   80°
       Weeta Bites   60°
       Cornflakes   120°
       Other cereals 100°

D5 (a) The student's completed table with frequencies

Gym	12
Swimming	3
Squash	6
Aerobics	9

(b) The student's labelled pie chart with sectors

Gym	144°
Swimming	36°
Squash	72°
Aerobics	108°

D6 (a) The student's labelled pie chart with sectors

Soccer	148°
Rugby	50°
Cricket	36°
Basketball	74°
Other	52°

(b) 21

E Drawing pie charts: percentages
(p 394)

E1 The student's labelled pie chart with sectors

Water	1%
Protein	5%
Fat	29%
Carbohydrate	65%

E2 (a) 25   (b) 4%   (c) 32%

(d) The student's labelled pie chart with sectors

Brown	52%
Blue	32%
Green	12%
Grey	4%

E3 (a) The student's labelled pie chart with sectors

Apple	16%
Orange	12%
Banana	40%
Grapes	18%
Other	14%

(b) The student's comment, for example: 'Bananas are the most popular fruit for both boys and girls.'

(c) The student's comment, for example: 'A higher percentage of the girls liked grapes best.'

E4 (a) 5493

(b) The student's labelled pie chart with sectors

Vehicle occupants	48%
Pedestrians	30%
Cyclists	12%
Motorcyclists	10%

F Handling real data (p 396)

F1 (a) The student's labelled pie chart with sectors

Ready salted	50° or 14%
Salt and vinegar	120° or 33%
Cheese and onion	154° or 43%
Other	36° or 10%

(b) The student's pie chart and comments

F2 (a) 27

(b) The student's labelled pie chart with sectors

Apple	67° or 19%
Banana	133° or 37%
Orange	40° or 11%
Grape	80° or 22%
Other	40° or 11%

F3 The student's labelled pie chart with sectors

Couple	285° or 79%
Widowed etc. mother	43° or 12%
Single mother	25° or 7%
Lone father	7° or 2%

F4 The student's labelled pie chart with sectors

Detached house	76° or 21%
Semi-detached house	115° or 32%
Terraced house	97° or 27%
Flat or maisonette	72° or 20%

Test yourself (p 397)

T1 (a) Overslept (b) 8

T2 The student's labelled pie chart with sectors

Have own	108° or 30%
Share	72° or 20%
Use only in school	120° or 33%
Never use	60° or 17%

T3 The student's labelled pie chart with sectors

National daily newspapers	170° or 47%
Echo	120° or 33%
Magazines and comics	70° or 19%

T4 The student's labelled pie chart with sectors

Ford	86° or 24%
Vauxhall	130° or 36%
Rover	43° or 12%
Toyota	36° or 10%
Other	65° or 18%

Practice book

Sections A and B (p 163)

1 (a) 150 (b) 60 (c) 80 (d) 25

2 (a) 90 (b) 27 (c) 72 (d) 80

3 (a) Family tub (b) $\frac{1}{3}$ (c) 100
  (d) $\frac{1}{4}$ (e) 75 (f) 60°
  (g) 50 (h) 25

4 (a) $\frac{1}{4}$ (b) 480
  (c) (i) 120° (ii) $\frac{1}{3}$ (iii) 160
  (d) 60

Section C (p 164)

1 (a) 5
  (b) (i) 70° (ii) 350
  (c) 275 (d) 75

2 (a) Soaps (b) 75° (c) $0.6 \times 75 = 45$
  (d) (i) $0.6 \times 135 = 81$
      (ii) $0.6 \times 85 = 51$

3 (a) $\frac{1}{3}$ (b) 90 (c) 40 (d) 5

Section D (p 165)

1 (a) 30 (b) 12° (c) 60°
  (d) Labelled pie chart (12° per person) with sectors

Blonde	60°
Black	84°
Brown	144°
Red	24°
Other	48°

2 (a) 45 (b) 8°
  (c) Labelled pie chart (8° per person) with sectors

Romance	80°
Fantasy	120°
Science fiction	56°
Crime	32°
Other	72°

3 Labelled pie chart (2.5° per person) with sectors

Games	100°
Email	90°
Word processing	60°
Internet shopping	25°
Research	30°
Other	55°

4 (a) Labelled pie chart (0.4° per accident) with sectors

Kitchen	160°
Stairs	90°
Bathroom	60°
Living room	36°
Other	14°

(b) 150

Section E (p 166)

1 Labelled pie chart with sectors

Protein	25%
Carbohydrate	10%
Fat	51%
Fibre	7%
Other	7%

2 (a) 20   (b) 5%   (c) 20%

(d) Labelled pie chart with sectors

Milk	55%
Plain	20%
White	15%
None	10%

3 (a) Labelled pie chart with sectors

Football	45%
Motor racing	32%
Snooker	6%
Tennis	12%
Cricket	5%

(b) e.g. 'Football is still the favourite sport.'

(c) e.g. 'More senior citizens prefer tennis (or cricket).'
or 'Fewer senior citizens liked motor racing.'

4 Labelled pie chart with sectors

Skiing	46%
Cycling	20%
Walking	16%
Boating	18%

Section F (p 167)

1 Labelled pie chart with sectors

Channel tunnel	50° or 14%
Sea	91° or 25%
Air	219° or 61%

2 Labelled pie chart with sectors

Squared	103° or 29%
Wide lined	167° or 46%
Narrow lined	51° or 14%
Plain	39° or 11%

3 Labelled pie chart with sectors

Paper and card	133° or 37%
Compost	83° or 23%
Glass	58° or 16%
Co-mingled material	19° or 5%
Cans	5° or 1%
Other	62° or 17%

(Note: Percentages do not add to 100% so this needs to be dealt with.)

Review 6 (p 399)

1 $P = 4a + 2b$

2 (a) 80 minutes   (b) 110 minutes
   (c) $t = 30w + 20$

3 (a) tonne   (b) gram
   (c) kilogram   (d) metre
   (e) kilometre   (f) millimetre

4 (a) 5 miles is about **8** kilometres
   (b) 1 inch is about 2.5 **centimetres**
   (c) 2.2 **pounds** is about 1 kilogram
   (d) 1 gallon is about $4\frac{1}{2}$ litres

5 (a) 1   (b) 38   (c) 86

6 (a) 10   (b) 20
   (c)

	Present	Absent	Totals
Boys	8	2	**10**
Girls	15	**5**	**20**
Totals	**23**	**7**	30

   (d) $\frac{1}{4}$ (e) 20%

7 (a) 1   (b) ⁻1   (c) ⁻6   (d) 6
   (e) ⁻12 (f) ⁻10 (g) 10   (h) 100

8 (a) £36   (b) 5.6 g
   (c) 264 m   (d) 14.7 km

9 In maths she got 56.3%, in English 52.9%
   and in history 54.1% – so she did best in
   maths.

10 (a)
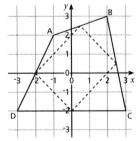

   (b) A rectangle

11 (a) 115°   (b) 295°

12 (a) $3x + 11$ (b) $10m - 2$ (c) $a^2 + 2a$

13 (a) $3(a + 4)$ (b) $2(2b + 3)$ (c) $c(c + 5)$

14
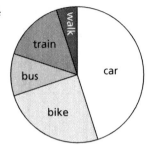

	Percentage	Angle
Car	45%	162°
Bike	25%	90°
Bus	10%	36°
Train	15%	54°
Walk	5%	18°

Mixed questions 6 (Practice book p 168)

> **Essential**
> Angle measurer or pie chart scale
> for question 18

1 (a) 4 m   (b) 2.5 m   (c) 4 cm

2 (a) 750 grams   (b) 400 millilitres
   (c) 1 metre 85 centimetres

3 (a) About 1 litre   (b) About 9 litres
   (c) About 6 litres

4 (a) 30°C   (b) 29°C
   (c) Wednesday and Thursday

5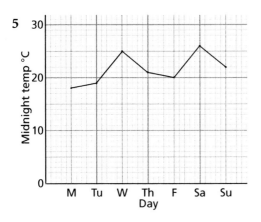

6 (a) 15 (b) 12 (c) 4
(d) 3 (e) $4\frac{1}{2}$

7 (a) 35 (b) $5(n + 3)$

8 (a) JACKIE (b) ELLIE
(c) DEBBIE (d) ABIGAIL

9 (a) 34% (b) 8%
(c) 32% (d) 4%

10 (a) £4.17 (b) £18.89
(c) £0.89 (d) £5.67

11 A (1, 2, 0)   B (1, 3, 2)   C (2, 4, 1)

12 500 ml bottle: 1p buys 6.94 ml
1.2 litre bottle: 1p buys 8 ml
3 litre bottle: 1p buys 7.14 ml
So a 1.2 litre bottle works out cheapest.

13 (a) £4.27 a tin (b) 7 tins

14 (a) $2(x + 3) = 2x + \mathbf{6}$
(b) $3(n - 4) = \mathbf{3n} - 12$
(c) $\mathbf{4}(h + 3) = 4h + 12$

15 (a) $12(n + 2)$ (b) $6(g - 2)$
(c) $6(3s + 4)$ (d) $4(3d - 4)$

16 (a) $2x + 11$ (b) $5d + 3$
(c) $5w + 2$ (d) $2w + 6$

17 (a) $\frac{1}{4}$ (b) $\frac{1}{6}$
(c) $120°, \frac{1}{3}$ (d) 75

18 (a) 16 people (b) 26 people

Essential	**Optional**
Sheets G84, G85	Tracing paper, mirrors, coloured pencils
Practice book pages 171 to 174	

𝔸 *Fractions* (p 401)

A3 Students could also try designing covers that are $\frac{1}{4}$ red, $\frac{1}{3}$ red, $\frac{3}{4}$ red and so on.

𝔹 *Block designs* (p 402)

'Hovering hawks was a good one to start with as they offered lots of answers before agreeing on $\frac{11}{16}$.'

◊ Ask students to copy the block onto squared paper and to think about what fraction of the block is red. They can compare their methods.

Some may consider the shape split into squares and triangles as shown.

The 10 red triangles make 5 squares giving 11 squares in total.

Hence $\frac{11}{16}$ of the shape is red.

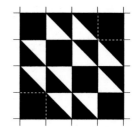

Others may consider the shape split into equal triangles as shown.

There are 22 red triangles.

Hence $\frac{22}{32}$ of the shape is red which is $\frac{11}{16}$ in its simplest form.

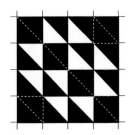

C **Symmetry** (p 403)

Sheets G84 and G85
Optional: Tracing paper, mirrors

◊ Remind students that a design with no rotational symmetry has order 1.

D **By degrees** (p 404)

TG

◊ The block is shown with and without dotted guidelines. The first diagram makes it easier to see the shape of the actual patchwork pieces. The second shows dotted grid lines so the angles are easier to calculate.

◊ Discuss right, acute, obtuse and reflex angles. Students should understand that a full turn is 360°, a straight line is equivalent to a half-turn (180°) and a right angle is equivalent to a quarter turn (90°).

They should also see that the diagonals of a square bisect its corners to give angles of 45°; hence angle *b*, for example, is 45°. Now some of the marked angles can be found by adding. For example, angle *f* is the sum of a right angle and a 45° angle and must be 90° + 45° = 135°.

E **It all adds up** (p 405)

TG

◊ Use the diagrams as a basis for a discussion on how to find missing angles in a right angle, on a straight line and round a point.

F **Triangles** (p 407)

Optional: tracing paper, coloured pencils

TG

◊ Students can construct their own strip of triangles for a cushion border using their own scalene triangle and tracing paper. Using three different coloured pens they can mark equal angles. They may then be able to see that the three angles that make up each triangle can be fitted on a straight line and that this works for all the different triangles students have used.

Hence the angles of a triangle add up to 180°.

Ⓐ *Fractions* (p 401)

A1 (a) $\frac{1}{2}$ (b) $\frac{1}{4}$

A2 (a) $\frac{1}{2}$ (b) $\frac{1}{2}$ (c) $\frac{1}{4}$ (d) $\frac{1}{3}$
  (e) $\frac{5}{9}$ (f) $\frac{2}{3}$ (g) $\frac{9}{25}$ (h) $\frac{3}{8}$

A3 The student's design

Ⓑ *Block designs* (p 402)

B1 (a) The student's copy
  (b) $\frac{1}{3}$ (c) $\frac{2}{3}$

B2 (a) 16 (b) 64
  (c) $\frac{1}{3}$ (d) 36 cm by 36 cm

B3 (a) The student's copy
  (b) $\frac{1}{4}$ (c) $\frac{1}{4}$ (d) $\frac{1}{2}$

B4 (a) 48 (b) 96
  (c) 20 cm by 20 cm

B5 (a) The student's copy
  (b) $\frac{3}{8}$ (c) $\frac{1}{4}$ (d) $\frac{3}{8}$

B6 (a) $16\,\text{cm}^2$ (b) $8\,\text{cm}^2$ (c) $32\,\text{cm}^2$

Ⓒ *Symmetry* (p 403)

C1 (a) 4 (b) 4

C2 The student's solutions on G84

Block	No. of lines of symmetry	Order of rotation symmetry
Windmill	0	4
Churn dash	4	4
Beggar's block	2	2
Pieced basket	1	1
Milky way	0	2
Prickly pear	0	4

C3 Big dipper

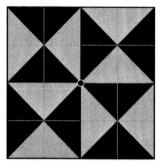

Order of rotation symmetry 4

Old tippecanoe

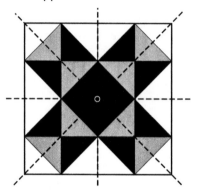

Order of rotation symmetry **4**

Northumberland star

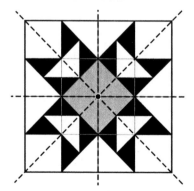

Order of rotation symmetry 4

Flower basket

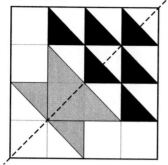

Order of rotation symmetry **1**

Jacob's ladder

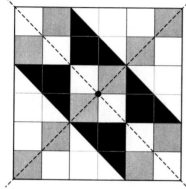

Order of rotation symmetry **2**

Jack in the box

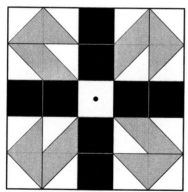

Order of rotation symmetry 4

C4 (a) The student's design with four lines of symmetry and order of rotation 4

    (b) The student's design with no lines of symmetry and order of rotation 4

Ⓓ **By degrees** (p 404)

D1 (a) $h = 90°$ $i = 45°$ $j = 45°$
         $k = 90°$ $l = 135°$ $m = 180°$
         $n = 45°$ $p = 135°$ $q = 90°$

    (b) l and p (c) 3   (d) 8

D2 (a) $r = 180°$ $s = 135°$ $t = 90°$
         $u = 180°$ $v = 360°$ $w = 135°$
         $x = 270°$ $y = 225°$ $z = 315°$

    (b) x, y and z

Ⓔ **It all adds up** (p 405)

E1 $a = 65°$ $b = 35°$ $c = 129°$
    $d = 95°$ $e = 33°$ $f = 53°$

E2 $a = 35°$ $b = 145°$ $c = 60°$

E3 $a = 100°$ $b = 71°$ $c = 117°$
    $d = 36°$ $e = 20°$ $f = 52°$

E4 $x = 128°$ $y = 38°$

E5 $60°$

Ⓕ **Triangles** (p 407)

F1 $a = 50°$ $b = 60°$ $c = 55°$
    $d = 23°$ $e = 119°$ $f = 12°$

F2 $a = 40°$ $b = 23°$ $c = 67°$

F3 (a) $a = 135°$ $b = 18°$ $c = 31°$
    (b) $d = 45°$ $e = 63°$ $f = 18°$
        $g = 14°$

*F4 $a = 60°$ $b = 120°$ $c = 70°$
    $d = 110°$ $e = 80°$ $f = 70°$
    $g = 65°$ $h = 128°$ $k = 80°$
    $m = 100°$ $n = 148°$

Test yourself (p 409)

T1 (a) The student's copy
    (b) $\frac{5}{9}$ (c) $\frac{2}{9}$

T2

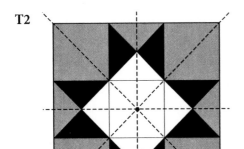

T3 $a = 45°$ $b = 40°$ $c = 90°$
 $d = 45°$ $e = 18°$ $f = 60°$

Practice book

Section A (p 171)

1 (a) $\frac{1}{2}$ (b) $\frac{1}{3}$ (c) $\frac{1}{3}$
 (d) $\frac{4}{9}$ (e) $\frac{5}{8}$ (f) $\frac{4}{9}$

2 Student's own design with $\frac{1}{4}$ black.

Section B (p 171)

1 (a) $\frac{2}{9}$ (b) $\frac{5}{9}$

2 (a) 125 (b) $\frac{2}{9}$

3 (a) $\frac{4}{9}$ (b) $\frac{8}{27}$ (c) $\frac{7}{27}$

4 (a) (i) $\frac{5}{18}$

 (ii) $\frac{13}{18}$

 (b) $40\,\text{cm}^2$

5 (a) (i) $\frac{1}{2}$ (ii) $\frac{1}{8}$ (iii) $\frac{3}{8}$
 (b) $24\,\text{cm}^2$

Section C (p 172)

1 (a) 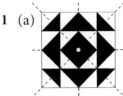 (b)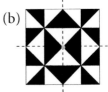

order of
rotation
symmetry 4

order of
rotation
symmetry 2

(c) 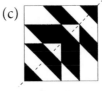 (d)

order of
rotation
symmetry 1

order of
rotation
symmetry 1

2 (a)   (b)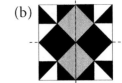

(c)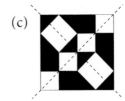

Section E (p 173)

1 $a = 54°$ $b = 53°$ $c = 96°$
 $d = 30°$ $e = 135°$ $f = 21°$
 $g = 123°$

2 $a = 135°$ $b = 120°$ $c = 72°$

Section F (p 174)

1 $a = 51°$ $b = 74°$ $c = 35°$ $d = 69°$
 $e = 111°$ $f = 50°$ $g = 130°$ $h = 50°$
 $i = 80°$ $j = 100°$

2 $a = 127°$ $b = 75°$ $c = 55°$ $d = 60°$

54 Travel

Essential	**Optional**
Sheets G87, G88, G89	Sheet G86
Dice	Local timetables, local maps
	Motion sensor, stopwatches, cones, chalk

Practice book pages 175 to 178

A Clocking on (p 410)

> Optional: sheet G86

◊ If students are familiar with 12- and 24-hour clocks the initial activity may be just a quick revision exercise. If they need more practice, sheet G86 can be copied on to a transparency or card and split into individual cards. They can then as a class or individually sort the cards into groups with the same time. Alternatively the cards could be used to play 'Snap'.

B Timetables (p 412)

> Sheets G87, G88
> Optional: dice, local timetables

◊ The introductory timetable gives an opportunity to ask questions orally before students consolidate skills with the questions in the exercise. The initial work will interest them more if your questions are based on a real local timetable.

Railroaded

This activity requires careful reading of timetables and the ability to add delays on to given times. If there are serious delays the students will not arrive in Victoria in time to catch the last train to Dover.

Timetables on the internet for trains and other means of transport could be used for an interesting exploration of other possible journeys.

C *Distance tables* (p 413)

> Sheet G89
> Optional: local maps

◊ Before asking students to fill in the distance table on sheet G89 it is worth asking for a few key distances. Emphasise that they need to look for the shortest distance each time.

This activity is more interesting if the area used is a local one. Most road maps give the distances along stretches of road. Route planning computer software is also a good source of information. You will need, however, to prepare a simplified map with distances between towns marked.

D *Average speed* (p 414)

◊ The key concept here is that the total distance is shared equally between each unit of time, for example 1 second, 1 hour and so on. It is useful to point out that the fastest child runs twice as fast as the slowest.

E *Distance–time graphs* (p 416)

> Optional: motion sensor, stopwatches, cones, chalk

◊ The initial activity can be used to show how the graph provides a picture of a moving object over a period of time. Alternatively a 50 metre course could be marked out in the playground with cones and lines marked at 10 metre intervals. Students could then walk, run, cycle or skateboard while other students record their times with a stopwatch at each 10 metre mark. The times can be used to generate distance–time graphs.

Motion sensors are available which can be connected directly to a computer or graphic calculator. When pointed at a moving object they record the distance the object is from the sensor. A distance–time graph will usually be drawn directly by the software. Asking students to walk to and from the sensor to produce particular shape graphs works very well. Other activities are usually described in accompanying literature and are very useful in introducing this topic.

F *Distance and time calculations* (p 419)

The students' text avoids an algorithmic approach to these calculations and tries to give students a visual picture to aid their memory.

Ⓐ Clocking on (p 410)

A1 (a) 15:40   (b) 00:30   (c) 01:40
      (d) 21:15   (e) 08:40   (f) 11:50

A2 03:05; 7:45 a.m.; 2:00 p.m.;
      17:35; 7:15 p.m.; 23:15

A3 17:15 or 5:15 p.m.

A4 20 minutes

A5 25 minutes

A6 (a)

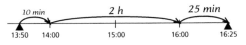

      (b) 2 hours 35 minutes

A7 (a) 3 hours 15 minutes
      (b) 2 hours 30 minutes
      (c) 4 hours 30 minutes
      (d) 1 hour 45 minutes
      (e) 1 hour 45 minutes
      (f) 2 hours 55 minutes

A8 (a) (i)   25 minutes
         (ii) 15 minutes
         (iii) 2 hours 10 minutes
         (iv) 45 minutes
      (b) 3 hours 50 minutes
      (c) CBBC and The Barefoot Contessa
      (d) CITV
      (e) 3.35   CITV
          5.20   The People Versus
          5.45   Crossroads

Ⓑ Timetables (p 412)

B1 4

B2 6

B3 0926

B4 1 hour 56 minutes

B5 (a) 1 hour 46 minutes
      (b) 10 minutes

B6 The 0817 train from Diss

B7 The 0807 train from Ipswich

B8 17 minutes

Ⓒ Distance tables (p 413)

C1

Cork	Dublin	Galway	Limerick	Longford	Roscrea	Tralee	Waterford
183							
126	143						
62	127	64					
188	80	63	126				
110	79	112	48	78			
75	190	127	63	189	111		
71	112	145	81	192	129	144	

C2 (a) 120 miles
      (b) Gatwick and Aberdeen

C3 (a) 445 miles   (b) 460 miles
      (c) 15 miles

Ⓓ Average speed (p 414)

D1 8 m/s

D2 (a) 10 m/s   (b) 5 m/s   (c) 3 m/s
      (d) 30 m/s   (e) 40 m/s

D3 (a) 70 km/h   (b) 15 km/h
      (c) 210 km/h   (d) 18 000 km/h

D4 (a) Flatford Flyer   25 km/h
          Walter   30 km/h
          Bolton Queen   29 km/h
          Caeredwen   24 km/h

      (b) (i)   Walter   (ii) Caeredwen

D5 (a) 10 m/s   (b) 280 m.p.h.
      (c) 40 km/h   (d) 37.5 m.p.h.

D6 (a) 48 km   (b) 48 km/h

D7 (a) 300 km/h   (b) 20 km/h
      (c) 24 km/h

D8 (a) 1.5   (b) 3.25   (c) 5.5   (d) 1.75

D9 (a) 40 m.p.h.   (b) 180 m.p.h.
     (c) 450 m.p.h.

E *Distance–time graphs* (p 416)

E1 (a) 15 m   (b) B
     (c) A 15 m/s   B 7 m/s   C 5 m/s
       D 2 m/s   E 1 m/s
     (d) A   (e) E

E2 (a) P   (b) R   (c) R
     (d) Q   (e) Q   (f) Q

E3 (a) Going away   (b) 3 km/h
     (c) 2 km/h

E4 (a) 3 km/h   (b) 1 km/h
     (c) He stopped   (d) 5 km
     (e) $2\frac{1}{2}$ km/h   (f) $1\frac{1}{2}$ km/h
     (g) 10 a.m. and 12 noon

E5 (a)

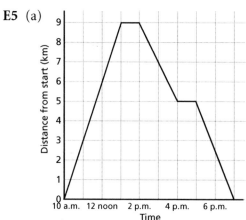

     (b) $2\frac{1}{2}$ km/h

E6 (a) Between 4 and 5 hours she was
       walking home at a speed of 6 km/h;
       after 5 hours she stopped for half an
       hour; she then took $2\frac{1}{2}$ hours to
       cover the last 6 km back home.
     (b) CD – between 4 and 5 hours
     (c) 4 km/h

F *Distance and time calculations* (p 419)

F1 (a) 20 m   (b) 45 m
     (c) 65 m   (d) 125 m

F2 (a) 50 m   (b) 80 m
     (c) 260 m   (d) 300 m

F3 (a) 150 miles   (b) 2400 km
     (c) 240 km   (d) 480 km
     (e) 125 km

F4 (a) 30 miles   (b) 210 miles
     (c) 135 miles   (d) 375 miles

*F5 2 metres

     A tricky problem
     The wildebeest would catch you, and so
     would the lion!

F6 3 hours

F7 4 hours

F8 6 hours

F9 (a) 6 seconds   (b) 10 seconds
     (c) 8 seconds   (d) 4 seconds

F10 18 seconds

F11 $2\frac{1}{2}$ hours

F12 $3\frac{1}{2}$ hours

G *Mixed examples* (p 420)

G1 (a) 540 miles   (b) $2\frac{1}{2}$ hours

G2 (a) 40 minutes   (b) 90 miles

G3 (a) 225 miles   (b) 45 m.p.h.

Test yourself (p 421)

T1 (a) 20 minutes   (b) Britain Today
     (c) Off the Shelf and World News

T2 (a) 0715   (b) 32 minutes
     (c) 0623

T3 (a) 90 m.p.h.   (b) $4\frac{1}{2}$ hours

T4 (a) 37 miles

    (b) (i) 185 miles

        (ii) 2.30 p.m.

        (iii) 6 hours 35 minutes

T5 (a) (i) 1300   (ii) 20 km/h

    (b)

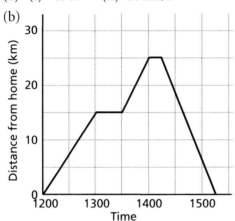

Practice book

Sections A, B and C (p 175)

1 (a) 16:15   (b) 06:30

   (c) 00:40   (d) 18:45

2 (a) 3.20 p.m.   (b) 15 minutes

   (c) 55 minutes

   (d) 1 hour 50 minutes

   (e) 6 hours 45 minutes

   (f) 25 minutes

3 (a) 13:25   (b) 29 minutes

   (c) 12:20

4 (a) 200 miles   (b) 100 miles

   (c) 504 miles

Section D (p 176)

1 (a) 30 m/s   (b) 29 m/s

   (c) 18 m/s

2 (a) 80 km/h   (b) 530 km/h

   (c) 21 000 km/h

3 (a) 70 m.p.h.   (b) 22 m/s

   (c) 18 km/h

Section E (p 176)

1 (a) 30 km/h   (b) He stopped.

   (c) Between 2 p.m. and 3 p.m.

   (d) 2 p.m.   (e) 120 km

2 (a)

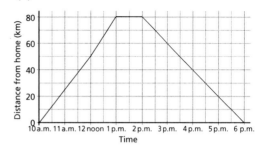

   (b) 20 km/h

Section F (p 177)

1 (a) 120 miles   (b) 180 miles

2 4 hours

3 (a) 420 m   (b) 340 m

   (c) 1650 km   (d) 2 km

   (e) 12.5 miles

4 (a) 30 minutes   (b) 4 hours

   (c) $2\frac{1}{2}$ hours   (d) 45 minutes

Section G (p 178)

1 (a) 40 m.p.h   (b) 178 m.p.h.

   (c) 48 m.p.h.

2 (a) 6 km/h   (b) 4 km/h

   (c) BC

3 14.44 m/s

4 (a) 20 m.p.h.

   (b) 1 hour 15 minutes

   (c) 135 miles

55 Cuboids

Essential	Optional
Empty cuboid cartons Centimetre cubes Centimetre square paper, scissors	Newspaper
Practice book pages 179 to 182	

A **Volume** (p 423)

> Empty cuboid cartons, centimetre cubes

Maximum volume

The maximum volume of the lidless cuboid will be obtained by cutting out a square of side 3.44 cm (to 2 d.p.). You may wish to treat this as a simple search in whole units or get students to use a decimal search method.

 Some students may be capable, with guidance, of using a spreadsheet to investigate this problem.

B **Cubic metres** (p 427)

> Optional: newspaper

◊ The cube in the photograph in 'Living in a box' was made by rolling up several sheets of newspaper very tightly to form the struts and taping the corners together. This gives a cheap, safe metre cube to work with if you wish to test how many students can actually fit inside this cube. Alternatively a demonstration cube could be made with metre rules.

Suppliers of gravel and similar bulk materials often sell in units of m^3.

C *Changing units* (p 428)

Some calculators may revert to standard form when dealing with volumes using centimetres and this may cause problems. It may be easier to complete this section without calculators.

D *Surface area* (p 429)

Students should have met surface area in key stage 3. This section revises this and extends to cases involving the areas of triangles.

A *Volume* (p 423)

A1 (a) (i) 10 (ii) 40
(b) (i) 12 (ii) 36
(c) (i) 4 (ii) 24
(d) (i) 20 (ii) 60
(e) (i) 21 (ii) 84

A2 (a) $40\,cm^3$ (b) $48\,cm^3$ (c) $54\,cm^3$
(d) $30\,cm^3$ (e) $16\,cm^3$ (f) $60\,cm^3$
(g) $48\,cm^3$ (h) $24\,cm^3$ (i) $125\,cm^3$

A3 (a) $60\,cm^3$ (b) $36\,cm^3$
(c) $28\,cm^3$ (d) $36\,cm^3$

A4 Totley's Tea $455\,cm^3$
Colour-run $126\,cm^3$
Biscuits $1600\,cm^3$
Toothpaste $240\,cm^3$

A5 $300\,cm^3$

A6 $12\,000\,cm^3$

A7 (a) $9\,cm^3$ (b) $42.9\,cm^3$
(c) $7.92\,cm^3$

A8 All volumes are $48\,cm^3$.
$a = 4\,cm$ $b = 16\,cm$
$c = 1.5\,cm$ $d = 4\,cm$

*A9 (a) $2\,cm$ (b) $0.5\,cm$

B *Cubic metres* (p 427)

B1 Removal van $30\,m^3$
Container $60\,m^3$
Paddling pool $2.5\,m^3$
Filing cabinet $0.48\,m^3$

B2 (a) $375\,m^3$ (b) $0.8\,m$

C *Changing units* (p 428)

C1 (a) $24\,m^3$
(b) $300\,cm, 400\,cm, 200\,cm$
(c) $24\,000\,000\,cm^3$

C2 (a) $1.5\,m^3$
(b) $150\,cm, 200\,cm, 50\,cm$
(c) $1\,500\,000\,cm^3$

C3 (a) $52\,500\,000\,cm^3$
(b) $5\,m, 3.5\,m, 3\,m$
(c) $52.5\,m^3$

C4 (a) (i) $5.4\,m^3$ (ii) $5\,400\,000\,cm^3$
(b) (i) $28.8\,m^3$ (ii) $28\,800\,000\,cm^3$

D *Surface area* (p 429)

D1 (a) $108\,cm^2$ (b) $220\,cm^2$
(c) $157.4\,cm^2$

D2 (a) $1048\,cm^2$ (b) $442.5\,cm^2$

D3 $136\,m^2$

D4 (a) Isosceles triangle

(b) The student's accurate net for prism

(c) 152 cm² (height of triangle = 4 cm)

*D5 (a) 38 cm²   (b) 356 cm²

Test yourself (p 430)

T1 (a) 48 cm³   (b) 88 cm²

T2 (a) 7 m³   (b) 0.2 m

T3 (a) 11.34 m³

(b) 150 cm, 420 cm, 180 cm

(c) 11 340 000 cm³

Practice book

Section A (p 179)

1 (a) (i) 8   (ii) 40

(b) (i) 9   (ii) 45

(c) (i) 12   (ii) 60

2 (a) 63 cm³ (b) 50 cm³ (c) 60 cm³

(d) 36 cm³ (e) 64 cm³ (f) 60 cm³

(g) 24 cm³ (h) 75 cm³ (i) 90 cm³

3 (a) 250 cm³   (b) 10 000 cm³

4 (a) 360 cm³   (b) 240 cm³

5 (a) 4830 cm³   (b) 1070.16 cm³

(c) 233.92 cm³

6 (a) 272.16 cm³   (b) 2.736 cm³

7 (a) 10 000 cm³   (b) 1000 cm³

8 $a = 5$ cm $b = 2$ cm $c = 2$ cm

9 (a) 5 cm   (b) 5 cm   (c) 4 cm

Sections B and C (p 181)

1 (a) 4200 m³   (b) 124.8 m³

(c) 0.432 m³   (d) 31.59 m³

2 (a) 30 m³

(b) 300 cm long, 400 cm wide, 250 cm high

(c) 30 000 000 cm³

3 (a) 80 cm   (b) 288 000 cm³

(c) 0.6 m by 0.6 m by 0.8 m

(d) 0.288 m³

Section D (p 182)

1 (a) 10 cm by 4 cm by 6 cm

(b) 240 cm³

(c) 248 cm²

2 (a) 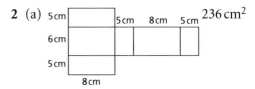 236 cm²

(b) 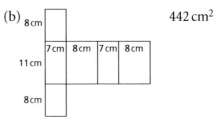 442 cm²

3 (a) 168 cm²   (b) 336 cm²

(c) 604 cm²   (d) 928 cm²

56 *More circle facts*

This unit revises how to find the circumference of a circle and introduces finding the area of a circle.

Essential	Optional
Sheets G90, G91	OS maps of a local area
Compasses, centimetre squared paper	Old CDs, vinyl singles and LPs
Tracing paper or acetate with centimetre square grids	
Practice book pages 183 to 185	

B *Areas of awkward shapes* (p 432)

This section uses square-counting methods to find the areas of shapes.

> Sheets G90, G91
> Tracing paper or acetate with centimetre square grids
> Optional: OS maps of a local area

◊ The usual method of finding the areas of shapes with a grid is to count all squares that are at least half covered by the area in question. You may wish to refine this by getting students to count half squares or even quarters of a square. The area of Scalpay is about 25 or 26 km².

B3 Using a grid copied on to acetate or tracing paper will greatly enhance students' understanding of irregular area. If this is impracticable then the shapes could be traced on to centimetre squared paper.

Forests and lakes

Squares on all scales of Ordnance Survey maps are 1 km apart. This is useful in estimating areas directly from a map.

C *Areas of circles* (p 433)

> Tracing paper, compasses
> Optional: old CDs, vinyl singles and LPs

◊ The aim of the initial activity is for students to notice that the area of a circle is roughly 3 times the area of a square with side length equal to its radius. They should be able to express this rule in words and as a formula. You may wish to use a graph of results to lead students to this rule as in similar work in algebra units. Once the rough rule is established, having previously used 3 as a first approximation in work on circumference, students should easily realise that π gives a better approximation. When using πr^2 students often confuse the order of operations so it is worth keeping alive the initial idea of the area being roughly 3 times the area of the square.

Which looks bigger?

This is a useful exercise in comparing different areas. Ask students to vote for the area they think looks biggest before measuring them.
Areas: circle 12.6 cm²; rectangle 13 cm²; triangle 12.5 cm²; parallelogram 12 cm².

In the groove!

The dimensions of the various recording media are approximately

Type	Radius	Total area
CD	6 cm	113 cm²
Vinyl LP	15 cm	707 cm²
Vinyl single	8.5 cm	227 cm²

It is interesting to note that a CD has half the total area of an old vinyl single. Clearly the playing area of each type is smaller than the total area and will vary with different recordings.

D *Around about* (p 437)

This section uses a mixture of circumference and area in a variety of contexts.

Largest area

This is an extension of question D6 and could lead to a useful mini-investigation into which shape contains the largest area for a given perimeter.

Ⓐ Circumference (p 431)

A1 (a) 24 cm (b) 36 cm
(c) 18 cm (d) 30 cm

A2 (a) 3 cm (b) 5 cm (c) 100 cm

A3 (a) 5 m (b) 2.5 m

A4 (a) 219.8 cm (b) 220 m

Ⓑ Areas of awkward shapes (p 432)

B1 Kerrara is roughly 12 km².
Ulva is roughly 18 km².

B2 (a) Roughly 26 cm² (b) Roughly 24 cm²

B3 (a) Roughly 29 m² (b) Roughly 19 m²

Ⓒ Areas of circles (p 433)

C1 (a) 12 cm² (b) 108 cm²
(c) 147 cm² (d) 300 cm²

C2 (a) 12 cm² (b) 13.5 cm² (c) 12 cm²

C3 (a) 50.3 cm² (b) 78.5 cm²
(c) 201.1 cm² (d) 706.9 cm²

C4 (a) (i) 6 cm (ii) 113.1 cm²
(b) (i) 7 cm (ii) 153.9 cm²
(c) (i) 10 cm (ii) 314.2 cm²
(d) (i) 20 cm (ii) 1256.6 cm²

C5 (a) 19.6 cm² (b) 176.7 cm²
(c) 128.7 cm² (d) 40.7 cm²

C6 (a) (i) 6.5 cm (ii) 132.7 cm²
(b) (i) 12.5 cm (ii) 490.9 cm²
(c) (i) 4.2 cm (ii) 55.4 cm²
(d) (i) 12.3 cm (ii) 475.3 cm²

C7

Coin	Diameter	Radius	Area
(a) 10 cent	2.0 cm	1.0 cm	3.1 cm²
(b) 1 euro	2.3 cm	1.15 cm	4.2 cm²
(c) 2 euros	2.5 cm	1.25 cm	4.9 cm²

C8 63.6 m²

C9 (a) 14.1 cm² (b) 19.6 cm²
(c) 57.1 cm² (d) 63.3 cm²
(e) 714.2 cm² (f) 2120.6 cm²

C10 (a) 113.1 cm² (b) 201.1 cm²
(c) 88 cm²

C11 (a) 12 cm by 8 cm (b) 96 cm²
(c) 12.57 cm²
(d) 96 − (6 × 12.57) = 20.6 cm²

C12 One large pizza has area 1256.6 cm².
Two smaller pizzas have area
2 × 314.2 cm² = 628.4.
So two smaller ones have half the
area of one large one.

*C13 (a)

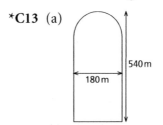

(b) Area = $\frac{1}{2}(\pi \times 90^2) + (180 \times 450)$
= 93 723.5 m²

(c) 1362.7 m

Ⓓ Around about (p 437)

D1 176.7 m²

D2 138 m

D3 (a) 25 cm (b) 200 times

D4 122.2 cm

D5 15.9 cm

D6 (a) 12 m (b) 144 m² (c) 15.3 m
(d) 184 m² (e) The circular pen

Test yourself (p 438)

T1 19 cm²

T2 (a) 78.5 cm² (b) 19.6 cm² (c) 50.3 m²

T3 628.3 cm²

T4 (a) 23.9 m (b) 45.6 m²

Practice book

Sections A and B (p 183)

1 Student's diagram showing radius, diameter and circumference

2 (a) 12 cm (b) 30 cm
   (c) 36 cm (d) 24 cm

3 (a) 47.1 cm (b) 471 cm

4 (a) Roughly 37 cm^2
   (b) Roughly 29 cm^2

Section C (p 184)

1 πr^2 or (radius)$^2 \times \pi$

2 (a) 28.3 cm^2 (b) 113.1 cm^2
   (c) 78.5 cm^2 (d) 706.9 cm^2

3 (a) (i) 4.4 cm (ii) 2.2 cm (iii) 15.2 cm^2
   (b) (i) 4.8 cm (ii) 2.4 cm (iii) 18.1 cm^2
   (c) (i) 2.8 cm (ii) 1.4 cm (iii) 6.2 cm^2

4 (a) Circle 12.6 cm^2
       Semicircle 6.3 cm^2
       Quadrant 3.15 cm^2
       Large square 16 cm^2
       Small square 4 cm^2
   (b) (i) 16 cm^2 + 6.3 cm^2 + 2 × 3.15 cm^2
            = 28.6 cm^2
        (ii) 4 cm^2 + 2 × 3.15 cm^2 = 10.3 cm^2
        (iii) 2 × 3.15 cm^2 = 6.3 cm^2

Section D (p 185)

1 (a) Length: 16 cm Width: 4 cm
       Height: 4 cm
   (b) 16 cm × 4 cm × 4 cm = 256 cm^3

2 (a) Sam runs 160 metres.
       Tom runs 251.3 metres.
   (b) Tom runs further by 91.3 metres.

3 (a) White circle: 2 cm
       Shaded circle: 4 cm
   (b) 12.6 cm^2 – 3.1 cm^2 = 9.5 cm^2

4 (a) $\frac{1}{2}(\pi \times 1.5^2)$ cm^2 = 3.53 cm^2
   (b) $\frac{1}{2}(\pi \times 3^2)$ cm^2 – 3.53 cm^2 = 10.6 cm^2

5 20 cm^2 + 20 cm^2 + $\frac{1}{4}(\pi \times 40)$ cm^2
   = 71.4 cm

57 Interpreting data

This unit revises key stage 3 work on the mean, median, mode and range for small data sets. It also revises frequency tables and graphs for discrete data, including stem-and-leaf tables and cases where data is grouped. Grouping is developed further to include frequency tables and graphs for continuous data.

Essential	**Optional**
Sheets G92, G93 on card, G94	Large sheets of paper and coins
Dice and counters	OHP transparency of sheet G92
Practice book pages 186 to 188	

Ⓐ *Just a few* (p 439)

> Sheets G92, G93 on card
> Dice and counters
> Optional: OHP transparency of sheet G92

TG

'I encouraged them to share their comments on the interpretations in the questions.'

◊ The initial activities are designed to give students practice in finding the mean, median and range of small data sets. The mode is not asked for in this section: it is an inappropriate measure to use with small data sets. You may wish to remind students of the terms before doing the activities.

Mean streak

This is a larger version of a game used in the SMP Interact key stage 3 materials. The board could be copied on to a transparency and the game played by the class before students play it themselves. As students check each other's answers, any errors that an individual might make should be picked up.

On the cards

These puzzles should test students' understanding of mean, median and range. They could be carried out as a class activity by asking the questions orally and students holding up the cards they think are the right ones. Alternatively, split the class into groups of four or eight students, each with a set of cards shared out equally among themselves. When the problem is set students must discuss which of the cards their group will hold up. Larger sets of cards would be an advantage here. The solutions are

- 3, 4, 5 or 3, 3, 6
- 3, 4, 6, 7 or 3, 4, 5, 8 or 3, 3, 6, 8
- 3, 3 or 4 or 5, 6, 6, 7 or 4, 5, 6, 6 or 7, 8 or 4, 6, 6, 7, 8
- 3, 4, 6, 8 or 3, 3, 7, 8
- 4, 5, 6, 6, 7, 8 or 3, 4, 5, 6, 7, 8

Families

These are useful problems for students to work on in small groups to generate discussion. The solutions are

- Mum and Dad are 41 and 47.
- The children are 8, 9, 13, 15 and 25.

A5 This question shows that the mean and median may lead towards different interpretations of the data. You may wish to discuss why there are two such measures in the first place.

B *Frequency tables* (p 441)

Some students may still have difficulty in interpreting frequency when the data is numerical. For example, in the initial example they may give the mode as 17 because it is the highest number. Writing the data out in full should help overcome this.

C *Grouping data* (p 442)

Sheet G94

◊ This work should be familiar to students from previous units. A useful discussion could be generated on what are the advantages of either a stem-and-leaf table or a frequency table.

◊ In drawing the frequency graph we have adopted the convention that as the data is discrete we leave gaps between the bars and each bar is labelled with the group description. The figures '40–49' etc. are just labels, so the width of the bars and the gaps between them are arbitrary. Using a continuous scale and not leaving gaps is generally acceptable though you would be advised to check examination boards' individual expectations.

Ⓓ *Continuous data* (p 444)

> Optional: large sheet of paper and coins

TG

◊ Playing the game themselves and collecting their own data will help students' understanding of this section. They need to understand that when dealing with continuous data the group limits need to be described more accurately.

Some examination boards may require the use of inequalities to describe group limits.

Frequency diagrams

The dividing lines between bars are sometimes drawn at 10.5, 20.5 etc. to allow for rounding. In reality, it makes little difference to the visual impact of the bars.

Ⓐ *Just a few* (p 439)

A1 (a) 2, 2, 2, 3, 8, 9, 9; median = 3

(b) $35 \div 7 = 5$ (c) $9 - 2 = 7$

A2 (a) $80 \div 5 = 16$

(b) 18   (c) 10

A3 (a) 5   (b) $174 \div 12 = 14.5$

(c) The girls' marks have (i) a smaller mean but (ii) a wider range.

A4 (a) $945 \div 9 = 105\,g$ (b) 19 g

(c) South African apples have
(i) a higher mean weight but
(ii) the same range as French apples.

A5 (a) $35 \div 5 = 7$

(b) $68 \div 8 = 8.5$

(c) Boys

(d) (i) 7   (ii) 6

(e) (i) 9   (ii) 14

(f) The girls have a higher median but the boys have a much wider range.

Ⓑ *Frequency tables* (p 441)

B1 (a) 30   (b) 7   (c) 5

(d) 13   (e) 13   (f) 390

(g)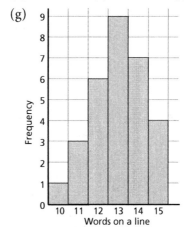

Ⓒ *Grouping data* (p 442)

C1 (a) 2   4 6 8
3   2 3 3 4 6 7 8 8
4   0 1 2 4 5 6 6 7 8 8
5   1 2 5 7 8 8

(b) Median = 42; range = $58 - 24 = 34$

(c) Median = 37; range = 38

(d) Males have a higher median but smaller range.

C2 (a)

Male age (years)	Frequency
20–29	3
30–39	8
40–49	10
50–59	6

(b) 40–49   (c) 30–39

(d)

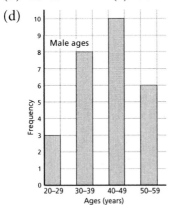

C3 (a)

Number of pets	Tally	Freq.
0–1	ЖЖ ЖЖ III	13
2–3	ЖЖ III	8
4–5	ЖЖ I	6
6–7	III	3
8–9	II	2

(b)

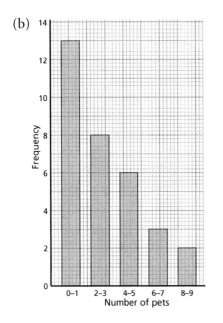

Ⓓ **Continuous data** (p 444)

D1 (a)

Distance (cm)	Frequency
$0 \leq x < 10$	3
$10 \leq x < 20$	5
$20 \leq x < 30$	6
$30 \leq x < 40$	10
$40 \leq x < 50$	6
Total	30

(b) $30 \leq x < 40$

D2 (a)

Max. temp. (°C)	Frequency
$12.0 \leq t < 13.0$	9
$13.0 \leq t < 14.0$	7
$14.0 \leq t < 15.0$	13
$15.0 \leq t < 16.0$	1
$16.0 \leq t < 17.0$	1
Total	31

(b) $14.0 \leq t < 15.0$ (c) 16

D3 (a) (i) 6.3 cm   (ii) 12.4 cm

(b)

Length of line (x cm)	Tally	Frequency
$0 \leq x < 4$	I	1
$4 \leq x < 8$	ЖЖ I	6
$8 \leq x < 12$	II	2
$12 \leq x < 16$	III	3
$16 \leq x < 20$	I	1

(c) $4 \leq x < 8$

D4

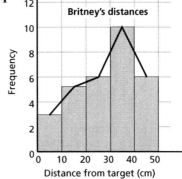

D5 (a) $40 < w \leq 50$ (b) $30 < w \leq 40$

(c)

Weight w (kg)	Frequency
$30 < w \leq 40$	4
$40 < w \leq 50$	11
$50 < w \leq 60$	8
$60 < w \leq 70$	6
$70 < w \leq 80$	1
Total	30

(d) $40 < w \leq 50$

(e) and (f)

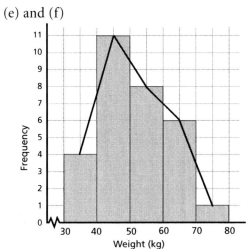

Test yourself (p 447)

T1 (a) $53 \div 10 = 5.3$

(b) 2 3 3 3 4 6 6 7 8 11; median = 5

(c) $11 - 2 = 9$

T2 (a) (i) 6.1s

(ii) $164 \div 12 = 13.7$s (1 d.p.)

(b) The girls' mean is higher but the range is smaller.

T3 (a)
2	5 5 5 6 6 8
3	0 3 3 4 5 5 5 6 8 8
4	0 2 3 3 4 5 6
5	0 1 4

(b) (i) 35.5   (ii) 29

T4

Number of beans	Tally	Frequency
1–5	Ⱶ I	6
6–10	Ⱶ II	7
11–15	Ⱶ I	6
16–20	I	1

T5

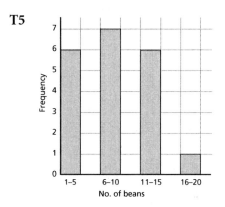

T6 (a)

Time (t seconds)	Tally	Frequency
$0 \leq t < 5$	III	3
$5 \leq t < 10$	Ⱶ II	7
$10 \leq t < 15$	Ⱶ IIII	9
$15 \leq t < 20$	IIII	4
$20 \leq t < 25$	II	2

(b) $10 \leq t < 15$

T7 (a) $5 < w \leq 10$

(b)

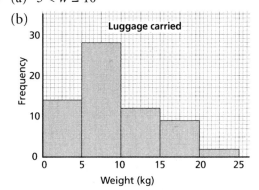

Practice book

Sections A and B (p 186)

1 (a) 4   (b) 6   (c) 5

2 (a) 17   (b) 14   (c) 20   (d) 9

(e) The range of goals scored, and the mean number of goals are both greater in the 2001–2002 season.

3 (a) 35   (b) 7   (c) 8   (d) 9

(e)
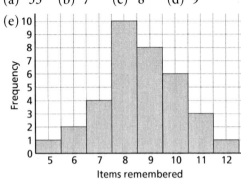

Section C (p 187)

1 (a)
```
2 |
3 | 3  7  9
4 | 0  1  2  4  5  5  9
5 | 0  0  1  1  2  3  3  6  6  9
6 | 0  5  6  6  6  9
7 | 1  4
8 | 4
```

(b) Median = 52; range = 51

(c)
```
2 | 8
3 | 8
4 | 2  7  8
5 | 3  4  5  6  7  9
6 | 1  1  2  2  4  7  8
7 | 1  1  2  2  3  4  4  4  5  8
8 | 1
```

(d) Median = 62; range = 53

(e) The median of the second paper is higher so more people scored high marks on the second paper.

2 (a)

Marks	Frequency
30–39	3
40–49	7
50–59	10
60–69	6
70–79	2
80–89	1

(b) 50–59

(c)
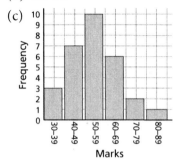

(d) 70–79

3 (a)

Fish	Frequency
5–7	1
8–10	18
11–13	2
14–16	6
17–19	0
20–22	1

(b)
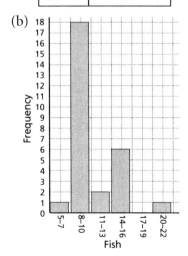

Section D (p 188)

1 (a)

Length l (cm)	Frequency
$19.0 \leq l < 22.0$	7
$22.0 \leq l < 25.0$	6
$25.0 \leq l < 28.0$	10
$28.0 \leq l < 31.0$	5
$31.0 \leq l < 34.0$	2
Total	30

(b) $25.0 \leq l < 28.0$

(c) 13

(d) and (e)

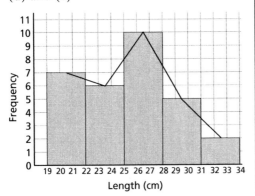

2 (a)

Jump j (m)	Frequency
$10.0 \leq j < 11.0$	1
$11.0 \leq j < 12.0$	3
$12.0 \leq j < 13.0$	7
$13.0 \leq j < 14.0$	5
$14.0 \leq j < 15.0$	1
Total	17

(b) $12.0 \leq j < 13.0$

(c) and (d)

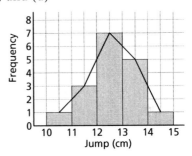

58 Sequences

Practice book pages 189 and 190

A *Next term* (p 449)

◊ One way to introduce this section would be to write on the board 1, 3, … and invite the class (without opening their textbooks!) to suggest what the next number is. When a number is suggested, write it up and ask for the next number. Continue until you think it is time to ask for an explanation of how you get the next number from the previous one(s).

Then write the numbers 1, 3, … on the board again, and ask if anyone can suggest a different next number, and continue as above.

(As an alternative you could say that you are thinking of a particular sequence – perhaps 'Add 2', but don't say so – that starts 1, 3, … Ask students to suggest what the next number is. When the correct next number is suggested, write it up, and continue writing up correct numbers until you think that most of the class know your rule.)

You could then repeat this until a sufficient variety of sequences have been suggested.

Then ask students to write down in secret a (simple) rule of their own for a sequence. Invite a student to come up to the front and write down their first five terms. The rest of the class have to try to guess the rule. If they cannot, then the student must write up another term, and another, and so on until the rule is found.

◊ Ensure that students understand the use of the word 'term', meaning one of the numbers in the sequence. When describing sequences on the board, take the opportunity to familiarise students with language such as 'How do we get the third term from the second term?' 'What do you think the fifth term will be?'

> 'This was a really useful unit to do as preparation for investigations coursework.'

B *Patterns* (p 451)

◊ Students need to be able to explain how they can find the number of matches if they are given a pattern number. In the introduction, ensure that the following points are made.

• As the pattern number goes up by 1, so the number of matches goes up by 3.

Pattern number	1	2	3	4	5	6
Number of matches	4	7	10	13	16	19

+3 +3 +3 +3 +3

So the number of matches has something to do with multiplying the pattern number by 3. At this point students may find it useful to copy the table and to write the multiples of 3 under it.

Pattern number	1	2	3	4	5	6
Number of matches	4	7	10	13	16	19
	3	6	9	12	15	18

Now we can see that adding 1 to the multiples of 3 gives us the number of matches. So the rule is to multiply the pattern number by 3 and then to add 1.

• Students can now use the rule to find the number of matches for other pattern numbers.

◊ Some students may be able to see the rule direct from the geometry of the pattern. In this case, pattern 4 (for example) is made of 4 sets of three matches and another one at the end.

◊ When they have found the rule for the pattern, ask which pattern has 100 matches. This could be found by simple trial and improvement, but some students may be happy to use the more formal method of solving an equation.

A *Next term* (p 449)

A1 16, 19, 22

A2 (a) 10, 12, 14   (b) 16, 26, 42
(c) 32, 64, 128   (d) 82, 244, 730

A3 (a) 17, 19; add 2 (b) 20, 23; add 3
(c) 26, 30; add 4 (d) 320, 640; double
(e) 21, 34; add the previous two terms together.

A4 (a) ⁻6, ⁻8; take off 2
(b) ⁻15, ⁻19; take off 4
(c) ⁻1, ⁻3; take off 2
(d) 3, $2\frac{1}{2}$; take off $\frac{1}{2}$

A5 (a) 16, 19   (b) Add 3

A6 (a) 17; add 4   (b) 16; double

A7 3, ⁻3

A8 (a) 18   (b) ⁻10

A9 (a) 34, 55   (b) 3

Ⓑ ***Patterns*** (p 451)

B1 (a) 8   (b) 10

(c)
Pattern no.	1	2	3	4	5	6
No. of btns	2	4	6	**8**	**10**	**12**

(d) 20

(e) Double the pattern number.

(f) Pattern 21

B2 (a)
Pattern no.	1	2	3	4	5
No. of matches	3	5	**7**	**9**	**11**

(b) Pattern 7

(c) Double the pattern number (12) and add 1.

B3 (a)
Shape no.	1	2	3	4	5
No. of matches	5	9	**13**	**17**	**21**

(b) 49; multiply the shape number by 4 and add 1.

B4 (a)

(b)
Pattern no.	1	2	3	4	5
No. of dots	3	5	7	**9**	**11**

(c) (i) 25

(ii) Double the pattern number and add 1.

B5 (a)
Shape no.	1	2	3	4	5
No. of matches	8	**13**	**18**	**23**	**28**

(b) 103; multiply the shape number by 5 and add 3.

(c) Shape 29

Test yourself (p 453)

T1 (a) 18, 21, 24; add 3

(b) 23, 27, 31; add 4

(c) ⁻3, ⁻5, ⁻7; take off 2

(d) 2, 1, $\frac{1}{2}$; divide by 2

(e) $3\frac{1}{2}$, 4, $4\frac{1}{2}$; add $\frac{1}{2}$

T2 80, 242

T3 No, the next term is (6 + 16) × 2 = 44. Deepak forgot to multiply by 2.

T4 (a)
Pattern no.	1	2	3	4	5
No. of dots	5	**8**	**11**	**14**	**17**

(b) 62; multiply the number of dots by 3 and then add 2.

(c) Pattern 28

T5 (a) (i) 41.

(ii) Multiply the term number by 4 and add 1.

(b) (i) 7   (ii) 127

Practice book

Section A (p 189)

1 (a) 17, 21, 25

(b) 16, 32, 64

(c) 121, 364, 1093

2 (a) 23, 28; add 5

(b) 96, 192; double

(c) 18, 29; add last two terms

3 (a) ⁻4, ⁻7; take 3 away

(b) ⁻8, ⁻13; take 5 away

(c) 3, $2\frac{1}{2}$; take $\frac{1}{2}$ away

4 (a) Double the last term.

(b) 80, 160

5 23, 37

*6 (a) Jo's rule:
    'Add the next multiple of 2.'
    or, Add 2, add 4, add 8 ...

(b) Peter's rule:
    'Double the previous term and
    add 1.'

Section B (p 190)

1 (a)

Pattern	1	2	3	4	5
No. of matches	9	13	**17**	**21**	**25**

(b) Pattern 7

(c) Multiply the pattern number (10) by
    4 and add 5.

2 (a)   Pattern 4

(b)

Pattern	1	2	3	4	5
No. of dots	6	10	**14**	**18**	**22**

(c) 42; multiply the pattern number by
    4 and add 2.

3 (a)

Shape	1	2	3	4	5
No. of matches	7	**12**	**17**	**22**	**27**

(b) 77; multiply the pattern number by
    5 and add 2

(c) Shape 20

Enlargement

This unit revises enlargement and deals with enlargement from a given centre. Students also investigate the effects of enlargement on perimeter and angle.

p 454 **A** *Using squares*		Enlarging using squared paper
p 455 **B** *Using a centre*		Enlarging using a given centre
p 457 **C** *Effects of enlargement*		Investigating the effect of enlargement on perimeter and angle

TG
TG

> **Essential**
> Sheets G95, G96, G97, G98
> Centimetre squared paper
>
> **Practice book** pages 191 and 192

Ⓐ *Using squares* (p 454)

> Centimetre squared paper

Ⓑ *Using a centre* (p 455)

> Sheets G95, G96, G97, G98
> Centimetre squared paper

TG

'It was unusual that finding the centre preceded the mechanics of enlargement but it worked well and the students enjoyed it.'

◊ The initial investigation should lead to the result that there is always a 'centre' of enlargement from which rays pass through corresponding points. It should also be established that the distances from this point to a point on the object are magnified by the scale factor of the enlargement on to the new point. This leads to the ray method of enlargement used in question B3. The distances, to the nearest 0.5 cm, from X to the original points should be:

A 5 cm, B 8.5 cm, C 9.5 cm, D 10 cm, E 9 cm

Where squared paper is used, the L method in 'Using a grid' on page 456 is more accurate and depends less on drawing skill.

C *Effects of enlargement* (p 457)

| Centimetre squared paper |

◊ In the initial investigation students should arrive at the result that the perimeter of a shape increases by the scale factor of the enlargement but the angles remain the same.

Perimeter of original = 19 cm, perimeter of enlargement = 38 cm
Angles: EAB = 53°, ABC = 127°, BCD = 143°, CDE = 127°, DEA = 90°

◊ Questions C3 and C4 deal with the fact that given any two squares or circles one is always an enlargement of the other. The same is not true of all rectangles.

A *Using squares* (p 454)

A1 The student's scale factor 2 enlargements of shapes

A2 B not an enlargement   C scale factor 2
D not an enlargement   E scale factor 3

B *Using a centre* (p 455)

B1 (a) and (b)

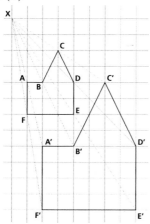

(c)

Point	X to original (D1)	X to enlargement (D2)
A	4.1 cm	8.2 cm
B	4.5 cm	9.0 cm
C	3.6 cm	7.2 cm
D	5.7 cm	11.4 cm
E	7.2 cm	14.4 cm
F	6.1 cm	12.2 cm

(d) The student's check that each D2 is 2 × D1.

B2 (a)

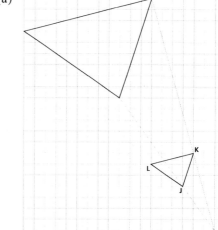

(b)

Point	(D1)	(D2)	D2 ÷ D1
J	5 cm	15 cm	3
K	7.3 cm	21.9 cm	3
L	8.5 cm	25.5 cm	3

(c) D2 ÷ D1 is always 3.

B3 (a)

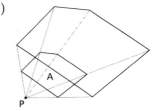

(b)

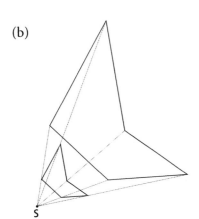

B4

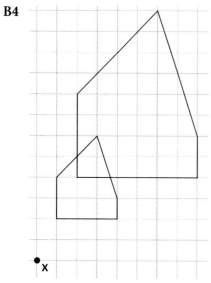

B5

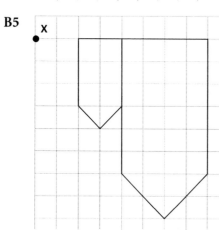

B6

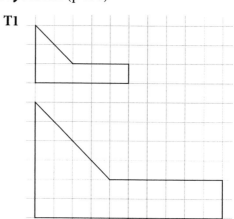

ℂ *Effects of enlargement* (p 457)

C1 (a) 12 cm   (b) 24 cm
     (c) 48 cm   (d) 37°

C2 (a) 8 cm   (b) 36°, 68° and 76°

C3 (a) B: 2   C: $1\frac{1}{2}$ (b) No

C4 (a) No   (b) Yes

Test yourself (p 458)

T1

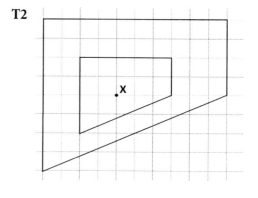

T2

Practice book

Sections B and C (p 191)

1

scale factor 2

2

scale factor 3

3

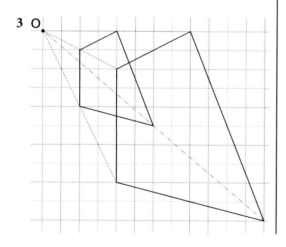

4

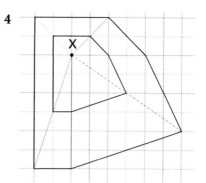

5 (a) 2   (b) 3

6 16 cm and 24 cm

7 (a) 48°, 99°, 66°, 147°

    (b) 90 cm

60 *Calculating with fractions*

Essential

Sheet G99, preferably on card

Practice book pages 193 to 195

ℂ *Calculating 1* (p 461)

Sheet G99

𝔻 *Comparing fractions 1* (p 463)

◊ It is intended that students see that they can compare unit fractions by looking at the denominators: for example, $\frac{1}{3}$ must be larger than $\frac{1}{4}$ as one out of three equal pieces must be larger than one out of four equal pieces.

◊ By the end of the discussion students should see that, where the denominator of one fraction is a multiple of the other, one fraction can be written with the denominator of the other so they can be compared.

D9 Encourage students to list fractions equivalent to the fraction with the smaller denominator as this leads to the general methods in sections F and G.

E Calculating 2 (p 464)

◊ By the end of the discussion students should see that, where the denominator of one fraction is a multiple of the other, one fraction can be written with the denominator of the other so they can be added or subtracted. Students may find it helpful to draw diagrams.

◊ You may wish to show students how to use the fraction key on a scientific calculator to check their answers.

F Comparing fractions 2 (p 465)

◊ The introduction could be put into a practical context such as: 'Which would you rather have, 2 pieces of a bar of chocolate cut into 3, or 4 pieces of a bar cut into 7?'

◊ When writing out sets of equivalent fractions, a common mistake is to repeatedly double the numerator and denominator and hence to miss the common denominators. For example: $\frac{2}{3} = \frac{4}{6} = \frac{8}{12} = \frac{16}{24} = \dots$ (missing out $\frac{6}{9}, \frac{10}{15}$ etc.) and $\frac{4}{7} = \frac{8}{14} = \frac{16}{28} = \dots$

A Review (p 459)

A1 A, S ($\frac{1}{3}$ is one third)

B, Q ($\frac{3}{4}$ is three quarters)

C, R ($\frac{3}{5}$ is three fifths)

D, T ($\frac{5}{6}$ is five sixths)

E, P ($\frac{4}{9}$ is four ninths)

A2 (a) $\frac{1}{2} = \frac{5}{10}$　(b) $\frac{1}{4} = \frac{3}{12}$

(c) $\frac{2}{5} = \frac{8}{20}$　(d) $\frac{2}{3} = \frac{4}{6}$

A3 $\frac{2}{3}$

A4 (a) $\frac{1}{2}$　(b) $\frac{1}{5}$　(c) $\frac{1}{6}$

(d) $\frac{4}{5}$　(e) $\frac{3}{4}$

A5 $\frac{1}{3}$

A6 (a) $\frac{6}{12}, \frac{3}{6}, \frac{10}{20}$　(b) $\frac{2}{8}, \frac{4}{16}$

(c) $\frac{6}{10}, \frac{9}{15}$

B Mixed numbers (p 460)

B1 (a) $\frac{5}{2}$　(b) $\frac{5}{4}$　(c) $\frac{6}{5}$　(d) $\frac{4}{3}$

(e) $\frac{9}{4}$　(f) $\frac{5}{3}$　(g) $\frac{13}{10}$　(h) $\frac{7}{2}$

(i) $\frac{13}{5}$　(j) $\frac{22}{5}$

B2 (a) $1\frac{2}{5}$　(b) $1\frac{3}{4}$　(c) $1\frac{1}{10}$　(d) $1\frac{1}{6}$

(e) $4\frac{1}{2}$　(f) $2\frac{3}{4}$　(g) $2\frac{1}{5}$　(h) 2

(i) $3\frac{1}{4}$　(j) $2\frac{1}{3}$

B3 $\frac{9}{2}$ ($4\frac{1}{2}$)

B4 $\frac{8}{7}$ ($1\frac{1}{7}$), $\frac{17}{10}$ ($1\frac{7}{10}$), $\frac{11}{4}$ ($2\frac{3}{4}$), $\frac{15}{5}$ (3), $\frac{10}{3}$ ($3\frac{1}{3}$)

B5 19

B6 16

C Calculating 1 (p 461)

C1 $\frac{3}{5}$

C2 (a) $\frac{2}{3}$ (b) $\frac{4}{5}$ (c) $\frac{5}{7}$ (d) $\frac{4}{5}$ (e) $\frac{7}{10}$ (f) $\frac{2}{7}$ (g) $\frac{1}{5}$ (h) $\frac{5}{8}$ (i) $\frac{2}{9}$ (j) $\frac{1}{6}$

C3 $\frac{1}{4}$

C4 (a) $1\frac{2}{5}$ (b) $1\frac{1}{3}$ (c) 1 (d) $1\frac{1}{7}$ (e) $1\frac{4}{9}$

C5 A, R $(\frac{1}{2})$ B, P $(\frac{1}{3})$ C, S $(1\frac{1}{2})$ D, Q $(\frac{2}{5})$ E, U $(\frac{3}{4})$ F, T $(\frac{2}{3})$

C6 (a) $\frac{1}{2}$ (b) $\frac{1}{2}$ (c) $\frac{2}{3}$ (d) $\frac{1}{4}$ (e) $\frac{3}{5}$

C7

$1\frac{1}{7}$	$\frac{4}{5}$	$\frac{5}{9}$	$\frac{1}{3}$
1 · $1\frac{2}{7}$	$1\frac{1}{5}$		
	$1\frac{1}{4}$	$1\frac{1}{2}$	$\frac{1}{2}$
$\frac{5}{11}$	$\frac{1}{4}$		
$\frac{1}{2}$			$\frac{3}{4}$
$\frac{2}{3}$	$1\frac{2}{11}$ · $4\frac{1}{7}$		$\frac{3}{8}$

C8 (a) $3\frac{1}{2}$ tins (b) 10 days

C9 3 pints

C10 (a) $1\frac{1}{2}$ (b) $1\frac{1}{4}$ (c) 2 (d) $1\frac{2}{3}$ (e) $2\frac{1}{3}$ (f) $2\frac{1}{4}$ (g) $1\frac{3}{5}$ (h) $1\frac{2}{6}$ or $1\frac{1}{3}$ (i) $1\frac{4}{8}$ or $1\frac{1}{2}$ (j) $1\frac{3}{9}$ or $1\frac{1}{3}$

C11 8 tins

C12 (a) 5 (b) $2\frac{2}{5}$ (c) $3\frac{1}{2}$ (d) $4\frac{4}{5}$ (e) $3\frac{1}{4}$

C13 (a) 5 (b) $3\frac{3}{4}$ (c) $6\frac{1}{2}$ (d) $6\frac{2}{3}$ (e) $4\frac{1}{3}$

C14 (a) $1\frac{3}{5}$ (b) $2\frac{1}{4}$ (c) $2\frac{1}{3}$ (d) $1\frac{1}{2}$ (e) $\frac{4}{5}$

C15 $10\frac{1}{2}$ pints

D Comparing fractions 1 (p 463)

D1 (a) $\frac{2}{3}$ (b) $\frac{1}{2}$ (c) $\frac{1}{3}$ (d) $\frac{2}{3}$

D2 Brooke

D3 $\frac{1}{2}$ P $\quad$ $\frac{3}{12}$ A $\quad$ $\frac{1}{4}$ R $\quad$ $\frac{2}{15}$ K

D4 The student's two different fractions between $\frac{1}{8}$ and $\frac{3}{4}$, such as: $\frac{1}{4}, \frac{3}{8}, \frac{1}{2}, \frac{5}{8}$

D5 Poppy and her friends

D6 $\frac{7}{9}$ C $\quad$ $\frac{2}{5}$ R $\quad$ $\frac{7}{8}$ A $\quad$ $\frac{3}{8}$ M $\quad$ $\frac{5}{7}$ P

D7 The student's fraction between $\frac{3}{4}$ and $\frac{14}{16}$, such as: $\frac{13}{16}$

D8 (a) $\frac{1}{5}, \frac{1}{4}, \frac{1}{2}$ (b) $\frac{1}{10}, \frac{1}{5}, \frac{2}{5}$ (c) $\frac{1}{6}, \frac{1}{3}, \frac{4}{9}$

D9 $\frac{1}{4}, \frac{11}{20}, \frac{4}{5}, \frac{9}{10}$

E Calculating 2 (p 464)

E1 (a) $\frac{3}{4}$ (b) $\frac{1}{4}$ (c) $\frac{3}{8}$ (d) $\frac{3}{8}$ (e) $\frac{3}{10}$

E2 (a) $1\frac{1}{4}$ (b) $1\frac{1}{8}$ (c) $1\frac{3}{4}$ (d) $2\frac{1}{4}$ (e) $1\frac{1}{8}$

E3 (a) $\frac{3}{5}$ (b) $\frac{1}{2}$ (c) $\frac{2}{3}$ (d) $\frac{1}{3}$ (e) $\frac{1}{5}$

E4 $\frac{1}{2}$

E5 (a) $\frac{5}{6}$ (b) $\frac{5}{8}$ (c) $\frac{1}{3}$ (d) $\frac{1}{4}$ (e) $\frac{1}{2}$

E6 (a) $1\frac{1}{14}$ (b) $1\frac{1}{3}$ (c) $1\frac{1}{2}$ (d) $1\frac{1}{9}$ (e) $1\frac{3}{8}$

*E7 (a) $2\frac{1}{4}$ miles (b) 5 miles (c) $2\frac{3}{4}$ miles

F Comparing fractions 2 (p 465)

F1 $\frac{3}{4}$ is smaller ($\frac{15}{20}$ is smaller than $\frac{16}{20}$).

F2 $\frac{2}{5}$ M $\quad$ $\frac{3}{4}$ I $\quad$ $\frac{3}{4}$ L $\quad$ $\frac{3}{7}$ L

F3 $\frac{2}{3}$ is larger: $\frac{3}{5} = \frac{9}{15}$ and $\frac{2}{3} = \frac{10}{15}$

F4 $\frac{1}{2}, \frac{5}{8}, \frac{2}{3}$

F5 $\frac{1}{3}, \frac{2}{5}, \frac{3}{5}, \frac{2}{3}$

F6 $\frac{1}{10}, \frac{1}{4}, \frac{2}{5}, \frac{1}{2}, \frac{3}{5}$

*F7 The student's fraction between $\frac{3}{5}$ and $\frac{5}{9}$, such as $\frac{26}{45}$

*F8 The student's two fractions between $\frac{1}{3}$ and $\frac{1}{5}$, such as $\frac{1}{4}, \frac{4}{15}$

Ⓖ **Calculating 3** (p 466)

G1 (a) $\frac{10}{15}, \frac{3}{15}$ (b) $\frac{13}{15}$

G2 (a) $\frac{1}{2} = \frac{2}{4} = \frac{\mathbf{3}}{\mathbf{6}} = \frac{\mathbf{4}}{\mathbf{8}}$
   (b) $\frac{1}{3} = \frac{\mathbf{2}}{\mathbf{6}} = \frac{\mathbf{3}}{\mathbf{9}} = \frac{\mathbf{4}}{\mathbf{12}}$
   (c) $\frac{5}{6}$

G3 (a) $\frac{7}{12}$ (b) $\frac{11}{15}$ (c) $\frac{3}{20}$
   (d) $\frac{3}{14}$ (e) $1\frac{5}{12}$

Test yourself (p 467)

T1 Jim has $\frac{3}{4} = \frac{9}{12}$ and Mary has $\frac{4}{6} = \frac{8}{12}$.
$\frac{9}{12}$ is greater than $\frac{8}{12}$ so Jim has the most paint.

T2 $\frac{7}{12}, \frac{5}{8}, \frac{17}{24}, \frac{3}{4}$

T3 $\frac{1}{4}, \frac{1}{3}, \frac{1}{2}, \frac{2}{3}, \frac{3}{4}$

T4 $3\frac{2}{5}$

T5 $5\frac{1}{2}$ miles

T6 The student's two fractions between $\frac{1}{2}$ and $\frac{1}{4}$, such as $\frac{1}{3}, \frac{3}{8}$

T7 $1\frac{1}{4}$ inches

T8 5 tins

T9 (a) 2   (b) $1\frac{1}{8}$ (c) $\frac{2}{15}$ (d) $\frac{9}{12}$ or $\frac{3}{4}$

Practice book

Section B (p 193)

1 $\frac{8}{3} = 2\frac{2}{3}$ $\frac{9}{5} = 1\frac{4}{5}$ $\frac{7}{3} = 2\frac{1}{3}$

   $\frac{6}{5} = 1\frac{1}{5}$ $\frac{16}{5} = 3\frac{1}{5}$

2 (a) $2\frac{3}{5}$ (b) $1\frac{2}{3}$ (c) $1\frac{5}{7}$
   (d) $2\frac{1}{6}$ (e) $2\frac{3}{8}$

3 $\frac{12}{7}, \frac{10}{5}, \frac{13}{6}, \frac{13}{4}, \frac{14}{3}$

Section C (p 193)

1 $\frac{3}{7}$

2 (a) $\frac{3}{5}$ (b) $\frac{2}{3}$ (c) $\frac{1}{2}$ (d) $\frac{6}{7}$
   (e) $\frac{3}{4}$ (f) $\frac{2}{3}$ (g) $\frac{1}{3}$ (h) $\frac{2}{5}$
   (i) $\frac{1}{2}$ (j) $\frac{2}{3}$

3 (a) $\frac{2}{5}$ or $\frac{4}{10}$ (b) $\frac{3}{5}$ or $\frac{6}{10}$

4 (a) 1   (b) $1\frac{1}{3}$ (c) 2   (d) $\frac{2}{5}$
   (e) $\frac{3}{4}$ (f) 3   (g) $2\frac{1}{7}$ (h) $4\frac{2}{7}$
   (i) $\frac{3}{5}$ (j) $\frac{1}{5}$

5 (a) 5   (b) $1\frac{3}{4}$ (c) $2\frac{2}{3}$ (d) $3\frac{3}{4}$
   (e) $4\frac{4}{5}$ (f) $4\frac{1}{2}$ (g) 9   (h) $16\frac{2}{3}$
   (i) $7\frac{1}{3}$ (j) $11\frac{1}{2}$

6 $13\frac{3}{4}$ hours

Sections D and E (p 194)

1 (a) $\frac{3}{5}$ (b) $\frac{1}{3}$ (c) $\frac{2}{5}$
   (d) $\frac{4}{9}$ (e) $\frac{5}{8}$

2 (a) $\frac{1}{2}$ $\frac{7}{12}$ $\frac{2}{3}$ $\frac{3}{4}$ $\frac{5}{6}$
      D   R   E   A   M

   (b) $\frac{1}{2}$ $\frac{3}{5}$ $\frac{7}{10}$ $\frac{4}{5}$ $\frac{9}{10}$
      B   R   A   C   E

   (c) $\frac{3}{8}$ $\frac{1}{2}$ $\frac{9}{16}$ $\frac{5}{8}$ $\frac{3}{4}$
      T   I   M   E   R

3 (a) $\frac{5}{8}$ (b) $\frac{1}{4}$ (c) $\frac{1}{4}$ (d) $\frac{1}{2}$
   (e) $\frac{3}{10}$ (f) $\frac{1}{8}$ (g) $\frac{3}{4}$ (h) $\frac{1}{4}$
   (i) $\frac{3}{5}$ (j) $\frac{1}{9}$

4 $\frac{3}{6}$ or $\frac{1}{2}$

5 $\frac{5}{8}$

6 (a) $1\frac{3}{8}$ (b) $1\frac{1}{10}$ (c) $1\frac{3}{4}$ (d) $1\frac{7}{8}$

  (e) $1\frac{1}{4}$ (f) $1\frac{2}{9}$ (g) $1\frac{1}{2}$ (h) $1\frac{1}{6}$

  (i) $1\frac{3}{4}$ (j) $2\frac{1}{8}$

7 (a) $1\frac{3}{10}$ litre   (b) $\frac{7}{10}$ litre

Sections F and G (p 195)

1 $\frac{5}{6}$ is larger: $\frac{3}{4} = \frac{9}{12}$, $\frac{5}{6} = \frac{10}{12}$

2 (a) $\frac{1}{2}$ $\frac{3}{5}$ $\frac{3}{4}$ $\frac{4}{5}$

    H O S T

  (b) $\frac{1}{4}$ $\frac{1}{3}$ $\frac{5}{12}$ $\frac{1}{2}$

    A R T S

  (c) $\frac{1}{2}$ $\frac{8}{15}$ $\frac{3}{5}$ $\frac{2}{3}$

    C O L A

3 $\frac{15}{20} + \frac{8}{20} = \frac{23}{20} = 1\frac{3}{20}$

4 (a) (i) $\frac{1}{4} = \frac{2}{8} = \frac{3}{12} = \frac{4}{16} = \frac{5}{20}$

    (ii) $\frac{2}{3} = \frac{4}{6} = \frac{6}{9} = \frac{8}{12} = \frac{10}{15}$

  (b) $\frac{3}{12} + \frac{8}{12} = \frac{11}{12}$

5 (a) $\frac{5}{6}$ (b) $\frac{5}{12}$ (c) $\frac{4}{15}$ (d) $\frac{9}{20}$

  (e) $\frac{1}{15}$ (f) $\frac{5}{28}$ (g) $\frac{9}{10}$ (h) $\frac{7}{12}$

  (i) $\frac{17}{30}$ (j) $\frac{1}{24}$

6 $\frac{8}{15}$

7 $\frac{31}{24} = 1\frac{7}{24}$

61 Substitution

Essential

Sheet G100

Practice book pages 196 to 198

B *What an expression!* (p 469)

The emphasis here is on the order in which expressions are evaluated:

- first what is in brackets (if any), then
- any powers, then
- multiplication or division, and last
- addition and subtraction

Stress that in expressions like $5a^3$ we evaluate a^3 first, then multiply by 5.

D *Decimals* (p 472)

Sheet G100

E *Forming and solving equations* (p 473)

◊ Students should by now be confident about substituting a value of a variable in a formula to find the value of the subject.

But sometimes the value of the subject is given, and they are asked to find the value of the variable. For example, in the introduction, $BC = x - 6$, and therefore the perimeter of the triangle is $x + x + x - 6 = 3x - 6$.

We are told that the perimeter (the subject) is 21 cm, so
$$21 = 3x - 6, \text{ and hence } x = 9. \text{ (AC = AB = 9 cm and BC = 3 cm.)}$$

Forming an equation in this way may be quite difficult for some students. You may wish to discuss questions like E3 with them before they tackle the section for themselves.

Ⓐ Review (p 468)

A1 (a) 14　(b) 14　(c) 10　(d) 20

A2 A and F: $6 + 4 \times 5 = 6 + 2 \times 10$
B and H: $6 \times (2 + 7) = 6 \times (4 + 5)$
C and E: $8 \times 3 + 5 = 6 \times 4 + 5$
D and G: $(6 + 4) \times 5 = (8 + 2) \times 5$

A3 (a) 7　(b) 10　(c) 8　(d) 11

A4 (a) $p + 999$　(b) p^2

A5 (a) 9.9　(b) 9.6　(c) 8　(d) 5

A6 (a) ⁻6　(b) ⁻5　(c) ⁻20　(d) ⁻8

*A7 $r - s = 3.7$; G　　$t + u = 8$; R
$u - 2s = 9.4$; E　　$5t = {}^-10$; A
$t - r = {}^-6$; T　　　GREAT

Ⓑ What an expression! (p 469)

B1 (a) 6　(b) 11　(c) 16　(d) 5　(e) 13

B2 (a) 16　(b) 5　(c) 3　(d) 24　(e) 16

B3 (a) $p(q + r) = 18$; K　$p^2 + q^2 = 13$; O
$\dfrac{pq}{r} = 1$; A　　　　OAK

(b) $pqr = 36$; R　　$\dfrac{pq}{2} = 3$; H
$r(p + q) = 30$; B　$3p^3 = 24$; I
$\dfrac{4pq}{r} = 4$; C　　　BIRCH

(c) $3q^2 = 27$; L　　$1 + pr = 13$; O
$\dfrac{r^2}{2} + q^2 = 27$; L　$q^3 - q = 24$; I
$\dfrac{r}{q} = 2$; W　　　$\dfrac{2r}{pq} = 2$; W WILLOW

B4 (a) ⁻6　(b) ⁻3　(c) ⁻9　(d) ⁻24　(e) 40

B5 A and F: $mp = 4n = {}^-8$

B and G: $mp - n = \dfrac{p}{m} - n = {}^-6$

C and E: $2mn - p = \dfrac{p}{n} = {}^-4$

D and H: $n + p = {}^-3n = 6$

B6 $R = 4$

B7 (a) 37　(b) 23

B8 (a) 1　(b) ⁻91

B9 (a) 15　(b) 46　(c) 512　(d) 3.8　(e) 26

B10 (a) 13　(b) 80

B11 About 860 or 900 cm²

B12 (a) 15 mg　(b) 2.5 mg

(c) The student's reasoning, such as 'If $A = 47$, then the dose would be 60 mg – twice the adult dose.'

B13 (a) 68°F　(b) 24°F

Ⓒ Brackets and fractions (p 471)

C1 $10 + (s + t)$ is bigger.

C2 (a) $80 + (5c - b)$ is bigger.
(b) $a + (c - b)$ is bigger.

C3 (a) 9　(b) 10　(c) 9

C4 (a) When $a = \frac{1}{2}$ and $b = \frac{1}{4}$,
$T = 2 - (\frac{1}{2} + \frac{1}{4})$
$= 2 - \frac{3}{4}$
$= \mathbf{1\frac{1}{4}}$
(b) $T = 1$

C5 (a) 7　(b) $9\frac{3}{4}$　(c) 3　(d) 0

C6 (a) 20　(b) 16 cm　(c) 12 cm
(d) 18 cm　(e) 19 cm　(f) 7 o'clock

C7 (a) 49 m.p.h.　(b) 45 m.p.h.
(c) 44 m.p.h.

Ⓓ Decimals (p 472)

D1 £128.00

D2 (a) 13.2　(b) 20.5　(c) 13.3

D3 (a) 64.8　(b) 27　(c) 1.92
(d) 1.2　(e) 86.4

D4 7 rolls (6.975 rounded up to nearest whole number)

D5 (a) 27°C　(b) 66°C
(c) ⁻37°C　(d) ⁻7°C

D6 (a) (i) $S = 15$, $n = 356$, $p = 0.12$

  (ii) £57.72

  (b) P: Units used 680
        Total charge £93.00
     Q: Units used 18 750
        Total charge £1372.50
     R: Units used 10 800
        Total charge £914.00
     S: Current reading 4200
        Units used 700

D7 $2.1\,\text{m}^2$

D8 (a) $0.775\,\text{m}^2$ (b) $45\,\text{cm}^2$

  𝔼 *Forming and solving equations* (p 473)

E1 (a) $y = 29$ (b) $y = {}^-19$ (c) $x = 9$

E2 (a) $l = 22$ (b) $l = 1$ (c) $r = 7$

E3 (a) £175 (b) 48 pages

E4 (a) 2900 (b) 8

  (c) 6 rooms (6.66... rounded down)

E5 (a) $2a$ (b) $6a$

  (c) $6a = 30$; 5 cm by 10 cm.

E6 (a) $s = 18$ (b) $t = 4$

  (c) $t = 19$ to nearest whole number, so
     $s \approx 2 \times 19 + 32 = 70$

E7 (a) $y - 3$ (b) $4y - 6$ (c) $y = 5.25$

E8 (a) £67 (b) $6n + 7$

  (c) $6n + 7 = 85$; she bought 13 trees.

E9 (a) $80x$ pence (or £$0.80x$) (b) $80r + 60t$

  (c) $80g + 120 = 1080$ (d) $g = 12$

Test yourself (p 475)

T1 (a) 24 (b) 18 (c) 6 (d) 5 (e) 8

T2 (a) 1 (b) $^-6$ (c) $^-1$ (d) $^-8$ (e) 5

T3 (a) 3 (b) 8 (c) $\frac{1}{4}$ (d) $\frac{5}{8}$

T4 (a) $36\,\text{cm}^2$ (b) $24\,\text{cm}^2$ (c) $17\frac{1}{2}\,\text{cm}^2$

T5 (a) $p = 25$ (b) $p = 11$ (c) $q = 7$

T6 (a) £30 (b) 8 inches

T7 (a) $x + 3$ (b) $x - 1$ (c) $3x + 2$

  (d) $3x + 2 = 44$

  (e) $x = 14$; AB = 14 cm, BC = 17 cm,
     CA = 13 cm

Practice book

Sections A and B (p 196)

  1 (a) 17 (b) 25 (c) 11

  2 C and E, B and F, G and H

  3 (a) $(2 + 3) \times 4 + 5 = 25$

   (b) $(2 + 3) \times (4 + 5) = 45$

  4 (a) 18 (b) 27 (c) 45 (d) 5
   (e) 45 (f) 54 (g) 57 (h) 2

  5 (a) 0 (b) 4 (c) 8 (d) $^-2$
   (e) 8 (f) $^-32$ (g) 10 (h) 0

  6 $252\,\text{cm}^2$

Sections C and D (p 197)

  1 A is biggest (24); B is 11; C is 12

  2 (a) A is biggest (38); B is 25; C is 22

   (b) C is biggest (39); A is 21; B is 36

  3 (a) 22 (b) 14 (c) 18

  4 (a) 11 (b) 8 (c) 3

  5 (a) 12 (b) 57 km (c) 54 km

   (d) 5 hours

  6 (a) 9.2 (b) 5.2 cm

Section E (p 198)

  1 (a) $v = 20$ (b) $t = 6$

  2 (a) $C = 2100$ (b) $m = 100$

   (c) £23.00 (d) 40 miles

  3 (a) $ah - bh$ or $h(a - b)$

   (b) $39\,\text{m}^2$ (c) $47.1\,\text{m}^2$

  4 (a) $x, x + 4, 2x$ (b) $4x + 4$

   (c) $4x + 4 = 24$

   (d) $x = 5$; sides are 5 cm, 9 cm and 10 cm

Review 7 (p 476)

1 (a) (i) 2   (ii) $\frac{1}{3}$

   (b) (i) 6   (ii) $\frac{1}{2}$

   (c) (i) 3   (ii) $\frac{1}{2}$

2   $0.072\,\text{m}^3$

3 (a)

Pattern no.	1	2	3	4	5	6
No. of tiles	4	7	10	**13**	**16**	**19**

   (b) Pattern 8

   (c) 31 tiles. Multiply the pattern number by 3 and add 1.

4 (a) $37.7\,\text{cm}$ (b) $113.1\,\text{cm}^2$

5   56 m.p.h.

6   $\frac{3}{10}, \frac{7}{20}, \frac{2}{5}, \frac{1}{2}$

7 (a)

$$
\begin{array}{c|ccccccc}
3 & 1 & 5 \\
4 & 2 & 4 & 6 & 6 & 7 & 8 \\
5 & 0 & 1 & 1 & 2 & 7 & 8 & 8 \\
6 & 3 & 4 & 5 & 6 & 8 & 9 \\
7 & 0 & 3 & 4 & 8 \\
\end{array}
$$

   (b) Median = 57; range = 47

8   27, 51

9

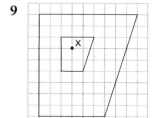

10   $1\frac{2}{3}$ pints

11 (a) ⁻6   (b) 6   (c) 2   (d) ⁻8

12 (a) £95   (b) £82.50

Mixed questions 7 (Practice book p 199)

1   $a = 35°$ $b = 138°$ $c = 42°$ $d = 138°$
    $e = 60°$ $f = 30°$ $g = 80°$

2 (a) $4410\,\text{cm}^3$ (b) $1974\,\text{cm}^2$

3 (a) 44

   (b) The student's explanation, e.g. 'You multiply the term number by 6 and subtract 4.'

4   63 cm

5 (a) 147 miles   (b) 192 miles

   (c) 42 m.p.h.

6 (a) 9 hours   (b) 8 hours

   (c) $7\frac{1}{2}$ hours

7   2

8 (a) $\frac{7}{12}$ (b) $\frac{3}{10}$ (c) $3\frac{3}{4}$ (d) $\frac{5}{8}$

9   $\frac{2}{3}$ is larger because $\frac{5}{8} = \frac{15}{24}$ and $\frac{2}{3} = \frac{16}{24}$

10 (a) $7x + 1$ (b) $x = 7\,\text{cm}$

11 (a) $1\frac{1}{2}$ (b) $\frac{1}{4}$ (c) 5   (d) 0

12 (a) 20 km   (b) 20 km/h

   (c) He stopped.   (d) 35 km/h

   (e) 70 km

62 Probability

62 Probability

This unit revises earlier work on calculating probabilities as a fraction and introduces decimals by considering experimental probabilities.

Essential

Cottage cheese pots or similar
Sheet G101 on card
Blank dice or wooden blocks

Practice book pages 201 to 203

B *Off the table* (p 479)

Students will have a much better feel for a set of information if they have collected one about their own group. For example, they could record whether they can roll their tongue, whether their earlobes are attached, or whether they see faces or a candlestick in the picture on the right.

With all tables stress the importance of finding the totals, and in the case of two-way tables of working out all the row and column totals.

D *Experiments* (p 481)

> Cottage cheese pots or similar

It will be better if all students use an identical pot so that results can be compared and combined as necessary. A supermarket or other grocery store may be willing to donate a supply of the tubs used at delicatessen counters.

◊ The two main objectives of the initial activity are for students to
- appreciate that results will vary when an experiment is repeated
- appreciate that the greater number of times an experiment is carried out, the more accurate the probability estimate is likely to be

In order to compare the estimates of the probability at each stage of the experiment they are converted into decimals. This is the first time students will have done this.

Students could continue, or combine results with other groups who have used an identical pot, to give results for 100 and 200 trials. A graph could be drawn plotting trials along the *x*-axis and probability up the *y*-axis with straight lines drawn between each consecutive point for each of the three ways. This would show how, after many trials, the estimates of the probability settle down to a fairly consistent result.

E *Theory or experiment?* (p 483)

Sheet G101 on card, blank dice or wooden blocks

Bear necessities

Students should first play this game 50 times and record the number of times A wins, B wins or the game is drawn. The experimental probabilities can then be calculated.

The theoretical probabilities can be calculated by using a grid.

	Bear	B	B	X	A	A
Player A	Bear	B	B	X	A	A
	Rifle	X	X	A	X	X
	Man	X	X	B	X	X
	Man	X	X	B	X	X
		Rifle	Rifle	Bear	Man	Man

Player B

So probability A wins $= \frac{5}{25} = 0.2$
probability B wins $= \frac{6}{25} = 0.24$
probability of a draw $= \frac{14}{25} = 0.56$

Chinese dice

Allow the students a little time to play with the dice and think about the outcomes, then ask them if they can see a strategy. The students could then carry out an experiment to see what happens when they play with different pairs of dice.

Once the students have a good estimate of the probability of A beating B, B beating C and C beating A the theoretical probabilities can be calculated. The game of A against B can be shown on a grid:

```
        6 | X   X   X   X   X   X
        6 | X   X   X   X   X   X
Score on 2 | X   X   O   O   O   O    X shows A winning
dice A   2 | X   X   O   O   O   O    O shows B winning
        2 | X   X   O   O   O   O
        2 | X   X   O   O   O   O
          |_____
            1   1   5   5   5   5
            Score on dice B
```

So the probability A beats B is $\frac{20}{36} = 0.56$.

Similarly the probability that B beats C is $\frac{2}{3} = 0.67$ and C beats A with probability $\frac{2}{3} = 0.67$.

The trick of Chinese dice is always to 'generously' let the other player choose a dice first and then choose the dice that has a higher chance of beating it.

The DIME probability kit available from mathematical product suppliers offers some excellent experiments for which the experimental probability can be calculated and then the theoretical probability analysed.

Ⓐ **Simply chance** (p 478)

A1 (a) Q   (b) P   (c) R

A2 (a) $\frac{1}{6}$ (b) $\frac{4}{6} = \frac{2}{3}$
    (c) $\frac{4}{6} = \frac{2}{3}$ (d) 0

A3 (a) $\frac{1}{8}$ (b) $\frac{1}{2}$ (c) $\frac{3}{8}$ (d) $\frac{1}{2}$

A4 (a) (i) $\frac{5}{8}$ (ii) $\frac{3}{8}$
    (b) (i) $\frac{4}{9}$ (ii) $\frac{5}{9}$
    (c) (i) $\frac{7}{10}$ (ii) $\frac{3}{10}$
    (d) (i) $\frac{6}{9} = \frac{2}{3}$ (ii) $\frac{3}{9} = \frac{1}{3}$

Ⓑ **Off the table** (p 479)

B1 (a) 50
    (b) (i) $\frac{3}{50}$ (ii) $\frac{15}{50} = \frac{3}{10}$
       (iii) $\frac{38}{50} = \frac{19}{25}$ (iv) 0

B2 (a) 25   (b) 10   (c) $\frac{10}{25} = \frac{2}{5}$
    (d) (i) $\frac{15}{25} = \frac{3}{5}$ (ii) $\frac{10}{25} = \frac{2}{5}$
       (iii) $\frac{15}{25} = \frac{3}{5}$

Ⓒ **Listing outcomes** (p 480)

C1 (a)

Boy	Girl
Aaron	Donna
Aaron	Evelyn
Aaron	Fatima
Aaron	Gill
Baljit	Donna
Baljit	Evelyn
Baljit	Fatima
Baljit	Gill
Colin	Donna
Colin	Evelyn
Colin	Fatima
Colin	Gill

    (b) 12

    (c) (i) $\frac{1}{12}$ (ii) $\frac{4}{12} = \frac{1}{3}$ (iii) $\frac{9}{12} = \frac{3}{4}$

C2 (a)

Red	Red
Red	Blue
Red	Green
Blue	Red
Blue	Blue
Blue	Green
Green	Red
Green	Blue
Green	Green

    (b) (i) $\frac{1}{9}$ (ii) $\frac{3}{9} = \frac{1}{3}$ (iii) $\frac{6}{9} = \frac{2}{3}$

C3 (a)   Set B

+	4	5	6	7
1	**5**	**6**	**7**	8
2	6	**7**	**8**	**9**
3	**7**	**8**	**9**	10

Set A for rows 1, 2, 3

    (b) (i) $\frac{2}{12} = \frac{1}{6}$ (ii) $\frac{3}{12} = \frac{1}{4}$

       (iii) $\frac{3}{12} = \frac{1}{4}$ (iv) $\frac{6}{12} = \frac{1}{2}$

       (v) 1

Ⓓ *Experiments* (p 481)

D1 (a) After 25 tries, an estimate of the
       probability of landing jam-down
       $= \frac{17}{25} = \frac{\mathbf{68}}{100} = \mathbf{0.68}$

    (b) (i) $\frac{36}{50}$ (ii) 0.72

D2 (a) 0.69

    (b) The result from 100 trials

D3 (a) 0.4   (b) 0.3   (c) 0.4

    (d) 0.52   (e) 0.46

D4 (a) (i) 0.5 (ii) 0.55   (iii) 0.6

    (b) Yes – it is quite close.

    (c) The council's

D5 (a)

Number of drops	5	10	20	25	50	100
Number of times landed up	3	7	11	15	32	63
Probability	0.6	0.7	**0.55**	**0.6**	**0.64**	**0.63**

    (b)

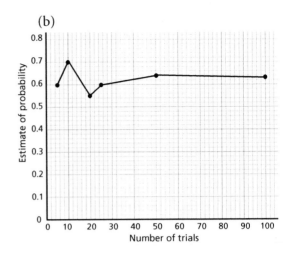

    (c) About 0.6 or 0.63

Ⓔ *Theory or experiment?* (p 483)

E1 (a) $\frac{1}{5} = 0.2$

    (b)

Colour	Red	Blue	Green	Yellow	White
Frequency	8	13	10	7	12
Prob.	0.16	**0.26**	**0.20**	**0.14**	**0.24**

    (c) Red and yellow

    (d) Blue and white

    (e) He could carry out more trials.

Ⓕ *Sum to 1* (p 484)

F1 0.44

F2 0.65

F3 0.25

F4 (a) 0.26   (b) 0

F5 (a) 0.2   (b) 40

F6 They add up to less than 1.

F7 They add up to more than 1.

G *Mixed questions* (p 485)

G1 (a) $\frac{2}{6} = \frac{1}{3}$ (b) $\frac{3}{10}$ (c) $\frac{3}{7}$

G2 (a) $\frac{3}{5}$ (b) 0

(c)   Differences

5	**4**	**3**	**2**	**1**	**0**	
4	**3**	**2**	**1**	**0**	**1**	
3	**2**	**1**	**0**	**1**	**2**	
2	**1**	**0**	**1**	**2**	**3**	
1	**0**	**1**	**2**	**3**	**4**	
	1	**2**	**3**	**4**	**5**	

Second spinner (vertical axis), First spinner (horizontal axis)

(d) (i) $\frac{5}{25} = \frac{1}{5}$ (ii) $\frac{8}{25}$ (iii) $\frac{12}{25}$

G3 (a) 0.9

(b) $\frac{8}{30} = \frac{4}{15}$

(c) The national survey will be more reliable as there were a lot more people in it.

G4 (a) 0.3   (b) 24

Test yourself (p 486)

T1 (a) $\frac{3}{8}$ (b) $\frac{1}{8}$ (c) 0.75

T2 (a) About 300

(b)

1, heads	1, tails
2, heads	2, tails
3, heads	3, tails
4, heads	4, tails
5, heads	5, tails

(c) (i) 0.14   (ii) 0   (iii) 1

T3 $\frac{20}{50} = 0.4$

Practice book

Sections A, B and C (p 201)

1 (a) M   (b) J   (c) L

2 (a) $\frac{1}{6}$ (b) $\frac{3}{6} = \frac{1}{2}$ (c) $\frac{5}{6}$ (d) 0

3 (a) 30

(b) (i) $\frac{15}{30} = \frac{1}{2}$ (ii) $\frac{14}{30} = \frac{7}{15}$

(iii) $\frac{16}{30} = \frac{8}{15}$

4 (a)

1 H	1 T
2 H	2 T
3 H	3 T
4 H	4 T
5 H	5 T
6 H	6 T

(b) (i) $\frac{1}{12}$ (ii) $\frac{3}{12} = \frac{1}{4}$

5 (a)

+	1	2	3	4	5	6
1	2	3	4	5	6	7
2	3	4	5	6	7	8
3	4	5	6	7	8	9
4	5	6	7	8	9	10

(b) (i) $\frac{1}{24}$ (ii) $\frac{4}{24} = \frac{1}{6}$

(iii) $\frac{6}{24} = \frac{1}{4}$ (iv) 1

Sections D and E (p 202)

1 (a) 0.7   (b) 0.65

(c) 0.46   (d) 0.55

2 (a) (i) 0.6   (ii) 0.55   (iii) 0.62

(b) Yes, the probabilities are quite close.

3 (a)

Score	1	2	3	4	5	6
Frequency	30	44	26	32	50	18
Estimated probability	0.15	**0.22**	**0.13**	**0.16**	**0.25**	**0.09**

(b) 1, 3, 4, 6   (c) 2, 5   (d) Yes

Section F (p 203)

1 0.82

2 0.37

3 (a) 0.1   (b) 4

4 They add up to less than 1.

5 (a) 0.76   (b) About 12 days

6 (a) 0.22   (b) 55

(c) No, the probabilities are roughly equal.

63 Getting more from your calculator

> **Practice book** pages 204 to 206

B *Order of operations* (p 487)

◊ In this unit it is assumed that the calculators used by the students will obey the priority rules (multiplication and division before addition and subtraction, and so on).

If you allow the use of 'simple' calculators that do calculations from left to right, then you will need to adapt the material in the unit.

Students might need reminding that they should not round their answers during the calculations.

E *Brackets* (p 489)

◊ You may need to explain why brackets are needed when entering $\frac{7+8}{5}$ in a calculator.

G *Square roots* (p 490)

◊ You may need to remind students of the meaning of square root and to build up a list of square roots that they know, such as $\sqrt{25} = 5$.

To start with, they could use the calculator to find known square roots, in order to familiarise themselves with how the $\sqrt{}$ key is used on their calculator.

Ⓐ *Rounding: review* (p 487)

A1 (a) 47   (b) 133   (c) 30   (d) 37

A2 (a) 3.4   (b) 17.2   (c) 21.0   (d) 6.0

A3 (a) 0.58   (b) 9.04   (c) 6.40
(d) 13.86

A4 (a) 3.2   (b) 15.95   (c) 7.30
(d) 2.1

Ⓑ *Order of operations* (p 487)

B1 (a) 19   (b) The student's check

B2 (a) 26   (b) 1   (c) 19   (d) 22
(e) 20

B3 (a) 178   (b) 6   (c) 622   (d) 256

B4 (a) 66.8   (b) 67   (c) 15.1

B5 (a) 66   (b) 60   (c) 52

B6 (a) 90.1   (b) 152.8   (c) 46.2

B7 (a) 24.88   (b) 152.65   (c) 25.07

Ⓒ *Division* (p 488)

C1 (a) 8   (b) The student's check

C2 (a) 7   (b) 1   (c) 16
(d) 13   (e) 20

C3 (a) 49   (b) 64   (c) 62   (d) 6
(e) 512

C4 (a) 57   (b) 108   (c) 15   (d) 5

C5 (a) 8.1   (b) 94.7   (c) 0.5

C6 (a) 18.07   (b) 16.93   (c) 43.66

Ⓓ *Negative numbers* (p 489)

D1 (a) 5   (b) ⁻5   (c) ⁻4   (d) 12
(e) 10   (f) ⁻5   (g) 3   (h) 1.5
(i) 7   (j) 2

D2 (a) 37   (b) ⁻43   (c) ⁻360   (d) 289
(e) ⁻2.5   (f) 12   (g) ⁻4.2   (h) 23.45

D3 395.6 degrees

Ⓔ *Brackets* (p 489)

E1 (a) 12   (b) The student's check

E2 (a) 27.9   (b) 6.2   (c) 2.7
(d) 3.3   (e) 135.8   (f) 22.6

E3 (a) 1.33   (b) 2.83   (c) 0.40

E4 (a) ⁻2   (b) 96   (c) 4.32

Ⓕ *Squares and other powers* (p 490)

F1 (a) 22.47   (b) 0.72   (c) 1.64
(d) 2.70

F2 (a) 5.81   (b) 61.78   (c) 5.72
(d) 9.18

F3 (a) 4.91   (b) 530.84   (c) 0.88
(d) 166.96   (e) 57.05

Ⓖ *Square roots* (p 490)

G1 (a) 4.3   (b) The student's check

G2 (a) 28   (b) 0.54   (c) 32.4

G3 (a) 23 cm   (b) 1.6 m
(c) 8.5 cm   (d) 0.84 m

G4 (a) 34   (b) 1.9   (c) 48.4
(d) 2.25   (e) 21.95   (f) 8.09
(g) 4   (h) ⁻1.46

G5 (a) 124   (b) 26   (c) 9
(d) 15   (e) 0.288   (f) 1.296
(g) 0.72   (h) 4.4

G6 (a) 4.93   (b) 6.01   (c) 0.89

Ⓗ *Reciprocals* (p 491)

H1 (a) 0.5   (b) 0.125   (c) 0.05
(d) 0.01   (e) 8   (f) 20
(g) 2.5   (h) 40   (i) 0.625
(j) 0.015625

H2 (a) 0.0625   (b) 0.02   (c) 0.3125
(d) 0.008   (e) 1.5625

H3 (a) 0.13   (b) 7.46   (c) 0.31
    (d) 5.76

Test yourself (p 491)

T1 (a) 2.65   (b) 343

T2 (a) 420   (b) 41.939 865…

T3 (a) 7.6   (b) 311.1696
    (c) 250   (d) 284

Practice book

Section B (p 204)

1 (a) 13 (b) 15 (c) 8 (d) 40

2 (a) 173   (b) 21
    (c) 1089   (d) 151

3 (a) 18   (b) 29

4 (a) 56.9   (b) 1.7

5 (a) 24.58   (b) 9.92

Section C (p 204)

1 (a) 9 (b) 4 (c) 15 (d) 10

2 (a) 20 (b) 56 (c) 32 (d) 2.5

3 (a) 7   (b) 78

4 (a) 47.3   (b) 1.2

5 (a) 5.18   (b) 13.95

6 K I L O G R A M
   1 4 5 6 7 9 10 23

Section D (p 205)

1 (a) 11   (b) 11   (c) $^-$414
    (d) 11   (e) $^-$4.5   (f) 15.54
    (g) 5.8   (h) $^-$4.2   (i) $^-$5

2 (a) 55.6°C   (b) 26.1°C

Sections E and F (p 205)

1 (a) 6.5   (b) 29.3   (c) 7.4
    (d) 1.4   (e) 8.1   (f) 8.6

2 (a) 2   (b) 8   (c) $^-$5.5

3 (a) 39.06   (b) 50.30
    (c) 5.52   (d) 6.49

4 (a) 21.95   (b) 676.52
    (c) 6.05   (d) 0.53

Section G (p 206)

1 (a) 26   (b) 8.2   (c) 0.67

2 (a) 1.1   (b) 45.36
    (c) 1.4   (d) 13.04

3 (a) 421 (b) 29 (c) 4 (d) 4

4 (a) 16.74   (b) 0.95   (c) 4.77

5 C   E   N   T   I
  1.08 1.26 2.02 4.37 4.48
   M   E   T   R   E
  7.13 14.52 14.53 79.63 79.64

Section H (p 206)

1 (a) 0.2   (b) 0.0625   (c) 0.025
    (d) 0.005   (e) 50   (f) 4
    (g) 80   (h) 0.3125

2 (a) 0.125   (b) 0.05
    (c) 0.15625 (d) 0.004

3 (a) 0.625   (b) 9.325   (c) 0.4

64 Transformations

This unit reviews transformations met in key stage 3 and extends this work to coordinate grids. Students are encouraged to use methods which do not rely on tracing paper. The term 'congruence' is also introduced.

Essential	**Optional**
Sheets G102, G103, G104, G105 Centimetre squared paper	Tracing paper, OHP transparency of sheet G102
Practice book pages 207 and 208	

A *Patterns* (p 492)

> Sheets G102, G103
> Optional: tracing paper, OHP transparency of sheet G102

◊ The initial activity is intended as a diagnostic exercise to review students' familiarity with transformations. Discussion should emphasise describing each transformation fully, for example describing a rotation by giving both the centre and the angle of rotation. Sheet G102 could be copied on to a transparency and used on an OHP. A separate blank transparency can then be used to demonstrate tracing-paper methods. Many students will still rely on tracing paper at this stage and later sections in this unit will show how to use a grid rather than tracing paper. The terms 'map' and 'image' are used throughout this unit and may need explaining.

B *Reflecting coordinates* (p 494)

> Centimetre squared paper

B6 Students should be familiar with the equations for lines parallel to the axes.

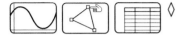 ◊ Much of the exploratory work in this unit, such as seeing what happens to coordinates under a reflection in the axes, can be carried out using suitable software such as *Omnigraph*, dynamic geometry packages or spreadsheets with appropriate routines to list the coordinates.

C *Translations* (p 496)

> Centimetre squared paper

At this level students are not required to use vectors. Questions C4 to C6 show that the horizontal and vertical shifts of a translation are added on to the *x*- and *y*-coordinates respectively. Describing a translation by distance and direction is covered in work on bearings.

D *Rotations* (p 497)

> Sheet G104, centimetre squared paper

By copying sheet G104 on to a transparency and using a separate sheet with the shape on it, the way that the L moves through 90° can easily be shown.

Fractions of a turn and degrees are used in this section.

E *Enlargement* (p 499)

> Centimetre squared paper

Students should be familiar with both techniques for enlargement from unit 59 'Enlargement'. Question E2 should reveal that when (0, 0) is used as a centre of enlargement, the coordinates of a shape are simply multiplied by the scale factor.

Test yourself (p 503)

> Sheet G105

Ⓐ *Patterns* (p 492)

A1 (a) K   (b) H   (c) H
     (d) A   (e) O   (f) J

A2 (a) Reflection in line L4
     (b) Rotation of a half turn, centre P8
     (c) Translation of 8 right and 10 up
     (d) Rotation of a half turn, centre P4
     (e) Reflection in line L5
     (f) Translation of 8 right

A3 (a) E   (b) K   (c) D
     (d) O   (e) N   (f) B

A4 (a) Rotation of a half turn, centre (14, 12)
     (b) Rotation of a quarter turn anticlockwise, centre (9, 9)
     (c) Translation of 2 left and 8 down
     (d) Rotation of a quarter turn anticlockwise, centre (14, 12)
     (e) Rotation of a half turn, centre (10, 13)
     (f) Rotation of a quarter turn clockwise, centre (4, 6)

A5 to A8

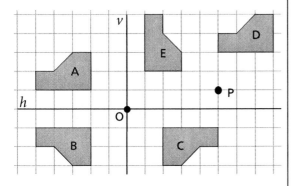

A9 (a) Reflection in line *v*
     (b) Point P as on diagram above

Ⓑ *Reflecting coordinates* (p 494)

B1 (1, 1), (2, 1), (2, 2), (1, 3)

B2 and **B3**

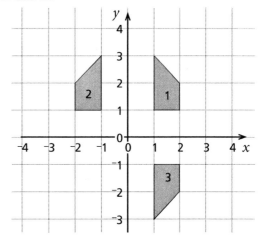

B4 (a) and (b)

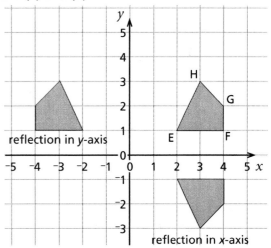

(c)

Original shape	Reflection in x-axis
E (2, 1)	E′ (2, ⁻1)
F (4, 1)	**F′ (4, ⁻1)**
G (4, 2)	**G′ (4, ⁻2)**
H (3, 3)	**H′ (3, ⁻3)**

(d) (i) (5, ⁻3)   (ii) (4, 0)
     (iii) (15, ⁻10)   (iv) (3, 2)

B5 (a) See diagram for B4.

(b)

Original shape	Reflection in y-axis
E (2, 1)	E' (-2, 1)
F (4, 1)	F' (-4, 1)
G (4, 2)	G' (-4, 2)
H (3, 3)	H' (-3, 3)

(c) (i) (-4, 5) (ii) (0, 3)

(iii) (-12, 15) (iv) (-3, -2)

B6 (a) $x = 3$ (b) $y = 3$

(c) $y = 1$ (d) $x = {}^-1$

B7 The x-axis has the equation $y = 0$, and the y-axis has the equation $x = 0$

B8 (a) B (b) C (c) I

B9 (a) Reflection in $x = 3$

(b) Reflection in $y = 3$

(c) Reflection in $x = 0$

ℂ **Translations** (p 496)

C1 (a) 2 (b) 3 (c) 4

C2 (a) Translation of 2 right and 3 up

(b) Translation of 4 right and 2 down

(c) Translation of 5 left and 3 down

C3

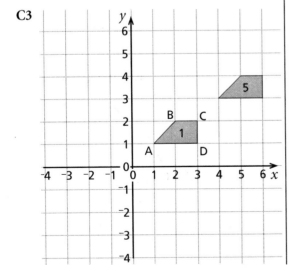

C4

Shape 1	Shape 5
A (1, 1)	A **(4, 3)**
B (2, 2)	B **(5, 4)**
C **(3, 2)**	C **(6, 4)**
D **(3, 1)**	D **(6, 3)**

C5 (a) (7, 4) (b) (15, 11) (c) (0, 6)

(d) (8, 2) (e) (5, -3) (f) (3, 6)

(g) (-3, -2) (h) (0, 0)

C6 (a) (9, 6) (b) (3, 5) (c) (-3, 6)

(d) (7, -2) (e) (-2, -1) (f) (0, 0)

𝔻 **Rotations** (p 497)

D1

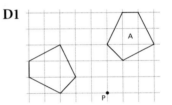

D2 (a), (b), (c) and (d)

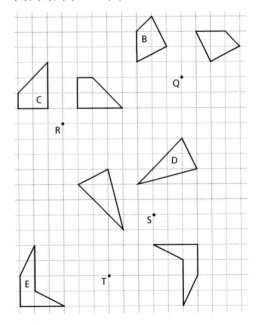

D3 (a), (b) and (c)

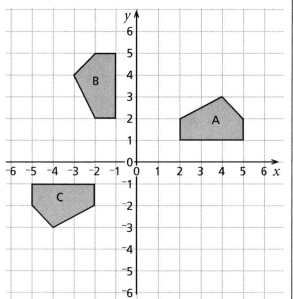

(d) $\frac{1}{4}$ turn clockwise rotation using centre (0, 0)

D4 (a) A (b) E (c) B (d) C

D5 (a) 90° anticlockwise rotation using centre (0, 0)

(b) 180° rotation using centre (0, 0)

(c) 90° clockwise rotation using centre (0, 0)

(d) 90° anticlockwise rotation using centre (0, 0)

D6 (a) 180° rotation using centre (0, 0)

(b) 90° clockwise rotation using centre (0, 0)

(c) 90° anticlockwise rotation using centre (0, 0)

D7 (a) Flag E (b) Flag A

(c) Flag C (d) Flag A

D8 (a) 60° clockwise rotation centre O

(b) 120° anticlockwise rotation centre O

E *Enlargements* (p 499)

E1 (a), (b) and (c)

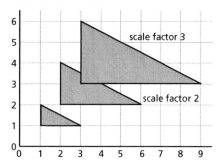

E2 (a), (b) and (c)

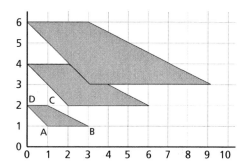

(d)

Original	Enlarged by scale factor 2	Enlarged by scale factor 3
A (1, 1)	A′ **(2, 2)**	A″ **(3, 3)**
B (3, 1)	B′ **(6, 2)**	B″ **(9, 3)**
C (1, 2)	C′ **(2, 4)**	C″ **(3, 6)**
D (0, 2)	D′ **(0, 4)**	D″ **(0, 6)**

(e) They are all multiplied by 2.

(f) They are all multiplied by 3.

F *Mixed transformations* (p 500)

F1 (a) Translation of 4 right and 4 up

(b) Reflection in the *x*-axis

(c) Reflection in the line $x = 4$

(d) 180° rotation, centre (0, 0)

(e) Reflection in the *y*-axis

(f) 90° anticlockwise rotation with centre (0, 0)

(g) Translation of 7 left and 2 up

(h) 90° clockwise rotation, centre (0, 0)

F2 (a)

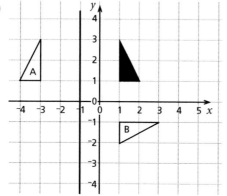

(b) 90° clockwise rotation, centre (0, 0)

F3 (a) Reflection in the *y*-axis

(b) 180° rotation, centre (0, 0)

(c) and (d)

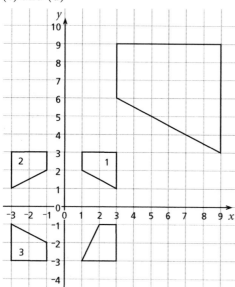

F4 (a) 90° clockwise rotation, centre (0, 0)

(b) and (c)

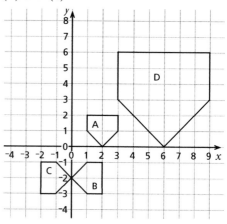

ⓖ *Congruence* (p 502)

G1 (a) C, F, G, L and O

(b) H, K, N and P

G2 Q, S, U and V

G3 J

Test yourself (p 503)

T1 (a)

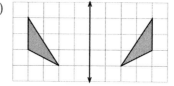

(b)

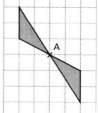

(c)

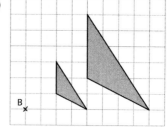

T2 90° anticlockwise rotation using centre $(0, 0)$

T3

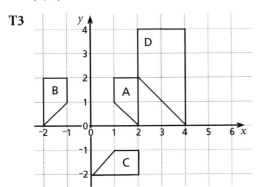

T4 A and F; B and G

Practice book

Sections B, C and D (p 207)

1 (a), (b), (c), (d) and (e)

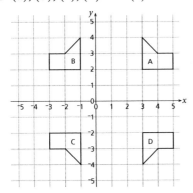

(f) $x = 1$

2 (a) 4 left and 1 down
(b) 1 left and 5 down
(c) 1 right and 4 up
(d) 4 right and 0 up

3 (a) $(8, {}^-5)$ (b) $({}^-1, 2)$

4 (a) Rotation 90° clockwise centre $(0, 0)$
(b) Rotation 180° centre $(0, 0)$
(c) Rotation 90° anticlockwise centre $(0, 0)$

Sections E and F (p 208)

1 (a) and (b)

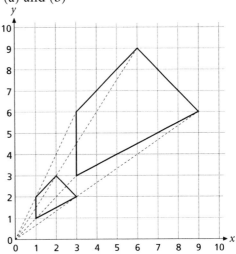

2 (a) Rotation 90° anticlockwise centre $(0, 0)$
(b) Reflection in the line $x = {}^-4$
(c) Reflection in the x-axis or $y = 0$
(d) Rotation 90° clockwise centre $(0, 0)$
(e) Translation 3 right and 2 up
(f) Reflection in the line $x = 4$
(g) Translation 2 left and 5 up

3 (a) to (g)

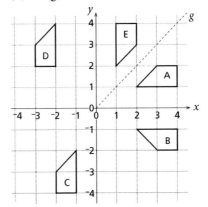

Written calculations with decimals

Practice book pages 209 and 210

Ⓐ *Review* (p 504)

Three different methods of long multiplication are shown, as a reminder. Students should be encouraged to use the method they find easiest.

Ⓑ *Multiplying with decimals* (p 506)

A revision of rounding to one significant figure and estimation may be useful. Students may also need to be reminded how to multiply decimals such as 20×0.3 and 0.2×0.5.

B7 You may need to point out that to find 2.5×6.50 we only need to multiply 2.5×6.5.

Ⓐ **Review** (p 504)

A1 (a) 7.65　　(b) 8.13
　　(c) 9.15　　(d) 15.62

A2 (a) 110.6　　(b) 10.72
　　(c) 2.6　　(d) 3.02

A3 (a) 2.3 kg　　(b) 2.05 kg

A4 (a) 7.44 kg　　(b) 2.64 kg
　　(c) 14.4 kg　　(d) 1.26 kg

A5 (a) 675　　(b) 1296
　　(c) 609　　(d) 2232

A6 (a) 2160　　(b) 6912
　　(c) 7820　　(d) 32 562

A7 825 words

A8 700 tiles

A9 (a) £2250　　(b) £1428
　　(c) £1680　　(d) £2142

A10 1050 kg

Ⓑ **Multiplying with decimals** (p 506)

B1 (a) 3　　(b) 16　　(c) 14
　　(d) 600　　(e) 0.04

B2 (a) 5.28　　(b) 52.8　　(c) 52.8
　　(d) 0.528　　(e) 0.0528

B3 (a) 8.84　　(b) 88.4　　(c) 88.4
　　(d) 0.884　　(e) 0.0884

B4 A and F: 164.5
B and G: 16.45
C and H: 1.645
D and E: 0.1645

B5 (a) 19.04   (b) 14.82   (c) 23.85
(d) 4.9   (e) 27

B6 (a) 75.6   (b) 240.8   (c) 1.344
(d) 0.702   (e) 0.85

B7 (a) £16.25   (b) £14.88   (c) £10.53

B8 (a) $3.68\,m^2$ (b) $9.18\,m^2$ (c) $4.845\,m^2$

B9 £172.80

B10 (a) 3.75 cm   (b) 6.75 kg
(c) 32 km   (d) 3.42 litres
(e) 38.25 litres   (f) 0.75 m, 1.2 m

ℂ *Mixed questions* (p 508)

C1 47.6 km

C2 (a) 22.6 cm   (b) 24.4 cm
(c) 111.2 cm   (d) 94 cm

C3 (a) £2.98   (b) £0.76
(c) £1.14   (d) £3.64

C4 £7.94

C5 Yes, 12 copies are only 7.2 cm thick.

C6 (a) 5.98 kg   (b) 0.82 kg

C7 (a) 1.6 km   (b) 12 km

C8 19.8 m

C9 8

Test yourself (p 509)

T1 (a) 3.2 m   (b) 6.8 m

T2 £1.69

T3 (a) £336
(b) (i) £66   (ii) 180 packets

T4 £63

Practice book

Section B (p 209)

1 (a) 10.81   (b) 1.081   (c) 10.81
(d) 0.1081   (e) 1.081

2 (a) 25   (b) 3.5   (c) 24
(d) 12   (e) 1.4

3 (a) 24.99   (b) 3.692   (c) 25.42
(d) 11.21   (e) 1.564

4 697p or £6.97

5 £30.45

6 (a) $6.82\,m^2$ (b) $9.57\,m^2$
(c) $15.12\,m^2$

7 (a) $336\,cm^2$ (b) $86.4\,cm^2$
(c) $21.06\,cm^2$ (d) $70.56\,cm^2$
(e) $22.95\,cm^2$

8 'Jennifer is 1.5 m tall. She weighs 44.1 kg.
Her handspan is 13.75 cm. On average,
she drinks 0.798 litres of water a day.
She lives 1.12 km from her school.'

Section C (p 210)

1 (a) Carrots £0.29, tomatoes £0.72,
turnips £1.02
(b) £17.97

2 (a) 1.35 m   (b) 0.45 m

3 (a) 6.3 kg   (b) 56.7 kg

4 (a) (i) £18.90   (ii) £6.50
(iii) £6.30
(b) £31.70

5 (a) $0.09\,m^2$ (b) $0.04\,m^2$
(c) $0.13\,m^2$ (d) $10.4\,m^2$
(e) 4.5 m

The solution is clear

This is the final unit on solving linear equations with integer coefficients. It deals with equations involving brackets and where unknowns or constants may be subtracted.

p 510 **A** *Review*	Equations of types already met
p 511 **B** *x subtracted*	Equations where an unknown is subtracted
p 512 **C** *Brackets*	
p 513 **D** *Mixed questions*	

Essential

Sheet G106

Practice book pages 211 and 212

B ***x subtracted*** (p 511)

Sheet G106

◊ When equations involve subtraction we can no longer appeal to the balancing image. Instead, the emphasis needs to be on doing the same thing to both sides.

◊ You will want to ensure that students write out their solutions in a logical way. One way of explaining what is done to both sides would be like this.

$$x + 4 = 16 - 2x$$
$$3x + 4 = 16 \quad [+ 2x]$$
$$3x = 12 \quad [- 4]$$
$$x = 4 \quad [÷ 3]$$

However, you may well have your own preferences, so we have not provided an exemplar in the student's book.

B5 Students often find equations of the type $1 = 9 - 2x$ hard to solve. Here x already appears only on one side, but with a negative coefficient. It is probably safest to add $2x$ to both sides first, though this does not seem a natural thing to do.

ℂ *Brackets* (p 512)

> Sheet G106

◊ The worked example in the introduction suggests multiplying out the brackets as the first step. In the example shown, it would of course be equally valid to first divide through by 2. But in examples of the type $2(x + 5) = x$ dividing will only confuse, so we suggest expanding the brackets as the first step.

C12 It may help to remind students that they have met solving equations involving division when solving 'Think of a number...' problems.

𝔻 *Mixed questions* (p 513)

> Sheet G106

𝔸 *Review* (p 510)

A1 (a) 12　(b) 5　(c) 6　(d) 11

A2 (a) $x = 6$　(b) $x = 3$　(c) $x = 3$
　　(d) $x = 3$　(e) $x = 8$　(f) $x = 5$

A3 (a) $n = 4$　(b) $w = 5$　(c) $m = 4$
　　(d) $x = 3$　(e) $n = 6$　(f) $h = 10$

A4 (a) $6x = 180$; $x = 30$
　　(b) $3x - 30 = 180$; $x = 70$
　　(c) $3x + 60 = 180$; $x = 40$

𝔹 *x subtracted* (p 511)

B1 $2x + 7 = 19 - 4x$
　　$6x + 7 = 19$
　　　$6x = 12$
　　　　$x = 2$

B2 (a) $x = 3$　(b) $r = 2$　(c) $p = 4$
　　(d) $x = 4$　(e) $x = 2$　(f) $x = 4$

B3 (a) $n = 4$　(b) $q = 5$　(c) $s = 3$
　　(d) $x = 5$　(e) $x = 3$　(f) $x = 4$

B4 (a) $n = 3$　(b) $n = 4$　(c) $n = 3$
　　(d) $n = 4$　(e) $n = 4$　(f) $n = 1$

B5 (a) $a = 2$　(b) $b = 4$

B6 (a) $x = 5$　(b) $e = 14$　(c) $x = 6$

B7 A: $x = 7$, C　　B: $x = 4$, H
　　C: $x = 4$, E　　D: $x = 2$, S
　　E: $x = 1$, T　　F: $x = 8$, E
　　G: $x = 7$, R　　CHESTER

B8 (a) $2x + 1 = 10 - x$; $x = 3$
　　(b) The plank's length is 7.

B9 (a) $x = 2$　　(b) $x = 2$

B10 (a) $x = {}^-1$　(b) $n = {}^-2$
　　(c) $r = 3$　　(d) $f = {}^-3$

B11 (a) $n = 2\frac{1}{2}$　(b) $m = \frac{2}{3}$
　　(c) $x = 3\frac{1}{2}$　(d) $d = \frac{3}{4}$

ℂ *Brackets* (p 512)

C1 (a) $x = 4$　(b) $x = 5$　(c) $x = 16$
　　(d) $n = 1$　(e) $n = 6$　(f) $n = 7$

C2 (a) $p = 10$　(b) $q = 5$　(c) $r = 14$
　　(d) $s = 6$　(e) $t = 6$　(f) $u = 3$

C3 (a) $d = 4$　(b) $f = 6$　(c) $v = 6$

C4 $3(2x - 5) = 9$
$6x - \mathbf{15} = 9$
$6x = \mathbf{24}$
$x = \mathbf{4}$

C5 (a) $n = 4$ (b) $n = 6$ (c) $n = 3$

C6 A: $x = 4$, B B: $x = 2$, R
C: $x = 8$, I D: $x = 7$, G
E: $x = 8$, H F: $x = 5$, T
G: $x = 6$, O H: $x = 4$, N
BRIGHTON

C7 (a) $x + 11y$
(b) (i) $x = 9$ (ii) $x = 1\frac{1}{2}$

C8 (a) $x = 3$ (b) $x = 4\frac{1}{2}$

C9 RABBIT

C10 $2(x + 5) = 17 + x$
$\mathbf{2x} + 10 = 17 + x$
$x + 10 = 17$
$x = \mathbf{7}$

C11 (a) $x = 7$ (b) $n = 7$ (c) $f = 5$

*C12 $\dfrac{x - 5}{2} = 3$
$x - 5 = \mathbf{6}$
$x = \mathbf{11}$

*C13 (a) $h = 18$ (b) $x = 18$ (c) $j = 8$

Ⓓ Mixed questions (p 513)

D1 (a) $x = 17$ (b) $x = 8$

D2 (a) $x = 7$ (b) $x = 23$

D3 (a) $x = 4$ (b) $x = 6$

D4 (a) $x = 6$ (b) $x = 3$ (c) $x = 5\frac{1}{2}$

D5 (a) $p = 7$ (b) $q = {}^-3$ (c) $r = 2.6$

D6 (a) $x = 7$ (b) $y = 5$

D7 (a) $q = {}^-4$ (b) $a = {}^-0.8$

D8 (a) $360°$ (b) $5x + 160$
(c) $5x + 160 = 360$ (d) $x = 40$
(e) A is $50°$, B is $120°$

D9 A: $x = 3$, S B: $x = 2$, W
C: $x = 7$, A D: $x = 4$, N
E: $x = 7$, S F: $x = 8$, E
G: $x = 3$, A SWANSEA

D10 (a) $8a - 4b$ (b) $x = 6$ (c) $7x - 21$

D11 (a) $9x°$ (b) $9x = 180, x = 20$

D12 (a) $3x + 2\,\text{cm}$ (b) $3x + 2 = 23, x = 7$

Test yourself (p 515)

T1 (a) $n = 5$ (b) $m = 4$ (c) $n = 4$
(d) $n = 3$ (e) $n = 6$ (f) $h = 10$

T2 (a) $a = 3$ (b) $b = 4$ (c) $c = 4$
(d) $d = 5$ (e) $e = 3$ (f) $f = 9$

T3 (a) $h = 5$ (b) Length $= 4$

T4 (a) $n = 6$ (b) $n = 8$ (c) $n = 21$
(d) $n = 3$ (e) $n = 5$ (f) $n = 6$

T5 (a) $x = 6\frac{1}{2}$
(b) (i) $^-7$ (ii) $y = 4\frac{1}{2}$

T6 (a) $x = 3$ (b) $x = 2$

T7 (a) $x = 3$ (b) $x = 1.4$
(c) $x = {}^-4$ (d) $x = 7$

T8 (a) $6x = 180$ (b) $x = 30$

T9 $x = 57$

Practice book

Sections A and B (p 211)

1 (a) $3x + 5 = x + 11$
$2x = 6$
$x = 3$
(b) $5x + 12 = 3x + 20$
$2x = 8$
$x = 4$

2 (a) $x = 4$ (b) $x = 2$ (c) $x = 3$
(d) $p = 3$ (e) $b = 10$ (f) $f = 2$

3 (a) $10p = 360$, $p = 36$

(b) $3p + 180 = 360$
$$3p = 180$$
$$p = 60$$

4 (a) $n = 2$ (b) $p = 7$ (c) $n = 2$
(d) $n = 2$ (e) $p = 3$ (f) $x = 1$

5 (a) $x = 3$ (b) $x = 3$ (c) $x = 3$

6 (a) $12 - 3x = 7x + 2$
$$10 = 10x$$
$$x = 1$$

(b) $37 - 6x = 3x + 10$
$$27 = 9x$$
$$x = 3$$

7 (a) $x = {}^-1$ (b) $n = {}^-3$ (c) $x = \frac{2}{3}$
(d) $d = \frac{3}{4}$ (e) $x = 4\frac{1}{2}$ (f) $x = \frac{4}{3}$

8 (a) $n = 3$ (b) $n = 2$
(c) $p = 1$ (d) $p = 0$

Sections C and D (p 212)

1 (a) $x = 6$ (b) $x = 9$ (c) $n = 13$
(d) $x = 10$ (e) $u = 8$ (f) $y = 4$

2 (a) $x = 1$ (b) $x = 1$ (c) $x = 2$
(d) $y = 1$ (e) $x = 2$ (f) $x = \frac{1}{2}$

3 (a) $x = 4$ (b) $n = 5$ (c) $x = 7$

4 (a) $3x = 36$, $x = 12$
(b) $y + 3 = 28$, $y = 25$
(c) $3p - 2 = 10$, $p = 4$

5 A: (a) $(80 - x) + (60 - 3x) + (100 - 2x)$
$$= 180$$
$$240 - 6x = 180$$

(b) $x = 10$

(c)

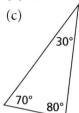

B: (a) $3x + 100 + (x + 20) + (90 - x)$
$$= 360$$
$$3x + 210 = 360$$

(b) $x = 50$

(c)

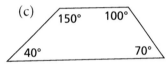

6 (a) $10x + 11$
(b) $10x + 11 = 51$
$$x = 4$$
(c) Sides are 16 cm, 9 cm, 2 cm, 24 cm

67 *Multiplying and dividing fractions*

> **Practice book** pages 213 and 214

TG

ℂ *Finding a fraction of a quantity: fractional results 2* (p 518)

The point to get over here is that $\frac{a}{b}$ **of** n is equivalent to $\frac{a}{b} \times n$.
So, for example, $\frac{2}{5}$ of $9 = \frac{2}{5} \times 9 = \frac{18}{5} = 3\frac{3}{5}$.

𝔻 *Dividing a unit fraction by a whole number* (p 519)

Once students have completed the questions, you could discuss the results and make explicit the rule that $\frac{1}{n} \div a = \frac{1}{na}$.

𝔼 *Dividing a fraction by a whole number* (p 520)

Again, once students have completed the questions, you could discuss the results and make explicit the rule that $\frac{m}{n} \div a = \frac{m}{na}$.
Include examples such as $\frac{2}{5} \div 2$ in your oral work and emphasise that this is an 'easy' problem which can be done directly. There is no need for $\frac{2}{5} \div 2 = \frac{2}{10} = \frac{1}{5}$.

𝔽 *Multiplying fractions* (p 521)

TG

◊ Different approaches are possible here.
Students can turn all multiplications into divisions (as only unit fractions are considered) so, for example, $\frac{1}{2} \times \frac{1}{3} = \frac{1}{2}$ of $\frac{1}{3}$ (using the equivalence of 'of' and '×' developed in section C) $= \frac{1}{3} \div 2 = \frac{1}{6}$.

Students could use the rule that $\frac{1}{a} \times \frac{b}{c} = \frac{b}{(a \times c)}$ as a special case of the more general rule for multiplying fractions: it depends on the receptiveness of the class!

'Area' diagrams for multiplying fractions could be helpful.

Ⓐ Review (p 516)

A1 (a) 4   (b) 3   (c) 3   (d) 10

A2 30 grams

A3 £5

A4 (a) 6   (b) 6   (c) 12   (d) 10

A5 21

A6 40 kg

A7 C ($\frac{1}{4} \times 10$)

A8 6

A9 (a) 2   (b) 4   (c) 4   (d) 5   (e) 2

A10 (a) $1\frac{1}{2}$ h   (b) $4\frac{1}{2}$ h   (c) $5\frac{1}{4}$ h

A11 (a) 3   (b) 4   (c) 6   (d) 8   (e) 6

A12 (a) $1\frac{1}{2}$ (b) $1\frac{1}{4}$ (c) $2\frac{1}{3}$
   (d) $1\frac{2}{3}$ (e) $1\frac{2}{5}$

Ⓑ Finding a fraction of a quantity: fractional results 1 (p 517)

B1 $1\frac{1}{2}$

B2 A, S   ($\frac{1}{4}$ of 5 and 5 ÷ 4)
   B, P   ($\frac{1}{5}$ of 4 and 4 ÷ 5)
   C, R   ($\frac{1}{4}$ of 6 and 6 ÷ 4)
   D, Q   ($\frac{1}{6}$ of 4 and 4 ÷ 6)

B3 (a) $3\frac{1}{2}$ (b) $1\frac{1}{4}$ (c) $3\frac{1}{3}$ (d) $3\frac{1}{2}$
   (e) $1\frac{1}{5}$ (f) $5\frac{1}{3}$ (g) $5\frac{1}{4}$ (h) $1\frac{1}{2}$

Ⓒ Finding a fraction of a quantity: fractional results 2 (p 518)

C1 (a) B ($\frac{1}{4} \times 7$)   (b) $1\frac{3}{4}$

C2 (a) $3\frac{3}{4}$ (b) $1\frac{2}{3}$ (c) $2\frac{2}{5}$
   (d) $4\frac{1}{2}$ (e) $1\frac{3}{4}$

C3 (a) $1\frac{1}{2}, 2\frac{3}{4}, 1\frac{2}{5}, 3\frac{3}{4}, 2\frac{1}{2}$
   BCHNE → BENCH
   (b) $4\frac{3}{4}, 1\frac{3}{5}, \frac{2}{3}, 2\frac{1}{2}$
   DKSE → DESK
   (c) $\frac{3}{4}, 2\frac{1}{3}, 1\frac{4}{5}, \frac{3}{4}, \frac{2}{3}$
   OTLOS → STOOL

C4 (a) D ($\frac{3}{4} \times 3$)   (b) $2\frac{1}{4}$

C5 (a) $2\frac{2}{3}$ (b) $5\frac{1}{4}$ (c) $1\frac{3}{5}$
   (d) $4\frac{1}{2}$ (e) $6\frac{2}{3}$

C6 (a) $1\frac{1}{3}, 1\frac{1}{5}, 2\frac{1}{4}, 2\frac{2}{5}, \frac{6}{7}$
   DABER → BREAD
   (b) $1\frac{1}{2}, 3\frac{1}{5}, 3\frac{1}{3}, 2\frac{4}{5}$
   SIFH → FISH
   (c) $6\frac{3}{4}, 3\frac{3}{4}, 1\frac{1}{2}, 1\frac{1}{5}, 1\frac{1}{5}$
   PTSAA → PASTA

Ⓓ Dividing a unit fraction by a whole number (p 519)

D1 (a) C   (b) $\frac{1}{8}$

D2 (a) A, Q   B, P   C, S   D, R
   (b) A $\frac{1}{5} \div 2 = \frac{1}{10}$ B $\frac{1}{3} \div 3 = \frac{1}{9}$
      C $\frac{1}{4} \div 3 = \frac{1}{12}$ D $\frac{1}{3} \div 5 = \frac{1}{15}$

D3 (a) $\frac{1}{4}$ (b) $\frac{1}{15}$ (c) $\frac{1}{12}$ (d) $\frac{1}{12}$ (e) $\frac{1}{8}$

D4 $\frac{1}{8}$

D5 (a) C   (b) $\frac{1}{6}$

D6 (a) $\frac{1}{8}$ (b) $\frac{1}{16}$ (c) $\frac{1}{12}$ (d) $\frac{1}{6}$ (e) $\frac{1}{8}$

E Dividing a fraction by a whole number (p 520)

E1 (a) B (b) $\frac{2}{9}$

E2 (a) A, R B, Q C, P

(b) A $\frac{3}{5} \div 2 = \frac{3}{10}$ B $\frac{5}{6} \div 2 = \frac{5}{12}$

C $\frac{2}{5} \div 3 = \frac{2}{15}$

E3 $\frac{2}{5}$

E4 (a) $\frac{2}{6}$ or $\frac{1}{3}$ (b) $\frac{2}{12}$ or $\frac{1}{6}$

(c) $\frac{3}{12}$ or $\frac{1}{4}$ (d) $\frac{3}{16}$

E5 (a) $\frac{2}{10}$ or $\frac{1}{5}$ (b) $\frac{3}{10}$

(c) $\frac{5}{16}$ (d) $\frac{2}{12}$ or $\frac{1}{6}$

F Multiplying fractions (p 521)

F1 (a) $\frac{1}{10}$ (b) $\frac{1}{16}$ (c) $\frac{1}{12}$ (d) $\frac{2}{15}$

F2 (a) $\frac{2}{5}, \frac{1}{9}, \frac{3}{4}, \frac{1}{6}$

ERMO → ROME

(b) $\frac{1}{12}, \frac{1}{4}, \frac{3}{16}, \frac{1}{8}, \frac{1}{9}$

SPAIR → PARIS

(c) $\frac{1}{5}, \frac{1}{5}, \frac{3}{4}, \frac{1}{9}, \frac{3}{16}, \frac{1}{8}$

DDMRAI → MADRID

(d) $\frac{3}{8}, \frac{1}{10}, \frac{1}{2}, \frac{1}{12}, \frac{1}{6}, \frac{3}{16}, \frac{1}{10}$

WGLSOAG → GLASGOW

Test yourself (p 522)

T1 5

T2 6

T3 $\frac{1}{2}$

T4 $\frac{3}{4}$

T5 (a) $2\frac{1}{3}$ (b) $1\frac{2}{5}$

T6 $6\frac{3}{4}$

T7 $\frac{1}{4}$

T8 $\frac{1}{20}$

T9 $\frac{1}{12}$

T10 $\frac{3}{12}$ or $\frac{1}{4}$

T11 (a) $\frac{3}{16}$ (b) $\frac{3}{48}$ or $\frac{1}{16}$

Practice book

Sections B and C (p 213)

1 $1\frac{1}{4}$ bars

2 (a) $1\frac{2}{3}$ (b) $3\frac{3}{4}$ (c) $1\frac{2}{5}$ (d) $2\frac{1}{6}$

3 (a) $5\frac{1}{2}$ (b) $2\frac{1}{2}$ (c) $2\frac{1}{2}$ (d) $3\frac{2}{3}$

4 (a) $2\frac{1}{2}$ $1\frac{1}{2}$ $4\frac{3}{4}$

　　　E　　B　　D　→ BED

(b) $1\frac{4}{5}$ $2\frac{2}{3}$ $2\frac{1}{2}$ $2\frac{1}{3}$ $1\frac{1}{2}$

　　　L　　A　　E　　T　　B　→ TABLE

(c) $2\frac{1}{3}$ $2\frac{1}{2}$ $2\frac{3}{4}$ $1\frac{2}{5}$ $\frac{2}{3}$

　　　T　　E　　C　　H　　S　→ CHEST

5 (a) $1\frac{2}{3}$ $\frac{6}{7}$ $3\frac{1}{5}$ $2\frac{2}{5}$

　　　C　　R　　I　　E　→ RICE

(b) $2\frac{2}{5}$ $2\frac{1}{4}$ $3\frac{1}{3}$ $2\frac{2}{5}$

　　　E　　B　　F　　E　→ BEEF

(c) $1\frac{1}{2}$ $3\frac{1}{5}$ $6\frac{3}{4}$ $1\frac{2}{3}$ $2\frac{4}{5}$

　　　S　　I　　P　　C　　H　→ CHIPS

6 (a) $2\frac{2}{5}$ inches (b) $7\frac{1}{5}$ inches

Sections D and E (p 214)

1 (a) $\frac{1}{12}$ (b) $\frac{1}{10}$ (c) $\frac{1}{10}$

2 $\frac{1}{3} \div 3 = \frac{1}{9}$

3 (a) $\frac{1}{12}$ (b) $\frac{1}{20}$ (c) $\frac{1}{10}$

4 $\frac{3}{4} \div 2 = \frac{3}{8}$

5 (a) $\frac{2}{15}$ (b) $\frac{2}{12}$ or $\frac{1}{6}$ (c) $\frac{3}{20}$

(d) $\frac{1}{5}$ (e) $\frac{3}{32}$ (f) $\frac{2}{15}$

Section F (p 214)

1 (a) $\frac{1}{8}$ (b) $\frac{2}{20}$ or $\frac{1}{10}$ (c) $\frac{3}{8}$

2 (a) $\frac{3}{10}$ (b) $\frac{2}{15}$ (c) $\frac{2}{3}$ (d) $\frac{2}{21}$

(e) $\frac{3}{32}$ (f) $\frac{5}{24}$ (g) $\frac{3}{16}$ (h) $\frac{1}{2}$

3 A and H: $\frac{5}{60}$ or $\frac{1}{12}$　　B and E: $\frac{5}{18}$

C and D: $\frac{5}{12}$　　F and G: $\frac{5}{24}$

68 Constructions

This unit reviews simple construction skills and asks students to consider what defines a triangle uniquely.

Essential

Set square, compasses, angle measurer, scissors

Practice book page 215

A *Using lengths* (p 523)

Set square, compasses, angle measurer, scissors

Triangle puzzle

◊ The purpose of this activity is to allow students to practise drawing triangles from SSS information. They can check the accuracy and, importantly, the uniqueness of their triangles by comparing their shapes with others in the group.

Ensure that students realise that, provided the two shorter lengths add up to more than the longer length, a unique triangle can be drawn.

This is the solution to the puzzle.

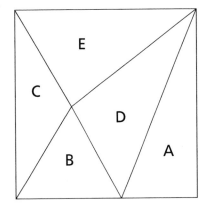

B *Using angles* (p 525)

This section asks students to construct triangles given ASA information.

> Rulers, angle measurers

C *Two sides and an angle* (p 526)

This section asks students to construct triangles given SAS or SSA information.

> Compasses, angle measurers

◊ In the initial activity students should realise that giving two sides and an angle produces a unique triangle when the angle is formed by the two given sides, but otherwise does not. A demonstration of why two cases arise from SSA in a compass construction is helpful here, as is measuring the angles in the two cases.

C3 This question asks students to look at the special case of SSA where the angle is a right angle, leading to a unique triangle.

D *Scale drawings* (p 527)

> Compasses, angle measurers, set squares

An accuracy of ±2 mm and ±2° seems appropriate in most answers.

A *Using lengths* (p 523)

A1 (a) The student's accurate triangle with sides 13 cm, 12 cm and 5 cm

(b) A right angle (c) 30 cm²

A2 (a) The student's accurate triangle with sides 10 cm, 10 cm and 12 cm

(b) 53° (c) Isosceles triangle

(d) 48 cm²

A3 (a) The student's accurate drawing with lengths 5.4 cm and 6.6 cm

(b) 39°

A4 (a) and (b) The student's accurate quadrilateral with side lengths 8 cm, 8 cm, 5 cm and 5 cm

(c) A kite

B *Using angles* (p 525)

B1 (a) The student's accurate drawing of triangle;
BC = 6.7 cm and BCA = 88°

(b) The student's accurate drawing of triangle;
BC = 11.5 cm and BCA = 32°

(c) The student's accurate drawing of triangle;
BC = 9.6 cm and BCA = 49°

B2 (a) Sides diverge rather than converge to a point. This is because CAB + ABC > 180°.

(b) (i) No   (ii) No
(iii) Yes   (iv) No

B3 (a) The student's accurate drawing of quadrilateral

(b) A trapezium

ℂ *Two sides and an angle* (p 526)

C1 (a) (i) and (ii) The student's accurate drawings of triangles

(b) (i) BC = 8.7 cm, CBA = 42° and ACB = 63°

     (ii) DF = 11.2 cm, EFD = 24° and EDF = 36°

        Yes

C2 The student's two accurate drawings of triangles.
Check third side is 8.7 cm in one case and 4.1 cm in the other.

C3 (a) The student's accurate drawing of a right-angled triangle with side lengths 6.9 cm, 8.8 cm and 5.5 cm

(b) No

𝔻 *Scale drawings* (p 527)

D1 (a) (i) 12 cm   (ii) 8.5 cm

(b) The student's accurate scale drawing

D2 (a) The student's accurate scale drawing

(b) No, the total height of the building would be 8.9 m.

Test yourself (p 527)

T1 (a) The student's accurate drawing of triangle
Hypotenuse = 9.5 cm

(b) (i) 37°   (ii) Acute

(c) 21.66 cm²

T2 (a) The student's accurate drawing of triangle

(b) 7.4 cm

Practice book

Sections A, B, C and D (p 215)

1 The student's accurate diagrams
(a) $x = 80°$ (b) $y = 9.7$ cm
(c) $z = 8.5$ cm

2 (a) The student's accurate diagram
(b) 90°   (c) Right-angled
(d) 19.44 cm²

3 (a) The student's accurate diagram
(b) Trapezium

4 The student's accurate diagrams, with the third triangle like this

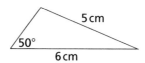

5 (a) and (b)

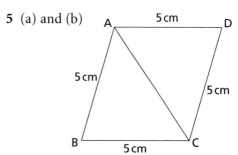

(c) Rhombus

6 (a) The student's accurate diagram
(b) Main Gate to Honeysuckle Gate 112 m

69 Percentage increase and decrease

Practice book pages 216 and 217

A *Review* (p 528)

TG

◊ This is revision of earlier work, but students may need to be reminded that finding 10% is the same as dividing by 10. This can lead to discussion of different methods of calculating the other percentages shown, using mental or pencil and paper methods.

B *Percentage increase* (p 529)

◊ Students should be encouraged to set out their working as shown in the worked example; this will help them to cope with the harder multi-stage questions later in the unit.

◊ Students may not understand how interest rates work, so this may need some discussion.

D *Increase and decrease with fractions* (p 531)

◊ Students may need to be reminded about how to calculate a fraction of a quantity. Only fractions are used in this section.

E *Percentages on a calculator* (p 532)

◊ It is important that students are clear about how to get the right answer to the calculation shown using their calculator. Three possible methods are shown, again as a reminder, but may need more explanation. Students should, however, use their one preferred method. They should be encouraged to write down the intermediate stages of their calculation.

F *In the real world* (p 533)

◊ VAT is introduced here. It could generate further discussion about what has VAT added to its price and what is zero rated.

Again three methods are shown. It should be pointed out that 17.5% is equivalent to 0.175 as a decimal, as students may have difficulty with this.

◊ Some builder's merchants and office supply companies produce catalogues which list prices excluding VAT, and these can be used as an extra resource for similar questions. The effect on prices of a different VAT rate could be investigated.

◊ Students could collect information about current interest rates from newspapers or banks and building societies and use these to investigate how much an investment could be worth at the end of a year in different accounts.

F6 'Time and a quarter' may need to be explained.

A *Review* (p 528)

A1 (a) £2.40 (b) £1.20
    (c) £3.60 (d) £4.80

A2 (a) £1.80 (b) 3 kg (c) £3.50
    (d) 0.8 m (e) £0.25

A3 (a) £2.80 (b) 8 cm (c) £70
    (d) £800 (e) 5 kg

A4 (a) 34 km (b) £3
    (c) 7 m (d) 18.5 kg

A5 (a) £2 (b) £0.08
    (c) £6.50 (d) £12.60

*A6 (a) £10 (b) £42
    (c) £1 (d) £144

B *Percentage increase* (p 529)

B1 (a) £25 (b) £275

B2 (a) 50 ml (b) 550 ml

B3 (a) 35p (b) £3.85

B4 (a) £264 (b) £660 (c) £19.80
    (d) £5940 (e) £2.09

B5 (a) 30p (b) £6.30

B6 (a) £60 (b) £1260

B7 (a) 18 minutes (b) 108 minutes

B8 1650 pupils

B9 60 m

B10 (a) £20 increased by 5% is greater.

(b) They are both the same.

(c) £42 increased by 10% is greater.

(d) £2000 increased by 25% is greater.

ℂ *Percentage decrease* (p 530)

C1 (a) £4   (b) £36

C2 5040

C3 38 hours

C4 A and T, B and R, C and P,
D and Q, E and S

C5 T-shirt £12, jeans £28.80, shirt £19.20,
shorts £15.20, jacket £44.80

𝔻 *Increase and decrease with fractions* (p 531)

D1 (a) £24   (b) £30

(c) £45   (d) £10.50

D2 (a) 250 g   (b) 750 g

D3 (a) 2 kg   (b) 625 ml   (c) 150 g

D4 £560

𝔼 *Percentages on a calculator* (p 532)

E1 (a) £22.68   (b) 16.8 kg   (c) £1225

(d) £16.15   (e) 300   (f) 6360

E2 (a) £0.68   (b) £1.03   (c) £3.75

E3 (a) 175   (b) 650   (c) 575

E4 (a) 6.4 litres   (b) 355.6 g

(c) 165.3 cm   (d) 31.85 ml

(e) 39.9 kg   (f) 2275 m

E5 (a) £840   (b) £12 840

E6 (a) £10 200   (b) £95 200

E7 2461 visitors

E8 (a) £2599   (b) £8701

E9 1725 blackbirds

𝔽 *In the real world* (p 533)

F1 Ballpens £2.35, A4 plastic pockets £6.11,
copy paper £11.15, envelopes £15.26

F2 Visionplus is cheaper; the
TV costs £258.50 at Best TVs.

F3 (a) £121.60   (b) £3921.60

F4 Sofa A costs £390. Sofa B costs £375.
Sofa B is cheaper.

F5 £44.44

F6 £64.50

F7 £1.02

F8 (a) £34.65   (b) £6.11

F9 (a) £88   (b) £31 350

F10 £91.40 to the nearest penny

F11 £329.60 per week

Test yourself (p 535)

T1 £63

T2 £91

T3 £36

T4 (a) (i) 0.125   (ii)   12.5%

(b) £2815.75

T5 £77

T6 Difference in price is £37
(Washing Power cost £277.50, Whytes
cost £314.50, Clean Up cost £282)

Practice book

Sections B, C and D (p 216)

1 (a) 33 ml   (b) 297 ml

2 (a) £8   (b) £88

3 (a) £15   (b) £285

4 (a) 16 cm   (b) 3 m 36 cm

5 (a) 1200   (b) 6000

6 £7200

7 £180 000

8 100

9 8 hours

Sections E and F (p 217)

1 (a) £31.82   (b) £180.60

    (c) 28 g   (d) 75.33 km

2 (a) £0.93   (b) £0.21   (c) £13.27

3 1431

4 (a) 1292   (b) 272   (c) 2448

5 371

6 (a) £29.79   (b) £199.99

7 (a) £10.32   (b) Yes, he has £250.32

8 (a) £57   (b) £405   (c) £419

p 536 **A** *Using a conversion graph*

p 538 **B** *Drawing a conversion graph*

Essential

Sheet G107 (for section B) and sheet G108 (for section B and 'Test yourself')

Practice book page 218

Ⓐ *Using a conversion graph* (p 536)

A1 (a) 32 km   (b) 43 km
    (c) 13 km   (d) 28 km

A2 22 miles

A3 (a) 25 miles   (b) 15 miles   (c) 6 miles

A4 You could convert 25 miles and then double (result 80 km).

A5 (a) 160 km   (b) 120 km
    (c) 37 or 38 miles (37.5 miles)
    (d) 62 or 63 miles (62.5 miles)

A6 88 km

A7 (a) (i) 2.5 litres   (ii) 1.6 litres
      (iii) 1 litre
    (b) (i) 5.3 pints   (ii) 2.6 pints
      (iii) 1.6 pints
    (c) 8.5 litres

A8 (a) (i) 1.8 kg   (ii) 2.5 kg
      (iii) 5.3 pounds   (iv) 2 pounds
    (b) (i) 5.5 kg   (ii) 22 pounds

Ⓑ *Drawing a conversion graph* (p 538)

B1 (a) The student's graph on diagram A
    (b) (i) 31 km/h   (ii) 22 knots

B2 (a) The student's graph on diagram B
    (b) (i) 96 km^2 (ii) 33 square miles

B3 (a) The student's graph on diagram C
    (b) (i) 6.2 m^3 (ii) 190 cubic feet

B4 (a) The student's graph on diagram D
    (b) (i) €28 (ii) £22 (iii) £12

B5 (i) The student's graph on diagram A
    (ii) 27°C   (iii) 14°F

Test yourself (p 539)

T1 (a) $8   (b) £10.50

T2 (a) The student's conversion graph
    (b) (i) €3.60 (ii) About £57

Practice book

Sections A and B (p 218)

  1 (a) 12.5 m^2 (b) 18 m^2
     (c) 24 square yards
     (d) 11 square yards

  2 (a) The student's graph
     (b) (i) 500 ml   (ii) 9 fluid ounces.

Review 8 (p 540)

1 (a)

		Second spinner			
	×	1	2	3	4
First spinner	1	**1**	**2**	**3**	**4**
	2	**2**	**4**	**6**	**8**
	3	**3**	**6**	**9**	**12**
	4	**4**	**8**	**12**	**16**

(b) (i) $\frac{1}{16}$ (ii) $\frac{4}{16} = \frac{1}{4}$ (iii) $\frac{12}{16} = \frac{3}{4}$

2 (a) 14.64   (b) 13.66   (c) 7.91

3 (a) 90° anticlockwise rotation using centre $(0, 0)$

(b) Translation of 1 right and 2 up

(c) Reflection in the x-axis

4 (a) 5.6 m   (b) 0.4 m

5 (a) $p = 1.8$ (b) $r = \frac{1}{3}$ (c) $s = {}^-4$

6 (a) $e = 7$ (b) $f = 4$ (c) $g = \frac{2}{3}$

7 (a) $\frac{1}{32}$ (b) $\frac{3}{8}$
(c) $\frac{1}{8}$ (d) $\frac{1}{9}$

8 (a) The student's accurate drawing
(b) 4.2 cm

9 £166.85

10 £240

11 (a) (i) $110   (ii) £68
(b) $330

12 (a) £279.30   (b) £312   (c) £123.30

Mixed questions 8 (Practice book p 219)

1 (a) 0.35   (b) 32

2 (a)

Number	1	2	3	4	5
Frequency	38	42	26	51	43
Estimated probability	0.19	0.21	0.13	0.255	0.215

(b) Yes, the probabilities vary by a large amount

3 (a) 46   (b) 0.6   (c) 5.94

4 (a), (b) and (c)

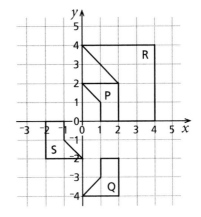

5 (a) 40 or 30   (b) 36

6 40 km

7 4

8 (a) $6x + 90°$ (b) $6x + 90° = 360°$, $x = 45°$

9 (a) The student's accurate drawing (b) 104°

10 (a) $x = 11$ (b) $y = 5$ (c) $n = 2$

11 (a) £4.08   (b) £1.47
(c) £3.69   (d) £5.47

12 £200

13 (a) £16.80   (b) £496.80

14 (a) (i) 5.1 cm   (ii) 3.5 inches
(b) (i) about 25.5 cm
(ii) about 5.9 inches

General review (Practice book p 221)

1 (a) Trapezium   (b) (1, 6)
   (c) 5.4 cm   (d) 18.4 cm
   (e) 20 cm^2

2 (a)

Fraction	Decimal	Percentage
$\frac{1}{4}$	0.25	25%
$\frac{1}{10}$	0.1	10%
$\frac{3}{10}$	0.3	30%

   (b) $\frac{1}{6}$ (c) $\frac{2}{3}$

3 (a) 4   (b) 414   (c) 16

4 (a) Bombay   (b) Moscow
   (c) 17 degrees   (d) $-13°C$

5 (a) 2, 12 and 16   (b) 12
   (c) 2   (d) 16 and 25

6 (a) $3x$ (b) $3x - 6$ (c) $5(x + 3)$

7 0.09, 0.099, 0.1, 0.19, 0.2

8 (a) Kilograms   (b) Cubic metres
   (c) Tonnes   (d) Litres
   (e) Grams   (f) Millilitres

9 (a) 14
   (b)

Pattern no.	1	2	3	4	5
No. of dots	5	8	11	14	17

   (c) (i) 92
       (ii) You multiply the pattern
           number by 3 and add 2.

10 (a) $\frac{5}{15} = \frac{1}{3}$
   (b) (i)   30   (ii) $\frac{25}{30} = \frac{5}{6}$

11 (a) 17   (b) £6.08   (c) 12

12 (a) 17
   (b) (i) Subtract 2   (ii) -11, -13

13 (a) 36 000   (b) 16 020

14 £49 + (232 × £0.12) = £76.84

15 (a) 3.77 or 3.8 metres
   (b) 1.77 or 1.8 m^2
   (c) 1.60 or 1.6 m

16 (a) 1.7   (b) 2.6   (c) 4.0

17 (a) £5.55   (b) $65n$
   (c) $90x + 65y$

18 (a) 50   (b) 13   (c) $19\frac{1}{2}$

19 (a) $5x + 20$
   (b) $5x + 20 = 180$
   (c) $x = 32$; the angles are 64°, 94°
      and 22°

20 (a)

	Mean	Range
Ann	1.55 m	0.17 m
Beth	1.60 m	0.53 m

   (b) Choice of jumper with 2 reasons
      based on data, e.g.

      Beth – she has the highest jump and
      the higher mean jump.

21 (a) and (b)

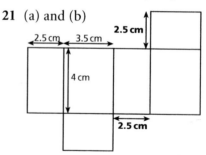

   (c) 35 cm^3 (d) 65.5 cm^2